CARIBBEAN VISIONARY

CARIBBEAN STUDIES SERIES
Anton L. Allahar and Shona N. Jackson
Series Editors

CARIBBEAN
VISIONARY

A. R. F. Webber
and the Making of the Guyanese Nation

Selwyn R. Cudjoe

University Press of Mississippi
Jackson

www.upress.state.ms.us

The University Press of Mississippi is a member of the Association of
American University Presses.

Copyright © 2009 by University Press of Mississippi
All rights reserved
Manufactured in the United States of America

First printing 2009
∞

Library of Congress Cataloging-in-Publication Data

Cudjoe, Selwyn Reginald.
Caribbean visionary : A. R. F. Webber and the making of the
Guyanese nation / Selwyn R. Cudjoe.
p. cm.—(Caribbean studies series)
Includes bibliographical references and index.
ISBN 978-1-60473-106-4 (cloth : alk. paper) 1. Webber, A. R. F.
(Albert Raymond Forbes), 1880–1932. 2. Guyana—History—
1803–1966. 3. Guyana—History—Autonomy and independence
movements. 4. Statesman—Guyana—Biography. 5. Authors,
Guyanese—20th century—Biography. I. Title.
F2384.W43C83 2009
328.881092—dc22
[B]
2008015568

British Library Cataloging-in-Publication Data available

To
Ewart Williams,
for his encouragement and friendship

We are a people. A people do not throw their geniuses away. And if they are thrown away, it is our duty as artists and *as witnesses for the future* to collect them again for the sake of our children, and, if necessary, bone by bone.

—ALICE WALKER, *In Search of Our Mothers' Gardens*

CONTENTS

CONTENTS

ABBREVIATIONS

BGEIA	British Guiana East Indian Association
BGLU	British Guiana Labor Union
EIYMS	East Indian Young Man's Association
IFTU	International Federation of Trade Unions
MFGB	Miners' Federation of Great Britain
NPC	Negro Progress Convention
PPP	People's Progressive Party
UNIA	Universal Negro Improvement Association

NOTE ON NOMENCLATURE

GUYANA POSSESSES A VERY DIVERSE POPULATION with many interlocking and changing definitions. The population consists of the American Indians, who are now called "First Nation" or the "First People." The term "Boivanders" refers to persons of American Indian and African ancestry. There are the Europeans who colonized the land, Africans who were brought to the colony and who were called Negroes. Until the end of the nineteenth century, negroid people were called Africans and Creole Africans. A recent study even speaks of race and politics among Africans and Indians. Today, we generally refer to Guyanese of African descent as Afro-Guyanese, even though they were called Africans during the nineteenth century. During the period within which this study is set, the upper and middle classes viewed the term "African" with derision. East Indians refer to the people who were bought from India to Guyana in 1838 as Indians. Those who stayed after indentureship ended were referred to as Creole Indians. Today they are referred to as Indo-Guyanese. There are also the Chinese who came from China and the Portuguese who, although they are Europeans, were never placed in the same social category or standing as northern Europeans. In Guyana and Trinidad, they were looked down upon as being less than Europeans. There is also the colored population, those of mixed stock, "who while coloured in appearance, possessed 'a large infusion of European blood.'" Webber was of this colored stock, even though he referred to himself as being a "black man" and would be so considered today.

All of these terms are used interchangeable in this study with the necessary qualifications.

CARIBBEAN VISIONARY

INTRODUCTION

Every acre at present in cultivation has been the scene of a struggle with the sea in front and the flood behind. As a result of this arduous labour during two centuries, a narrow strip of land along the coast has been rescued from the mangrove swamp and kept under cultivation by an elaborate system of dams and dykes.
—JAMES RODWAY, *History of British Guiana*

Each historical narrative renews a claim to truth.
—MICHEL-ROLPH TROUILLOT, *Silencing the Past*

ON THURSDAY, JUNE 30, 1932, the *New Daily Chronicle* shocked the consciousness of Guyanese people when it reported the sudden death of Albert Raymond Forbes Webber, one the country's most brilliant statesmen. For a person who seemed to be in the best of health and relatively young (he was fifty-two years old at the time), and who enjoyed tremendous popularity among the people, his death came as a great shock to the community and represented the passing of an important symbol of his people's resistance to colonial domination. A day later, in an apparent reference to the bravery and loyalty of Sir John Moore, the distinguished British soldier, to his nation, a poet who signed his name as Z called upon his fellow Guyanese to remember "the good points of his [Webber's] life" and "the fame fight he made" on behalf of his people.[1] Even as they were devastated by the *New Daily Chronicle*'s announcement, Webber's death marked the end of one of the Caribbean's most distinguished politicians, scholar, activists, and man of letters. Seventy-seven years after Webber's death, a virtual silence envelops his name. His story needs to be told.

Webber was born on New Year's Day, 1880, in Scarborough, Tobago, and christened in the Wesleyan-Methodist Church by Rev. A. H. Aguilar on February 1, 1880.[2] In 1899, after receiving the rudiments of an education, Webber immigrated to Guyana to join his father, James Frances Webber, and uncles, S. E. R. (Ernest) and Percival Forbes, partners in Crosby and Forbes, one of the largest traders in the goldfields of Bartica.[3] A prominent member of the colored middle class of Guyana, Ernest Forbes was held in such high esteem that he was asked to submit his views on the development of Bartica to the West India Royal Commission when its members visited Guyana to inquire into the sugar industry in 1897.[4] One year after he arrived in Guyana, Webber married Beatrice Elizabeth Glassford, and from their marriage came two children: Ivy Emma Forbes Webber (1901–) and Edith May Forbes Webber (1902–88). Ivy married Colin Whitehead; they had two children, Derek and Barbara. Edith married A. C. Dummett, with whom Anne and Jennifer were conceived. From 1903 and 1906, as he tried to settle down in his new environment, he sent his daughters to live with his aunts in Tobago. During this period, Webber's brother, George, and his uncle-in-law, Edward Percival Ross, were overseers on the Davson plantation.[5] Although Louis Ross, Webber's first cousin, was not willing to confirm it, he hinted that Webber may have acted as an overseer on one of Davson's sugar estate for a short period of time. If this is true, it would explain Webber's intimate knowledge of East Indian life on the sugar estates, which he chronicled in *Those That Be in Bondage* (1917), and his dedication of the novel to the memory of T. Gordon Davson, an accomplished musical composer and a member of the Davsons, a prominent English family that settled in Guyana.

By 1906 Crosby and Forbes had fallen on hard times. The gold bars it shipped to London were stolen and replaced by lead, and that led to the company's ruin. In 1906 Webber became the secretary of British Guiana (Purini) Gold Concession. In 1907 he branched out into Water Street, Georgetown, the business center of Guyana, and became a clerk at J. J. Chapman, a post that he held for a short while. In 1908 he left J. J. Chapman and became the secretary to Peter's Mine, an American-run gold-producing company that specialized in quartz mining but which ended its gold-mining operations when the boom in the balata and rubber industries led to the "ever-increasing cost of wood fuel" and, as a consequence, "a wane in the corporate activities in the gold industry."[6] In 1909 he joined the Mara Mara Gold Company. Dissatisfied with the gold prospecting business, he joined the advertising department of the *Daily Argosy* as an advertising agent in 1910. A few years later, he became an advertising clerk at Bookers Brothers, the largest conglomerate in the colony.

Webber's advertising work at the *Daily Argosy* changed the course of his life and prepared him for the career that he was about to undertake. A report in the *Daily Chronicle* suggests that it "gave him valuable knowledge of publicity methods which served him in good stead as the politician and journalist which he subsequently became."[7] Undoubtedly, Webber's change of career led to a greater intellectual and political awakening and points to a young man who was becoming more interested in public affairs and writerly pursuits. From this point on, Webber read much more and developed a greater interest in world affairs. As he matured, he turned more of his attention to political pursuits. Keeping these two vocational imperatives in balance became a major challenge of his later life.

Between 1899 and 1915, Webber gained an enormous amount of knowledge of Guyana's interior and its people. He came into contact with a large cross section of the Guyanese population, which proved to be of great value in his subsequent political, literary, and journalistic pursuits. During this period, he did a lot of free-lance work and polished his writing skills. In 1915, when he was asked to write an article on the rise and wane of the colonies' industries, all of his experience had prepared him for this task. In 1917 he wrote *Those That Be in Bondage*, a novel about East Indian indentures in Guyana, thereby becoming the first Caribbean novelist to write about the conditions of East Indians in the Caribbean. Coming three years after Herbert de Lisser's *Jane Career* (1914), *Those That Be in Bondage* was among the first wave of Caribbean novels that mined the poverty and dis-possession of the underclass and set the stage for several novels in this genre.[8] *An Innocent's Pilgrimage* (1927), one of the earliest travelogues in Caribbean litera-ture, records Webber's impressions of England when he visited there in 1926 as one of Guyana's representatives to the West Indian Conference. Another visit to London, Trinidad, Barbados, and Jamaica allowed him to offer his impressions in "From an Editorial View-Point," a series of articles that appeared in the *Daily Chronicle* in 1928. Webber saw himself as a litterateur and felt comfortable in that role. As one of the earliest Caribbean writers, he made important contributions to Caribbean literature.

In 1921 Webber entered the political arena when there were urgent calls throughout the Caribbean for more representative governments.[9] By 1925 Webber had emerged as the leader of the Africans and East Indians in Guyana and had be-gun to link up his activities with those of other Caribbean people. In 1926, when the British government sought to reduce the electorate and transform Guyana into a Crown Colony, Webber and his colleagues (particularly Nelson Cannon) fought back against such political retrogression and formed the Popular Party, the first political party in the West Indies, which preceded Marcus Garvey's People's Popular Party by two years. In its manifesto, the Popular Party pledged to fight for self-government, the right of women to vote, and the promotion and protection of trade unions. Morley Ayearst asserted that the party was also formed to assist Henry Ford, who was interested in building a road from Georgetown to his rub-ber plantations in Brazil.[10] On several occasions, Webber traveled to London to argue for better representation for his people and to urge the Colonial Office to nullify the backward constitution that took away most of their political rights.

As Webber became more involved in the political struggle of his people, his work began to merge with that of the British Guiana Labour Union (BGLU), whose members selected him to represent them at various labor conferences in England. Together with Hubert Critchlow, secretary-treasurer of the BGLU,

Webber fought for an old-age pension, worker's compensation, an eight-hour day for workers, and a widening of the franchise. As a legislator, he held his own with the most skillful legislators in the Caribbean. Reno Rohini described Webber as having

> made a distinctive mark in local politics and one which has somewhat reverberated throughout the West Indies. Indeed, in thought, he is the most West Indian of British Guiana's public men.... He is a proficient debater and an able and poignant critic with a sound knowledge of parliamentary procedure. He may truly be an asset to the British Labour Party and bear fair comparison with any standard type and caliber of present-day British politicians.[11]

Many Caribbean politicians shared these characteristics. Speaking of the prodigious skills of Captain Arthur Cipriani and L. A. P. O'Reilly of Trinidad, C. L. R. James observed that "during the last two generations our best men have been consistently superior either in intellectual gifts or political strength of character to the large majority of the official class."[12] James was speaking of lower-level Englishmen who were sent to run colonial affairs in the Caribbean.

Webber also fought for universal suffrage, a self-governing constitution, a West Indian press union, the creation of a West Indian Federation, and other progressive causes that clarified the liberation goals of his people and set the political agenda of his society and the Caribbean. He also evinced considerable interest in the East Indians and the American Indians. There can be no doubt that his frequent trips to the United Kingdom, the people he met there, and the ideas he encountered shaped his approach to politics and later to economics. When Sir Arthur Lewis argued that the two major outcomes of the social upheavals of the 1930s were "the rise of trade unions and the entry of the working classes into West Indian politics,"[13] he had Webber in mind. Webber was involved in these activities twelve years before these labor disturbances occurred.

As the editor of the *Daily Chronicle* (1919–25) and the *New Daily Chronicle* (1925–30), the two most influential Guyanese daily newspapers of the 1920s, Webber helped to shape the social and political views of his society. Apart from his using these newspapers to influence his people's views of things, he also used them to educate people as they positioned themselves in the fight against colonial oppression and constructed themselves as a class. Thus his journalistic calling enhanced his political activities. He devoted himself to both pursuits and became a relentless champion of his people, feared by his foes, admired by his friends, adored by his followers, and respected by his political and journalistic colleagues around the Caribbean.

Webber recognized the press as a necessary medium of communication among the islands and a vehicle for laying the foundation for West Indian nationalism. As a result, he worked assiduously to unite the West Indian press into one organization. Through his hard work, representatives from thirteen newspapers throughout the region came together in Barbados in 1929 to form the first West Indian Press Association. Among its objectives were promoting a freer exchange of the news, preserving press freedom, and establishing a high standard of journalism throughout the West Indies. A columnist from Dominica recognized the importance of this endeavor. He saw the press "as laying the foundation on which West Indian nationalism is to be built" and Webber as the chief architect of this movement.[14]

Webber also produced two pioneering works in economics and in history. In one short article, "Why I Am an Economic Heretic," Webber anticipated John Maynard Keynes, the celebrated economist, in that he was one of the earliest promoters of government spending to boost the economy and advocated liberal reforms in the economy. Although Webber may have overemphasized the importance of underconsumption in the crisis of capitalism (and the depression), he was certainly correct in calling upon the government to invest more monies into the economy rather than balance the budget on the backs of the working people. Karl Case, an economist at Wellesley College, said of Webber: "His analysis of the economic situation in Guyana in 1930 was 'pure Keynes.'"[15] Eric St. Cyr, a noted Caribbean economist, saw Webber as an early practitioner in the field.[16]

Webber was equally astute and progressive in his *Centenary History and Handbook of British Guiana*, in which he analyzed the development of British Guiana from its unification in 1831 and interpreted his people's history through their eyes and activities. As a reviewer of the time suggested about another book on Guyana's history, *Centenary History* sought to "look into cause and effect, conditions and their results, rather than to memorize the dates that certain kings lived and died or killed each other."[17] In other words, rather than offer descriptive accounts of Guyanese history, Webber outlined the economic problems and causes of Guyana's development during its first century of existence. He was one of the first Caribbean scholars—in this case, a literary journalist—to do so. Although James's *The Black Jacobins* may have "laid the foundation for the development of a modern West Indian historiography,"[18] Webber's *Centenary History,* which predated it by seven years, began to set *the* standard (a people's-oriented emphasis) for the writing of West Indian history by West Indians.

At the beginning of his career in Guyana, Webber may have been conservative or even indifferent to the political situation that surrounded him, even though his uncle was involved in the social uplift of his people. Webber first worked in the cause of the planters but later began to espouse liberal causes and identify with issues that concerned working people. At the end of his career, he identified with the ideas of Fabian socialism. Throughout all of these transformations, he held a strong belief in self-reliance and the power of the will to triumph over negative situations. In a poem to his daughter in 1920—she may have been going through her own private crisis—Webber reminded her that whatever problems she may have had,

Your own strong soul must guide you,
Your own will standing clear,
For nothing ever matters,
But what we build and perfect.[19]

Webber was determined to be his own man. Later in life (that is, in his early forties), he demonstrated his sensitivity to the sufferings of the East Indians, the Africans or Afro-Guyanese, the poor Europeans, and the American Indians that he saw around him.[20] Although he did not believe that socialism along the classical Marxist line could work in Guyana—he thought it was applicable for industrialized England and the slums of London—he was certainly influenced by its explication of social reality, and that guided his understanding of the problems that faced the working people of his country. In 1930 Rohini described Webber as "a theoretic socialist rather than a practical one."[21] Such a description coming at the end of Webber's career suggests that even in his time, Webber was seen by many Guyanese as a socialist. Rohini's views certainly coincided with Jennifer Welshman's (nee Dummett) recollection that the first indication that she had of her grandfather's political importance was when, on a public stage, Sir Lionel Lucky, one of Guyana's most successful lawyers, described him as Guyana's first socialist.

When Webber became an elected official in 1921, he was content to think, to build, and "to do," as his poem to his daughter suggested. However, the poverty that he saw around him and the pressures that were brought upon working people were a tremendous challenge to him. As the British colonial powers moved to remove all of the self-governing powers of the Guyana legislature and convert Guyana into a Crown Colony (which it achieved in 1928), Webber began to embrace the socialist way of interpreting the world. By the end of the decade, he identified with the political and social ideas of the Fabians and the economic thoughts of A. J. Cook, the famous Welsh Marxist and trade union leader, and he displayed a heightened level of working-class consciousness and solidarity. Although he was never a union leader, he associated himself with the work of unions and identified with their issues. Harold Perkin has observed that the struggle of the early English working class for universal suffrage and other such progressive reforms served not only as an "awakening to consciousness . . . of their conflict of economic and political interest with the aristocracy" but also as an indicator of their potential strength.[22]

At that moment of his career, Webber represented the most advanced political awareness of West Indian people. In this, he shared similarities with Theophilus

Albert Marryshow of Grenada and Captain Arthur Cipriani of Trinidad and Tobago. Their struggle against the ruling elite, their demands for self-government, and
their activities among the working class and the laboring poor raised the level of the
social and political consciousness of Caribbean people. Their radical thinking also
set the stage for the nationalist agenda of the 1930s, the socialist agenda of the 1940s,
and the emergence of figures such as Cheddi Jagan, Forbes Burnham, Norman
Manley, Alexander Bustamante, and Eric Williams and their pro-independence
parties of the 1950s.[23] Webber's excursion into economics and his fidelity to the
working people anticipated the demands of the working class in the 1930s and the
development of the modern Caribbean. Much of Jagan's socialist agenda would
take its impetus from Webber's and Critchlow's progressive activities of this
earlier era.

Webber's erudition, his rhetorical, debating, and well-honed journalistic skills,
together with his spellbinding oratory made him a formidable presence and an intellectual match for any other legislator in the British Commonwealth. His intellectual production between 1915 ("The Rise and Wane of the Colony's Industries")
and 1931 (*Centenary History and Handbook*) constituted the most sustained intellectual work by any West Indian during that period and emerges as an intellectual
bridge between J. J. Thomas's *Froudacity* (1889), "one of the earliest and clearest
challenges to the ideological validations of colonial rule,"[24] and C. L. R. James's
Black Jacobins (1938), a work that, as James says, demonstrates that the people of
African descent "would themselves be taking action on a grand scale and shaping
other people to their own needs."[25] Although Webber devoted his adulthood to
politics, he still retained a love for writing. He loved literature, took a delight in
reading, and, as he acknowledged, was really a litterateur. He never renounced this
primary way of seeing or theorized about the relationship between writing and
politics. Writing was his vocation; politics was his avocation.

Webber belonged to a generation of scholars and politicians who challenged
English colonialism, "with its disproportionate privileges for the heirs of the old
plantations and the dwindling minority of European descent."[26] Whether they
stayed at home or traveled abroad, they were distinguished by "their ability to
transcend the limitations of their socioeconomic status and locale. They grasped
whatever small opportunities were offered and in serving themselves they served
their countries well."[27] His struggles at home gave him an intimate sense of the
beast he had to deal with, while his encounter with the mother country fertilized
his ideas and took him leaps and bounds beyond what he reasonably could have
been expected to achieve given the social and economic conditions in which he
lived. In fact, his contributions loom even larger when one recognizes that he
was an active politician rather than a savant who devoted himself exclusively to
academic pursuits. Few activists-scholars were doing the innovative work that
Webber was doing.

Little scholarship has been devoted to Webber or the politics of 1915–32. In his "Year by Year Bibliography," Kenneth Ramchand lists Webber's novel *Those That Be in Bondage* but does not mention it in his text. In his explication of the beginning of West Indian literature, Anthony Boxhill notes woefully but incorrectly that after Webber wrote *Those That Be in Bondage*, "nothing more" was heard from him.[28] Harold Lutchman's *From Colonialism to Cooperative Republic* and "Middle Class Colonial Politics" offer the most comprehensive political reading of this period.[29] Clem Seecharan's *Tiger in the Stars: The Anatomy of Indian Achievement in British Guiana, 1919–1927* is an impressive record of East Indian achievements during this period. Although he speaks generously about Webber's empathy and support of the East Indian cause and calls him "an astute observer of Guianese society,"[30] he does not devote any time to Webber's work. Jagan's *The West on Trial* mentions Webber's name once, although he recognizes the existence of the Popular Party and the important work Webber and others did on constitutional reform.[31] In *The British West Indies: The Search for Self-Government*, Ayearst mentions Webber's name twice in his study.[32] Other studies such as Roy Arthur Glasgow's *Guyana: Race and Politics among African and East Indians* and Peter Simms's *Trouble in Guyana* have elided over Webber's contributions.[33]

Some writers have tried to distort or diminish Webber's role in the making of Guyana. Nigel Westmaas observes that Webber "betrays his anti-working class vibes" when he analyzes the 1905 rebellion in *Centenary History*.[34] Nothing can be farther from the truth. In *Tiger in the Stars*, Seecharan describes Webber as that "progressive fighter for the working people."[35] Webber worked closely with Critchlow to improve the conditions of the Guyanese working people, and he became a member of BGLU's Advisory Committee. He also accompanied Critchlow as a British Guiana delegate to the British Commonwealth Labour Conference that was held in London in July 1930, where Webber was one of the major spokespersons for the working people of Guyana.[36]

Jagan distorts the history of the working-class struggle in Guyana and Webber's place in it when he claims that his (Jagan's) election to the British Guyana Legislative Council in 1947 "brought a consciousness to the Council that was *never* there before."[37] Such a statement was intended to belittle the important work of Critchlow, Ayube Edun,[38] and Webber in building the working-class movement in Guyana and to promote Jagan as the most progressive person ever elected to the Guyanese legislature. Although no one can gainsay Jagan's long and principled struggle for the Guyanese people, his observation can be characterized as just another bit of "local iconolatry" that seeks to promote Jagan's stature out of all proportion to his contribution to Guyana's history.[39]

It is not possible to offer the most insightful discussion of the work of Burnham, Jagan, and the events of the 1950s—as important as they and the period were—without an understanding of the work of Webber and his generation. No Caribbean scholar has made the connection between the 1920s and the 1950s in Guyanese political history and intellectual thought. Although enormous attention has been devoted to Jagan and the overthrow of his government by Britain (with U.S. assistance) in 1953, little work has been done on Guyana's political and social history in the period leading up to that historic juncture. If it is true, as Cary Fraser has argued, that "the crisis of 1953 in Guyana was a product of political immaturity (if not naïveté) of the People's Progressive Party (PPP) leadership and its collective failure to understand the constraints under which it operated,"[40] then how much more important it is to know the events that preceded this political "naïveté," particularly since it coincides with the time when Jagan, the son of East Indian sugar workers, was born (in 1918) and a period in which there was tremendous political turmoil in Guyana.[41] Any work on Guyana's modern political history that does not take into consideration the preparatory work of Webber and the activities of Critchlow does not do justice to this rich period of Guyana's history.

Webber was an intellectually gifted man. Although he may have lacked the structure of high school and university training in his formative years, his inquisitive mind made up for this lack. He was exposed to the best minds of his time, and he picked up much from his tutors at Queens College and his extensive travels to London, New York, and the Caribbean. He was steeped in English literature and New World history. His journalistic work brought him face to face with most of the leading Caribbean intellectuals and activists of his time, while his legislative duties granted him a deep and intimate knowledge of the economic problems that faced his society. His travels to London brought him into contact with leaders from other colonial territories such as India, Ceylon (Sri Lanka), and Africa. He was aware of the works and activities of Marcus Garvey, Mahatma Gandhi, and Booker T Washington. He did not accept the exclusionary nature of Garvey's politics and treated it in much the same way that Norman Manley treated it.[42] His political work with West Indians such as Captain Cipriani, T. A. Marryshow, P. W. Sangster, Dunbar Wint, and others and his meeting with members of the British Labour Party kept him abreast of things and a major participant in what was taking place in the Caribbean and the British Empire.

Webber was a quintessential product of his age. His life and times were important bases upon which his and succeeding generations reasserted their historicity and constructed their human agency. As Jean Paul Sartre and Frantz Fanon understood only too well, "Freedom is constituted by taking responsibility to transform oneself back into an agent."[43] In trying to understand Webber's appeal to his people and how they took him to their hearts, I draw on the example of A. J. Cook, one of the most inspiring orators and working-class leaders of Great Britain in the 1920s. In comparing himself with Cook and trying to explain Cook's charisma, Arthur Horner, one of Cook's comrades in arms, observed: "I was speaking *to* the meeting. Cook was speaking *for* the meeting. He was expressing the thoughts of his audience, I was trying to persuade them. He was the burning expression of their anger at the iniquities which they were suffering. It was the sort of demagogic appeal which in unscrupulous hands would be dangerous, the sort of appeal that a dictator might have, but Cook was utterly honest and selfless."[44]

Webber spoke *for* his generation in an eloquent manner as he burned with anger at the treatment that he and his people received from the colonizers. Through his tireless work, he emerged as *the* major spokesman and ideologue of the working people and laboring poor of Guyana during the second and early part of the third decade of the twentieth century (1915–32). Although he served as a spokesperson for the dominant capitalist class for a short while, the social and political circumstances of his adopted country soon transformed him into the people's spokesman as he began to be influenced by their ideals and their truths. He transformed the Guyanese people into agents of their destiny (that is, he historicized them), made them into the people they became, and set the stage for those who came after him. His profound belief in the Caribbean people marked him as a true patriot and a devoted son of "Mother West India." As Marryshow exclaimed when he heard of Webber's death: "Webber dead? Then the cause of West Indian freedom has lost a finished fighter."[45]

After 1932, Webber's life and work drifted from the national and historical memory of Guyana and the Caribbean. No one knows why his voice was silenced—in some ways the historians and political scientists had to clear a space for the exploits of Jagan and Burnham—or why the historians and political scientists neglected the period (1915–32) so shamefully. This silence may have been due to scholarly laziness, a lack of interest in our history unless it is sanctified by the other, or an unequal control over the means of historical production. After all, Guyana only gained international attention in 1953 after Britain invaded it and suspended its constitution, and a more dubious notoriety in 1978 when Jim Jones induced hundreds of Americans to take their own lives in the jungles of Guyana. In other words, Guyana assumed international prominence only when it was touched by others and whiteness showed its ugly face.

Caribbean Visionary seeks to break this silence, recover Webber's life, and fill an important lacuna in Guyanese and Caribbean history. It also chronicles Webber's contributions to the making of the Guyanese nation at an important period of its development. I first outline Webber's origins; then discuss *Those That Be in Bondage* (1917), *Glints from an Anvil* (1919), and his other poems; explicate the factors that shaped his life (1917–21); trace his political ascendancy (1921–25); and explain his involvement with the constitutional crisis of 1925. I examine his leadership during the deepening constitutional crisis (1926–27) and the quest for self-government, his travel writings during this period (*An Innocent's Pilgrimage* [1927], "From an Editorial View-Point" [1928], and "New York versus London"

[1929]), the effects of the world economic depression on the Guyanese sugar industry, and the continuing battle for constitutional reform in 1929.

On this biographical journey, I travel with Webber as he explores new regions of his country, with him during his first experience flying in an airplane, and with him in his struggle to be reelected to the Legislative Council in 1930. I examine his last travel writings ("Exploring Unbroken British Guiana" [1930] and "Hors D'Oeuvre of the Ocean Passage" [1930]); analyze *Centenary History and Handbook of British Guiana* (1931); sketch out a connection between Webber's work and that of Sir Arthur Lewis, Nobel Laureate in Economics; and discuss Webber's anticipation of John Maynard Keynes's theory of employment as is elaborated in *The General Theory of Employment, Interest and Money* (1936). I also examine the rising nationalism (or better still, the sense of nation-ness) as the original colonies of Guyana (Berbice, Demerara, and Essequibo) sought to construct a nation; look at Webber's final attempt to eradicate the Crown Colony form of government that was imposed upon Guyana in 1928; and discuss the international response to Webber's demise. As a follower of Fabian socialism, Webber sowed the seeds for a radical dimension in Caribbean political thought and provided the foundation for the intellectual outpourings that erupted in the English-speaking Caribbean at the beginnings of the 1930s.

Michel-Rolph Trouillot has argued that each historical narrative is a "particular bunch of silences" that "renews a claim to truth."[46] *Caribbean Visionary: A. R. F. Webber and the Making of the Guyanese Nation* seeks to wrench Webber from the silence that has enveloped his work and to offer a rich and nuanced understanding of our past. Hopefully, it can generate a better appreciation of Caribbean people and their stories. It's time that the story of Webber and his time was told.

I have incurred many debts along the way. First I want to thank the members of Webber's family who were so kind to me and who offered so much of their time and materials: Edith Dummet, Webber's daughter; Jennifer and Howard Welshman, Webber's granddaughter and her husband; Derek Whitehead, Webber's grandson; Barbara Cox, Webber's granddaughter; Clarence Webber and his wife; Yvonne Bissesser, granddaughter of Sarah, Webber's mother; Zena Webber, Webber's niece; Louis Ross, Webber's first cousin; Dolores Thompson, a relative of Beatrice, Webber's wife; Wilson Harris, nephew of Beatrice Webber who wrote an insightful introduction to *Those That Be in Bondage*; Joan Christiani, former head of the Guyanese National Library; Tommy Payne, former archivist of the Guyanese archives; Cecelia McAlmont, lecturer at the University of Guyana; Harold Lutchman, author; and Edward Rodway, Bernard Matthews, Clarence David Kirton, and Terence Roberts.

I want to thank Karl "Chip" Case, my colleague at Wellesley College; Ewart Williams and Shelton Nichols, governor and deputy governor, respectively, of the

Central Bank of Trinidad and Tobago, especially for their assistance with chapter 12; Nana Tagoe-Wilson, a former professor at the University of London, for being a perceptive reader and making me rewrite the introduction; Maxie Cuffie, for his patience in listening to and reading an initial draft of the manuscript; Carl Cambridge, for his suggestions; Kwadwo Osei-Nyame and his wife, for their hospitality and friendship; Aamer Khan, for his friendship and intellectual curiosity; Betty Ann Tyson, for helping me get the manuscript into shape; and Seetha Srinivasan, director of the University Press of Mississippi, for demanding that I produce the best manuscript I was capable of. The suggestions of the anonymous reader of the manuscript were also helpful.

I want to thank Henry Louis Gates Jr., director of the Du Bois Institute for Research, and Evelyn Higginbotham, chair of the African and African American Studies Department, both at Harvard University, for granting me an associate status with the African and African American Studies Department that allowed me to access the Harvard Library Collection; the support of Biodum Jeyifo, my lifelong friend who, better than most, remembers the beginning of the journey and the perils along the way; Abiola Irele, a firm supporter of my work; Louis Lee Sing, my brother and my friend; and Jerome Lewis, for listening. My thanks also goes out to Yashica, my soul mate; my daughters, Frances and Kwamena; my many friends in Trinidad (Oscar, Rianella, Resa, Brian, Rose, Giles, Mavis, Judith, Brader, Denisse, and Nicole); the New York posse (Margaret, Marva, Rhonda, Anthony, Fatima, Ronald, Judith, and Michele) who helped me dry my tears many times; and my many nieces and nephews (Jaael, Terrel, Shanelle, Akil, Anton, Akila, Ibrahim, and Maryam). They all know what I put them through.

I want to thank Wellesley College for the many faculty awards; Karen Jansen for facilitating the many interlibrary loans; the library and staff of Wellesley College for putting up with me; and the staff at the British Library, Colindale Library, the Public Record Office, Widener Library at Harvard University, the Guyana Archives, and the West India Collection at the University of the West Indies (St. Augustine).

In the end, I have to thank Terry Eagleton, professor of cultural theory at the University of Manchester, for demanding that I quote from *Those That Be in Bondage* after I asked him to critique my manuscript on V. S. Naipaul, later published as *V. S. Naipaul: A Materialist Reading*.[47] His question, "Why don't you quote Webber?" sent me in search of a book I had never seen and which I discovered subsequently in British Guiana archives. Without his query this book would never have been written.

CHAPTER ONE

THOSE THAT BE IN BONDAGE

As the ships dropped anchor in the river, no cannon from Fort William Frederick boomed forth the great event; no strains of music from the City band greeted the landing of the new-comers. There were no outward demonstrations of joy, as one friend greeting friend. Their coming was marked by a mute reception, save, perhaps, by the rude gibes and taunts of Africa's liberated sons, drawn thither by idle curiosity to look with pitying, if not with wondering eyes, on those whom they could regard in no other light than as the unfortunate victims of a new slavery.
— PETER RUHOMON, *Centenary History of the East Indians in British Guiana, 1838–1938*

I knew A. R. F. Webber as a child. My mother's sister was his wife. My memories are somewhat vague and imprecise, but I recall something of his turbulent political career and news of his sudden death on a river steamer bound for Bartica on the Essequebo River. This news seemed to plunge the entire country into grief. I recall the odd visit he paid to my home. He wore a red rose in his buttonhole and this, I was told, was characteristic of his style of dress.
— WILSON HARRIS, "A Note on A. R. F. Webber's *Those That Be in Bondage*"

WEBBER BEGAN HIS LITERARY CAREER BY WRITING POETRY. When his work appeared in 1916, he enjoyed two advantages. He had a good understanding of the problems of the laboring classes, and he knew the geography of his adopted country well. He described himself as "an old bushman" and boasted that he had walked from one end of the country to another.[1] Many Guyanese believed that he was awarded a Fellowship of the Royal Geographical Society "solely on his knowledge of the hinterland of British Guiana."[2] Louis Ross believes that his elder brother, Everil Ross (1893-?), and Webber started a literary magazine around 1910, about seven years before Webber published *Those That Be in Bondage*. In fact, there is evidence to suggest that *Those That Be in Bondage*, which ended with the Brickdam Cathedral fire of March 1913, must have been completed some years (perhaps in 1913–14) before it was published in 1917. Webber might have also tried his hand at other literary pursuits when he began to work for the advertising department of the *Daily Argosy* in 1910. However, his first known published poems, "What of a Night," "Wisdom Cometh in the Morning," and "The Jealous Scribe," appeared in various issues of the *Daily Chronicle* in January and February 1916.[3] When *Glints from an Anvil*, Webber's book of poems, appeared in 1919, it offered us the closest, most searching glimpse of Webber's way of thinking.

Webber's first substantial effort at writing prose, "The Rise and Wane of the Colony's Industries," appeared in 1916 when he accepted an invitation from the editor of the *Chronicle* to submit an article on the colony's industries in the place of one that was to have been written by Cecil Richter, who was out of the country at the time. Webber was well prepared to carry out the task, and the article demonstrated his erudition and his knowledge of the country's industries. He condemned "the abominable slave trade," which, when it was abolished, brought "no statesmanlike move for the reinforcement of the colony's labour supply under some more humane system. The planter stubbornly refused to recognize the rising tide of the voice of humanity; but was content to sit down and inveigh against the foolhardiness of the anti-slavery party, meanwhile he extolled the excellence of a system which compelled him to treat his 'property' well, and to take care of its offspring."[4]

Webber also argued that a lack of population rather than a lack of capital led to the rise and wane of the country's industries (that is, timber, gold, balata, and sugar production). Because capital always chased after a fast dollar, it led systematically to the ruin of the country's industries. Thirty years later, Eric Williams acknowledged that "British Guiana suffers not from the population pressures of the West Indian islands, but from a serious shortage of labor," and that it was "as dependent on capital as it is on labour. Without both of these factors, its hinterland will remain undeveloped and its potentialities the subject of the most extravagant schemes."[5] Williams had benefited from reading Webber's *Centenary History and Handbook of British Guiana*.

In his discussion on the sugar industry, Webber noted that the industry brought into "bolder relief . . . the fortunes of war between capital and labour" and that the sugar industry better suited "the Negroes" who preferred the rhythm of the sugar industry to the East Indians who preferred the rhythms of coffee and cocoa. Although Webber seemed to empathize with the East Indians' condition in the colony, he saw the immigration of East Indians as leading to "the disappearance of serious labour competitors" and the further increase of the "indents" as one way of preventing the "bleak days which succeeded 1807 [the year in which the British slave trade was abolished]."[6] In this early piece, Webber correctly identified the central contradiction of the society as one between labor and capital and saw the resolution of this problem as the way out of the constant rise and fall of the country's economy.

The editor of the *Chronicle* was pleased with the article. Since Webber had contributed to the *Christmas Annual*, the newspaper's literary supplement, the editor was acquainted with his work. He was pleased with Webber's nonfictional efforts. When he received Webber's article, he noted: "It would have been difficult for us to choose a more vigorous or better informed writer."[7] Given its academic rigor and its lucid prose, it is clear that Webber was thoroughly at ease in the literary/journalistic milieu of his time. Undoubtedly, he was offered the editorship of the *Daily Chronicle* in 1919 precisely because of his advertising experience, his journalistic skills, and his writing ability.

In "The Rise and Wane of the Colony's Industries," Webber empathized with the suffering and deprivation of East Indians (conditions that he had known on a firsthand basis because of his association with the sugar industry), and pondered "the higher value set on males in recruiting, and consequently, the existence of a disproportion of the sexes" within the Negro community.[8] In *Those That Be in Bondage*, he used a similar theme—the shortage of East Indian women and their sexual exploitation by European overseers on the plantation—as his point of departure to examine the exploitation of East Indians in a colonialist-capitalist society. Rev. C. F. Andrews, a visiting Indian reformist and confidant of Gandhi, saw the shortage of women as "the fatal flaw of the [immigration] system" that poisoned the system for the ninety years the British government allowed it to exist.[9] The liaisons between the European overseers and East Indian women, another source of trouble for the colonial authorities, also had a destabilizing effect on the social order of the plantation.[10]

Set in Guyana, Tobago, and Trinidad between 1890 and 1913, this historical romance traces the lives of two generations of the Walton family as they work out their destinies in those societies. Like Conrad's *Heart of Darkness*, it touches upon the crossing of boundaries and how Europeans are seduced and destroyed by colonized lands. Chapters 1 through 6, the first part of the novel, examine the life and death of John James Walton, "sugar oracle and Planting Attorney" for one of the largest sugar plantations in Guyana, and his brother-in-law, Edwin Hamilton, bred on the English sense of "fairplay" and reared "far from Colonial influences."[11] Hamilton is the perfect gentleman, the romantic stereotype untouched by the abhorrent influences of colonialism and racial dogmas. In his attempt to cross the racial and geographical boundaries of the society, he marries Bibi, "that smooth-skinned, bare-toed East Indian young lady" (*Bondage*, 4), the quintessence of rustic beauty, whose "strong Caucasian features had brought many men to her feet with all manner of proposals" (*Bondage*, 25).[12] Through this marriage, a daughter, Marjorie, is born. As the story develops, Harold eventually becomes a priest in the Dominican Order. He breaks his vow of celibacy when he enters into a sexual relationship with Marjorie and thereby enters into the heart of darkness, signifying a crack in the hegemony that the white, European world possessed over the black, creolized world of the Caribbean.

Webber was also concerned about the unjust manner in which the colored people of the society were treated. His being colored and his family's history made him interested in discrimination against them. The racist attitudes of those who controlled the fortunes of the industry prevented any "coloured Creole" from being appointed to a management position. According to the narrator: "They may have every qualification under the sun: they may be as able as Attila: but they may not aspire to such appointments" (*Bondage*, 52). On the other hand, the young Europeans who were recruited to fill management positions, no matter how unqualified they were for those positions or how little they understood the conditions of tropical agriculture, were always preferred over local black persons of merit.[13] As a result of such racist behavior, the narrator argues, the industry strangles itself.

Such racist behavior had practical consequences for the industry. It prevented any innovations or forward-looking transformation among the workers or the bosses from taking place. He asks: "What are the inventions recorded for the last hundred years? What generations have you had of boys and men, bred in the atmosphere of agriculture and sugar; generations from whom an Arkwright or an Edison could arise?" (*Bondage*, 204). Such is the pernicious nature of plantation society that nothing worthwhile can come out of it, hence his conclusion:

> Each generation sees a scratch team of raw Englishmen, who have never seen a cane field in their lives—and often not even a hop or a potato field—of rawer Scotsmen, and of broken Creoles. Death or dismissal closes all the effort and study of their minds; they bequeath their thoughts to no offspring; the barren die, and those few who rise to positions of affluence, and, are blessed with sons see that they take to the learned professions, to the Army or Navy, and to every other walk of life except planting. (*Bondage*, 204)

As a legislator, he would make a similar point about the colonial officials who were sent to govern Guyana.

The conflict between Eastern and Western ways of perceiving also comes in for scrutiny under Webber's scrupulous gaze. He depicts this encounter through a fearsome and forbidden sexual relation between Edwin, a European overseer, and Bibi, an East Indian indenture, that brings together all of the anxieties of racial purity and male sexual desire. Karin, a former admirer of Bibi, is aghast that a European should wander into his community and appropriate the most desirable of "their woman" with a certain degree of impunity. Not only does such an incident allude to a presumed European superiority, it also negates the sexuality of the colonized male other and renders him impotent. Karin's resort to violence to vindicate his loss only confirms the barbarity of the colonized as opposed to the relative sophistication and culture of the colonizer.

However, it is Karin's legal counsel, an East Indian of nationalist sentiments, who articulates the parameters of the contesting ideologies when he speaks about the "grievous wrong that was frequently done to these immigrants who were brought across two oceans to be shot down, or hanged; their liberty impaired and their wives stolen, or suborned" (*Bondage*, 66). In presenting his arguments to the jury, Karin's legal counsel argues that his client was not being judged by a jury of his peers. He implores them to

> divest themselves of all Western ideas of ways of thought, and codes of eti-
> quette or honour. . . . Here we find the gorgeous East, with its riot of colour
> and extremes, its patriarchal standard of honour, and its restrictions and privi-
> leges of caste, all exemplified and stamped on the brain of the accused, facing
> practically what is a Western Court of Honour, steeped in a rigid sense of law
> and justice, drawing its ideals from Mayfair, and saturated with centuries of a
> different standard of right and wrong. (*Bondage*, 66)

While it's true that both the East and West are depicted in stereotypical terms, the novel highlights the privileging of Western/Occidental over Eastern/Oriental values and the implicit attempt to normalize Western values and thereby present them as better, more desirable, and valuable in and of themselves.

In chapters 7 through 16, the narrative action shifts to Tobago and Trinidad, where the Waltons went to seek refuge and where Marjorie Hamilton and Harold, Mrs. Walton's son, grew up and went to school. It explores the lives of Marjorie and Harold and the plight of the English overseers overseas. The narrator seems to be sympathetic to the plight of the latter, who, like the East Indians, also find themselves abandoned and lost in a strange land. He is also concerned with a spiritual bondage that denies a person the possibility of sharing a warm, loving, and sexual relationship with another person of a different race. In this section of the text, Harold commits his most "heinous" crime and is expelled (or expels himself) from the church.

The narrative action from chapter 17 to the end of the novel shifts to British Guiana, where Harold (and later, Marjorie) returns to meet his destiny. Initially, he is employed as an overseer on Plantation Waterloo, where he is eventually fired for leaving the plantation without permission. Later he gets a job as an architect working on the tower of Brickdam Cathedral. While working there, a fire breaks out that destroys the cathedral. He is accused of setting the fire while he was "in some inhumane frenzy" (*Bondage*, 221).[14] Harold believes that his infidelity to the church has caused the destruction of God's holy edifice, which leads him to plead: "O Lord! Spare the Church! Oh God! Visit not the sins of an infidel upon a defenseless people! Oh Almighty Master . . . spare the faithful this frightful desolation, and stay the wrath of Thy vengeance" (*Bondage*, 211).[15] When he tries to make amends for what he believes is his fault by offering to rebuild the cathedral with his family's fortune, he is denied an opportunity to do so. Therefore he leaves the country to start life anew in another country. Such is the ambivalence that we find at the end of the story.

In the end, Webber seems to suggest that a person is the master of his or her own fate and should not be controlled by any creeds, a theme he elaborates upon in his poems. One should struggle for freedom whenever one has the opportunity. When Harold attempts to take his own life, he is foiled by Dr. St. Aldwyn, an ex-clergyman, who cries: "You are the architect of your own fortunes and the master of your own destiny. Don't you forget it! . . . There you are. No man can be master of anything, unless he takes masterful precautions to be master" (*Bondage*, 214). Only with such control and balance can one construct a life that is reflective of one's own native genius. This is the synthesis toward which the novel moves.

Wilson Harris was fascinated by Dr. St. Aldwyn, whom he calls the "mirror image of Harold himself, ex-priest mirroring ex-clergyman." Harris argues that St. Aldwyn may represent "the first appearance of the trickster in written West Indian literature in the twentieth century." He continues:

> It is the trickster apparition of St. Aldwyn which jolts us into perceiving a strand in the novel that subsists upon a dark, sometimes flamboyant, admiration for Napoleonic and Czarist figures of destiny. That such "masters" are inherently doomed yet remain a source of hero worship tells us something about the conventions of the novel, the conventional dress or restricted ambience, in which the eruptive capacity of the trickster to stand outside rigged institutions, rigged ceremonies, etc., etc., becomes hypothetical if not an illusion.
>
> Perhaps such a mixture of grave hypothesis and the pathos instinctive to illusory freedom is a reflection of a stifled cry from the heart, unspoken prayer, a necessary prelude to a revisionary apparatus and self-judgment. But such revisionary insight departs in the given shape of the novel. There arrives in its place an element of anticlimax as the narrative draws to a close. It seems incongruous that Harold and Marjorie contemplated departure for England in 1913 and an ideal estate or carefree existence there, conditions of work as well through which Harold's talents would blossom, that no inkling possessed them of the end of an age and the impending outbreak of the Great War. It seems particularly incongruous after the prophecies of St. Aldwyn. Perhaps they knew but were unable to say what they knew, as they held each other within a "sweetness" akin to "death."[16]

The contemplated departure of Harold and Marjorie to England and the eventual outbreak of World War I suggest that the system of indenture was coming to an end; that, in fact, it had exhausted itself.

Ten years after he published *Those That Be in Bondage*, Webber was in a much better position to sketch out what he strove to say in his novel. In his travelogue *An Innocent's Pilgrimage*, he speaks about the important part the church played in building Oxford University but warns against the church's tendency to subvert its true function and to use its doctrines and prestige against the aspirations of colonial people. Although he acknowledges the importance of schooling, he also recognizes the ideological role that schools play in the indoctrination of colonial subjects and asks us to be on our guard:

> Let therefore those who gird at denominational education in our colony and elsewhere remember that, however the denominations may use schools for other purposes at the beginning of any educational system, and until it has reached sturdy self-supporting adolescence, the Church is the best foster parent. The Church made Oxford possible. Let us be accordingly grateful, without losing our right to stop abuses, whether it be for the old Obediahs or the fanatical John Knoxes; both types of which will recur to eternity.[17]

In *An Innocent's Pilgrimage*, he is also more explicit. He says that the Roman Catholic church and capitalism (represented by the power of Standard Oil) are the "two great organisations" of the world of which he was writing.[18] Harold, it seems, strove "to build not only a great Church, but a Church which would pulse of his native land and its people" (*Bondage*, 229). This impulse drove him to encounter St. Aldwyn, "a figure who appears to defy a rigid professional identity or *persona* and stands outside of any given or preordained frame."[19] Although "the scandal-mongering world . . . [sought] to overturn Harold's good name with accusations of arson,"[20] his commitment to his people, his willingness to give his total being without coercion, allowed him to realize his spiritual freedom ultimately. Neither the church, the colonial-capitalist authorities, nor an anestheticizing school system should prevent colonial people from realizing their possibilities in their own land.

Those That Be in Bondage is somewhat roughly hewn, but it is a very valuable achievement. A. J. Seymour says that the work suffers from "the shapelessness of being successive episodes" and argues that the "characters are not fully round, although they have vitality, and, in the Eighteenth Century manner, the author keeps interjecting moral comments. Four chapters are merely descriptions of Tobago, in the best guide book fashion, there is the account of a riot on a sugar estate and many instances occur of the florid oratory and rhetoric that are characteristic of Webber the politician."[21] Although there is much truth in Seymour's observation, the text remains a vigorous protest against the evils of the plantation system, as Seymour acknowledges in his criticism.[22]

There is also much truth in Harris's observation that "Webber's vision of 'bondage'—though apparently rooted in political and economic legacies—is determined by a psychology of fate, fate so restrictive that the characters in his novel seem unable to breach certain formulae, certain structures of ornament."[23] This is ironic since Webber, in his protest against the treatment of East Indians and the colonial system, tries to open new terrain and new ways of seeing for his characters. But then, at that moment of his development, Webber was trying to extricate himself from the strictures of the system in which he may have been trapped. In time, his populist strain would give way to that of a socialist orientation toward the world. He, too, would have "to breach certain formulae [and] certain structures of ornament" to become the person he became.

In spite of its shortcomings, *Those That Be in Bondage* represents a transition from the oral literary tradition and its episodic dimension and the more developed West Indian novel. It is a transitional piece that inaugurates a realist tradition in West Indian literature that explores the dawning social and political consciousness of a people, which continued in works such as Ralph Boissiere's *Crown Jewel* (1952), V. S. Naipaul's *A House for Mr. Biswas* (1961), and Earl Lovelace's *The Dragon Can't Dance* (1970). Harris notes: "When one reflects on the distinguished body of writing that has come from Trinidad born authors, who include C. L. R. James, Alfred Mendes, Ralph de Boissiere, V. S. Naipaul, Samuel Selvon, Earl Lovelace, and others, one looks to the 'first' in such a faculty of design for seeds of impulse both ominous and instructive within the medium of the twentieth century that spans areas of colonialism and post-colonialism, empires and revolutions."[24]

Those That Be in Bondage, a pioneering work, signified yet another challenge to colonialism and its inability to deal with the irrationalities the colonial system was causing among the East Indians, the most vulnerable of the colonized subjects, and the Europeans who had come to the colony to superintend them. Drawing heavily on plantation life in British Guiana, the novel probes the question of how Englishness came into conflict with the lives and practices of the indentures, how it subverted their lives and distorted their psyches. In tackling "the great tragedy" that grew out of indentureship, Webber challenges obvious injustices and demonstrates perspicacity in his understanding the deleterious effects of the mental or physical bondage that inheres in the colonialist-capitalist system. Harold's major problem lay in his inability to break away from the temporal laws of the church and give himself to the eternal laws of human progress and brotherhood. Such sentiments are captured in Harold's last words as he leaves Tobago for London: "Men's heart in its rise and fall is as changeless as the tides of the sea; on the banks of the Nile, the Euphrates, or the Ganges: on the Tiber or the Thames, under the white peaked tops of the Himalayas, or by the sunny waters of the Caribbean: those that are not as well as those that be in bondage" (*Bondage*, 236).

In other words, wherever one goes, people possess similar dreams of freedom. Wherever they find themselves, they all seek varied avenues to express that freedom of body and spirit. In this context, physical or spiritual bondage is never conducive to the well-being of people. Such is the profound concern of this difficult novel. It raises troubling philosophical questions about the nature of existence and the need for men and women to struggle against the conditions that keep them in bondage. It also illustrates an important dimension of the Caribbean tradition of resistance that we find in literature, to which Daly alludes in *West Indian Freedom and West Indian Literature*, and a theme I developed in *Resistance and Caribbean Literature*. In many important ways, *Those That Be in Bondage* articulates the aspirations of West Indian people via the medium of literature and speaks to their constant quest for freedom and justice.

CHAPTER TWO

THE PRIVATE THOUGHTS OF A POLITICAL MAN
The Making of A. R. F. Webber, 1917–19

If love could bring you joy
I would abundance spread thee:
If pride could bring you safety
Mountains I will build thee

But naught that I can wish you,
Nor still undying feel
Will strew your path with roses,
Or buy you free from care.

The world's a stage by setting
And you must be a playwright,
And actor too, and "prompter":
For the band that fain would help you,
Will be forbid and useless.
—A. R. F. WEBBER, "Poem to My Daughter"

Wouldst thou be Great?
Then grapple to the soul these primal truths.
Greatness is neither born of intolerance nor schism,
But 'tis a sturdy growth of open minds,
And fierce competing.
—A. R. F. WEBBER, "Guiana!"

THE END OF THE GREAT WAR (1914–18) ushered in new social and political relations in the Caribbean and the colonial world and made questions of self-determination and racial awareness even more urgent. Not that there were no indigenous liberation movements prior to the war, but the contradictions in the colonial-capitalist world simply gave colonial peoples a better opening and a greater determination to continue their struggle for liberation. In a way, it allowed more people to speak about their liberation in their countries with greater confidence and assurance. A. J. P. Taylor, a British historian, noted: "In 1917 European history, in the old sense, came to an end. World history began. It was the year of Lenin and Woodrow Wilson, both of whom repudiated the traditional standards of political behavior. Both preached Utopia, Heaven on Earth. It was the moment of birth for our contemporary world; the dramatic moment of modern man's existence."[1] By inclination and training, Caribbean people were positioned to etch themselves into this phase of social development. C. L. R. James noted that Caribbean people descended from the same stock of people as the Haitians and lived a similar life on the plantations that "made them what they were." Such a tendency inhered in people who had made the Middle Passage and who "had to learn all that they can and build a new life with what they gathered from the standards, the ideas and the ideologies of the people and the new civilization in which they live."[2] He emphasized that African people did not come to the Caribbean as empty vessels. By looking at the past, one could get a good idea about what Caribbean people could achieve. James noted:

> The Negro people in the Caribbean are of the same stock as the men who played such a role in the history of their time. We are the product of the same historical past and the same type of life, and as long as we are not being educated by the Colonial Office (or the stooges of the financial interests), we shall be able to do whatever we have to do. We have to remember that where slavery was abolished by law, the great mass of the Negro slaves had shown that they were ready to take any steps that were necessary to free themselves. That was a very important step in the making of the Caribbean people.[3]

The war also had a tremendous liberating effect in that it opened up new possibilities for the people of the Caribbean. Those who went abroad to help "make the world safe for democracy" demanded more democracy at home when they returned from the war. This resulted in a greater intensity of the nationalist struggle and a rise of racial pride throughout the Caribbean and other parts of the colonial world after the war had ended. The war also had an important impact on those who served in it. James remembered seeing soldiers from Trinidad going to war, many of whom had never left the narrow confines of their villages, many of whom "wore shoes consistently for the first time."[4] They became first-class soldiers to the astonishment of all those who saw them perform. Speaking specifically about Captain Arthur Cipriani, one of the leading proponents of self-government and a West Indian federation, James averred: "From that time he advocated independence, self-government, and federation on the basis that the West Indian rank and file, 'the bare-foot man' as he called him, was able to hold his own with any sort of people anywhere. He had seen it in war, a stern test. That was the basis of his ceaseless agitation from island to island in the British Caribbean [and British Guiana], mobilising labour against capital for independence and federation."[5]

In Grenada, the Grenada Association demanded greater representation of Grenadians in running their government. Several of the leaders who emerged in Grenada and other West Indian islands "had a tour abroad before they began their political career. . . . They contended that West Indians were now sufficiently educated to have a say in their government and they recommended that elected members be included in the legislature."[6] As a result of the growing discontent and violence in the islands and on the mainland and the many petitions sent to His Majesty's government, the Hon. E. L. F. Wood, undersecretary of state for the colonies, was sent to the West Indies and Guyana to survey the conditions of the people of those colonies. His visit lasted from December 1921 to February 1922. He reported that several reasons made it likely

> that the common demand for a measure of representative government will in the long run prove irresistible. The wave of democratic sentiment has been powerfully stimulated by the war. Education is rapidly spreading, and tending to produce a coloured and black intelligentsia, of which the members are quick to absorb elements of knowledge requisite for entry into learned professions, and return from travel abroad with minds emancipated and enlarged, ready to devote time and energy to propaganda among their own people. Local traditions of representative institutions reinforce these tendencies.[7]

As with most of these reports on conditions in the colonial territories, the authors thought it necessary to slander the intelligence of the working people.[8] Wood and his group were no exception. They reported that the demands for elective representatives among the West Indian communities were far less substantial than among the leaders who championed these ideas. To an "ignorant and uneducated population," it was "comparatively simple for good organisers to arrange effective mass meetings to advance a cause, with regard to which not one person in twenty, if cross-examined as to what it was all about, would be able to give an intelligent reply."[9] He blamed the teachers for this state of behavior and noted: "Practically all elementary school teachers in the West Indies are of unmixed negro descent. They are actively interested in politics, and in Jamaica and British Guiana are, in the opinion of some, inclined to take an excessive part in political disputation and organization."[10] It did not trouble Wood or his party that the Trinidad Workingmen's Association that greeted them when they arrived at Port of Spain, Trinidad, on January 23, 1922, came into existence as early as 1897 and that throughout its history had shown a firm grasp of the issues that concerned their liberation.[11] Wood did not know Caribbean history and so, as James suggested, could not appreciate the freedom-loving spirit of Caribbean people.

The issues that were important to people of the West Indies at the end of the war were the same issues that plagued the people of Guyana, although there was more poverty and illness there than in the other West Indian territories.[12] In his *Centenary History*, Webber reported that approximately 800 Guyanese fought in the war.[13] In 1918 several hundreds of these veterans returned to Guyana. Although Webber, an army reservist, did not fight in the war, he spent a few months in London in the fall of 1918, where he heard lots of discussions about the destructiveness of the war (over nine million soldiers died) and the importance of "national self-determination," one of the great principles of the war.[14] Voracious reader, political animal, conversationalist, and raconteur that he was, he picked up a lot of what was happening to the men who were fighting to save (and in some instances to expand) His Majesty's empire. Such energy and intelligence would serve his country well.

When Webber returned home, he must have been informed about the state of affairs on the other islands. As a newspaperman, he was in touch with the sentiments of the radical movements and organizations in the regions, such as the Trinidad Workingmen's Association, T. A. Marryshow's group in Grenada, and C. D. Rawle's group in Dominica. It has been argued that Webber's politics were influenced by the work of Marryshow, Cipriani, and Rawle.[15] As a part of the "coloured and black intelligentsia" of the society who, as Wood noted, were powerful enough "to mold the thoughts of the majority of to-morrow," Webber knew that his work was cut out for him. The rise of an indigenous bourgeoisie and an active working class was at hand. His activities on their behalf and his address to the Wood Commission supported this position. The Great War had drawn Guyana into the currents of world affairs. The Guyanese were no longer isolated islanders or colonists. They were caught up in the grand struggle against imperialism and the imperative "to make the world safe for democracy."[16]

At a personal level, the Great War had profound effects on Webber in that it prodded him to examine his own life and to ask serious questions about life and death, love and hate, war and peace, belief and unbelief, and truth and untruth, and a host of other questions. Undoubtedly, at the age of thirty-five, with a calamitous war raging, he had to question what was happening around and within him. Hence, his first task after returning to Guyana in 1918 was to assemble his published poems into a slight volume, *Glints from an Anvil: Being Lines of Song*, which was published in 1919.[17] An extended study of these poems allows us to appreciate the issues that engaged Webber for the last fourteen years of his life and how he approached them. It reveals a deep philosophical mind that engaged his ontological concerns, his society, and its future in an unflinching manner.

The seventeen poems contained in *Glints from an Anvil,* written between 1915 and 1918, reflect the disillusionment Webber felt during this period and the comfort he received from his Christian beliefs and certain fundamental truths of life. In reading his poems, one cannot help but feel that Webber was fascinated by death, perhaps even a premonition of his early death, a point I demonstrate as the work proceeds. "Wisdom Cometh in the Morning" (1915) celebrates the power of love rather than the destructive poison of hate. In it, he advises:

> *That to love is life's great blessing:*
> *That to hate is a sinful waste,*
> *And to once forgive is better*
> *Than to drain full draughts of pleasure!*

In "Peace or War" (1917), written during the height of the war, he emphasizes the right of people/nations to control their own affairs and the contradiction that is inherent in war itself. First, he declares, "The cry is Peace!" Then he asks, "But what if Peace means future War, / And yet more savage warfare?" One would remember that the slogan of the Great War was "the war to end all wars" that would "make the world safe for democracy." Sensing the need for peace, he asserts:

> *Then let there be no Peace*
> *Till War is banished;*
> *Till People's free may cleave to light*
> *And none shall claim dominion.*
> *A man's a man the right to choose*
> *The way he shall be governed.*
> *No swords shall conquer will*
> *To live and breathe and have our being.*
>
> *When caste of war shall know its end:*
> *When arrogance gives way to right:*
> *When justice sits enthroned in peopled will,*
> *And equal rights be chartered all;*
> *When war is banished rapine stayed,*
> *When all may breathe a free man's air,*
> *Let there be peace!*

Webber's belief in the self-determination and self-government of his people would play a powerful role in his life. He was aware of the contradiction between the call for peace and the intractable nature of war. Although he believed that peace was worth fighting for, he was acutely aware that the conduct of war is demonstrably bad at ensuring peace, hence his admonition: "The cry is peace! / But what if Peace means future war?" Inherent in the war and the cry for peace was people's right to be free.

Yet if truth is war's first casualty, then certainly God is its first conscript. In 1914, on Christmas Day, war stopped, and British and German soldiers along the trench lines set aside their weapons, greeted one another, "gossiped, exchanging cigarettes." In some places they played football. They met again the next day. Then, after strong rebuke from headquarters, firing gradually started again. In the churches at home, prayers were offered for victory and for the slaughter of the men who were exchanging cigarettes. An English poet (J. C. Squire) wrote:

> *God heard the embattled nations sing and shout:*
> *"Gott strafe England"—"God save the King"—*
> *"God this"—"God that"—and "God the other thing."*
> *"My God!" said God, "I've got my work cut out."*[18]

I am not sure that Webber was aware of Squire's epigram, which was first published in May 1916,[19] but in December 1915 Webber offered "What of the Night?" a poem that posed similar questions about the use/role of God in the mayhem of the war. He asks:

> *Christians, what of the night?*
> *The light has failed: the earth is dark*
> *Man's hand is 'gainst his brother:*
> *Cain unloosed stalks abroad*
> *And earth is drunk with blood.*
> *Centuries of work undangered stand*
> *And effort seems in vain*
> *Christian, what of the night?*
>
> *The cloud is low: the night is dark;*
> *Grim War escheats thy tenets fair.*
> *Didst not thine enemies declare*
> *For war prepare?*

If the church has failed and God has been vanquished, we should not blame the doctrine of love and truth the church proclaims:

We [should] blame those guardians clothed in purple,
Who hear and smile at evil,
So silks and gold engird it.

These are the persons who have failed humankind and failed to preach the true life-giving messages of the gospel. Therefore, he avers:

The Greater Good prevail,
The spurious faith must under fall,
And light alone shall reign!
Warring nations shall be still
And lay aside the spear;
Truth, Knowledge and the Right
And Peace and Love and Grace:
These shall be: but not until
All men shall be thy equal brother,
And all be one in God.

This is his assertion of faith. The power of Truth, Knowledge, Peace, Love, and Grace should be the guiding principles of all people.

In Webber's schema, however, women/mothers play a central role in keeping the family together. They should be given the responsibility of keeping the national/global family together. He believed that if mothers/women ran the world, they would bring the same care to the larger family of nations as they do to their immediate families. As a result, there would be less death and destruction to all. In "The Mother," he says a mother makes all the difference:

I am the pillar of the house—
The keystone of the arch I am:
Take me away, and roof and wall
Would fall to ruin utterly.

I am the twist that holds together
The children in its sacred ring
Their knot of love, from whose close tether
No lost child goes a wandering.

Having established the centrality of a mother's role in binding the family together, he extends this notion to the world and the troubling wars that beset us. In "L'Envoi," the only sonnet in his book, he counsels:

The canons rattle and wars dread battle
May for Kings decide
Blood is spilled and men are killed
For dreams and conquests bold.
Yet none are long enduring.
Mothers pay and cease to pray
For all seems lost in holocaust
And none to cry, "we halt!"
Oh! mothers strong, I am not wrong
There is a long to-morrow!
When ye who cradling, rule the world,
Shall bid all war to cease.
Cry Peace! and true Fraternity!
And Who shall say thee Nay?

Romantic love also held an important place in Webber's life. In "A Phantasie," he speaks of his enduring love of a woman and presumably what he is willing to bear to win her over. In "A Thing of Beauty," he celebrates an inner love and a beauty that is more lasting and more sublime than mere physical beauty:

The beauty that from souls do shine,
That 'lumines smile and look.
Such beauty bears the withering blast,
And earns a soul's repose!
For know it now, my charming lass,
It never fades to nothingness.

In "Vigil Keeping," he is willing to wait as long as it takes to snatch

That great reward,
And drink nectar
From those lips
That smile and burn.

Love, he believes, is the greatest gift. For him,

The Soul full grown
That's loved and loves
Is joy to God

> *And takes its absolution*
> *From its own intent.*
>
> *Then Peace be still—*
> *And let it be!*
> *For joy is love*
> *And love is peace—*
> *And all but everlasting joy.*

As is to be expected in a soul as deep and searching as Webber's, a meditation on death had a prominent part in his poems. This concern was always on his mind. Four of the most touching poems in this volume, "The Life in Death," "Distance," "He Wrought His Trade," and "Oh! Banish Fear," revolve around the theme of death. The passing of O. E. L. Sharples, a distinguished Guyanese lawyer whom Webber knew very well, left him saddened, apprehensive, and deeply reflective about life.[20] To Webber, death and life were part of "one eternal whole—Life—Love—Death—All?" or, as he says in "He Wrought His Trade,"

> *And now I know and sense*
> *That Life may be but moving death,*
> *And Death but'st manifest of life;*
> *For accomplishment is all.*

But if death is a part of life and vice versa, Webber asks, why then "at Death we shrink and shiver" since it "joins us to Eternity." His answer echoes similar sentiments in St. Paul's Epistle to the Corinthians (13:13): "For now we see through a glass, darkly; but then face to face: now I know in part; but then shall I know even as I am known." Webber, however, puts it in his own inimitable way as he muses tantalizingly to Sharples:

> *Time shall tell me; you may not.*
> *I must eat the great Passover:*
> *I must tread the hidden way.*
> *Our souls shall meet—through years forever:*
> *Knowing all, and yet the past forgotten,*
> *Struggling, fighting, still embracing—*
> *All created, all forgiving;*
> *All to one Great Silken Throne.*

"Oh! Banish Fear" is an extended examination of death. In this poem, the poet sits on a riverbed and ponders the mystery of life and death even as he asks "Kingly nature's God," "Teach me then to fear not Death." To Webber, death is but another stage in an unending journey of a person's existence. Meditating this mighty stream, he beckons all to sit with him,

> *And learn from fullness of the deep,*
> *The calm and peace that comes to all*
> *Who can but feel the easy stage that God ordains*
> *Shall mark each movement of this sphere;*
> *From birth to death; each but a shifted scene.*

In "The Life and Death," he indicates that only time will reveal the whole mystery of life, which we, in our blinded state, cannot but fathom from this standpoint of our existence. Yet there are things we can do to make ourselves ready for death, or, as some wise sage noted, "I will live for a cause. If I die in the process, then so be it."

What, then, should we fear about death? According to Webber, we should only fear the life not lived well, which, to him, is really living life in death—or as a Caribbean aphorism suggests, acting as "a living or walking dead." Thus he advises:

> *This then, let's lisp it well:*
> *If on life's great way you go*
> *Scattering deeds of cheer, not woe:*
> *If a brother met is glum,*
> *Tilt your chin and cry, "What cheer!*
> *Brother hasten, yon is clear."*
> *If lame dogs you helped o'er stiles*
> *Death is naught save evening miles.*
>
> *Shun the narrowing forms of creed,*
> *Practise broader, wider, need—*
> *String your rosary with deeds,*
> *Each will grow on what it feeds.*
> *If your life has selfish been,*
> *Death will have a fearsome mien;*
> *Lead you out a darkened room,*
> *Through a long and gathering gloom.*
>
> *But the soul wide pressed with joy*
> *Finds in death but life's alloy:*
> *Never lonesome, never dull,*
> *Leading ways most merciful.*

Each good deed a beacon sign.
Lighting all along the line.
Others woven, bright and clear,
Making garlands for your hair.

The life well spent is cause for cheer;
The life ill ordered stays its growth,
And turns exhaust to source, or tries again;
But fear nor helps nor hinders these.
Spend less time in fear of death
And more in ways to live.
Learn great lessons from life's all:
The moving flood, the stately palm,
The industrious bee: the ants great psalm:
And let all discord banished be.
The earth's attuned to life and death,
Each birth and death, and sorrows fall,
Each sign and pulse is sired by God—
And let that truth suffice for all.

This was Webber's creed. He lived and died by it. His was a magnanimous life that took in every aspect of the world around him. His interests were wide and all encompassing. He believed in giving fully of himself. He was a man in search of life even if death necessarily would catch up with him, as it does us all. But he feared not death. As he said in his poem:

The fear of death should only be:
What trails of love we leave?
The welling tears around a bier,
Of what is their express?

In 1929, less than three years before he died, he meditated upon life publicly and penned the following lines:

No sunset and evening star for me,
Nor twilight and vesper bell.
Let me fall on the raging battle field
With banners gaily flying,
In full throated battle cry
With drums a throb and bugles calling[21]

Webber's destiny was always tied up with the economic and social development of Guyana. It is no wonder then that he used the sentiments contained in "The March of Time" (1916) and "Guiana" to spur on his compatriots to greater heights. Slavery and indentureship may have played their parts in keeping most of the country's inhabitants down, but that was not a sufficient reason for the lack of initiative on the part of the colonists, whom he felt were not doing as much as they could to push their country forward. The colonists had not taken up the challenges of developing their land, hence he warned:

> *Colonist, what of the day?*
> *Have we lain enslumbered,*
> *While the tide did steal and race,*
> *To wide and open sea?*

In other words, he is asking his fellow colonists if they had done enough to make our land prosperous. Then he admonishes:

> *The hour has struck to struggle,*
> *And the time to fight has come.*
> *Challenge destiny to combat:*
> *And be silent as the wolf.*

> *Colonist, the way to greatness is endeavour,*
> *And the road untrod is barren.*
> *Then; shall we not be up and doing,*
> *And be reapers in boundless harvest time?*

> *Yes my brethren: with the bugles—*
> *If ye would the children say:*
> *With the morning ye had acted,*
> *And had wrought the Golden Way.*

In "Guiana," he strikes a similar note as he celebrates his people and calls upon them to do the things that would make the country great. The poem celebrates a gritty stoicism and envisions a land where manly Spartan glory prevails. He asks of his countrymen, "Wouldst thou be Great?" and then calls upon them to grapple with certain "primal truths" such as the "sturdy growth of open minds / And [the acceptance of] fierce competition." "Thou shall be great," he says, "When thy broad and fertile acres / Teem with husbandmen and industry." In that world, equality, nobility, and honor shall rule—the utopia Lenin and Wilson sought to create (according to Taylor) and which garnered the support of some people at the beginning of the Great War. It was the "socialist strain" in Webber to which Reno Rohini alluded when he offered his biographical sketch of this great patriot. This, however, is Webber's version of the world he envisioned:

Thou shall be Great
When thy sons, reared in the school of stern endeavour
Shall scorn all aid to preferment
Save only merit.
Thou shalt be Great
When to claim office on the accident of birth
Shall be deemed ignoble and unworthy
By thy gallant sons.

Thou shall be Great
When thy sons, reared as men who, grappling
In the fierce struggles of the stadium
Fought and fell, scorning all aid but majesty of strength,
Shall shun the languid couch of safety
And into the open world advance,
Armed only with the shield of merit,
And the mighty sword of valour:
And there combating with the opposing tides
Win their laurels.

Thou shall be Great
When, returning with their shields, they
Shall say they won in open combat fair
And be hailed as heroes fit to stand
Midst gathering throngs of noble men;
When all shall hail thee as the mother
Of those who labour to be strong,
Then shall thou be Great.

These early poems give us a sense of the philosophy that guided Webber's life. According to Norman Cameron, these poems reflect Webber's "courageous and patriotic" tendencies.[22] They also show us the breadth of his concerns, his innate abilities, and his wide-ranging interests. As a self-made man, he needed as much self-motivation as was possible. He may have been the Edgar Guest of his country. As he emphasized in a poem to his daughter, Ivy, in 1920 when she was in the dumps:

Your own strong soul must guide you,
Your own will standing clear,
For nothing ever matters
But what we build and perfect

Elaborating on these principles, he noted, "What we are, and will be, / Is born of naught save wishes." But wishes are not enough, hence his admonition: "Then have a care in wishes, / And think, and build and Do!" These lines were so important to Ivy that she kept the poem throughout her life. She passed it on to her daughter Barbara, who, in turn, kept it.

As Webber entered the later phase of his life, he was guided by these simple, stoic principles that informed everything that he did. Reading Webber, one might have thought that he was a fan of Guest, who offered:

You are the one that has to decide;
Whether you'll do it or toss it aside;
You are the one who must make up your mind;
Whether you will lead or will linger behind;
Whether you'll try for the goal that's afar.
Or just be contented to stay where you are.
Take it or leave it. Here's something to do!
Just think it over—It's all up to you.

In today's jargon, one would say that Webber's challenge to the Caribbean people was not so much to go through life as victims but to live life courageously. It was the message he tried to convey to his daughter and other Caribbean people through his poems.

CHAPTER THREE

WEBBER'S ENTRANCE TO THE
POLITICAL ARENA, 1919–21

Several reasons combine to make it likely that the common demand for a measure of representative government will in the long run prove irresistible. The wave of democratic sentiment has been powerfully stimulated by the War. Education is rapidly spreading, and tending to produce coloured and black intelligentsia, of which the members are quick to absorb elements of knowledge requisite for entry into learned professions, and return from travel abroad with minds emancipated and enlarged, ready to devote time and energy to propaganda among their own people.

—E. F. L. WOODS, "Visit to the West Indies and British Guiana," 1922

I do not desire to say much about the [election] struggle, but if one thing is patent, I have always fought for the black man's place in the sun both in and out of columns of the *Daily Chronicle*.

—A. R. F. WEBBER, *Daily Chronicle*, 1921

THOSE THAT BE IN BONDAGE AND *GLINTS FROM AN ANVIL* established Webber as a literary light in his society and made him more respectable to the business community. Up until then, Webber saw himself as a litterateur, as he defined himself in "How I Won My Election" in 1921.[1] Additionally, there is every indication that Webber had risen in the estimation of the dominant commercial group since he became the secretary of the Colonization Committee, a group that concerned itself with the colony's irrigation and drainage problems. At the very least, his association with the planters and the commercial class gave him an intimate knowledge of the workings of the society's business elite, and this positioned him to understand how that sector functioned and what was important to them. However, he was becoming a bit restless serving in the business community since he had seen himself primarily as a litterateur.

In 1919 he was appointed editor of the *Daily Chronicle*, succeeding C. W. Marchant, and served in that capacity until 1925, when the newspaper went into liquidation. Such a position conferred immense influence upon Webber and, to a greater degree, brought him closer to the politics of the community. The local press was perhaps the most important instrument of political advocacy and information in the community. As one reader of the *Daily Chronicle* noted on October 6, 1921, "The masses looked largely to the press for political guidance." In addition to being editor for the *Daily Chronicle,* Webber became the secretary of the British Guiana Sugar Planters' Association, publicity secretary of the Georgetown Chamber of Commerce, and editor of the latter's official journal. It is safe to say that at that moment of his career, Webber was close to and apparently courted the favor of the members of the commercial class. According to Harold Lutchman, Webber also secured a concession from the Crown to explore for oil in the country.[2]

A very good example of Webber's support for and service to the commercial class manifested itself during the controversy that arose around the passage of the Shop Assistant's Hours Bill in 1921. This bill allowed shops to open at 7:30 A.M. rather than 7 A.M., a measure that cut into the time that the workers would have to serve the commercial class and certainly gave them more time to spend with their families. In his capacity as publicity secretary of the Chamber of Commerce, Webber was selected to a committee that was responsible for sending a letter to the governor to withhold his assent to the bill until the chamber had time to study it. It is likely that his advocacy of the Chamber of Commerce's interest must have conflicted with his feelings for working people. However, as we follow Webber's career, we begin to detect the ambivalence that characterizes individuals from his strata: his uncertainty as to which class he really ought to serve. Looking at the example that his uncle had set, he could not have been entirely happy in his position. By the middle of the year, he began to change his tune and started to support the interests of working people.

Even as a spokesperson for the Chamber of Commerce, Webber continued his activities in the community and subsequently offered himself for elections. On Friday, February 24, 1921, he attended a meeting of the (Wesleyan) East Indian Young Men's Society (EIYMS), where he delivered an address entitled "The Psychology of Communities" to a "fairly large gathering" of people. Peter Ruhomon, the secretary of the EIYMS and one of the first Creole historians on indenture, was present at that meeting.[3] When he wrote *The East Indians in British Guiana,* he quoted Webber to prove how cruel the conditions of East Indian indentureship were. In July Webber attended a meeting at Georgetown Town Hall that was chaired by Hubert Critchlow, secretary treasurer of the BGLU, to protest the excessive rents that the tenants of Georgetown were being charged, particularly at a time when wages had dropped drastically. At that meeting, Webber supported the tenants and complimented Critchlow for the organizational work he was doing among working people. The *Daily Chronicle* noted: "Mr. Webber expressed his sympathy with the movement and in the course of his remarks stated that the tenants had a great organizer behind them in Mr. Critchlow and that the same weapon which had been used on the employers could again be used with similar results on the landlords provided the cause was righteous."[4] A day later, his paper ran an editorial, presumably written by Webber, against those landlords "whose scandalous exploitation" of the tenants had reached "such a pitch that public opinion must be aroused." The editorial continued: "Wednesday night's meeting in the Town Hall endeavored to call attention to the grievous burdens now being carried by the people in the outrageous rents that some landlords find it possible to impose on their tenants. We are anxious not to be misunderstood on this question of landlords; there are many landlords who are beyond reproach but also many unfortunately who are not."[5]

Although he was very cautious, this broadside seems to be Webber's first public attack against the commercial class. Since the commercial class needed workers, and the prohibitive rents made it more difficult for them to recruit workers, Webber's tentative opening was safe enough. Since some of the leading civil servants who lived on fixed incomes (about $75–$120 per month) were forced to pay about 45 percent of their salary toward rent, Webber may have thought that he could attack the "landlord class," as he called them, with a certain amount of impunity. In the same editorial, he noted: "Sugar manufacturers are now faced with almost certain ruin, and wages have had to be brought down and possibly will be brought down further again; merchants are losing money every day in Water Street through the grave industrial crisis in which we are now caught; and it is ridiculous to suggest that the landlord class alone is to be set apart as a favoured cult and not be asked to bear their share of the industrial burden."[6] In this episode, Webber is still pleading the cause of that privileged strata about whom he spoke so passionately in *Those That Be in Bondage*—that group of colored persons whose ability and talents were not recognized or rewarded sufficiently by the colonial authorities.

Webber, however, may have been beginning to find his position intolerable— that of serving the business class but being sympathetic to working people. In August 1921, we glimpse his giving thought to seeking elective office. In its editorial of August 31, the *Daily Chronicle* announced that in spite of rumors to the contrary, Webber would not take part in the elections scheduled for October of that year. To do so, the editors argued, would make it difficult for them "to pronounce impartially on the issues and therefore we must keep free of personal participation in the conflict." In making such a cavalier statement, the editors left room open for the specific circumstances under which their editor might change his mind:

> The time might come when the interests of our party [one is not sure of the party to which they are referring] may be so threatened and jeopardised that even editorial well being must be relegated to the background, and the respon-

sibility assumed for a contested election; but we envisage no such danger in the immediate future and we see nothing to be gained by asking any constituency to divide on the subject of whether our editor is to be entrusted with their suffrages [*sic*] or no.[7]

The first indication that Webber may have changed his mind about taking part in the general elections occurred on September 27, when the *Daily Chronicle*, in a news item, "Mr. A. R. F. Webber: A Likely Candidate," reported that Webber's name "was mentioned as a likely candidate for the seat of F.R. [Financial Representative] for the [Berbice] County at the coming general elections." The report went on to speak of the incumbent's (Joseph Eleazer's) increasing unpopularity and the "solid support" that Webber was beginning to receive from the small electorate. The increasingly "solid support" for Webber was reiterated in another *Daily Chronicle* news story of September 29.[8]

Having nudged the electorate a bit, the *Daily Chronicle* continued to push Webber's candidacy very strongly. Presumably, "the interests" of the newspaper's party were being "threatened or jeopardized," and thus its "editorial well being" could be thrown aside for a while. The newspaper's professed "impartiality" would also have to take a backseat in light of Webber's electoral interest. Eight days after Webber was mentioned as a "likely candidate," another news story reported that an unnamed "representative" was gratified that Webber had offered "no opposition" to his name being put forward as a candidate for the county of Berbice. The representative then painted Webber's accomplishment in terms most glorious and agreeable:

I have been watching his career ever since he was placed in charge of the *Daily Chronicle* newspaper. He has manifested a very keen interest in the affairs of the colony generally, and in a particular manner he has championed irrigation and drainage schemes. Constitutionally, Mr. Webber has the courage of his convictions and cannot be bought. He is not a toad to any particular party, and he is never fearful of expressing his opinions, even though those opinions may run counter to the opinions of any particular party in the colony, or to the Government itself. He is an old colonist and has studied local conditions very closely, and is intimately informed as to other aspects of Colonial affairs.[9]

At this point of his career, Webber had been thoroughly absorbed into the community (he is considered an "old colonist"), was aware of the major problems the colony faced, and, more important, was accepted by the community as one of them. Needless to say, an informed position on irrigation and drainage was a necessary prerequisite for anyone who hoped to serve his or her constituents' needs. That Webber had served as the secretary of the Colonization Committee must have worked in his favor. Given such strong encouragement, Webber broke his promise not to contest the general elections and on October 1 announced his candidacy for one of the Financial Representative seats on the Court of Policy for the county of Berbice.

Having made the plunge into electoral politics, the first image that Webber had to live down was the conception in some people's mind that he was the "planters' man." As publicity secretary of the Planters' Association, Webber represented the interest of the planter class, and the people were not about to be taken in by his newly avowed interest in working people. In refuting this notion, Webber took pains to point out that it was not true "to suggest that I am a Planters' candidate; or that I am coming forward under the aegis of the planters."[10] If he were going to represent the people, the first image he had to eradicate from the voters' minds was that of being the "planters' candidate" or the "planters' man." Only time would tell how successful he would be in this endeavor. From this point on, we begin to see Webber leaning in a more populist direction, the interest of the working people taking precedence in his work.

Once Webber decided to run, he had the immediate support of the *Daily Chronicle*, where he retained his position as editor of the newspaper. Within two weeks of his announcement for the Berbice seat, the *Daily Chronicle* ran two editorials (on October 11 and 18, respectively) and several news reports that were favorable to his candidacy. An editorial of October 11 outlined why its editors changed their position of August 31. It argued that "the political situation [had] changed considerably" since Webber promised not to stand for election. They sought to clear away "the mist of apprehension" that their sudden turnaround had caused in the public's mind and used an insect image to explain their position: "As time went on, however, and the situation emerged from the chrysalis stage and took more definiteness of shape it became increasingly evident that the people wanted a man of action and of ideas; one who not only had a policy but had the courage to give expression to his convictions regardless of whom they might offend; and it was also borne upon us that man was Mr. A. R. F. Webber." The editorial also referred to what it called Webber's "high sense of public duty" and his newspaper's consistent championing of "the right of the people to vote in the ordering of their affairs." It concluded that Webber's "mature judgment and precision" would serve him in good stead if he were elected to the Court of Policy.[11] At that moment in Guyana's history, the destinies of the *Daily Chronicle* and Webber were deeply intertwined, and thus their fortunes were linked together. Needless to say, the newspaper promoted and supported Webber's candidacy assiduously and unashamedly.

On October 13, in a letter to the editor, D. G. Pahalan, of New Amsterdam, Berbice, supported Webber's candidacy because of what he called Webber's knowledge of the "Ways and Means" of doing things, his proximity to power since he resided in Georgetown, and his association with the *Daily Chronicle*, which allowed him to apply what Pahalan called "the elements of the Press, your only means of making known your grievances to the public and to the outside world."[12] On October 14, in another letter to the editor of the *Daily Chronicle*, a reader calling himself or herself "East Indian Voter" also used some of the above arguments to support Webber's candidacy. "East Indian Reader" observed that Webber was far superior to Eleazer, and reminded the paper's readers that Webber "fearlessly fought the rice question last year and through the medium of the *Daily Chronicle* has always championed the cause of the masses and tried to have their lot ameliorated." "East Indian Voter" also believed that because Webber was the editor of the *Daily Chronicle*, his election to the Court of Policy would grant him an important advantage over Eleazer in publicizing the plight of working people.

On October 18 the *Daily Chronicle* ran another editorial in support of Webber's candidacy. The editorial noted Webber's "twenty-five years' experience in local commerce and politics" (not quite accurate since Webber arrived in Guyana in 1899) and reminded its readers that the directors of the *Daily Chronicle* selected Webber as manager and editor in chief of the paper because of his "commercial ability and his literary capacity. 'Earnest, thoughtful, persuasive' he withal wields a virile pen. . . . As to his business acumen the improvement of the commercial side of the organization bears abundant testimony [to that fact]." The editorial continued:

> The rice farmers of the colony will not easily forget, we are persuaded, the strenuous battle which he put up on their behalf. . . . His bold outspoken policy in that [latter] connexion is only equaled by the courageous fight which he has always put forward for drainage and irrigation. These he has always recognized as two of the primary considerations for our progress as a people and he has never failed in season and out of season to urge upon the Government the necessity for adopting such schemes. The general trend of political thought today is in favour of irrigation and drainage, but it must not be forgotten that Mr. Webber was a pioneer in this respect, and as a result of his assiduous efforts there is every likelihood of irrigation and drainage being made a Colonial question in the near future.[13]

The sentiments in the news reports and letters to the editor that supported Webber's candidacy that appeared in the *Daily Chronicle* invariably wound up in the editorials, which used the same language of support. On the contrary, no letters or news reports favorable to Eleazer appeared in Webber's newspaper. These factors seem to suggest that the letters to the editor, the news reports, and editorials that appeared on Webber's behalf were part of a well-orchestrated strategy to elect him to the Court of Policy. Whatever the claims of neutrality that the *Daily Chronicle* espoused on August 31, they were all gone by the time the general elections rolled around in October, as the newspaper unapologetically supported and actively promoted Webber's candidacy. It did not hurt that R. E. Brassington, one of the most prominent members of the legislature, also supported Webber's candidacy.

On October 19 Webber was victorious at the polls (he defeated his opponent by 83 votes) and entered the history books of Guyana as "the first editor to secure a seat in the Legislature of the colony whilst still being actively connected with a local newspaper."[14] The election results were as follows:

District	Webber	Eleazer
Weldaad	46	22
Fort Wellington	23	5
Maica	7	0
Sisters	16	10
Canje	70	38
Whim	91	103
No. 53	14	14
Springlands	22	14
Total	**289**	**206**

In his victory speech, Webber felt vindicated of the charge that he was the "planters' candidate" and noted, "I do not desire to say much about the [election] struggle, but if one thing is patent, I have fought for the black man's place in the sun both in and out of the columns of the *Daily Chronicle*."[15] And, as if to support that position further, on November 4, 1921, the fortieth anniversary of the *Daily Chronicle*, Webber stated with vigor and some conviction that for the forty years of its existence, the *Daily Chronicle* always had been "on the side of the people and the avowed champion of their legitimate aspirations."

Webber had cleared the first hurdle. Whatever his links with the commercial and propertied class, the elections of 1921 forced him to take a position closer to the interests of the working people. When he started on his election journey, many persons saw him as the planters' candidate, beholden to their bidding.[16] His victory at the elections had freed him from the burdens of those obligations. After the election, Webber assumed the honorific post of "Whip and Secretary of the Electives." It was an attempt to bring cohesion to the activities of the elective members of the Combined Court. As time progressed, he vindicated the position he had taken in his victory speech: he would continue to serve the black people of his adopted home in a vigorous and forthright manner.

In winning a seat in the legislature, Webber had created history in Guyana. He was the first sitting editor of a newspaper to do so. He was also carrying on a tradition of service that his uncle had started. The same bravado and boldness that allowed him to seek an electoral seat in part of the colony that he didn't know quite well also allowed him to share the story of his victory with his people with a certain amount of honesty. Recognizing that he was "the first literateur [*sic*]" in the colony to win an election, he decided to tell "the inner story of an election fight," thereby granting his readers "a peep behind the scenes."[17] The four essays in which Webber revealed the inner dimensions of the election battle became his first attempt at autobiographical/travel writing, a genre that he would explore in the future.[18]

In these essays, Webber spoke not only about the personal traits that were necessary for a successful campaign but of some of the obstacles that he faced as well. The candidate, he said, cannot be bashful, must know something about "crowd psychology," and, most important, can be helped by certain photogenic possibilities.[19] In the final essay of the series, subtitled "The Last Stages," Webber recounted a very humorous but instructive episode about voting patterns that reflect contemporary echoes. Speaking of an encounter with a "lady friend," Webber noted:

> Knowing the influence of the eternal feminine I was soon engaged in a political canvass! "Sir," she said, "the minute I see your photo, I tell my brother-in-law if he don't vote for you he must never look me in my face again. Now I meet you," she continued, "I glad and I going to tell him so again. All of them got to vote for you," she continued triumphantly. . . . Evidently, the friendly personal touch of the photo was working its way home all right.[20]

He also spoke about another side of Caribbean politics that V. S. Naipaul captured in *The Mystic Masseur*, a situation in which a voter takes a candidate's refreshments (and in some cases his or her money) and then votes for the candidate's opponent. On the campaign trail, a "buxom" Guyanese woman reminded Webber of that fact of political life: "Sir, believe me, you gwine loss. Dey gwine drink you rum, drive in you car and voted for Mr. Eleazar." In his usually humorous manner, Webber took heart from the encounter and arrived at the following conclusion: "There was good, homely advice in that, and evidently also kindly meant. However, to be forewarned is to be forearmed: and the Constitution Ordinance forbids the providing of rum or motor cars: blessed be thee of Constitution Ordinance. I wonder what accounts for the enormous bills I have to meet, as disbursements and out-of-pockets of my generals and district managers?"[21]

Eleazar's charges that Webber was the "planters' candidate" also hurt Webber personally and cost him some votes. Webber noted:

One [charge] which he used unwittingly, but which I could never entirely counteract the effect of . . . was the canard that I was Secretary of the Planters' Association, and hence bound to obey the lawful or unlawful requests of the Planters! That cost me an immense slump in popularity and is possibly still believed by some who recorded their votes against me. Then came another [charge]: that Mr. Brassington, as chairman of the *Chronicle*, could dismiss me as Editor if I did not do the Planters' bidding![22]

The latter charge hurt Webber the most, although he didn't attempt to answer it in "How I Won the Elections." In spite of these charges, Webber was victorious in the election. What turned the battle for Webber was a simple, spontaneous act of discarding his blouse during one of his stump speeches when he was faced by what he called "the genus heckler." He says: "My dramatic touch brought forth bursts of applause, and thereafter I had the meeting my own way. Subsequently, I was told by my heckler that the fighting spirit then displayed did more to win his vote than all my studied phrases and arguments put together. Thirteen others—what a number—conceded similar conversions: for it was a fighter they wanted."[23]

Webber also described the tension-filled atmosphere as the votes were counted. As the votes from Whim, one of the polling areas in which he was weaker, were counted and Webber realized that he was victorious, perhaps had become "the senior Financial Representative" of the colony, he noted wryly: "I was scarcely elated." Recognizing the responsibility he faced and the major burden that was placed upon his shoulders, he ended his essay with the following reflection: "The battle has now been won [but] the remainder is left to be done. Confidence has been placed abundantly and has to be repaid. The recollection of this splendid struggle will remain green in my memory for evermore, and health sustaining I hope to secure for the progress of the country and the benefit of my fellow colonists as much as human endeavor and earnestness can secure."[24] Webber now had a chance to implement many of the ideals he expressed in "The March of Time" and "Guiana."

From his first election encounter, he had learned two lessons that would take him through the next eleven years of his life: his people wanted a fighter and a solemn commitment from someone to battle for their welfare. These two qualities, together with those he articulated in his poems, would shape his political career as he struggled against the colonial authorities in Guyana. As he noted in his victory speech, he would devote his energies to elevate "the black man" (the colonized) so as to ensure his rightful place within Guyanese and Caribbean society.

CHAPTER FOUR

WEBBER'S POLITICAL ASCENDANCY, 1921–25

His Excellency: What is that?

Mr. Webber: I said, sir, that he [the former governor] is now sitting in a quiet corner of London fiddling. I know he was fond of the fiddle.

His Excellency: I do not see what the observation of the Financial Representative has to do with the removal of a magazine.

Mr. Webber: In [the] process of time Your Excellency and your Lieutenant will also go into peaceful retirement in the happy possession of a pension and the people of the Colony will still be here bearing their burdens.

—EXCHANGE BETWEEN GOVERNOR GRAEME THOMSON AND WEBBER,
Combined Court, May 1925

As long as the Colony remains under a paternal sort of Government, manned chiefly by Administrators from abroad, the Citizens have to acknowledge their moral and intellectual inferiority to the peoples of the World and even to the neighbouring South American Countries. If the Citizens have within them pride and patriotism and above all else self-respect they cannot be satisfied forever to remain in the present subservient and ignominious state. Self-Government ought to be the Colony's ultimate aim.

—NAIVA TASYA, "Entre Nous"

WEBBER'S ELECTION TO THE COMBINED COURT IN 1921 coincided with strong calls throughout the West Indies for more representative government and the visit of the Hon. E. F. L. Wood, parliamentary undersecretary of state for the colonies.[1] During the early months of 1921, even before Webber was elected, the *Daily Chronicle* raised several issues about the constitution. On August 21 the newspaper criticized a policy in which the "colony's financial and economic policies are in the hands of one man, and at that, a bird of passage, with the inevitable result that there is no continuity of policy."[2] On October 2 the newspaper called for the greater participation of the Electives in running the country and argued: "The burdens of this country have to be borne by the men in the country. If the Colonial Office is prepared to foot the bill caused by the errors of the professional administrations sent us, we may smile and pass on; but since the course and charges have to be faced by us, it is only reasonable to contend that some control of Executive action should be vested in the hands of the electives." A. V. Crane, an African lawyer who later became a member of the Court of Policy, railed against the "antiquated" nature of the constitution and noted that an autocratic form of government was antithetical to the development of the country.[3]

In 1922 the economic situation worsened in Guyana. Webber noted that "the depression caused by the sugar slump was at its greatest depth," and so there was much misery in the colony.[4] In 1923 there was a severe economic dislocation in the country. Approximately 15,000 Guyanese were out of work, and businesses lost as much as $300,000. In January 1923 the police force went on strike, and by April of the following year the famous Ruimveldt Riot took place, when the dockworkers went on strike to protest the rising cost of living, a condition that was particularly harsh on working people. What began in Georgetown as a peaceful demonstration to protest "the inevitable wage question" resulted in the deaths of thirteen persons, twelve of whom were East Indians. One was African or Afro-Guyanese. Webber insists that what started as peaceful picketing was disrupted by

> unruly elements [who] invaded private homes for the purpose of driving out domestics and compelling them to join in the demonstration. . . . Meanwhile, similar demonstrations were being made on the East Bank, and the demonstrators decided upon a march to Georgetown to appeal to CROSBY, or the Governor, or probably anyone else. The Police resolved to prevent the demonstrants [sic] from joining forces with disorderly elements then threatening the city. The military formed up to hold the road at Ruimveldt. The Mounted Police charged the crowd rather than passively wait on its advance: stoning commenced, and the officer in charge ordered pot shooting at those he thought deserving it.[5]

Ravi Dev interprets this event in racial terms and argues that "the Indians were so traumatized by the incidents at Ruimveldt that there were no strikes recorded [by Indians] for the next three years. They also lost all faith in Critchlow's BGLU. The killings torpedoed a Colonisation Scheme, which envisaged re-opening Indian immigration" to Guyana so as to create an Indian state.[6] To him, the riot was part of the systematic violence that was practiced against the East Indians. Clem Seecharan argues that "there seemed to have been a deep undercurrent of Black manipulation of Indian workers' dissatisfaction, to court confrontation, in order to cripple the Colonisation Scheme and stem potential Indian domination. The disaster at Ruimveldt strengthened Indian fears of the motives of Black leaders."[7] The evaluations of Dev and Seecharan are caught in an Indocentric approach to the events that tends to reduce most of the problems of that period to a struggle between the two groups in which the Afro-Guyanese took advantage of East Indians. One is more inclined to accept Rodney's position that in British Guiana, particularly during that earlier period of its history, "contradictions between labourers did not always have a racial dimension, in the commonly accepted sense of the term 'racial.' By the same reasoning, conflicts between different race groups were not necessarily 'racial'—although disputes were always potentially more explosive when racial identifications were involved."[8]

In March 1923, however, Webber was buoyed by the election of Nelson Cannon, who, with Webber's help, won a by-election to the Georgetown seat on the Combined Court. Quickly thereafter, Cannon, a former mayor of Georgetown, aligned with Webber politically. They became close political friends and formed a political partnership that lasted for most of their political lives. Soon after Cannon's victory at the polls, Cannon and Webber began to devote their energies toward assisting the less privileged members of society and thus became identified as "the champions of the masses." As a result, they became popular figures. Harold Lutchman has argued that much to the chagrin of the middle and upper classes, Webber and Cannon used the language of the people and behaved in a manner that identified them with the lower classes. Because the Guyanese society was "greatly deferent to colour," Cannon's " 'whiteness' and Webber's 'colour' [were] a definite advantage vis-à-vis the bulk of the population, and in any case, with the largely Negro electorate." Lutchman acknowledges that Webber was regarded generally as being among "the foremost political thinkers in the country during the period," and that served him in good stead.[9]

Sir William Collet, governor of the colony and an arbitrary and authoritative figure, left his post in 1923. He was replaced by Sir Graeme Thomson, who initially seemed be a beneficent ruler. In his capacity as governor, he was more considerate of the Electives' views and did not see them always as adversaries. During the relatively short time he governed, he allowed the Electives to participate more in decision making and listened carefully to their views, although he later became an implacable foe of Webber. Lutchman observes: "He apparently appreciated the advantage, and importance of instilling in the Electives a sense of involvement with the Executive in the process of government. While his predecessor very often expressed contempt for their position, he treated them as if they had a legitimate and useful part to play."[10]

By 1925 Webber had become the acknowledged leader and champion of the Afro-Guyanese and East Indian peoples, while his relationship with Governor Thomson deteriorated. From being considered "the planters' candidate" in the election of 1921, Webber rose to become the most feared elected member of the Combined Court by 1925. In fact, he had challenged the government on so many issues that by 1925 he had become the implacable adversary of the governor, and the relationship between the latter and the Electives had changed drastically.

During this period, we begin to see the first suggestions about the need to change the constitution that gave the colony's representatives greater control over the society's finances. With this transformation in mind, on May 26, 1925, Thomson sent a detailed and confidential document to L. C. Amery, secretary of state for the colonies, that defamed Webber and the other elective members, and alerted His Majesty's government to the growing clamor of the people for self-government and the active part that these members, particularly Webber, were playing in this movement. In his document, Thomson noted the changed attitude of the Electives:

> Generally speaking, I understand that previous to my assumption of office [April 1923] the Elected Members acted and voted together, more or less as a matter of principle, in opposition to the official section.
>
> From 1923 until recently this attitude was considerably modified. Few points of difference arose and I found them ready to support the Government in most of its important proposals, including the schemes for drainage, irrigation and pure water supply and for municipal improvements in Georgetown. There was a welcome absence of irresponsible criticism and, inasmuch as none of these important questions affected the personal interests of members, [they displayed] an honest desire to treat them on their merits.
>
> Within the past few months however the situation has undergone a marked change and certain of the Electives have taken up an attitude of deliberate hostility to Government and at the same time have lost the goodwill of several of their colleagues from whom they are divided by sharp personal differences. The Members in question are A. R. F. Webber, Financial Representative for Berbice and Editor of the *Daily Chronicle*, who normally acts as Whip for the North Essequebo, and the Honourable N. Cannon, Junior Member of Georgetown. With these may be reckoned the Honorable J. J. Da Silva, Member for West Demerara, and the Honourable E. G. Woodford, K. C., Member for New Amsterdam.[11]

Webber was *the* major focus of attack in this document. The governor's wrath had fallen upon him. The governor was prepared to do everything in his power "to cut Webber down to size." In fact, he felt so antagonistic toward Webber that he described him derogatorily as

> a coloured man, born in Tobago, of undoubted ability but wholly venal and unscrupulous and devoid of any ambition other than to get what he can from the highest bidder in return for his support in the columns of the *Daily Chronicle* and in the Court for whatever scheme happens to be on foot at the moment. As he does not enjoy the respect of honest men he can only hope to retain

his political position and influence by securing the support of the dishonest and ignorant, and when it suits him to do so he does not hesitate to threaten Government with possible civil disorder or to do his best to bring about a situation which might produce it.[12]

In other words, the governor depicted Webber as a dangerous demagogue who was willing to do anything to advance himself and his cause. Several times in the course of his career, Webber's Tobago roots would be used to impugn his legitimacy —although not successfully—as a leader of the Guyanese people.

Governor Thomson did not confine his attack to Webber. He describes Dodds as being "thoroughly dishonest" and "practically a bankrupt"; Cannon as "an ignorant and opinionated man in bad financial circumstances" who, together with Webber, used his position on the Combined Court and his directorship of the Essequebo Land Settlement to make money for himself; Da Silva as "an uneducated Portuguese, recently convicted and fined for gambling, whose interests in the Court are confined to criticizing the Police and opposing any measure which would prejudicially affect his business as a purveyor of rum;" and Woodford, a colored barrister, as being "in serious financial difficulties owing to imprudent transactions in real estates. He is a man of ability with an English University education but devoid of any stability of character."[13] Recognizing the degree to which these men were dependent upon the largesse of the government, Governor Thomson penalized them where it hurt the most: he dropped Webber and Cannon from the directorate of the Essequebo Land Settlement scheme and dismissed Dodds as the manager of the company. He noted: "There is little doubt that the loss of their appointments deprived all of them of the opportunity of supplementing their incomes by the manipulation of the Company's funds and property. Mr. Dodds, who has been sued for debt by more than one business firm and is virtually insolvent although he has, in his wife's name, purchased a portion of the Company's estate and erected a residence on it. [He] has, as I have stated, been debarred from carrying out Government contracts." The struggle was drawn: Thomson would reduce these "champions of the peoples" (Thomson said they were only "posing as the champions of the people") to penury.[14]

What, then, had Webber done between 1923 and 1925 that antagonized Governor Thomson to such an extent? For one thing, Webber was not inclined to be intimidated by Thomson in any way. As a scholar of history, Webber was convinced that governors made little difference in the affairs of the colony since they were merely "passing through" the colony. Years later, in his *Centenary History*, he observed that Thomson, who assumed the reins of government in April 1923, came from "the Home Civil Service and was Deputy Minister of Transport during the war, a position in which he won a high reputation." When he arrived, he was hailed everywhere. With almost a sigh, Webber observed ruefully: "*The childish belief* that a change of Governors can change the fundamentals of the governance of the country dies hard, and Sir Graeme Thomson was feted everywhere."[15] In the end, Governor Thomson did not leave a huge mark on the island's history.

This attitude of defiance (perhaps a sense of condescension) is evident in Webber's many exchanges with Governor Thomson during debates in the Combined Court. A typical example of these exchanges occurred on May 6, 1925, during a discussion on the removal of an ammunition magazine from Camp Road:

> Mr. Webber: I move the deletion of this item. I regret that I have so often to repeat my charges against the extravagance of Government but I am left no other course when so many items come up which apparently could be avoided. Year after year the expenditure of Government is going up, and within a comparatively few years it has risen from 2½ million to over 5 million dollars.
>
> His Excellency: Yes, but I explained yesterday what the Financial Representative is well aware of, that the cost of labour and materials has practically doubled within that period and the expenditure must have gone up without extravagance from the Government.
>
> Mr. Webber: Oh yes, sir. I am aware of that and I am also aware of the fact that we paid $150,000 to Government Officers as bonus cheques. That may account for some of the increased cost of materials for all I know. I fear—and I say it more in sorrow than in anger—Government is too divorced, not maliciously, but, for instance, your predecessor ruined the rice industry, probably with the best intentions.
>
> His Excellency: That is the Financial Representative's opinion.
>
> Mr. Webber: Yes sir, you mean as to whether did he have every good intention or not. The fact remains that hundreds of men were reduced from affluence to beggary. I repeat that he ruined the rice industry, but he did so with the best possible intentions, and he is now in London happy and contented drawing a handsome pension and sitting in a quiet corner fiddling.
>
> His Excellency: What is that?
>
> Mr. Webber: I said, sir, that he is now sitting in a quiet corner of London fiddling. I know he was fond of the fiddle.
>
> His Excellency: I do not see what the observation of the Financial Representative has to do with the removal of a magazine.
>
> Mr. Webber: In [the] process of time Your Excellency and your Lieutenant will also go into peaceful retirement in the happy possession of a pension and the people of the Colony will still be here bearing their burdens.
>
> His Excellency: I must ask the Financial Representative to keep to the point.
>
> Mr. Webber: I cannot keep to the point until I get there. . . . I repeat that the Government is engaged in a rake's progress.[16]

Such biting exchanges increased the governor's resentment against Webber. The above was one of the many extracts from *Hansard,* a record of government debates that Governor Thomson sent to Amery when he lodged his complaint against Webber and the other Electives. It was one of the reasons why he sought to expel Webber from the Combined Court on May 12, 1925. Governor Thomson characterized the exchange as an example of Webber's "studied insolence . . . and his deliberate intent to show disrespect and to provoke the Chair."[17]

Webber also demanded that the Combined Court discuss the "Major Chancellor's Report on Police Force and Shooting at Ruimveldt."[18] In the debate on the encouragement of cotton growing and the setting of fixed prices for cotton in the country, he took the opportunity to accuse the governor of being the

> type of official that comes to this Colony–the type of Crown Colony bred official—[that] is without initiative, without constructive ability, without courage, without anything that makes for progress in the Country. He sits down and rules the Colony, sometimes well, sometimes ill, sometimes with financial success, sometimes not, but when it comes to taking the initiative for the development of the Colony he is entirely barren of resources and afraid of his shadow.[19]

Webber openly accused the government of being "in the grip" of the Sugar Planters' Association and the Chamber of Commerce, thereby making the government completely insensitive to the needs of poor people. This was a complete change from his posture prior to his becoming a member of the legislature. He chastises the governor in the following manner:

> If that section of the community says "Thou shall not have irrigation on certain lands of the Colony" the Government says "Aye, aye, masters, they shall not have it." If that section says "Cotton shall not be encouraged" the Government says "Aye, aye masters, it shall not be done." Here you are with your ear to the ground from morning to night listening to the tramp of feet of those whom you fear. *I fear none of them.* . . . So long as I hold my place in this Court I will go on; some day reward of success will come to me. I am talking to empty benches this morning. I had hoped that there would have been sufficient Electives here to trample down the puerile and cowardly attitude of the Government and endeavour to galvanise something into them carrying the motion. Whether the motion is carried or not does not matter to me. I had hoped that this Session would have marked a milestone in the history of the Colony by the initiation of a policy of something constructive, and I say this motion is an acid test of Your Excellency's and the Government's sincerity that the drainage of the coastlands is not for the purpose of window dressing and you have no intention of encouraging

the development of any industries. What are you draining the front lands for if there is no labour?[20]

Although Webber did not want to do or say anything that would injure the sugar industry, he was tired of the black population being "accused of being shiftless and worthless, with all the sense of the old Adam, who as a matter of fact is not going to work on sugar estates under any conditions whatever."[21] Webber was defending the integrity of the black worker in very much the same way that D. M. Hutson, another member of the middle class, defended "the black man" when G. H. Richter, a rich planter of an earlier generation, accused black men of being lazy before a West India Royal Commission that was investigating the state of the sugar industry in 1897.[22]

Webber's bravery in taking on the colonial system and his determination to be the people's representative in that august body came though in his indictment of the government. As could be expected, the governor did not take this indictment kindly. Six days later, on May 14, he returned to the court to chastise this "boldface" colonial who had the temerity to question his actions. He accused Webber of trying "to mislead . . . the more ignorant and less educated members of the community" and of showing "deliberate disrespect both to my predecessors and to myself." Therefore, he called on him to apologize to the chair and the court for "the unfounded observations that he made" and warned that if Webber repeated such statements, he would be compelled to take action under the standing rules and orders "to uphold the authority of the Chair and to preserve the dignity of the Court."[23]

Not apprised of this development and thus taken by surprise, Webber asked for an opportunity to respond to the governor when the court resumed that afternoon. His response was a masterpiece of courage and defiance, a demonstration of his superior debating skills and knowledge of parliamentary procedure, and an example of his tremendous intellectual acuity. After apologizing to the governor if he felt insulted in his personal capacity, Webber differentiated between the governor's role in his personal capacity and his role as the representative of the Crown, and he articulated the difficulty of speaking on national issues when the governor presided both in his own right as governor and as the representative of the colonial government. He observed:

> It means that when one has to address criticism to the Administration they almost become of a personal nature because one has to address them to His Excellency in the Chair, and it becomes difficult therefore to differentiate between one's criticism of the Administration and one's criticism of the person of Your Excellency. . . . I reiterate that everything I say now must be regarded as addressed to Your Excellency as Governor, Your Excellency

speaking, I believe with the advice of your constituent advisers and representing the views of Governor rather than Your Excellency personally. Personally,
I regard the remarks that Your Excellency made to-day as an attempt to ham-
per me in the discharge of my duties as a representative in this Court.

His Excellency: Nothing of the kind.

Mr. Webber: I do so regard it; it may not have been so intended. I regard it as
an attempt to stifle criticism. I regard it as an attempt to limit my usefulness in this Court by holding out threats to me, threats of course, which I
may say I regard as empty. I have never refused to obey any ruling in this
Court. I cannot find from the time I became a member of this Court where
I have been disrespectful to either Your Excellency, your predecessor or any
Chairman of Committee of Ways and Means, and therefore to charge me
with the rules of this Court, as far as I am concerned, falls on barren ground
because I cannot regard myself as having ever transgressed those rules. I do
not intend to transgress them. If Your Excellency calls upon me now, even
at this moment, to resume my seat I shall do so, but I shall hope always to
find some ways within the four walls of the Rules of this Court to explore
any avenue that I think advisable or desirable to gain my ends in representing the views of my constituents. I do not come to this Court to represent
my personal grievances, but, as I said before, the threats of this nature fall
upon a man who, I trust, from my boyhood up has never been guilty of either physical or moral cowardice, and in my approaching old age I shall not
allow that attack of nerves to seize me now. The Rules of the Court, Your
Excellency, provide ample powers.[24]

The sparring between Webber and the governor continued for about five minutes. The issue was not brought to a vote because the governor, as he admitted
later, feared that he didn't have sufficient votes to carry the motion to eject Webber
from the court. However, when he ruled finally that Webber should take his seat,
the latter reserved the right to take up the issue with the colonial secretary, which
he did some days later. The incident revealed the tremendous amount of power
the governor had over these representatives. Drawing on the example of another
colonized country, C. L. R. James observed that the governor of a Crown Colony
is three things in one.

He is the representative of His Majesty the King, and as such must have all
the homage and respect customary to that position. But the Governor is also
the officer responsible for the proper administration of the government. . . . In
Trinidad [and Guyana] the Governor is the Governor-General and the Prime
Minister in one. But that makes only two. When the Governor sits in the
Legislative Council he is the Chairman of that body. The unfortunate result is

that when a member of the Council rises to speak he is addressing at one and the same time an incomprehensible personage, three in one and one in three.[25]

Although James must have heard Webber when he addressed the Trinidad Workingmen's Association in Trinidad in 1928, neither James nor Webber mentions each other in their work. However, they were certainly speaking the same language and understood the governor's all-embracing powers.

The next day, the newspapers went to town on this issue. As was to be expected, the *Daily Chronicle* supported Webber and castigated the governor for threatening to eject Webber from the court. The *Outlook*, a weekly edited by A. A. Thorne, an Afro-Guyanese leader and former member of the Combined Court, disagreed with Webber's position.[26] In an editorial entitled "Recklessness of a Legislator," the newspaper noted that it was Webber's "misfortune" to have been born in Tobago, "among the most backward of the British West Indies, with no educational institutions to uplift its inhabitants and make them fit for sober responsibilities, and so poor that, despite its size, it became necessary for the Crown several decades ago to make it a ward of Trinidad." Bemoaning that from his birth Webber was not acquainted with representative institutions and "the dignity and responsibility of those honoured with selection to sit on such institutions," the editorial suggested that "we must not expect too much of him, but rather pity his shortcomings and remember that the first impressions of childhood on the mind are indelible, and that frequent observations in boyhood of the blind charges of a ram are likely to be reechoed in manhood in volleys of abusive language as entertaining to the unwashed as the pranks of the butting billy-goat careening madly along."

Part of Thorne's jealously toward Webber's political ascendancy was engendered by the respect Webber received from the masses of people and the hostility some of the locals felt against outsiders, be they from Tobago or Barbados. Thorne and his cohorts resented Webber's "sudden and accidental elevation to a seat in the Combined Court of the Colony." Coming from one section of the black middle class, such language must have wounded Webber deeply. It certainly hurt more because Thorne was a member of the Reform Association of 1891, a progressive group;, was considered to be "a staunch socialist";[27] and was born in Barbados. He must have known of the progressive work that S. E. R. Forbes did with this association. The attacks did not deter Webber from his vocation. He continued to struggle on behalf of the lower classes. Perhaps he could have forgiven Thorne. The *Daily Chronicle* observed that a radical change had come over Thorne's behavior "since he started to tread the carpeted stairs to Government House" and became "a recipient of [Governor] Collet's dinners and favours."[28]

Thomson's war against Webber did not stop at his attempt to eject him from the court. When the *Daily Chronicle* editorial appeared on May 16, Thomson inquired of his attorney general whether there were sufficient legal grounds to bring charges of libel against Webber. The attorney general advised him in the negative. Additionally, the police continued to spy on Webber and his colleagues to gather as much incriminating information as they could against them. On May 11 District Inspector Matthey reported to Colonel F. H. Blackwood, inspector-general of the police, a conversation that took place among Webber, Dodds, Cannon, and others aboard a ferry that transported them to work that morning. A report of this conversation was given to Governor Thomson and subsequently sent to the secretary of state for the colonies. According to Matthey, Webber and his colleagues did conspire to abuse the governor "until he resigned. If he did not resign, they would get up a petition to the secretary of state asking for his removal." On the afternoon back from work, Matthey followed Webber and his colleagues again and reported their activities to his superior. He concluded his report for that day by noting that he was "supposed to be a friend of Dodds and can at any time get information out of him as to his intentions and Webber's so I am asking that this information and previous information given about Dodds be kept secret otherwise I will be unable to get anything out of him."[29]

On May 26 Webber wrote to the secretary of state to protest how he was treated by Governor Thomson, who, as Webber charged, by "his grave misuse of privilege ... sought to limit my usefulness as a Financial Representative, and to intimidate me in the discharge of my duties, by an arbitrary use of his Powers as President of the Court."[30] After outlining his case against Thomson and defending his conduct of May 14, Webber argued that it was unparliamentary for the governor to bring action against him six days after the incident occurred. Therefore, he asked the secretary of state to rule whether his remarks violated the standing rules and orders of the Combined Court,

> whether it was competent for the Chair to rule that I would not be permitted to explain, or to amplify, or to justify any remarks made by me; and finally whether, having been given permission to make an explanation, it was competent for the Chair to ask me to resume my seat before my remarks had been completed, and without my having been guilty of any discourtesy to the Chair, without having broken any known canon of parliamentary debate, and without having outraged any of the Standing Rules or Orders of the Court.[31]

As was customary, when such appeals were made to the secretary of state, they usually went to the secretary's various advisers for their comments before a final response was made to the person seeking advice. Most of the colonial officials had a chance to reveal their attitudes toward the matter at hand, and in this circumstance, to give an indication of how they felt about Webber. Their responses suggest that Webber had become an anathema to the Colonial Office.

In his note on this matter, the secretary of state thought that Webber's remarks were made "with studied insolence and cunning," although he was "very doubtful" whether they went "beyond the limits of parliamentary language." However, he was inclined to follow the advice of a Mr. Wiseman, one of his advisers, "and certainly not say anything more favourable to Mr. Webber."[32] In a handwritten note of October 5 that was appended to this minute, Sir Gilbert Grindle also agreed that Webber was in the right, yet supporting his own, he concluded that "even if Sir Graeme Thomson went beyond what was strictly necessary when he took the matter up after a week's interval, one would like to snub Mr. Webber and show him that the S. of S. [secretary of state] will support the King's representative in maintaining his dignity. I would add to the proposed reply that the S. of S. sees no reason to question Sir Graeme Thomson's action."[33] In short, no matter how incorrect Governor Thomson was, the secretary of state would support "the King's representative" in order to preserve the dignity of the Crown. No black man should dare contradict His Majesty's representative and come out victorious. What was interpreted as Webber's insolence would not be tolerated by the Colonial Office.

Over and beyond Webber's perceived insolence, the second matter of obvious concern to the governor was the need to reduce the Electives' power in the Combined Court. Such a position arose from the solid manner in which the Electives voted and the inability of the governor to pass certain bills in the court. In writing to the secretary of state, Thomson noted that one of the more "serious disabilities" under which the colony labored "was the inevitable tendency of a system of popular representation based upon a grossly ignorant and often illiterate polyglot population, easily swayed by racial feeling and highly susceptible to outside suggestion, to bring to the top the type of unscrupulous and irresponsible demagogue who can only maintain his position by creating imaginary grievances and playing on the prejudices and lack of discernment of the people." While he called for the greater dissemination of "popular education" among the masses of people (he endorsed the recommendations of the Education Commission of 1925), he also urged the secretary of state to amend the constitution so that the government would always have "an official majority in the Combined Court."[34]

Thomson also believed that the addition of more Guyanese to the electorate, an inevitable position, would spell doom to the planter class since it would place more power in the hands of the Electives and their followers at the expense of the whites.[35] In fact, a dispatch sent to the secretary of state by the Hon. Reginald Popham Lobb, the acting governor, on July 27, to supplement Governor Thomson's dispatch of May 26, only spelled out this fear in greater detail. Lobb noted that with the continuing expansion of the electorate, "the European section which still controls the major interests of the Colony and comprises the great bulk of its wealth and intelligence, has been practically submerged, politically speaking, and is likely to disappear altogether from the elective side of the Legislature." Outlining the racial composition of the legislature in great detail (half of the elected members of the Combined Court and three-quarters of the Court of Policy were "non-White"), Lobb noted that

> the measure of popular representation and the complete financial control now wielded by the Electives are respectively enjoyed and exercised at the cost of efficiency in administration and the proper development of the Colony. It is a heavy price to pay, and nothing in my opinion can prevent it from becoming still heavier, . . . unless steps are taken to create, as suggested by the Governor in his Confidential dispatch of the 26th May, a counterpoise to the weight of ignorance and self-interest which now hampers the executive at every turn.[36]

At the base of their concerns was the increasing possibility that Afro-Guyanese and East Indians would control society. The calls for self-government and dominion status enjoyed by Canadian citizens managed to leave His Majesty's representatives a little shaken.

As a result of this "growing threat" by the Afro-Guyanese and East Indian sections of the community, Thomson, like Lobb, feared the economic implications of black control. He believed that if the fiscal system and financial policy of the colony were left to "the mercy of . . . [this] irresponsible and ignorant minority," foreign capitalists would be discouraged from investing in the country, and "the confidence of the investors who already have a stake in the country" would be shaken badly.[37] Moreover, Thomson believed that in the general election that was scheduled to take place in October of the following year (1926), an increased black and colored electorate would certainly result in "the displacement of some of the more desirable of the present members by negro and other extremists who are already engaged in paving the way for their return by stirring up class and anti-government, and therefore anti-white, feeling."[38] This position was supported by the *Daily Argosy*, the pro-government, planter-class mouthpiece, which labeled Webber, Dodds, Canon, and Da Silva "the Elective demagogues" who shed "crocodile tears" for the welfare of the poor.[39]

Adding fuel to the political fire, there was a perception among the Guyanese people that Thomson was a racist. They had not read Thomson's confidential dispatch to the Colonial Office that warned against the "stirring up" of "anti-white feeling," but from his behavior and pronouncements they discerned that he was acting against their interests. Thus, when he attempted to set up a promotions board that would discriminate against the colored colonial civil servants of the country, his proposal met with little favor from members of that stratum and their representatives. Beneath his claims of fairness they saw an attempt to deny the promotions that they had won through hard work and dedication to the Crown. No wonder that on the eve of his departure to London for a long leave, an editorial in the *Tribune* of March 17, 1925, noted that Thomson's term of office had been "a colossal failure." The author of the editorial hoped that before the expiration of his leave, "he should be promoted elsewhere and not return to benighted British Guiana." Thomson also included this editorial in his package to Lord Amery, calling it an "inspired and scurrilous personal attack upon the Government, the Colonial Secretary and myself."[40]

While he was in London, Thomson reported to the secretary of state personally on July 23, it having been agreed shortly after his arrival in London that he would not return to British Guiana as the governor. In the minutes of their meeting, they both agreed that Webber was "a dangerous demagogue." Precisely because of that reason, the secretary of state concluded that Webber's petition ("memorial") should be treated "with the utmost care." In agreeing with Webber's position, the secretary of state noted that while Webber's remarks were "extremely irritating to a Governor," the standing orders that Thomson cited as the source of his authority prescribed that the president's powers arose only if a member was " 'grossly disorderly.' The question of the interpretation of such a term is one of which I should be glad to receive the opinion of some authority of the House of Commons, but Mr. Webber's remarks prima facie do not appear to me to come within this description."[41]

Unfortunately for Webber, the preservation of the dignity of His Majesty's government and white solidarity clashed with the rights of colonial peoples and black "boldfaceness." The former had to be maintained, and so Webber was depicted as being in the wrong. Although Webber was correct, the secretary of state noted in this confidential minute: "It would be most undesirable to let the Governor down in the presence of a man like Mr. Webber, and I would suggest that we might perhaps get out of this difficulty by replying to 27548 [Webber's petition to the secretary of state] on the lines that the Governor does not appear to have exercised any power under the Standing Rules and Orders, and therefore no case appears to have arisen on which the Secretary of State could give a ruling."[42] Such a response demonstrated the solidarity of white power versus the rights of colonial people.

Webber received this response (almost verbatim) from the secretary of state on August 12 via J. Hampden King, acting colonial secretary. The secretary of state seemed intent on adding insult to injury by trying to chastise Webber and put him in his place: "I am to add that Mr. Amery [the secretary of state] observes that he has noted with surprise and regret the terms in which you permitted yourself to address the Governor in your letter of the 19th May."[43] Webber was not to be fooled in that he detected the secretary of state's palpable dishonesty. On September 26 he submitted yet another memorial to the secretary of state (which the latter never really answered) in which he asked: "What is the remedy of a member [of the Combined Court], when a motion constitutionally correct is ruled out of order through the caprice, ill-advice, or even misjudgment, of the Officer presiding over the deliberations of the Court?" The secretary of state understood Webber's argument and even agreed with him privately. He could not expose the shortcomings of his ministers to the eyes of "ignorant" colonial people. Webber and his people would continue to suffer though the malfeasance of these governors, who would continue to snub him even more. He would prove to be correct in his assessment of the governor and his behavior. It was his job to make the colonial regime know that he was "on the case" and that his major task was to look out for the interests of his people.

On the constitutional question, it was agreed that Sir Cecil Rodwell, the governor designate, should not seek to relieve the members of the Combined Court of their powers immediately upon his arrival in the colony but that he should proceed cautiously. Thomson believed that it would not have been sensible to precipitate "a constitutional crisis, as obviously the new Governor would not be in a position to say immediately on assumption of office that he had found the administration of Government impossible owing to the attitude of the Combined Court." After some time in office, Rowell would find the necessary excuse to force such a crisis and thereby deprive the Electives of the powers they possessed in fiscal affairs and policy matters. But the Colonial Office understood the psychology of colonial people. They realized that it was important to warn Rowell "that he should not take up this question without being very sure of his ground, since nothing would be more fatal to him in his conduct of the administration of the Colony than to let it be thought that the first thing he had come out to do was to induce the Combined Court to give up some of its privileges."[44] As the above constitutional ploy suggested and the secretary of state's response to Webber demonstrated, continued deception in the Colonial Office's relationship with the colony would remain at the center of the Colonial Office's general policy toward the Caribbean.

In the colony, however, the cries for self-government were being heard. In an article in the *Tribune* one day before Lobb sent his confidential dispatch to the secretary of state, a reader who called himself Naiva Tasya captured the essence of the independence sentiment that was in the air. First, he used an epigram from Shakespeare's *Julius Caesar* to head his article ("Men at some time are masters of their fates; / The fault, my dear Brutus, is not in our stars, / But, in ourselves, that we are underlings") before noting that "as long as the Colony remains under a paternal sort of Government, manned chiefly by Administrators from abroad, the Citizens have to acknowledge their moral and intellectual inferiority to the peoples of the World and even to many of the neighbouring South American Countries. If the Citizens have within them pride and patriotism and above all self-respect they cannot be satisfied forever to remain in the present subservient and ignominious state. Self-Government ought to be the Colony's ultimate aim."

Responding to charges that "the intelligentsia of the Colony, especially the political leaders, are not trustworthy and patriotic" and that the masses of the people were not "enlightened" and therefore could not exercise their franchise "wisely and well so as to place the right men in the right place," Tasya argued that such a position was false and merely put the proverbial cart before the horse. Without self-government, he argued, none of these grave political and economic matters could be dealt with effectively. Tasya argued that Britain was against self-government for the Guyanese people because "self-government means so many less appointments for eager ones from 'Home' perhaps so much less opportunity for exploitation. It is natural then, that it should be a matter of policy with them to keep the people of the Colony as ignorant as possible and grant them minimum facilities and enlightenment."

Tasya ended his article with a kind of patriotic assurance and implacable logic that must have left the secretary of state, the governor, and his minions in a very uncomfortable position. Since the subsequent years (1926–28) were filled with talk about constitutional matters, Tasya's concluding remarks were important and are worth remembering. He had "hit the nail on its constitutional head":

It is in the nature of things to progress. No one can completely arrest the onward march to better things and to Self-Government, but the ultimate attainment may be indefinitely delayed unless the people take the reins in their own hands. There are a good many Alarmists and Chickenhearts who predict the immediate ruination of the Colony if it should get Self-Government. We have no such mis-givings; on the other hand we believe that though for a few years the conditions may remain a little unsettled and nothing substantially good may be accomplished, it would not be long before the conditions commence to improve and the Government operates to the prosperity, enlightenment and exaltation of the people. This opinion is not founded on speculation but on rational faith that the people of the Colony are inherently endowed with the same qualities as the people of any other country as well as our faith that the people do not need the knowledge of the three Rs (reading, writing and arithmetic) to know the true from the false leaders and as soon as they realize that the men whom they elect will have a power for good or for evil, they will not fail to discard the false leader and to adhere to the true ones. Whether the colony is ripe for Self-Government or not it is certainly not too early to raise a political cry for Self-Government.[45]

It was almost as if Naiva Tasya had read the correspondences between the governor and the secretary of state, glimpsed at the notes of their advisers, anticipated Britain's reactionary posture, and then responded in kind. He certainly had put to rest a number of questions that were raised in response to the behavior of Webber and the other Electives. Lobb found the article interesting (perhaps alarming) enough to send a copy to the secretary of state. Webber understood his people's need for freedom and sought to argue their case with the colonial powers and their local representatives. In the process, he became the leader of his people and one of the most perspicacious leaders of the region.

CHAPTER FIVE

THE CONSTITUTIONAL CRISIS
The Bullet or the Ballot

It was the Marquis of Normandy, the only Peer in Holy orders, and a really earnest man, who said, here in England a day or two ago, that it was impossible to work in slum districts without becoming some measure of a Socialist.

—A. R. F. WEBBER, *An Innocent's Pilgrimage*

THE DROUGHT THAT GRIPPED BRITISH GUIANA from August 25, 1925, to May 1926 led to economic depression, unemployment, and financial loss to the colony. When the rains returned in May, they brought with them fever epidemics and intestinal diseases that resulted in a loss of children's lives. For example, in the village mission of Murko, over 100 children under the age of seven died as a result of these epidemics. Unfortunately, during this period there was as much havoc politically as there was physically, as Afro-Guyanese and Indo-Guyanese clamored for greater political representation. Moreover, the gradual loss of political power by the European population and the greater forcefulness of the Electives in the Combined Court led to a major constitutional crisis that eventually reduced Guyana to a Crown Colony.

The year 1926 also saw the articulation of a greater sense of class and racial consciousness as the labor unions, and the nationalist organizations such as the Universal Negro Improvement Association (UNIA), the African Communities League, the Negro Progress Convention (NPC), and the British Guiana East Indian Association (BGEAI) became more organized. Until the 1920s, Afro-Guyanese and Indo-Guyanese worked collectively against the planter class, whom they saw as their common enemy. Indeed, the pioneering work of Rev. E. R. O. Robertson, the first black Wesleyan minister in Guyana and president of British Guiana Farmers' Association, on behalf of the East Indian rice farmers demonstrated the unity that existed between the two groups. Clem Seecheran argues that Robertson "transcended the instinctive racial allegiances and parochial outlook of the time" and describes his work on behalf of East Indians as "an epic of imagination, magnanimity of spirit, and resolution" until his religious bosses transferred him to the Leeward Islands in 1924.[1] One is not too sure why the allegiances should have been "instinctive."

Founded in 1919, the BGLU gained increasing prestige in society and became a greater threat to the colonial order. The work of the union also "made an impression on the Indian workers on the Demerara estates and they were inclined to see him [Critchlow] as a replacement for the moribund 'Crosby,' the Immigration Agent General. Critchlow visited many rural areas in 1919–20, enrolling Indian workers for this union. They called him 'Black Crosby.'"[2] Cheddi Jagan reemphasized this point when he noted that "the Indian sugar workers accepted the African militant trade union leader, Hubert Critchlow, as their 'Black Crosby.'"[3] Unfortunately, Critchlow did not have sufficient resources to represent them as they ought to have been represented.

At this phase of its development, the work of the Afro-Guyanese nationalists and the labor union cohered. It was helped by Critchlow's affiliation with the NPC. The teachings of Marcus Garvey also had their effect on the growing consciousness of Afro-Guyanese, as the UNIA established several branches throughout the colony. Its street meetings posed a continuous threat to the colonial administration and strengthened black consciousness. R. J. Craig, an undercover police officer, in his semiannual report to the Colonial Office, noted: "The Association cannot cause much trouble on its own account, but in the event of trouble originating with the Labour Union, the latter would have the full support of the Universal Negro Improvement Association on colour grounds alone." Although the BGEIA recruited members aggressively it did not form a union to represent its members. However, the union "seems to have an understanding with the Labour Union," which allowed them to depend on the BGLU for labor representation.[4]

This unity between Afro-Guyanese and Indo-Guyanese frightened the planters and the colonial state. They interpreted the labor unrest as a serious threat to white power in the colony. Whereas prior to 1926, in a confidential memorandum to Secretary of State Amery, Lobb noted that "the Colony's political institutions were suited to the interests of a small white class and presumably ensured the election of Europeans of that class alone, that is to say of persons well fitted to represent the interests of the Colony under the social and economic conditions," by 1926, with the extension of the franchise, the planters believed that "the worst instead of the best elements . . . are brought to the front to represent . . . the community."[5] In 1926 European (read white) hegemony and control of the society were threatened severely by the political activities of the nonwhite population; thus the Colonial Office had to make plans to overcome nonwhite rule of the society by introducing a new constitution. Years later, Jagan observed that racial consciousness did not act as a barrier to common action on the political and industrial fronts. He noted that "Indians and Africans were aware of the peculiar disadvantages under which they lived. This led to a common assault against the colonial society. And the more moderate leaders were propelled forward by the militant struggles waged on the political and industrial fronts; Indian and African workers rallied together under the leadership of Critchlow in the industrial battles from 1906 to the 1920s for better wages, improved working conditions and the 8-hour day."[6] Later on, Afro-Guyanese and Indo-Guyanese would struggle among themselves for the control of the state.

After Governor Thomson left Guyana in 1925, he advised that Rodwell, the governor designate of the colony, should proceed cautiously before he attempted to change the constitution. Most of all, he wanted to curtail the power that the Financial Representatives of the Combined Court possessed and to give the governor a casting vote so that he could control the legislature. Realizing that the Financial Representatives' right "to control the appropriation of public moneys" was one of the oldest prerogatives the Electives possessed, Thomson had to come up with a plausible reason and strategy if he wanted to take away such power.[7] In his discussion with Amery on July 11, 1925, he outlined a scenario under which the constitution could be suspended. In a note prepared for Amery, Thomson worried that such a change could not take place unless "a real issue" occurred between the government and the Electives. He believed that such an issue would arise when a measure to effect the recommendations of a commission on education reform and another measure on sanitation was brought to the legislature. In utter disdain for the integrity of Afro-Guyanese, he boasted:

> The negro politicians both in the Combined Court and on the local boards do not care for sanitation and would oppose the effective control of sanitary improvements by the Government. If the Combined Court directly or indirectly rejected either of these contemplated measures he would like the full support of the Secretary of State in making an end of the existing constitution. He was of opinion [sic] that it would be necessary to carry the change through with a strong hand, but obviously do nothing until the actual time for action came.[8]

The stage was set to change Guyana's constitution, which fitted perfectly into what Rowell called "the Imperial ideal." Everything was put in place to effectuate a clash with the Electives. The single-chamber Legislative Council that was proposed would consist of six official members, including the governor; two members nominated by the governor; eleven legislative councilors chosen through the direct franchise of the people; and three members "indirectly elected" by certain recognized bodies such as the Georgetown Chamber of Commerce and the Sugar Planters' Association. The governor would have an original as well as a casting vote. By this reasoning, such an arrangement would "put the constitution on a sounder and more democratic basis than it is at present."[9] Such a "democratic" alteration of the constitution was needed since local legislators

> are not in a position to realize the wide repercussions that may result from the rejection of some particular measure or . . . sensible [*sic*] of the fact that such rejection may run counter to some settled line of policy which H. M. Government may be pursuing in its determination to bring about the industrial and agricultural expansion of the tropical territories of the Empire. Indeed, it must be recognized in any discussion of this matter that this determination as to the development of this settled line policy stands paramount and must take precedence over any local feeling of prejudice, however well-intentioned.[10]

This was the perfect colonial system—the imperial ideal as it were. British Guiana existed to serve the needs of the British Empire. Dev notes, "In Guyana, the *raison d'etre* for the local state—an agent of the metropolitan state—was primarily the protection of the planter interest."[11] Consequently, the aspirations of the Guyanese people had to be subsumed under the overall needs of the empire. The constitution was only another avenue through which this imperial ideal would be realized. It is instructive, therefore, to see how Rowell ended his remarks:

> In conclusion, I would like to refer again to the Imperial idea. Not only has British Guiana, to my mind, reached the parting of the ways, when it must decide whether it is going to play a part worthy of itself in the Imperial future or whether it is going to fall back into a slough of despond [*sic*], but the Empire itself has reached a critical point in its history. Steps will, I hope, shortly be taken by H. M. Government to stimulate the consumption in the markets of Britain the products of the Empire in preference to those of foreign countries. I hope that, as a result, the demand for the people of this country calls for reciprocal action on the part of the Empire producers in producing to the utmost of their resources. It is, as I have said, my earnest wish that British Guiana should take its share in this Imperial work, and it may rest assured that, in its endeavor to do so, it will always have my unqualified support.[12]

This line of reasoning set the stage for the constitutional struggle that ensued between 1926 and 1928. The governor and his colleagues saw Guyana's destiny as serving the imperial ideal, whereas Webber and his colleagues saw society as existing, first and foremost, to serve the interests of the Guyanese people. Inevitably, these competing ideas had to clash. Aided and abetted by a greater intensive pressure for more "representational government" in Guyana and the Caribbean, the Colonial Office invited the leaders of the various Caribbean countries to London to discuss these demands. This was the first time that local legislators from the West Indies would meet together in England, as a body, to discuss their future. Webber, staunch nationalist as he was, was named one of Guyana's delegates to attend the conference.

The conference, which took place in London from May 13 to June 5, 1926, was attended by delegates from all of the British West Indies and Guyana. His Majesty, King George V, received the delegates at Buckingham Palace to give the meeting a measure of importance. In his opening remarks to the conference, Amery noted that it was not "a Colonial Office Conference" but "a West Indian Conference ... one in which the initiative has come, not from the Secretary of State, but from the Colonial Legislators themselves, and it is in pursuance of their expressed wishes that the arrangements for this Conference have been made."[13] At the formal level, Webber's contribution was confined to the remarks he made on May 26 at a session devoted to the possibility of creating separate "currency arrangements" for the West Indies and British Guiana.[14] The discussion was opened by Edward Davson, chairman of the conference, and led by R. A. Wiseman, a member of the West Indian Currency Committee. Basically, it was intended that a system of currency in dollars and cents should be introduced into the West Indies and British Guiana. Davson argued that "the main point is that the West Indies have a bad currency and ought to have a good one."[15] In his turn, Webber argued that any discussion in British Guiana's legislature about "the desirability of establishing a currency ... would fizzle out as soon as you began it, unless there is going to be something practical put before it."[16] As far as he was concerned, any solution of the currency problem must be beneficial to the people of his adopted country.

Even in this discussion on currency, Webber's commitment to self-government came through, as he urged his colleagues "to accept the obligation" of controlling their country's currency. He reminded his colleagues that the British treasury had never

> repudiated the obligation, but is only treating us as it would treat importunate creditors, whereas they did not put off the others. We have not yet discussed the interior difficulties of our own so far as the currency is concerned. Those are our domestic concerns. We have our troubles with regard to the domestic details of our currency. This difficulty [of exchange] is an exterior one, because British currency is going to take up the coinage, but we want them to give us a show down for our money.[17]

In arguing for their own currency and its regulation on the basis of commercial exchange, George F. Huggins, a Trinbagonian delegate,[18] made it clear that because Britain controlled the "currency exchange," West Indian merchants suffered enormously, particularly when "shipping produce to the United States for which we were earning 40 per cent profit, but on bringing the stuff back we paid that away in exchange the other way, though as a matter of fact the balance of trade was in our favor."[19] Some of the delegates, particularly Huggins, a cocoa proprietor, recognized that because of their inability to control their own currency, West Indian proprietors lost enormous profits on their goods. Many of the West Indian delegates recognized this as just another form of indirect exploitation. Webber argued that it was only when "we have control of our own Currency Board and our own currency bank to guarantee them" that West Indians would be able to get the most out of their labor. He concluded: "The funds will have to be in West Indian silver. Therefore, control of the bank-notes would be an integral part of our currency system, because it would be tied to our currency."[20]

While they were in London, the British Guiana delegates met separately with the secretary of state on June 11 to discuss two of their special concerns: "the railway question" and immigration policies. Since 1924 Webber and his colleagues were interested in the possibility of constructing a railway in Guyana. Amery opened the discussion by saying that his dispatch of December 17, 1925, "was not to be regarded as . . . final, and that the door stood open if a powerful corporation like the Canadian Railway desired to enter the field and the forest enquiry showed a prospect of a railway which in a broad sense would really pay."[21] Webber argued that a railway was essential to the colony and left it to the secretary of state to determine whether the colony would be served better by a railway constructed by the government or by private enterprise.[22]

On immigration policy, Webber disagreed with the colonial ruling against organized immigration and argued that the colony should be free to secure indentured immigrants of Chinese agricultural families for its development, to which the secretary of state responded that there were "possible political objections . . . as to the advisability of introducing Chinese into the Western hemisphere on a large scale, and difficulties which were probably at the moment insuperable arising out of the disorders in China." Sir Alfred Sherlock noted that "such immigrants could not be housed in coolie lines, but required cottages. The planters could not find the capital to build such cottages in any large numbers."[23] The secretary of state agreed to report back to the delegates after he had the time to give their suggestions the attention they deserved.

On June 26 Webber addressed the Empire Parliamentary Association, which consisted of the Labour members of the House of Commons. The subject of his address was Guyana's development. He considered this address his most important political engagement, since he was able to bring to the attention of the imperial masters the "true" state of affairs in his country. He believed he had won them over to sympathize with his cause of self-government, so he need not pay much attention to it. This address, a fitting climax of Webber's labors on behalf of his people and an indication of his stature as a statesperson, called upon the parliamentarians to confer upon the Guyanese people the same democracy they enjoyed in their own country. He also repeated the ago-old fears of his countrymen and women that he had raised previously in *Those That Be in Bondage* and noted:

> We feel we are too often left to the tender mercies of men–old as well as young–who know not our country. Men who have never seen the mighty Essequebo River, nor the Picturesque Potaro: men whose horizon is inevitably circumscribed by dispatches: who set law and order as the object of their very existence, and who think a balanced budget the acme of statesmanship of a Colonial Governor.
>
> The untravelled officials in Downing Street find it difficult to visualize that the mouth of the Mighty Essequebo is as wide as the straits between Dover and Calais; men who live in the tradition that the less they hear from, and about a Governor sent to rule, the more successful has been and is his administration.[24]

Webber also demonstrated a broad knowledge about Great Britain and his society. He said his first duty was to find the delegates a "figurative idea of this great continental domain of the Crown." Although Guyana was as large as Great Britain, it was immensely richer in gold, diamonds, and other minerals, "with some of the most valuable forests in the world." Citing the sparseness of population because of the presence of diseases that were preventable and avoidable, he went on to note that it was "the labouring classes who suffer [most] from the ravages of these diseases through ignorance, and lower economic standards." The solution to the problems of colonial Guyana lay in getting better and more "remunerative markets for its principal products, and so increase its population, and broaden the basis of taxation." Reiterating the presence of Guyana's rich natural resources, Webber saw the construction of a railway as the principal means of opening up the country to its economic potential and thereby "converting British Guiana into one of the world's highways." He argued that the people of the country believed that "an officially constructed and owned railway, means the railway of a bureaucracy; where deficits will fall upon the Treasury, and pensionable officials increase and multiply." He regretted that the officials at the Colonial Office "were not ready to allow Guyana to embark on the construction of a railway outside official ownership, and there it has been deadlocked for fifteen years." Putting his argument in economic terms, Webber concluded: "A great continental highway of this kind is not only a dream but a practical possibility, which once achieved would convert British Guiana, from being a neglected heritage of the Crown, into a proud continental Dominion, carrying millions of people and importing as much goods from the United Kingdom, as New Zealand, or any other of the Australian states, increasing employment at home and opportunity abroad." Years earlier, his uncle Ernest made similar recommendations.

Webber's comments on the question of currency and the very sophisticated understanding of economic development that he demonstrated in his address to the Labour MPs made it obvious that he was knowledgeable about the affairs of state and the implications of running a government. Much of the understanding of economics that he gained in his encounters with the government and these international organizations would be placed on display when he wrote his seminal essay, "Why I Am an Economic Heretic" (1930). He also demonstrated a profound understanding of his society's history and its interconnection with the economics of the country, a fact that became more evident when he wrote *Centenary History and Handbook of British Guiana* (1931).

One of the concrete results of the West Indian Conference was the agreement that they would set up the West Indian Standing Conference, which would meet in England and the West Indies alternately to discuss matters of the area. Such a meeting would allow West Indians to put "forward a definite West Indian opinion for the information of the Imperial Government (which until now has been totally lacking, to the great loss of these Colonies) and possibly entitling it in due course to a voice in the deliberations of Imperial Conference thus at length raising [the islands of the] West Indies to their proper status in the Empire."[25] This was not necessarily a radical proposal, but these delegates had begun to appreciate the necessity of coming together to elicit concessions from the mother country, but knowing that the ultimate struggle for freedom lay with the desire of "the people" to fight for that goal. This conference allowed Webber another avenue to press for the greater self-government of his people.

Even as Webber discussed the political future of his country, he found time to give expression to his first love: creative writing. As a member of the Guyana delegation and guest of His Majesty's government, Webber had the freedom to travel wherever he wanted in England. At the beginning of the conference, Amery announced: "You will now be free, not only to attend this Conference with ease, but also, in the intervals of the Conference, to see something of England in the springtime, a sight worth seeing, and to enjoy some of the social amenities from which at one moment it looked as if you were doomed to be cut off altogether."[26] Webber took advantage of Amery's offer, and out of it came *An Innocent's Pilgrimage*, which records his impressions of what he saw in England during the springtime of 1926, "Being Pen Pictures of a Tender-foot Who Visited London for the First Time," as he announced on the title page of his book.[27]

This travelogue was published from May 5 to August 20, 1926, as a series of nineteen articles in the *New Daily Chronicle*; they were published subsequently as a book the following year.[28] While not much is heard of this travelogue in Guyanese or West Indian literature, and we are not aware of the reception it received when it was first published, we do know that it was actively promoted in the pages of the *New Daily Chronicle*. It furnishes us with one of the earliest responses of a black (colonized) person to the mother country—an ambivalent response—and suggests the beginning of a literary trend that would emerge in West Indian writing: the colonized writing back from the mother country to home.[29] This travelogue summarizes Webber's response to the West Indian Conference and his sense of where Guyana was in terms of its political development, and signaled that travel writing would become one of his outstanding contributions to West Indian literature.

An Innocent's Pilgrimage is characterized by its realistic descriptions and romantic responses to the mother country. It resembles Mark Twain's *The Innocents Abroad; Or, The New Pilgrims' Progress* (1869) in that it seeks to give the local reader "a taste" of England by comparing English sights and sounds to those in British Guiana so that Webber's readers would have a better basis upon which to understand and measure that distant land, which was available only in the master trope of the other.[30] Apart from giving Webber's impressions of London, the text reveals a great deal about Webber himself. At that moment of his development, whatever else he might have been, Webber clearly sees himself "as a newspaperman" trying to capture the feel and atmosphere of England.[31] As Webber describes his arrival in England and his excitement at reaching London, it seems as though the idea of London garnered from books struggles to come to terms with the reality that he encounters. Thus his exclamation: "This is the London which inspired the arrogance that cost the Empire the American colonies; the London which freed the slaves; the London which has been guilty of every sin under the sun; and has been in the van of every cause of righteousness. What mighty traditions, what fatal errors lay enshrouded in its folds" (*IP*, vi).[32] Webber also recounts his visits to the Throne Room of Buckingham Palace, where he met King George, and to Oxford University, where he became enraptured with Shelley's statue. He also displayed a great deal of admiration for the educational experience that took place at Oxford University.

Webber is enamored by the London of his dreams while he is terrified by the city's arrogance. As he reports on what he sees, we realize how well read he was. He was acquainted with the "great books" of the English tradition and employed the talents of many of those authors to support his description of the place and his historical knowledge of the empire to inform what he encounters. To him, history (or the master's story) became alive through this visit. His arguments, analysis, and rhetorical asides displayed his enormous erudition, humor, and good sense amid patches of maudlin prose.

Webber also tells us about his first ride in an airplane, his first visit to the London theaters and the London newspaper offices, his address to the Labour members of the House of Commons at Westminster Hall, and his speech over the British Broadcasting Company (BBC). Commenting on the hostile reception he received at Westminster Hall, he wrote: "They had me with my back to the wall and in that position one must be quick on his feet" (*IP*, 80). Given the novelty of radio at that time, he felt impelled to describe the recording procedures of his BBC address. Although the text shows Webber as a proud West Indian person, it also demonstrates his ambivalence as a colonial person: his capacity to worship the accomplishments of the colonizers while simultaneously hating the cruelty and inhumanity of their practices.

A careful perusal of the text also gives one an insight into the issues that were important to Webber. It becomes an important supplement to *Glints from an Anvil*, a prosaic rendition of his poetic sentiments. He notes the poverty that he found in London, compares it to what he was accustomed to in British Guiana, and condemns the former in the strongest possible terms. In one of his most powerful indictments of the ill effects of British capitalism, he writes:

England is fearfully cruel to the poor, despite the work of all her philanthropists. In British Guiana we have our problems. The grueling poverty of many: the cruel plight of the middle classes, who must pay a rent forced upon them by the wickedness of a certain type of politician, not only to serve private ends and not that of those whose votes they beg at Election time; but, let me say it, the plight of the poor in large towns in England is sufficient to make the very heavens belch forth! The match sellers at midnight, in the bitterest cold imaginable, and those without even matches to sell!! Across all this a veil is drawn in this mighty land of pleasure.... I have often wondered, after experiencing the bitter coldness of a late spring, which was almost wintry in its temperature, how any woman could remain virtuous who was offered a warm bed and blankets against bleak rags and sordid surroundings. Hunger is as heaven compared with the hell of cold—and when both are combined God help the victim. When the sun is up, resolve must be strong; but when the darkness of night descends, and shivering takes the place of sunshine, resolution must be a very poor substitute for roses and raptures, even if the price be chastity. (*IP*, 50)

Webber's sociological insights were particularly astute. He was not a trained sociologist, did not have the benefit of a degree from Cambridge or Oxford to guide him, or did not have Henry Mayhew's studies on poverty to draw upon.[33] Yet he recognized the tremendous social dissolution that poverty caused to those who lived in London and, by extension, other urban centers. Writing of the impact of the Industrial Revolution on English towns around the middle of the nineteenth century, Harold Perkin observed that the rapid growth of the new industrial towns and cities created new social problems (such as insecurity created fluctuations in employment) that aggravated and expanded the scale of old ones such as "the chronically depressed and abandoned urban poor. Closely connected with both was the vast increase in crime and prostitution which occurred in the towns in the first half of the nineteenth century, and swelled to a new peak in every economic slump."[34] Speaking of the specific role of prostitution under these conditions, Perkin noted:

> Prostitution rather than crime is the traditional resort of women in desperate straits, and it is significant that the number of women committed for trial [during the first half of the nineteenth century] increased much less than that of men. Contemporaries were convinced that prostitution was a vast and widespread evil—"*the* social problem," as many of them called it—and that it was rapidly increasing, but the statistics are naturally fugitive and unreliable. . . . Informed observers like [Leon] Faucher's [French politician and economist] translator thought that prostitution increased with commercial distress in exactly the same way as crime, and owing to similar economic causes. Others, like Joseph Fletcher [an early criminologist], put it down to the decay of morality and paternal social control in the urban slums.[35]

In his brief visit to London, Webber was able to put his finger on this important problem and its possible effect on English society. He was not willing to take a socialist path to solve the problems in Guyana, although he recognized how it might be applicable to the London slums. After speaking about the terrible cruelty of London and the terrible cold, he says:

> If I had to make a choice in those circumstances, I believe I would be profane enough to ask for a little warm hell rather than stay on such a biting cold earth without food, raiment, or shelter. These are the things which are filling England with Socialists. In rural England, no one ought to be a Socialist. In British Guiana, there is presently not much need for Bolshevism. But in Urban England, industrialized to the fingertips, the strong crushing the weak, and the poor gripped in unspeakable misery, the plant must flourish. (*IP*, 50)

That was 1926, and Webber did not think that socialism was the ideal tool to solve Guyana's problems. Twenty-five years later, Jagan thought it the only tool to solve Guyana's problems. Although he moved closer to accepting the socialist ideal as he went along, one wonders where Webber might have landed up if he hadn't died prematurely.

Edith Dummett, Webber's daughter, and some newspapers' reports noted that Webber was a humorous man. This, too, was reflected in *An Innocent's Pilgrimage*. "Sunday at the Zoo," perhaps the most clever and witty section of the text, shows

Webber at his humorous best. After admiring some of the animals in the zoo, Webber noted the objection that some of his "Guianese" friends had made against the removal of these animals from "their natural surroundings, paddocked, and labeled, merely for the curious to stare upon, without regard to their rights and happiness" (*IP*, 63–64). To this argument, Webber playfully responded:

> There is certainly something in the argument; but like most theses it requires a lot of qualification. Some of the birds might be unhappy, some quite indifferent. Looking at another paddock I am sure the peacock did not give two straws, so he got a square meal and space to spread his feathers. The lions and tigers maybe are unhappy; but the Polar bears seem to be having the time of their lives; while the sea lions would break their hearts, I verily believe, if removed from admiring crowds and favorite keepers. As to the reptiles, the best place I know for them, rights or no rights, is under lock and key; and as soon at the Zoo as anywhere else. Still there must be many who pine for their confinement to any transgressions of theirs—provided they are given introspective thinking and not endowed with some measure of philosophy. (*IP*, 64)

On July 2 Webber sailed back to Guyana, wanting desperately to get out of a city that he remembered as "cold, heartless and inhospitable.... London is so unreal. It is artificial in its life equally with its pleasures. Its traffic roar is like the ceaseless swell of the tractless [*sic*] ocean: its crowds hurry past each other in a constant stream of unknown humanity" (*IP*, 67). To him, the countryside reflected the better, more authentic dimension of England, and he was very much at home when he was farthest from London. Although he said little about the West Indian Conference in his book, he was sure of one thing: these conferences "touch only the upper strata: something more is needed for the man in the Street" (*IP*, 82). He believed that his society would be better served because of his visit and that the "entire Colonial Office has now a far greater respect and appreciation, both for British Guiana and its wants, and the caliber of its public men—elected and otherwise—than they had before the mission" (*IP*, 83). He left England convinced (although his speculation turned out to be incorrect) that the Colonial Office was willing to grant the colony "an informal measure of self-Government, within the limits of the present Constitution" (*IP*, 83), if only there was political unity in the colony.

Finally, he reiterated his call for an open, parliamentary democracy as one way to correct the wrongs of the society. He argued that "there can be no progress until those responsible for, or who pursued, this bitter fratricidal feud are placed where they can no longer wreak mischief; the means available are the ballot, bullet or bomb. Various patriots chose different methods: because of my inherent benevolence which desireth not the death of the sinner, I commend the ballot" (*IP*, 84). In this observation, Webber anticipated Malcolm X's radical formulation.

As Webber saw it, society had to pull itself together if its people were to achieve their liberation. On August 20, 1926, in the last article of his series, he noted: "The duty of the whole colony now lies ahead and forward. All those who stand in the way must be swept out, and kept out" (*IP*, 91). In light of his earlier comment that British Guiana did not need Bolshevism, Webber became more determined to work toward the liberation of his people and to bring them together politically. His eventual formation of the Popular Party with Nelson Cannon reflected one dimension of his seriousness to transform the political culture of Guyana.

An Innocent's Pilgrimage is a journalistic piece. His is an easy, readable style. Realistic descriptions of places abound, and certain observations of life are made. Sometimes there are powerful observations of social life. However, there is nothing particularly gripping or careful about his prose, nor does it reveal the calibrated prosaic observation of V. S. Naipaul or of his brother, Shiva. But then again, Webber does not want to position what he *sees* in England to the detriment of what he *knows* about Guyana. He is an "innocent on pilgrimage" who wants to give his readers his "first impressions" of a country of which they had heard so much. He loves Guyana and cannot wait to return to his home, a point he makes with abundant clarity at the end of the text:

> To London, let me say farewell, which, like a certain type of professional lady, can be adorable and enchanting in turns, even enslaving on occasion; but ever the sordid side of her nature will show up, to prevent the final conversion of transient relationship into perpetual and refined wifely domesticity. That is why one can never really love London: always attractive; but under the face of a painted doll is the heartlessness of stone. Some women one is always glad to get away from and glad to meet again. That is London. And with that I take my final farewell. (*IP*, 92)[36]

An Innocent's Pilgrimage gives us an extraordinary insight into how Webber thought and some of his powerful observations of English life. It is one of the earliest pieces of travel writing in West Indian literature that describes the colonial response to the (m)other country. It also tells of Webber's energy and talent and the seriousness with which he took his responsibility as a journalist and a patriot. Webber was enamored with this work. He published a second edition in 1929 and described it as "light and delightful reading. . . . There are chapters on Romance, Adventure, Humour [and] Pathos. Every chord of the emotion is touched."[37] His efforts certainly pleased him.

CHAPTER SIX

WEBBER'S LEADERSHIP, THE POPULAR PARTY, AND THE CONSTITUTIONAL CRISIS, 1926–27

It is not surprising that the famous tolerance leaves him almost entirely [when he arrives in the colonial territories]. At home he was distinguished for the liberality and freedom of his views. Hampden, Chatham, Dunning and Fox, Magna Charta and Bill of Rights, these are the persons and things (however misconceived) which Englishmen, undemonstrative as they are, write and speak of with subdued but conscious pride.... But in the colonies any man who speaks for his country, any man who dares to question the authority of those who rule over him, any man who tries to do for his own people what Englishmen are so proud that other Englishmen have done for theirs, immediately becomes in the eyes of the colonial Englishman a dangerous person, a wild revolutionary, a man with no respect for law and order, a self-seeker actuated by the lowest motives, a reptile to be crushed at the first opportunity. What at home is the greatest virtue becomes in the colonies the greatest crime.

—C. L. R. JAMES, *The Case for West-Indian Self Government*

In a society which was greatly deferent to colour, his [Cannon's] whiteness and Webber's "colour" would have been a definite advantage *vis-à-vis* the bulk of the population, and in any case, with the largely Negro electorate.

—HAROLD LUTCHMAN, *Middle Class Colonial Politics*

NINETEEN TWENTY-SIX USHERED IN A NEW ERA IN GUYANA POLITICS. It was the year in which locally based, rambunctious politicians took over the political leadership from wealthy, elite, "respectable" politicians whose representation primarily served the interests of owners who lived abroad. It was the year in which the Popular Party, the first political party in the West Indies, was formed and became victorious in the election.[1] In that new dispensation, with the exception of Webber, all of the victorious candidates were born in Guyana. It also proved to be "the most lively [time politically] in the history of British Guiana.... Political organization also reached its highest level of sophistication."[2] Webber, together with Norman Cannon, who was reelected to the Legislative Council in a by-election in 1923, formed a close-knit political association, acted as the champions of "the masses" or the "common people," and gained a reputation as the "chief opponents of the government." By 1926, Webber and Cannon had become the two most "prominent politicians of the day," Webber having gained the reputation of being "among the foremost political thinkers" and activist in the colony.³ In its battle to sway public opinion, the *Daily Chronicle* of which Webber was the editor became a major weapon in the political equation in that it always took "a popular stand on political issues. It was at the fore of 'progressive political thinking' and was, for example, the chief advocate of constitutional reform on popular lines, and this and other matters, owed very much, as was frequently acknowledged even by the *Daily Argosy* [its rival], to Webber."⁴

Webber continued his battle against the Colonial Office and the government after he returned from the West Indian Conference in July 1926. His first political battle took the form of "a major fight against attempts to reduce the powers of the British Guiana Constitution Ordinance of 1891 and to report, in detail, what changes were desirable owing to the lapse of time."⁵ Within three months of his arrival, the secretary of state and the governor set up three powerful committees to determine how best to wrest financial control from the hands of the Financial Representatives of the Combined Court. Recognizing that such a constitutional move represented a deceptive detour whereby the colonial government would introduce a Crown Colony government into the society, Webber and his colleagues organized themselves in a much more meticulous manner to confront the situation ahead.

At the end of September, the government's move to limit the powers of the Electives was aggravated further when, anticipating the dissolution of the Combined Court, the secretary of state notified J. B. Cassels, government trade commissioner, that he would send a parliamentary commission to Guyana in October to study the best way to limit the activities of local legislators.⁶ On October 16 the British Guiana Commission, appointed by Amery, left England in the S.S. *Samaria*, arriving in British Guiana on November 16 "to consider and report on the economic condition of the colony, the causes which have hitherto retarded and the measures which could be taken to promote development, and any facts which they may consider to have a bearing on the above matters."⁷ As it became evident afterward, this commission was a clever disguise to take away the powers of the Financial Representatives since it would be very easy to allege (even though it wasn't proven) that their power over the colony's financial purse strings contributed to the adverse development of the colony. Hence, the commission noted in its report:

In the Court of Policy the Government majority is subject to a potential veto which can be exercised by the elected members inasmuch as if seven of them abstain from attending they can prevent the formation of the quorum required. In the Combined Court, on the other hand, and consequently in matters of taxation or involving expenditure, the elected members possess a majority, and the only limitation to their powers is that they cannot increase, though they can reduce or reject, any item on the annual estimates which are prepared by the Governor in Executive Council. Thus this nominally two-chamber system is in fact merely a method of dividing the subjects of legislation into two classes, financial, in which the elected members possess a majority, and non-financial, over which they can only exercise a negative control. (*BGC*, 49)

This control that the elected members possessed appeared to be very threatening to the Colonial Office and the commissioners since the franchise, at that time, had been extended to anyone with an income of $300. The commissioners noted that the electorate was "principally composed of the black and coloured population and numbered at the last elections about 11,000 out of an adult *male* population of some 86,000" (*BGC*, 50).[8] Once they continued to be fractious, it was easy for the government or the Colonial Office to divide and rule. E. F. Fredericks, a member of the Popular Party, observed that as long as the Electives were seen "not only playing at chess with one another, but were actually in open warfare with one another, Government would simply sit and smilingly look on."[9] An expanding black and colored electorate under a unified party became an urgent concern of the Colonial Office and remained a pressing issue in the private correspondences between the secretary of state and the governor in confidential memoranda.

From November 16 to December 17, the commissioners went from Georgetown to New Amsterdam, from Corentyne to Port Mourant, to conduct their business. They met with government officials, the elected members, and members of the Bartica Village Council, Webber's old stumping ground. They inspected the prisons and the forest and visited the Sugar Planters Experimental Station, after which they presented their report to the secretary of state for the colonies in April 1927. The commissioners gave their impression of the colony before they got down to the gist of their conclusions: first, the existing "educational and political institutions" were inadequate to the needs of the society; second, the government could not enforce its economic responsibilities to society because it did not have full control over financial decisions. While they welcomed changes in the existing constitution that would give to the people's representatives "wider powers of usefulness and greater opportunity for constructive criticism," they could not see how it could be possible either to ensure a consistent financial policy or to exercise efficient control of the colony's sources of revenue, "unless Government have the power, in the last resort, and under proper safeguards, to enforce their own decisions" (*BGC*, 14).

As one examines the motives of the commissioners more closely, one discovers that their main concern was the realization that a black electorate had assumed powers they did not possess previously. Such a development threatened the control that the Colonial Office and the planters had over the society. They were explicit about "the disadvantages" of the political system "now that the control of the political machine has passed to a wider and more numerous but necessarily, in a racially composite community, where the great majority of the population are too indifferent or too ignorant to exercise political rights, to a relatively narrow and also inexperienced electorate" (*BGC*, 51). Therefore, the Colonial Office had to devise a plan, as innocuously as possible, to wrest political control from the hands of a greatly expanded electorate that were "too indifferent or to ignorant to exercise [their] political rights." Having made a distinction between the "representative" but "nonresponsible government" (that is, the elected element of the legislature) and the "nonrepresentative" but "responsible government," controlled by the secretary of state and the governor, the commission granted reserve powers to the governor, which in effect negated the rights of the elected representatives, who were defined as being "irresponsible" in their use of power. No wonder the commission saw the latter conflict as "*the* fundamental defect" of the constitution and argued that at its stage of development, "it is not merely desirable but essential that the authorities finally responsible for the Government of the Colony should have power in the last resort to carry into effect measures which they consider essential for its well being." They believed that "every effort should be made to enlist the assistance of the best brains of the Colony and of men with affairs. Especially we hope that the elected representatives of the people will take an active and constructive part in effecting the necessary changes, bearing in mind the desirability of securing the greatest possible measure of agreement on the spot and thus avoiding the necessity of an imposed reform of the constitution" (*BGC*, 53).

This was their case. Having made their argument for what they considered "the vital change" and chastising the people for "venerat[ing] what they are not presently able to comprehend," the commissioners concluded: "We are anxious not to tamper unnecessarily with a time-honoured and historic institution" (*BGC*, 53). Nonetheless, they recommended a single chamber Legislative Council, an expanded Executive Council, and the addition of a nominated element to accommodate the European members of society, who they feared would no longer be elected to the Legislative Council in numbers to which they were accustomed. Their racist logic for the last move ran as follows:

It is a general phenomenon in *tropical* colonies that the extension of the electorate and the greater frequency of contests make it extremely and increasingly difficult for anyone who is not able and prepared to embark more or less whole time on the career of politics to enter the Legislature by the avenue of the con-stituencies. The result is the loss to public life of no inconsiderable proportion of those who are *best qualified for it, or, in other words, of the small but extremely important European* class which still controls the principal agricultural and commercial activities of the Colony. (*BGC*, 55, my emphasis)

Such a formulation was apartheid Guyanese style, but the commissioners had pre-sented a rationale for what they intended to achieve when they left England on October 16, 1926. The victims would be the Guyanese people.

On July 12, 1927, Governor Rodwell appointed the commission that was rec-ommended by the secretary of state's fact-finding body to advise him on the steps that should be taken "to confer power upon the Governor to carry into effect measures which he and the secretary of state consider essential for the well-being of the Colony."[10] The seven members of the commission began their deliberations on July 15, reported back to the governor in September 1927, and presented their report to the secretary of state in November 1927.

Such a development was not entirely unexpected by Webber and his colleagues, who had had begun to prepare themselves for the general elections since the end of 1925. As a result, they began to attack government policies more frequently and paid much more attention to the demands of their constituents. Recognizing the need to carry forward a united struggle to safeguard the little self-governing au-thority they possessed through the Combined Court, they organized themselves more carefully into the Popular Party under the leadership of Cannon and Webber. Cannon was the more prominent leader of the party, which became known also as the Cannonites. It included several prominent citizens, among whom were J. P. Santos, J. Da Silva, P. A. Fernandes, J. Gonsalves, and S. M. DeFreitas (Portuguese); A. E. Seeram (East Indian); E. F. Fredericks (Negro); E. G. Woolford and Webber (colored); and Cannon and J. Dodds (whites).[11] The most militant members of the party were Fredericks, Fernandes, Dodds, Cannon, and Webber.

The party possessed a progressive manifesto. It proposed universal suffrage for the country and advocated self-government in the villages and the promotion and protection of trade unions. It promised to increase the salaries of the lower levels of the civil servants and government workers. However, the creation of jobs was the most important challenge the party faced. The party members believed that the construction of a railway from the coast to the interior would encourage eco-nomic development and go a long way to relieve the chronic unemployment that plagued the colony. Fredericks thought that unemployment "was so universal in the city of Georgetown as to be tantamount to a disgrace to the Government's existence."[12] The party was also "strongly in favour of reaching an agreement with Henry Ford who had made a tentative offer to build a road from Georgetown to the Brazilian frontier in order to connect with a road to his new rubber plantation on the Amazon."[13] Such a move would have opened up the hinterland and created more employment.

The election campaign was an intense affair. According to the *Daily Argosy*, it was "the longest and most determined election campaign Georgetown has ever known."[14] The Popular Party organized for about three months in advance of the election, held strategy sessions, canvassed widely, and registered eligible voters and made sure their names were on the voters' list. Candidates were even asked to contribute financially to the overall election campaign. They kept pounding away at the inefficiency of government and the Colonial Office while the "respectable" candidates sought to uphold the intelligence and well-meaning behavior of the two bodies. This proved to be the undoing of their opponents, who were not well organized. They "left everything to the last moment and devoted little more than three days to the task of organizing for victory."[15]

When the general election took place, the Popular Party succeeded beyond its wildest dreams. It secured majorities in the Combined Court and the Court of Policy. Zenophon, a reader of the *Daily Argosy*, averred: "The Popular Party got elected because of the promise to change the Constitutional Ordinance to admit these reforms."[16] At a victory meeting, Cannon informed his listeners that he would let "the Secretary of State for the Colonies know that I have been returned here with the principal object of seeing the railway proposal brought to a termination. . . . This is my mission and I have been returned to see that you get your railway."[17] The members of the Popular Party had worked hard and deserved their victory. According to the *Daily Argosy*, it was "a glorious victory for the people."[18]

In spite of the fears of the government and the Colonial Office, the predominantly African and East Indian electorate elected a majority of white candidates to represent their interests. In fact, some people called the Popular Party "the light skinned man's party."[19] Lutchman advanced that Webber's "color" and Cannon's whiteness were major assets of the Popular Party. Webber was extremely popular, and Cannon was seen as the government's major antagonist. Such staunch antigovernment credentials enhanced their success. Of the fourteen victorious Electives, three were Afro-Guyanese (Fredericks, J. S. McArthur, and J. Eleazer). The same electorate rejected some of the most prominent Afro-Guyanese, including the much-revered P. N. Browne (born in Barbados), A. A. Thorne, and A. V. Crane, none of whom was a member of the Popular Party. The electorate was willing to disregard the question of color and vote for the party that presented a better solution to their problems. Nonetheless, the respect for whiteness in a colonial society cannot be dismissed easily.

Needless to say, the plantocracy "was alarmed when the Popular Party swept the polls" and extremely angry in defeat.[20] They ascribed the sweeping victory "in the General Elections of the Graft, Gutter and Grab [Popular] party to organization, co-operation and combination, coupled of course, with the systematic diffusion of dastardly lies, gross misrepresentations and the most scurrilous stories, and slander."[21] They even alluded to the low educational level of the electorate, to whom "bluster is sometimes apt to be mistaken for bravery, insolence and impudence for an independent spirit and unmannerly conduct for manly resolution" and concluded that the lower class could not possibly know what they were doing when they voted for the Popular Party.[22] The candidates who stood for the Popular Party were described as "'men of straw' with little or no stake in the community."[23] Lutchman seems to be correct when he notes that there is "good reason to believe that the intelligence of the electorate, many of whom were among the more literate and intelligent section of the population, was underrated."[24]

Reeling from this unexpected defeat, the government set its legal machinery in motion to steal the elections from the people. What it did not accomplish in the political sphere it sought to achieve in the judicial arena. Accordingly, the attorney general challenged the results of the election in the courts, and four of the successful candidates were disqualified from taking their seats in the Combined Court. J. P. Santos, winner of the Berbice seat, was unseated because he was not a registered voter. John Dodds, winner of the North-West Essequebo seat; J. J. Da Silva, winner of the West Demerara seat; and P. A. Fernandes, winner of another seat, were unseated because they did not possess the requisite property qualifications. The court awarded the Da Silva seat to A. V. Crane. J. S. MacArthur, an independent candidate, was unseated also because "he had failed to file a declaration within a specified time."[25] More important, the Court of Policy addressed a memorial to the colonial secretary that set up the investigation commission that recommended the abolition of the Combined Court.

In the end, only eight of the fourteen elected members of the Popular Party were allowed to take their seats. Webber and his colleagues did not take this judicial and constitutional lynching lying down. Undaunted, they kept on fighting. On December 18, 1926, the Electives held a meeting in the Court of Policy Hall and "unanimously decided" to move a motion in the Combined Court asking for an inquiry "into the administration of justice in the Colony."[26] The next day, December 19, Webber wrote a stinging editorial in the *New Daily Chronicle* denouncing "a judicial scandal [that] had been perpetrated against the people." He opined: "[Justice] Berkeley has, by his conduct, outraged every canon of the judiciary, and reduced the bench to the scoffs of the multitude; as was evinced by the sorry scene enacted at the close of the judgment, when the crowds in Court declined to render the judge the ordinary courtesies usually accorded to all wearers of the King's ermine, and his Honour had to rebuke the crowd as he descended the steps from the bench." Webber argued that Justice Berkeley had "neither the will nor the intellectual capacity to be impartial," or "the mental caliber to disguise his flagrant partisanship." He called for Berkeley's impeachment and an inquiry into his conduct and noted that the Crown could not afford to have its judiciary hand down judgments that were "a disgrace to the community, and a grave reflection upon the whole administration of justice in the colony."[27]

The state was not prepared to sit idly by as Webber used his pen to assault its (lack of) integrity or as Anthony De Fraitas, the chief justice, said in his ruling, "scandalize[ed] a court or a judge of the court."[28] Necessarily, the court was an integral part of the machinery that was used to keep natives in their place. On January 10, 1927, the state brought contempt of court charges against Webber for the offending editorial. It was a tactic that the state had used before to silence Louis de Souza.[29] Although Webber admitted that he had written the editorial, he objected to how the court proceedings took place and asked that the case be dismissed. On March 15 the court overruled Webber's objections and found him guilty of contempt of court the next day. Two years later, the colonial authorities used the same legal language to jail Marcus Garvey and deny him a seat in the Jamaica legislature. Webber was more judicious. Realizing that he had little choice, he apologized and informed the court that he never "intended to impugn the honour or honesty of Mr. Justice Berkeley."[30] He was charged £200, a large sum in those days. The court ordered that he be imprisoned if he did not pay his fine by March 31. With the support of his friends, Webber raised much more than the amount needed, paid his fine on March 23, and thereby escaped imprisonment. He would live to fight another day. Four years later, Rohini seemed to be on target when he concluded: "The country paid the fine, and this no doubt compensated him [Webber] and represented a kind of moral victory, for the cause he advocated."[31]

Governor Rodwell was overjoyed when Webber was found guilty. He interpreted Webber's conviction as a significant public humiliation. On April 27, 1927, he reported to Amery with glee:

> Had the proceedings not been taken, or had they failed, I believe that the prestige not only of the Judiciary but of the Executive (the uneducated mind draws no distinction between the two) would have suffered serious damage. . . . I am informed that towards the close of the proceedings, Mr. Webber's usual bravado deserted him and that he cut a sorry figure. The incident has been a wholesome lesson not only to him but to large numbers of people whom he had led to believe by his utterances in the Press and on the platform that he could defy the authorities with impunity. One of his former adherents among the crowd in Court is reported to have remarked in the vernacular: "That man Webber no good. He eat dirt."[32]

In a curt reply to Rodwell, Amery observed: "The case was clearly one in which it was essential to take proceedings. I have noted your satisfaction and your view of the Attorney General's handling of it."[33] He did not support Rodwell's gloating over Webber's conviction.

Webber did not take this temporary setback lying down. In February 1927 he moved a motion in the Combined Court that the status and activity of Governor Thomson's Constitutional Commission be reviewed. By the middle of that year, the issue of constitutional reform had erupted into a full-blown "constitutional crisis." As a result of his ardor and passion for self-government, his fearlessness and eloquence in expressing his people's sentiments for freedom, Webber became the leading figure in the Guyanese people's struggle for liberation.[34] In July of that year Webber and the other Electives told the governor how the people whom they represented felt about constitutional reform. They believed that the proposed changes to the 1891 constitution were aimed primarily at taking away most of the basic rights for which they had fought for such a long time and making British Guiana a Crown Colony. Basically, the 1891 constitution had broken the power of the sugar interests and granted the franchise to more persons. Lutchman regarded 1891 "as a turning point in the political life of British Guiana, because of the belief that it was the year in which the planters were deprived of their power and influence and were superseded by middle class politicians."[35] Leo Despres argues that although the constitutional reforms of the time did not alter the power structure, "the extension of the franchise in that year, and again in 1909, marked a definite turning point in Guianese political life."[36] Even the size of the electorate had grown. Whereas the electorate was comprised of approximately 1,000 persons in 1891, by 1915 it consisted of 4,312 persons, of whom 62.7 percent were Africans, 9 percent were Portuguese, and 6.4 percent were Indians. Needless to say, Webber and the other Electives did not want to lose the gains that Africans, Indians, and other oppressed groups and classes had achieved through the 1891 constitution.

Webber and the Electives were most incensed by the proposed constitutional amendment that was aimed at scuttling the financial control that they had over internal affairs. On July 12, 1927, Webber argued that the proposed changes represented "a destruction of the Colony, as provided for by the Articles of Capitulation especially in relation to the control over the mode of taxation." He noted that the commission's terms of references "transgress[ed] the Imperial Law Offices of the Crown given in 1840, that it is not competent for the Crown-in-Council to raise revenue and determine its appropriation in British Guiana." On behalf of the other Electives, he tabled a motion in which he vigorously protested "against the terms of reference of the said Commission duly appointed and pledge[d] to pursue all legitimate means to prevent and resist the transference of financial control to the Government without the express sanction of a majority of Members of the Court and the inhabitants of the Colony."[37]

On August 11, 1927, in an editorial in the *New Daily Chronicle*, Webber placed the local elements who were arguing for the imposition of Crown Colony government in British Guiana in the same category as those who fought so arduously to prevent the slaves from being freed:

> The identical elements which struggled so bitterly for the retention of slavery are, by a sinister coincidence, the identical influences which are now agitating for Crown Colony government as being the best thing for British Guiana. The men who are hailing Crown Colony government, with the elimination of the control of the popularly elected representatives, are lineal descendants of the men who soaked this colony and many others in blood, in the vain attempt to bolster up slavery.[38]

As Webber continued his attack against the reactionary elements of the society, he compared the supporters of Crown Colony government to those who had betrayed Caribbean people in the past and argued that "the men who murdered [John] Smith in Demerara, and hanged [George William] Gordon, in Jamaica, are the prototypes of the men today who talk glibly, and write more loosely, of battleships and stirring up of traitors at the ships' yard arms."[39] In this spirited and erudite attack against the defenders of colonialism, Webber took on Sam Lumpton, editor of the *Daily Argosy* and a major spokesman for the reactionaries, whose newspaper supported the call for Crown Colony government. Lumpton, a displaced Englishman living in British Guiana who used the *Daily Argosy* to promote his brand of reactionary politics, became the embodiment of colonial reaction. Webber located his attack within the terrain of capitalist exploitation and the need of Lumpton and his group to defend the colonial-capitalist system in British Guiana. He argued:

> We could reconstruct his daily articles every morning, as to the benefits of slavery and what number of lashes to administer to local agitators; but best of all his choicest epithets would be reserved for Wilberforce and Buxton; Canning and Clarkson. They would have been doddering idiots; imbecile mischief makers; masked assassins. Phrase would have trampled upon the heels of phrase. Daylight would have been darkened with invective; vituperation would have hummed us to church by day and rocked us to sleep at nights. Mr. Lumpton's blood would have glowed at the opportunity of eternal service to be done to capital. Industry would have been his protégé; while the great benefits of slavery even to the slave himself would have been trumpeted from house tops daily. Every slave was sleek and fat; every free negro a mass of ulcers scarcely decently covered in rags, and fit only for the lethal chamber.[40]

Webber was at his eloquent best. He had read local, Caribbean, European, and New World histories deeply. His knowledge of slavery and its aftermath, his knowledge of trade and commerce, was vast. He understood the working of the colonial mind and the myriad ways in which the colonizer sought to keep colonized persons enslaved. His stance on the side of working people marked him as one of our earliest progressive thinkers and activists of the Caribbean. His invocation of Smith and Gordon demonstrated his awareness of the Caribbean struggle for justice, the two men having been involved in issues (such as unemployment, declining wages, high taxation, high food prices, lack of representation) similar to those with which the Guyanese people were engaged. Kim Blake has observed that the Morant Bay Rebellion with which Gordon was involved and for which he lost his life "served to highlight the absence of a legal political platform for the majority of black Jamaicans to air their grievances. Gordon was colored. Although there was a majority of 'coloured' representatives in the white-dominated assembly, the interests of black small farmers and labourers were overlooked."[41] Webber's article was a classic in its denunciation of Crown Colony rule and a scathing attack against those who wanted to turn the constitutional clock backward and deny working people their just due. This was Webber's "Massa Day Done" speech.[42] It preceded Eric Williams's speech by over twenty-five years.

During this period, Webber also argued for East Indian representation and urged the East Indians to come forward and support the majority's position against the imposition of Crown Colony rule. Up until this time, the East Indians were somewhat quiescent on political matters. At an open-air meeting that took place during the crisis, Webber urged them to unite with the Afro-Guyanese in common struggle. He argued that the best way for the East Indians "to get adequate representation was through the polls and by means of the ballot box. If they wished to become useful citizens, they must stand up for their rights in a manly way and not depend to be spoon-fed by Government's nominated members." Webber denounced as "fallacious" the position that the nominated members would offer East Indians more representation "and urged upon the necessity for [East] Indians and Negroes combining in this crisis."[43]

At that meeting, the Hon. E. A. Luckhoo, a legislative colleague of Webber and a founder of BGEAI, also objected to what he called "the monstrous proposal of the secretary of state" and gave "every support to his colleagues in the fight they were waging for the retention of the Constitution."[44] Although he supported the retention of the constitution, there were questions about whether Luckhoo and the BGEAI were against Crown Colony government, and this led to a lively debate in the local newspapers.[45] In 1919 Luckhoo went to India "to induce more Indians from the motherland to join our ranks, increase our numbers and so help us to make British Guiana an Indian Colony."[46] Probably such a posture reflected the unease that East Indians were beginning to feel in the colony. Undoubtedly, Luckhoo admired Webber, which suggests that he was appreciative of the work that Webber was waging on the East Indians' behalf. When Jennifer Welshman, granddaughter of Webber, says that she first became aware of her grandfather's importance through a speech by Sir Lionel Luckhoo, son of J. A. Luckhoo, it may not be such a stretch of the imagination. The elder Luckhoo must have conveyed Webber's greatness and his contribution to the people's cause to his son.

Webber used all the tools he had at his disposal to fight against the retrograde constitution the British wanted to impose upon Guyana. As part of the battle against the imposition of Crown Colony government, the *New Daily Chronicle* republished James Rodway's seminal article, published originally in 1891, on British Guiana's constitution, in which he examined the constitution from its origins in the first Dutch settlement to 1891.[47] Anticipating that the governor was prepared to adopt the new constitution without the consent of the governed or their representatives, on July 12, 1927, via a motion, Webber notified the governor that he would take the issue to the secretary of state and the British Parliament if the sentiments of the Guyanese people were not included in the making of the new constitution.

As the 1928 constitution was being adopted, Webber, H. C. Humphries, and E. G. Woolford, all Electives, went to England to see the secretary of state for the colonies to protest its adoption, but to little avail. Unfortunately, the weakening of the Popular Party proved to be of little assistance in this phase of the struggle. The inability to enforce party discipline and the unseating of several of its members in the Legislative Council led to the destruction of the party.[48] However, before Webber and his group proceeded to London, he appealed to the government "not to 'railroad' any matter on which the remaining Electives were unanimous, in the absence of these three delegates."[49] The secretary of state did not listen to the Electives and proceeded on his own counsel. It took a long time, but in 1962 Daly noted that the adoption of the 1928 constitution represented "a backward step on the road to independence," a judgment that confirmed Webber's foresight and political sagacity.[50] History confirmed the correctness of his insight.

CHAPTER SEVEN

WEBBER: A TRAVELING MAN

Texts that are inertly of their time stay there; those which brush up unstintingly against historical constraints are the ones we keep with us, generation after generation.
—EDWARD SAID, *Freud and the Non-European*

If I would convert one hundred million tropical heathen[s] to the worship of an UNKNOWN God I would lead them to see a heavy snowfall: not while it was falling for that is monotonous, and it is the accumulated effect that is required. I would lead them, most to the great snow-covered parks, and beautiful pastures where the snow lay. Then I would tell them that the Unknown God had willed such ethereal beauty, such rapturous loveliness, that none may look upon it, but weep at His name, His grandeur and His magnificence. And perhaps then I may have been a greater missionary than Livingstone or Chas. Wesley, or William Booth; or any in this or any other age—and that without book or bigotry.
—A. R. F. WEBBER, "New York versus London"

WHEN WEBBER TRAVELED TO LONDON IN 1928 to protest the proposed changes in British Guiana's constitution, he wrote nine sketches about his visits, which he called "From an Editorial View-Point." These sketches appeared in the *New Daily Chronicle* from February 19 through June 20, 1928, and discussed his impressions of Trinidad, Barbados, London, and Jamaica. Although Webber hoped to publish these sketches in book form, he never got around to doing so. In his personal notebook, which Edith, his daughter, kept and which is now in the possession of Jennifer Welshman, Webber made several corrections to the copy that appeared in the *New Daily Chronicle* in anticipation that the sketches would be published eventually. Circumstances, apparently, did not allow him to do so.

On this his third trip to London, Webber left Georgetown around January 20, 1928, stopping first in Trinidad, then proceeding to Barbados and Portugal before arriving in London on February 6, 1928. On January 24 he addressed an audience at the Princess Building, in Port of Spain, Trinidad, a report of which was published in the *Port of Spain Gazette* the following day. Captain Arthur Cipriani, Dr. Tito Achong, J. Ryan, A. V. Stollmyer, Mrs. Aubrey Jeffers, and the officers of the Trinidad Workingmen's Association attended his lecture. It is likely that C. L. R. James might have heard this lecture since he was a faithful follower of Cipriani and wrote a biography on him. Webber spoke on the "physio-graphical features of British Guiana," while Captain Cipriani spoke about the importance of a West Indian Federation. Acting in solidarity with British Guiana against the proposed changes that were to be made in the country's constitution, Cipriani protested against what he called the "big stick legislation under British rule." Although Webber discussed his visit to Trinidad in his first sketch, "Bird's Eye Sketches of Trinidad and Barbados," he does not mention his appearance at the Princess Building.

Unlike *An Innocent's Pilgrimage* in which Webber refused to discuss the political aspects of his second visit to London, he devotes a third of "From an Editorial View-Point" (or what he calls his "letters") to his delegation's meeting with the Colonial Office and the subsequent debate on the proposed measures on the constitution, particularly in sketches five and six.[1] Reading these accounts, one gets an understanding of how the colonial officials functioned. In his sixth letter, "Gathering Up the Ashes," Webber speaks of the frustration of his discussions of the constitution with officials from the Colonial Office after he cornered them into a meeting. At the conference, they were welcomed by Sir Robert Grindle, undersecretary of state, who counseled his colleagues to discount some of the official criticisms they were hearing about the elected members of Guyana. Webber continued:

> But, here was I [*sic*] facing the man who fathered those criticisms; for to me was allowed the venture of trying to convince him of the error of his ways. There was a distant handicap in that there was no immediate finality to the discussion. Except by intuition one could not tell whether to leave well alone, to shift ground, or to pass to another point. Everything was "to be considered." Our views would be transmitted to the Secretary of State for his decision, etc. A pretty game of make believe, but no doubt necessary under parliamentary institutions and representations. All fight against the Reserve Power had to be abandoned; all hope had to be concentrated on "hamstringing" it. Limit it over a period of years: make it a constitutional exercise in the Executive Council, etc. We won on the last point.[2]

At this meeting, Webber kept on pressing for the vindication of the "elective principle," but to no avail. Recognizing the power the Colonial Office had over his country, he could only note for posterity that he concentrated on "the necessity for preserving Elective preponderance under any circumstances. It seemed also that 'the Secretary of State would not approve.' But I hung on—hopelessly as far as my auditors were concerned. How successful eventually only time will tell!" He left the conference, and later England, with the thought that he had made British Guiana perhaps as well known, "as a political issue, as Kenya, and he would be a very bold Governor indeed who would venture to use his 'Reserve' power to flout the unanimous wishes of the Electives. British Guiana has now become a parliamentary issue of some importance."³

Having concluded his business, Webber left England for the West Indies on the S.S. *Patuca* on March 19. His first stop was Jamaica, where he landed on April 5 and lectured at the Ward Theatre on the economic conditions in Guyana. The *New Daily Chronicle* noted that on April 5, "Jamaica Legislators Lionize Mr. A. R. F. Webber." On April 6 he was the guest of the Hon. P. W. Sangster, "whose spontaneous championing of the cause of the Electives of British Guiana had warmed my heart towards him before we have ever met."⁴ On April 7 he went on a motor tour of the island. In Jamaica, he took his usually irrevocable position on the desirability of a West Indian Federation and the need for West Indians to know one another better. He argued that "whether Federation comes next year or the next generation be assured it will never come or if it does will be a ghastly failure until the men of each community know more of and appreciate more in each other. When that day comes the cry *floreat–West India* will be no empty slogan."⁵ Such a declaration would surely be an impetus for the West Indian Press Association that he would lead the way in forming one year later.

Webber was a staunch West Indian nationalist leader in the movement for self-determination in the colonies, West Indian unity, and the reclamation of the dignity of the West Indian person. The *New Daily Chronicle*, one of the most progressive newspapers in the region, published innumerable stories regarding the West Indian Federation, self-determination of the colonies, and works by Theophilus Albert Marryshow, Booker T. Washington (whose activities in those early days were seen by many as giving much dignity to black people), and J. A. Rogers, a Jamaican historian who resided in the United States and who spoke about the early achievements of African civilization. The newspaper also reprinted progressive articles that appeared in the *West Indian* (Grenada), the *Dominica Tribune*, and other West Indian newspapers.

Webber returned to Guyana on May 24, 1928, with many pleasant memories of Jamaica, stating, "Neither joy at home coming nor distresses of my country [can] obliterate the pictures of Jamaica."⁶ He really loved Jamaica and was swept away by the beauty of its scenery. While he found some of the roads tortuous, he ended his tribute to Jamaica and the last sketch, "Jamaica from Her Mountain Tops," with the following words: "Jamaica from her mountain tops or her plains is just one intoxicating feast of ravishing beauty and estatic [*sic*] joy."⁷

In November 1928 Webber left for New York City due to the "pressure of important business" and thus was absent for the municipal elections that took place in December 1928.[8] In a public letter to his constituents of Kingston, Guyana, dated November 2, 1928, he alerted them that he may be "a day or two late in returning to the colony for the General Elections at the end of December," but his absence should not prevent him from being reelected since "the Ordinance provides for such eventualities." He wanted to thank them for their support in the past and craved their votes in the forthcoming municipal general election as he pledged "to devote the same assiduous attention to municipal affairs as I have done in the past."[9] He ended his letter by asking his constituents for their support and pledging himself to serve their interests in the future. Webber, however, was not successful in this municipal election.

Webber was fascinated by New York City in a way that he was not by London. He became acquainted with London via books and intellectual ideas but was excited by what he calls the "hum" of New York City. In New York, he wrote about the conditions of women, the relationship between the races, and the city's architectural monstrosities. Most of all, he wrote about all the snow of Long Island. On December 20, 1929, he devoted his first essay to the "entrancingly beautiful" snow that he experienced in Long Island and, in the process, gave us some of the best descriptive prose of his career. He seemed to have been truly mesmerized by the enchanting beauty of the snow in New York's countryside. After advising his readers that New York was quite different from England, which he visited as early as 1917, he compared the former with the latter. Sounding like a modern-day Wordsworth, he inveighed:

> If London was a disappointment, New York was just a nightmare. But if England had its compensations so has greater New York. All God's beauty and man's humanity have not yet disappeared from New York. If the nightmare may be found in Manhattan, where things hum, and buildings raise their hideous crowns in defiance of God's heaven, so also may the peace that passeth all understanding be found in Brooklyn, in Queens, in Jamaica or any suburban district of Long Island.[10]

When Webber arrived in New York, prohibition was very much in the air. He compared the response to prohibition in New York with the consumption of alcohol by the people of British Guiana and noted the effects that prohibition was having on women in the United States. "Prohibition," he writes,

> has had its great evils; perhaps the worst of which is the nation wide demoralization that has followed in its train. In a lesser degree it is producing an unhappy effect among the women. Young women, who under normal conditions would never think of drinking, now drink as a matter of course and cleverness. But that has no general disastrous effects, and so may be passed over. I am nev-

ertheless inclined to believe that all this will evaporate, and a sane enforcement of the 18th amendment come to pass. It will never be enforced in the Eastern states while public opinion stands where it does. What the United States requires more than anything else at the moment is nation wide education on the subject; until then it will be defied.[11]

The beauty of the Long Island snow captured Webber's imagination and brought out the best of his descriptive talents. He rhapsodized about the beauty of snow as it was reflected in the sunlight:

I have read of the snow, of its dangers and its beauties, I have seen pictures of it in all phases, from the frosted Xmas cards of my youth to the more pretentious expositions of picture galleries; but no where did those pictures convey to me the ethereal, the poignant beauty of the real. Writers, it seems to me, never have conveyed the picture that might be. Perhaps they feel that all readers alike know what an everyday winter covering looks like, so why worry. May be, the writers themselves have grown stale watching snows year after year; nursing perhaps grievances of colds and coal bills; so that their admiration is but a grudging tribute. Fortunately, I had nothing but admiration, yea worship, to render; despite the fact that the precious winter had been anything but kind to me.[12]

To him, the snow appeared "whiter and whiter as you look into it, with the impression that there is something yet whiter below, or behind, if only you could penetrate the outer layers. Thus begins the first ethereal beauty of snow. Something hidden, something elusive, something yet to be seen; the yet more driven whiteness indiscernible."[13] Webber records his feelings and the kind of transcendence that takes place in that suburban countryside as he experienced "the physical effect of this ravishing beauty" of this natural world. As he admired the beauty of the place, he exclaimed:

Silence seized me, beauty beckoned; and my boundless admiration swept into that physical pain born of ecstasy. Let him smile who will. He whose adoration cannot be translated into the physical has no soul, and therefore cannot truly worship. I was mentally snow bound; my hands, heart, feet were transfigured into one great worship of the immeasurably beautiful. Oh, cruel remorseless beauty, the beauty of winter, that is beautiful only to destroy! . . .

[C]old as I was within a closed car; the snow without looked warm. Warm as a caress; ethereal and entrancing even unto the sexual. Whether it was day or night; whether it was chilly or warm, I was being wafted into the ecstasies of the infinite: perhaps even unto beyond the sexual, where male and female ceased to be![14]

As one reads Webber's description of the snow and the effects it had upon him, one gets the distinct impression that he was trying to discover a language to capture the "illusive beauty" of the snow and to contend with those areas of linguistic experience that were imprisoned within him because of his many years of colonial schooling and its attendant sociology. In many ways, his linguistic quest parallels that of V. S. Naipaul, who was always seeking to find language to interpret and to express areas of experience that were not his, experiences and images that had been appropriated/depreciated as a result of his colonial schooling, inundated as he was with images and realities of others.[15] Webber's experience of snow in Long Island made a deep impression on him. The make-believe of images that had seeped into his imagination as a result of foreign books and postcards had been disrupted violently by the immediacy of his encounter with the snow of Long Island.

In the second installment of his articles, "The Women and Worries of New York," Webber examined the newly evolving freedoms of women of the time. He is perceptive enough to recognize that many of the changes that women were undergoing (from changes in style to relationships with men) were due, in part, to their "changed economic status," which was more evident in places such as New York or London, "where the opportunities, equally for economic independence and the wider license, are greater." As evidence of this new condition, Webber drew on the story of a Jamaican "Negress" washerwoman, the breadwinner of her family, who scornfully rejects the suggestion of marriage from a man who is her common law husband, with the withering demand: " 'Who go tie theyself to yo'—yo' wutless nigger man?' The idea being that she retains her freedom of action to quit and choose another mate the moment the present sharer of her affections ceases to be of good behavior."[16] Looking at the negative side of the argument, Webber noted that under these new conditions of women's liberation, women were demanding the freedom to be childless "even in marriage." The saving grace of this situation, he seems to argue, is that "fortunately, this phase of modern life is now confined almost entirely to the larger cities; but no one can say when its boundaries will be reached and the species cease to be menaced."[17]

In his essay, Webber asks what should be men's response to this new condition, which he calls "this evil." "When he was the master and tyrant, the great economic panjandrum, he demanded all, took all, and perhaps gave nothing. Now that he has been dethroned he takes the position with much the same 'answering complex' as the lions of the forest take with complaisance [sic] the choice of the coveted lionesses. One nevertheless must feel with that hope which springs eternal in the human breast, that in the end all such evils will cure themselves; or else civilization is doomed."[18] While he displayed a rather sophisticated understanding of the causes of women's emancipation, he does not seem to accept its consequences fully, nor does he seem to understand women's quest to liberate themselves. That "all such evils would cure themselves" suggests that he is not too sure how he should respond to these less dependent roles that women have assumed. Indeed, he ends this installment by arguing that "so much space has been consumed by entrancing women that no room is left for the worries—which were mostly women or women bred."[19] Being a ladies' man may have shaped Webber's responses to this new freedom of women. However, Webber may have been among the first West Indian writers to address the question of feminism. While some of his observations may have been controversial, he shows an ability to face up to them.

Webber's third essay shows his fascination with the enormous height of the buildings he encountered in New York City. He says "the 20 storey building had made way for the 40; and now there is talk of the 50. The skyscraper has made way for the 'cloud buster.'"[20] Webber makes a very astute architectural suggestion when he notes that the height of the buildings makes it very difficult for one to really enjoy their "architectural beauty," and their apparent crowdedness gives the impression that "one burrows in and out of these buildings like a rodent." In this essay, he uses the same sociological lenses that allowed him to be so insightful in London on the questions of crime and prostitution. Coming from the West Indies, Webber couldn't help but observe the nature of the relationship between the races. He was visiting New York at the height of the Harlem Renaissance, a time when "the Negro was in vogue," and one can appreciate his joy at seeing how the black people of New York had become a part of the city's landscape. These were astute observations for someone who was visiting New York for the first time, but then, as a Caribbean person, he had always lived within the cocoon of the color question. His observations are worth quoting at length:

I am inclined to think colour lines are less rigidly drawn in New York than in either Canada or British Guiana. Of course no reference is made to the intense colour lines as drawn in the Southern States. New York is, speaking on the wide and the broad, developing a wider orientation and a broader outlook. For one thing, it is the greatest Negro city in the world. Coloured persons are met every two yards in 5th Avenue, Broadway, or anywhere else. White restaurants, it is true will not serve pronouncedly Negro persons; but these ride without let or hindrance on the tram cars, on the subways, on the elevated railroads or on buses. There is no segregation in traveling in New York. A Negro may sit by the side of a white person without comment. American steamship companies sailing south or back to New York grant Negroes first class accommodation, without hesitancy; and it has been left to the Canadian Government steamships, subsidised by the Negro Governments of the West Indies, to impose a colour bar and refuse Negroes first class accommodation. As to the grades of colour as understood in this colony and the West Indies, there are none in New York: a person is either white or Negro—with this peculiarity: all West Indians are Negroes, unless they can prove themselves white; and all South Americans

(including British Guiana) are white, unless some one else proves them coloured! . . . On this race question New York is producing a wonderful experiment, and the other great cities in a lesser extent, in annealing all the races of
the earth into one. Incidentally, it is in New York that the greater barriers of
colour prejudice will yet become submerged—25, 50 or 150 years hence. At the
present it is the great melting pot of the earth.[21]

In his fourth essay, subtitled "Getting Out and Getting Under," Webber
launches into a semiphilosophical discussion with one of the waiters at his hotel
about "the verities and humanities" and describes his visit to "the historic church"
in which George Washington once worshipped. Next he offers a description of
New York's rush hour and a subway experience at 5 o'clock in the evening ("sardine
time," he called it), which, to him, was one of "the most amusing and sometimes
exasperating experiences of the traveler." There is a sense of contemporaniety in
his observations in that he might have been describing a New York rush hour of
the first decade of the twenty-first century. Reacting as a West Indian man of his
time, he captures the possibilities of sexual misadventure that is possible in such
a situation:

In the rush hours, mostly at around 5 o'clock, passengers in the subway train
are stacked absolutely and literally like sardines. Everybody is good humoured:
but it has its embarrassing moments. Male and female are jammed together
without regard to sex. Just who does the pushing is nothing. You are pushed,
that's all. Not only just pushed: but squeezed tight and fast. Now, that is all
very well when a man happens to be wedged in between men; or women between women; but all are mixed trains! The whole world seems to be riding in
the subways at that hour, and it is a regular case of "male and female created
He them." As only standing room is available one has to be very cautious with
one's hands. An involuntary movement may be taken as a caress, welcome or
unwelcome. If the latter then your number is up. Fortunately as I said before,
the utmost good-humour prevails, and everybody takes it smiling. But there is
the potential danger of much embarrassment, when the sexes are jammed tight
together in a twenty minute ride, and when the slightest movement of a limb
may be misunderstood! Bad as it is in winter, when all wear overcoats and provide as it were dividing paddings, one wonders what must it be like in summer
when the clothing of both sexes is not quite so copious![22]

The presence of West Indians, their food, and their language is palpable in New
York City. Speaking of the economic possibilities of the plantain, a West Indian
staple, Webber believes that "an enormous trade can be done with New York in

both ripe and green plantains," the "king of vegetables." He speaks further about the benefits of the plantain in that temperate region: "I verily believe that 'when winter came' it was the absence of that bold, sustaining iron content of the resolute plantain that hurried me into deciding to get out and get under—the Tropic of Cancer."[23] Winter was approaching. Although he was fascinated with New York, Webber had decided to leave. In spite of his admiration for the beauty of the snow, he says that "when the mercury began to hit the floor I decided it was time, while there was yet life to flee from the wrath to come."[24] In his last essay, he describes Christmas and New Year's Eve in New York City and his departure from that city. Before departing from New York, Webber visited the Roxy, "the Great Paramount theatres," and "the Earl Carroll vanities." Carroll, it seems, was sentenced to prison for one year and a day for presenting to a party of guests "a nude beauty in a bath tub of champagne, from which they were supposed to drink."[25] From this, Webber enters into a discussion of where indecency ends and artistic creation begins. While we need not follow the intricacies of this debate, it is obvious that Webber was au courant with the ideas of his time and a very sophisticated observer of a changing world. Needless to say, discussion of these issues continues even today.

Webber remained in New York long enough to view the Christmas celebrations and the festivities of New Year's Eve, "or what we call Old Year's Day." He believes that Christmas has become much too commercialized and compares it to Christmas in British Guiana, where "merchants concentrate on toy land [and] selling activity is concentrated into catching the current trade that sets in to buy presents for the kids." In New York, he writes, "Selling forces are directed into stimulating the demand for presents; presents from son to father; wife to husband; friend to friend. Everybody is urged to buy a present. This fierce fanning, by show window display, advertising; and all the subtile [*sic*] ways known to the elect, has culminated into creating one huge bazaar of the whole commercial world."[26] He likens New Year's Eve unto Trinidad carnival. "Broadway is hell. Everybody seems determined to show just how mad he can be."[27]

From New York, Webber sailed to St. Thomas, then to St. Croix, to St. Kitts, Dominica, Guadeloupe, and Martinique. Of Guadeloupe, he says, "My dream of entrancing women proved nothing but a nightmare. I draw the veil over the misery of the place, and concluded that the cruel tidal wave must have swept away all the young and the beautiful and left nothing but the dregs." In Martinique, his quest to meet the beautiful women for which that island is famous reached the same unsatisfying conclusion: "The legend of the beautiful women of Martinique is a myth and a hoax. One can see more to gladden the eye and the heart in five minutes in Port of Spain, Trinidad, than in five months in Martinique! That was the average I worked out." As he leaves the island, he describes the "one really piquant face" he sees:

She was a bum-boat woman selling liqueurs at the gang way. She must have been 50, or 49! Her teeth were like pearls and her eyes shone like stars from the exquisite mahogany of her skin; her profile was exquisite, and she had lips and a chiseled chin that would have made a cinema star green with envy. She was the last of a dying tribe, apparently; for she was no longer in the first flush of her youth, and "mercenary" was written all over her gaudy costume—I fled from the wrath to come.[28]

There was something Naipaulian in this image; one that he evoked at the end of *An Area of Darkness*. Webber left Martinique for his final voyage to British Guiana, but not before he stopped off in Barbados, where he and his West Indian colleagues worked to form the West Indian Press Association, which was inaugurated on January 23, 1929. As a fighter for the rights of his people and a newspaperman, Webber understood the importance of press freedom and the significance of the Fourth Estate in upholding democracy, sharing information, and guiding public opinion. As early as July 1927, Webber moved in the British Guiana legislature that police officers be prevented from following persons who were taking part in any legitimate protest against the colonial government. His motion protested "any policy of intimidation on the part of the Government in the free expression of the public in the present Constitution."[29] Now, he sought to institutionalize that freedom throughout the West Indies. William Robinson, governor of Barbados, opened the conference, which was attended by several delegates from the Caribbean region who came together to ensure that "the formerly disconnected link of West Indian journalism might be forged into one, strong unbreakable chain."[30] The association aimed to get a closer understanding and a freer exchange of news. It also sought "(a) to further the interests of the West Indian Press, (b) to preserve its rights and privileges, (c) to extend generally the usefulness of the West Indian Press, and (d) to encourage a high standard of journalism in the West Indies for the benefit of the several communities concerned."[31] The conference also repudiated some of the archaic laws, passed some ninety years earlier, that were intended to prevent "the publication of newspapers by people who were not connected with the colony and who might publish sedition and blasphemy." A committee consisting of Webber, a Mr. Parker, Andre Paul Ambard, and Grantley Adams drafted the following resolution (subsequently carried) that condemned such behavior: "That in the opinion of this Conference some of the laws and ordinances governing newspaper publication in British Guiana and some of the West Indian islands are cumbersome, archaic and unnecessary and call urgently for modification; That the requirement of bonds and recognizances before the committal of any offence is un-British and an attack upon the dignity of the Press and uncalled for."[32] Herbert De Lisser, editor of Jamaica's *Daily Gleaner* and a prolific author and journalist, was named president of the association, his having been the chairman of the Empire Press Union. Webber and Marryshow were elected as members of the Management Committee.[33] Grantley Adams went on to lead the Barbados Workers' Union (1941–54), became the first premier of Barbados, and the first and only prime minister of the West Indian Federation (1958–62).

Although De Lisser noted that the first West Indian Press Conference was held in Jamaica in 1923 under the auspices of the Empire Press Union, Ambard, the editor of the *Port of Spain Gazette*, objected to that statement. He observed that many Caribbean editors did not attend the 1923 conference because its impetus arose from outside the region. The present conference had its impetus from inside the region. He observed: "It was indeed very pleasing to see a Conference had now been formed and he hoped that they would be able to do their business in such a way to command the respect of the entire press of the West Indies."[34] De Lisser's presidency did not last very long. In May 1929 he resigned. Webber was the major force behind the formation of the association. In welcoming the delegates to the conference, Clennell Wickham, a prominent social activist and columnist for the *Barbados Herald*, observed that Webber, "to whom in great measure this Convention was due, was another great West Indian. They had to tender him many thanks as this Convention would not have been possible had he not displayed such persistence and working to bring it about."[35] An editorial in the *Port of Spain Gazette* noted that the idea of the association originated with Webber, who believed the crusading role of the press was important for the liberation of West Indian people, while the *Port of Spain Chronicle* acknowledged that Webber showed "himself to be fertile in ideas and his work for the West Indian Press Conference will not soon be forgotten."[36] The *Daily Chronicle*, Webber's rival paper in Guyana, noted:

> Among the delegates was A. R. F. Webber, editor of the *New Daily Chronicle* of British Guiana, who not only conceived the idea of the conference but also worked for its development. It must have been a source of great pleasure and gratification to him to see the early reward of his labours; and he may rest assured that whenever and wherever the members of the West Indian Press Association foregather in the years, they will always regard him as the prime mover in a great scheme for their mutual progress and prosperity.[37]

Many West Indians supported the need to maintain a vigorous press. Ernest V. Bentham of Grenada argued that until West Indians realized the truth that one of the steps to enable them to lay claim to anything as a people "lies in preserving (by means of the written page) the glories of our sacred past, without which none ever dared to live, until then, we shall have learned nothing. What we must have as an organized [West Indian] people are historians, biographers, poets, novelists, dramatists, essayists and even our critics."[38] A columnist from the *Dominica*

Chronicle noted that the West Indian Press Association "arose from the spontaneous motion of West Indians themselves, and was not inspired from outside." He
observed: "A West Indian consciousness is developing. We are getting to know
each other better. Some men are gradually becoming West Indian as distinct from
local personalities, such as A. R. F. Webber, L. A. R. O'Reilly [from Trinidad],
Gaston Johnson [from Trinidad], Marryshow, [and] H. G. De Lisser." He saw the
press "as laying the foundation on which West Indian nationalism is to be built"
and Webber as the chief architect of this movement.[39]

Shortly after Webber returned from Barbados, a meeting of the Guyanese legislature on March 8 inadvertently turned out to be a trigger that caused the British
Guiana Department of Education to examine British Guiana's past and to take
stock of what was being taught to its children. On that day, Major W. Bain Gray,
director of education, moved that the government contribute to a program set up
by the secretary of state for the colonies that would establish an advisory committee of education in the British colonies that would review educational matters in
all of the British dependencies. In return for its financial contribution, the advisory
committee would advise the government on educational matters and publish a
bulletin that dealt with educational matters generally. Although Guyana was only
asked to pay a small amount of money—£184 annually for three years—Webber
attacked the bill with unusual ferocity. He was suspicious about handing over
Guyanese education to persons outside of Guyana and feared that the education
of the country would be reduced to a level of those of African dependences. He
also remarked that in the Colonial Office, there was a tendency

> to confuse the higher standard of civilization and culture of British Guiana and
> the West Indies with that of the African dependencies. I have not one word
> to say about culture of Africa in its highest walks and of its native races and
> processes. But where you have millions of illiterate people, practically naked
> savages, you cannot compare them with the clothed people of British Guiana
> and the West Indies. It is a mistake to endeavour to bring them down to a com-
> mon level.[40]

One does not know if Webber meant to play upon the prejudices of the governor and the educated elites of the colony or if he really saw Africans existing
in such a "savage" state. In Guyana during that period, Africa "conjured up ideas
of an 'uncivilized' [state] and a very low level of social development." Describing
someone as African was tantamount to calling him or her "a barbaric creature
barely, or hardly, human." Prominent Afro-Guyanese individuals boasted that they
were in possession of a "British civilization. [They] knew no other."[41] Paradoxically,
Webber seemed ambivalent about aspects of African practices and was not aware
(he could not possibly be) of the connections among African, Caribbean, and

African American people's struggle for independence, of which he was a part.[42] Therefore when the president of the legislature (the governor) drew to Webber's attention that Africa was merely one part of the British Empire, Webber hastened to advise him that C. R. L. Fletcher and Rudyard Kipling's *A School History of England*, a very derogatory school text that replicated all of England's racial biases of the nineteenth century, was being taught at Queen's College, the premier high school in the colony, to the detriment of the students who were studying there. The offending part of the text read as follows:

> The prosperity of the West Indies, once our richest possession, has very largely declined since slavery was abolished in 1833. There is little market for their chief products, and yet a large population, mainly black, descended from slaves imported in previous centuries, or of mixed black and white race; lazy, vicious and incapable of any serious improvement or of work except under compulsion. In such a climate a few bananas will sustain the life of a negro quite sufficiently; why should he work to get more than this? He is quite happy and quite useless, and spends any extra wages which he may earn upon finery.[43]

These were the sentiments of Thomas Carlyle, James Anthony Froude, Joseph Chamberlain, and other English writers of that ilk. G. H. Richter had repeated this slander in his testimony to the West India Royal Commission. Webber rejected this position many times. He would not necessarily have considered himself a Pan-Africanist in the way that J. J. Thomas, Theophilus Scholes, Sylvester Williams, Norman Cameron (whose work I discuss in the next chapter), or James did—he was more a Pan-Caribbeanist—but he certainly was among those who were fighting against imperialism and racism during the height of British colonialism.[44] In fact, his disdain for the "abominable slave trade" and his assertion that he had given his life to liberate "the black man" best captured his sentiments. Webber's work in Guyana was a part of Pan-Africanism, "an ideology of emancipation [that] maintained the principle that all races are equal and therefore should enjoy equal rights."[45]

When Webber made his contribution to the debate in the Legislative Council, he could not remember the precise wording of the extract, but he was aware that it was offensive. Although the governor prodded him to cite the text from which the extract came, he only remembered that the text was "an insult, a scandal, and a libel against the educated and culture of people of these communities. It may be suitable for the curriculum in the schools of African Tropical Dependencies but it is a gratuitous provocation to the goodwill of the community that such a book should be [still in use in the colony]." He also strongly objected to the proposal that the colony's educational policies should be subjected to an advisory board that existed 4,000 miles away from Guyana.

Taken by surprise, the governor agreed that the textbook in question should be reviewed to determine whether it should still be used in the colony's schools. Granted that concession, Webber withdrew his objection to the bill. Two days later, the *Daily Chronicle* reproduced the offending paragraph and supported Webber's objections. A few days later, the Negro Progress Convention (NPC) took up the issue with the government and wrote the director of education, demanding that the offending book be removed from the curriculum.[46] On March 19 the director of education withdrew the book from the school curriculum and introduced a new set of history books into Queen's College. Thanking the NPC for its work, the *Daily Chronicle* noted that through the NPC's efforts, "One of the libels against the Colony has been removed, and another nail put on the canard that people of African descent are lazy, vicious and incapable of any serious improvement."[47]

Webber deserves much praise for bringing this book to the attention of the public. When he raised his objections in the Legislative Council, he did not expect such a quick, successful response. In fact, Webber never called for the removal of the book from the curriculum. Although he seemed to have libeled millions of Africans in the process, something overlooked by the NPC, he got the Education Department to bury a piece of libel against African peoples and their descendents in Guyana and the Caribbean that had remained a part of its educational curriculum for all of the nineteenth and the early part of the twentieth centuries.

This incident also illustrated an important principle. At that moment, the people of Guyana and the Caribbean not only waged a struggle for political self-government but also a struggle for the liberation of their minds from a pernicious miseducation that had become endemic within the educational system. Webber and the NPC demonstrated the gigantic stride that the people of Guyana and the Caribbean had made in recapturing their historic identity in the face of an intransigent political and economic system.

CHAPTER EIGHT

THE QUEST FOR SELF-GOVERNMENT

As I look ahead to the future of these Colonies, I do not see the question of present day conception of Empire as one of the greatest issues and I would prefer, and many of my friends would agree with me, to count the Empire dead and, out of its ashes, Phoenix like, expect to see raised up a Commonwealth of Free Nations with the West Indies filling her own part as a confederate whole and taking her place in the administrations and Councils of the Commonwealth of Free Nations. The task of touring the entire West Indies is one which is not easy of realization and as much as I would like to preach Federation and Self-Government throughout the length and breath of the British West Indies, the time necessary is not at my disposal.

 —CAPTAIN ARTHUR CIPRIANI, "W. I. Federation Delegates for Labour
     Party Conference in 1930"

It is not with our lips only that we are loyal to King George V, it is with our hearts also. The crown is not only the "golden circle" that binds the Empire together; it is the greatest thing in that Empire.

 —C. R. L. FLETCHER AND RUDYARD KIPLING, *A School History of England*

ALTHOUGH WEBBER, THE DAILY NEWSPAPERS, and the Afro-Guyanese were angry that Fletcher and Kipling depicted Africans in such a negative light, they could not have missed the equally dangerous paragraph that preceded the one I quoted in the previous chapter. The offending paragraph reads as follows: "There are other countries, like Ceylon, the West Indies, several stations on the Northwest African coast, Singapore on the Straights of Malacca, Guiana on the north coast of South America, and islands too numerous to mention, both in the Pacific and Atlantic Oceans, which belong to Great Britain. But most of these are called 'Crown Colonies' and do not enjoy any form of Parliamentary government *nor need it*."[1] Written in 1911, these sentiments revealed the prevailing views of the British conservatives of the 1920s and suggested that every move the British government made during that period was designed to reduce British Guiana to

Crown Colony status, which was thrust upon it in 1928. However, the victory of the Labour government under Ramsay MacDonald in 1929 brought great hope to Guyana nationalists and gave them renewed impetus to continue their struggle for representative government. Too many citizens saw the withdrawal of the 1928 constitution as a retrograde step and vowed to fight for a more progressive, self-governing constitution. John Lucie Griffith, a progressive nationalist and member of the BGLU, argued that they had to work harder than ever "to prevent Capital from giving us [in labor] the knockout."[2] He praised the efforts of the Afro-Guyanese and Indo-Guyanese who built the country and noted that while they were forging ahead in spite of the obstacles that the white planters placed in their way and

> the scandalous failure of Government to give these hardy pioneers of the gold, diamond and rice industries the necessary assistance in the form of roads or railways in the interior and drainage and irrigation on the coast lands for which the industries were prepared to pay, Capitalists after a campaign of the most wicked misrepresentation got the late Conservative government to rob us of our Constitution, the Constitution under which Negroes and East Indians proved themselves excellent colonists when "British colonising enterprise" failed.[3]

On June 9, at a mass meeting, the Labour movement passed a resolution demanding that British Guiana take every "lawful step" to obtain a constitution that "enabled the inhabitants of the Colony, through their elected members of the Legislature, to have greater control of their own destinies by having a majority over the Government members, but still leaving the power of the veto in the [hands of the] Secretary of State for the Colonies."[4] The resolution also authorized the leadership of the union to confer with the members of the legislature to achieve their ends.

Such a resolution fitted into Webber's program of action since he had stepped up his drive for self-government and the creation of a West Indian Federation. Closely associated with the labor movement, Webber had established many contacts with other West Indian nationalists and had the power of a newspaper at his disposal. He was participating in a struggle that was part of a Caribbean movement that demanded full internal self-government and the creation of a West Indian Federation. He was fighting against a reactionary constitution that gave the governor reserve powers that ensured he would always have his way in the legislature. Under the new constitution, the Electives became mere figureheads destined always to protest the actions of the government rather than initiate programs that benefited their constituents. This legislative roadblock, as it were, caused much frustration among the elected representatives. Webber declared: "The Constitution of today is good for nobody, not even the Government. The people get careless of political issues; the Electives are tempted to get careless because they find . . . they are struggling behind a gag; and the Government gets careless for lack of virile opposition. It is high time, therefore, to settle what course [of action] should be adopted *for,* rather than *at,* the general elections booked for next year."⁵In May 1929, in response to C. C. Briston, one of his constituents of West Berbice, Webber proposed that in any new constitution, the Electives should be given a majority of two votes over the combined totals of the ex-officio, nominated officials and unofficial members so that the people's will could be realized. He noted: "There is a good deal to be recommended in the theory that the Government of the day must be in possession of a majority, and command the power to govern; but this majority must be a majority of the Government of British Guiana; and not merely a majority of the chosen officials and 'court' friends of His Excellency the Governor." Webber objected most to Order 59 of the new constitution, "under which the Council may not impose any tax, or according to my reading, reduce any tax without the approval of the Government." He concluded his letter by demanding that the constitution be amended and warned: "I am firmly of the belief that the Colony must cease prating about 'changing of Constitution,' 'greater powers,' 'Self government,' and all such nebulous 'no wheres.' Let us determine what we want, say why we want it, and nail our colours to the mast until we get it. With a united front, firm resolution, and determined demand, the present Constitution can be amended within two years of the next general election."⁶

The same day Webber's letter appeared, the *New Daily Chronicle* observed that although the Colonial Office would object to a movement toward self-government, there was some merit in the Colonial Office's position. "Why," the newspaper asked, "should the whole machinery of Government be upset, and the Crown Law Officers sent scurrying from room to room, and from precedent to precedent, merely because Mr. Webber writes a letter to a correspondent, or Capt. Cipriani holds a public meeting?" The editorial concluded:

If the principal colonies [Trinidad, Guyana, and Jamaica] . . . would but get together, either in agreement on a constitution common to all three, or even over what is most desirable for each, and all decided to support each, we know of no power on earth which could withstand such a demand. . . . A rising united demand from Jamaica, Trinidad and British Guiana, pressed by a strong combined delegation representative of each, is as assured of victory as the rising sun. Thereafter, the Leeward and Windward Islands have only to take a leaf out of the book of the senior colonies to secure success.⁷

The *Daily Chronicle* also supported the government's position and warned that the progressive forces should go slow in demanding a new constitution. On June 13, 1929, after a stinging condemnation by John Lucie Griffith, the *Daily Chronicle* noted it was foolish to believe that "because a Labour Government is now in power in Britain, *ipso facto*, it would follow that if sufficiently strong representations were made, the old order of things would be reverted to, and the Constitution of which we were deprived on July 18, 1928, would be restored to us." Griffith responded to this apologia in a scathing manner:

> Yours is the counsel, not as you say of watchful waiting, calm patience, and resolution, but rather the counsel of delay, despair, death. You cannot escape the conclusion that if we accept your advice, we would never do anything until doomsday. Surely, sir, if our old Constitution was worth having, as you all along contended, it was certainly worth fighting for, not only for a few weeks, but for any length of time it became necessary, and no reverse however severe could justify you or anyone else in abandoning the cause.[8]

Necessarily, the battle lines were drawn between those who accepted the 1928 constitution and urged caution in fighting for a new constitution and those, like Webber and Griffith, who rejected the 1928 constitution and were prepared to fight to have it scrapped. In fact, the new legislation was stacked against the elected representatives. The Legislative Council proposed by the new legislation was

> comprised of 29 members, 4 of whom were *ex-officio*, 6 nominated official, 5 nominated non-official and 14 elected. The *ex-officio* members were the Governor, the Colonial Secretary, the Attorney General and the Colonial Treasurer. . . . The Executive Council, the policy-making body, consisted of the Governor as chairman, 6 official members and 6 non-officials. All the members, both official and non-official, were appointed by the Governor, and only 2 of them were chosen from among elected members of the Legislative Council.[9]

Webber and his friends could not accept a constitution that took away financial power from the Electives and gave it to the executive branch of government. They believed that their constitutional prerogatives could be restored only through public agitation.

Given this strenuous objection to the new constitution, Webber and his party believed that they could better confront the British by intensifying the struggle for self-government within the context of a West Indian Federation and by deepening his link with the trade union movement. At an open-air meeting of the BGLU that he addressed in the presence of Hubert Crichlow, Webber noted that "when all sections of labour were combined together in the Labour Union they would be able to secure attention to their legislative demands." He insisted that the people must combine to struggle for a constitution "in which the people of the colony would have a greater share in the management of their own affairs."[10] In speaking of the Electives' inability to have any impact on the government as set out in the

1928 constitution (they could only give advice to the governor when they were "invited" to do so), Webber reminded his audience of the daunting challenges English governors encountered once they took up their duties in the colony and wondered if they could really work efficiently with the people in a new environment. He noted: "Governor Bruce, a former administrator of the colony, stated that one half of the time of the Colonial Governors was taken up with learning what their predecessors had done, and the other half in reversing their policies. That was the kind of governors who accounted for the stagnation of British Guiana today and they certainly desired that the new constitution should put an end to that scandalous state of affairs."[11] He called for a shared democracy rather than a one-man show in which all power resided in the hands of the Executive Committee. He believed they should adopt a constitution in which "all sections of the community would be able to have a share in the Government [and] which would enable them to pull their weight for the progress and prosperity of the country." Finally, he argued that the Guyanese people "were entitled to self-government." Such efforts, he said, would be "in vain if they did not have the support of the masses."[12]

In November 1929 the governor decreed that the electoral boundaries should be changed. Other measures were making it difficult for electors to register to vote. Suspicious of the governor's strategy, Webber declared that a "multiplicity of barriers" were being put in the way of the prospective voters to prevent them from registering to vote. Subsequently, a series of meetings were held throughout the country to bring this matter to the governor's attention. The New Amsterdam Progressive Association called together over 3,000 persons to protest the government's shortsightedness, and Webber hotly debated the issue in the Legislative Council, requesting that the date of registration be extended to accommodate the voters. He assured His Excellency that "if that was done . . . a good deal of their difficulties would be met and he appealed to Government to accept his motion."[13] The Electives, as well as the various civic and political organizations, supported Webber on this point.

Meanwhile, life had become very hectic for Webber, given the pivotal place he had assumed on the national landscape. Greater agitation on behalf of the people meant increased visibility and a corresponding danger to his life. On November 29, 1929, the headlines of the *New Daily Chronicle* announced in sensationalist tones, "Life of A. R. F. Webber Threatened." Robert Lindsay, a "well known Boot and Shoe Maker . . . called at the residence of Mr. A. R. F. Webber, in Main Street, accused him in loud tones of having sold the cause of the people to the planters; and demanding to be told why he [Webber] had not yet appeared before the Sugar Commission to state the cause of the people, who hitherto supported him through thick and thin." Lindsay had threatened Webber's life because an article appeared in the *Daily Argosy*, the planters' paper, suggesting that Webber had sold out to the planter class. In fact, Webber had difficulties in obtaining an audience with the West Indian Sugar Commission, headed by Lord Olivier, which came to the West Indies to investigate the plight of the sugar industry. The morning after this incident, Webber appeared before the commission. Realizing his indiscretion, Lindsay apologized to Webber, whom he had threatened while he was under the influence of alcohol. Webber, having no desire to punish Lindsay unduly, asked the court to forgive him in view of his respectability and good character.[14]

Webber, in his turn, had to make his own public apology to P. N. Browne for an article that appeared in his newspaper that impugned the integrity of Browne and his wife, Elisa. He noted that a young reporter was carried away by his pen, and that led to the offending article. Although Webber had not seen the article before it was published, as editor of the newspaper he assumed responsibility for everything that appeared in it. Therefore, he "publicly assure[ed] the said defendant that he regrets that the language used in the said newspaper was culpable . . . would never have permitted anything to appear in the paper under my editorship that would reflect on Mr. Browne's relationship with his wife. . . . As there was no foundation for the imputations as applicable to the plaintiff and his wife the said defendant unreservedly apologizes to Mrs. Browne for any annoyance she suffered by reason of the said publication."[15] Webber supplemented his spoken apology with a written one and shook Browne's hand publicly in court to demonstrate his goodwill and apologies. It is good that he did, for Browne, a distinguished lawyer, had sued Webber, Cannon, and R. A. Small for the sum of $10,000 for defaming his wife's name.

Webber's quest for self-government in British Guiana and the construction of a federated West Indies were a part of the larger regional effort on the part of Caribbean leaders to ensure that their people participated more fully in their own development. Cipriani, Marryshow, and Rawle of Dominica were all copartners in this effort. Their activities signaled a new and sustained involvement of Caribbean people to achieve their liberation. When Cipriani addressed his Labour colleagues in St. George's, Grenada, he observed that the time had come when West Indians, owing to their culture and civilization, must take charge of the administration of their own affairs. He indicated that the British Labour Party and the Labour and Socialist International had pledged to support the West Indian thrust for self-government if all of the colonies united around that demand. He believed that the colonies should get together

and run our administration through a West Indian Parliament. I am not at all satisfied that we are going to get the unanimous support throughout these Colonies, but I am looking forward to having the unanimous support of the labouring classes, and even if the majority of the employer class and representatives of capital will not help, or even if they are out to oppose it, the labouring classes need not be disappointed at any such gesture. But, instead, it should act more as an incentive for them to co-operate and get together in one big Labour Union and present a solid front in the demand for Self-Government.[16]

Caribbean leaders recognized that if they wanted to achieve their objectives, they had to bring the laboring classes into the struggle. The most oppressed section of the population, the laboring classes were being taxed "out of all proportion to [their] income and in contradiction of the clear democratic policy that the broadest back should carry the heaviest weight."[17] To move forward, there needed to be improvements in housing and education policies. Convinced that the employer or capitalist class would give "neither their help nor their co-operation," Cipriani believed that "the movement must be made whole-heartedly from the labouring classes. I therefore look to them for their generous and united support which will make a tremendous difference in the economic state of these countries, their women and their children, and those who shall come after them."[18] Cipriani placed the attainment of dominion status within the British Empire as a necessary step along the road to Caribbean liberation. In British Guiana, the workers were making similar demands of the Colonial Office. They had even gone further. In a well-attended meeting in Georgetown, Critchlow demanded universal adult suffrage and that one of the five nominated members in the Legislative Council should be a representative of the Labour movement.

While this labor "agitation" was occurring, there was also a strong movement to develop black and brown consciousness, which was discouraged during the earlier period. The persistence of racial discrimination, particularly against those in the professions, led to more vociferous demands for equal opportunities in the field of employment. Particularly pernicious was Governor Wilfred Collect's refusal to appoint a black man to the post of surgeon general because "men of purely European descent" were not likely to work under his charge. A European was preferable because, in the words of the governor, "rightly or wrongly, there is the general impression amongst all races in the colony that impartiality is more likely to be found amongst men of pure Anglo-Saxon descent than among others."[19] In 1919 the authorities were alarmed by the formation of the Caribbean League by members of the British West India Regiment who believed that "the black man should have freedom and govern himself in the West Indies and that force must be used, and if necessary bloodshed to attain the objective." They were concerned "that white non-commissioned officers were being appointed in place of the black although the black was not inferior."[20]

The NPC, the leading proponent of black consciousness, was founded in 1922 by E. F. Fredericks, who became its president; Critchlow; E. P. Bruvning, barrister-at-law; and other outstanding Africans in the colony. It held several meetings and functions throughout the country and sought in every possible way to bring the Afro-Guyanese in the country "to a realization of their responsibilities to themselves and to the State, and also to assist them in working out their industrial salvation."[21] The leaders of the organization warned its members to refrain from selling their lands to East Indians and urged them to grow economic crops "to revive the village economy" that was gradually dying.[22] As was customary, on August 1, 1929, the NPC commemorated the abolition of British slavery, Guyana being the first country in the New World to commemorate the abolition of slavery on August 1, 1888.[23] In 1929 Webber and his wife—one of the few times we see them together—attended the emancipation celebration that was put on by the NPC. By 1933 the NPC had over 5,000 members, with twenty-five branches throughout the country.

The NPC also petitioned the governor and the larger community to respect the rights of Africans and to grant them the economic opportunities they richly deserved. On several occasions they came together with the East Indians, most conspicuously when they welcomed Rev. C. F. Andrews, a confidant of Mahatma Gandhi, who went to Guyana to inquire into the educational, social, and labor conditions of East Indians in the colony. Eventually, the NPC hoped to build an educational and industrial institution along the lines of Booker T. Washington's Tuskegee Institute. In furtherance of their plans, they sent two students to study at Tuskegee "to fit them as exponents of the kind of industrial training necessary to be given to the members of the Negro race to enable them to pull their weight as important factors in the industrial life of the Colony."[24]

In 1925 Governor Graeme Thomson informed the secretary of state for the colonies that he had issued instructions that "no film is to be exhibited in which there is the least suggestion of intimacy between men of Negro race and white women."[25] This directive was meant to maintain the separation of the races and thereby reinforce the notions of white superiority in the colony. In 1929 Norman Eustace Cameron, a Guyanese scholar who received an advanced degree from Cambridge University, published the first volume of *The Evolution of the Negro*, which contested the racial sense of exclusiveness on the part of the Europeans. The second volume, published in 1934, outlined "Negro Development from Emancipation to the Present [1934]."[26] Both of these volumes followed the major template of books written about Pan-Africanism: "rejection of the doctrine that the races were unequal; reference to the history of Africa, especially ancient Egypt, as proof that Africans were able to produce an advanced culture, if even only in the past; and emphasis on individuals of African descent who had achieved success in various fields."[27]

Cameron believed that his work was a necessary antidote to the racism that existed in the society at the time. He thought that

the absence of a clear, well-defined, philosophic view of slavery, and ignorance of the attainments and civilization of our ancestors are partly responsible for

the fact that such taunts [the inferiority of the Negroes] often have some effect, and also for what some have observed in Afro-Americans as an "inferiority complex," i.e., a tacit admission of inferiority to other races—an admission
which greatly hampers vigorous effort, confidence in self and success in an undertaking.[28]

He believed that "every Afro-American would do better who keeps deep down
within himself a consciousness of ancestral achievement in the not distant past."
Through his work, he hoped to awaken a sense of pride in those persons of African
descent by providing them with knowledge of "the culture and achievement of
their race in the years of long ago, and even in the present, in order that the inferiority complex from which it is alleged many suffer should be dispelled."[29]
Significantly, when Cameron returned from Cambridge, Queen's College, his alma
mater, which at the time promulgated the views of Kipling, refused him a teaching
position at the college. This led him to found the Guianese Academy.

An early review in the *Daily Chronicle* welcomed the book and observed that
it seldom saw "a coloured man who is consciously proud of the Negro blood in
his veins."[30] In a later review, the same newspaper observed that Cameron's book
was "not only a valuable landmark in local literature [the book was published locally by Argosy Press], but an exceedingly creditable contribution to the growing
bibliography of the Negro race." It hoped the book would also be of service to the
Europeans and

would contribute to the general assault on the race prejudice of the Caucasians,
by proving that the African *in his home land* was a child of culture and the arts,
and fully entitled to be received into the boson of cultured peoples. Doubtless,
the first objective [the awakening of race pride] can be reached by a diffusion
of knowledge, and through the awakening of racial pride consciousness; but
the battlements of Nordic prejudice have to be carried by something far more
effective than mere proof of early culture of the banned races.[31]

The newspaper recommended that the book be included in the school curriculum,
particularly in "the upper classes of the primary ones." *The Evolution of the Negro*
was a welcome antidote to *A School History of England.*

Cameron's intellectual work, the educational work of the NPC, the thoughts
of Marcus Garvey, and Garvey's activities in the United States and Jamaica encouraged a nascent black nationalism that was building in the colony. In July 1929
Amy Ashford Garvey, Garvey's first wife, addressed the women's session of the
NPC's emancipation celebrations. She also addressed the Young Women's Mutual
Improvement Association, and a "silver collection" was taken.[32] Her presentation
was well received by her audience. Meanwhile, Marcus Garvey's political activity

in Jamaica was also having an impact on the politics of Guyana and other West Indian islands.[33] Spurred on by his political defeat in Jamaica (he was defeated by George Seymour), the *New Daily Chronicle* warned about the negative aspects excessive racism could have on Guyana and observed:

> The West Indian voter has a sanity of outlook not always conceded by his detractors. He has the uncanny horse sense of being able to judge the real from the tinsel: he declines to be exploited on colour or race. . . . In evaluating the lessons to be drawn from the Jamaica elections, it must be noted that Garvey is the world's most spectacular Negro. Jamaica is his native country: he is a great journalist, and a platform speaker of great magnetism. But his native country would have none of him: because, in our opinion, he sought to exploit race and colour. . . . The man who hopes to win [in Guyana] must show that he has the capacity and the will to serve. In conclusion, perhaps we had better say, lest unscrupulous persons seek to distort our remarks, that we have nothing but the warmest sympathy for any efforts made to awaken consciousness, pride or self-respect among the Negroes, or any community in our midst for these are assets to the benefit of the whole. But the doctrine of race hatred is both foolish and dangerous.[34]

The *New Daily Chronicle* declined to tell its readers that masses of the laboring people in Jamaica were not allowed to show their preference for the candidates. Only those who paid ten shilling rates on real estate or thirty shillings on personal property were eligible to vote. Of the 900,000 persons in Jamaica, 700,000 were of African descent. However, only 78,000 persons were eligible to vote. Garvey's newspaper, the *Blackman,* bemoaned: "In Jamaica there is no universal suffrage. The bulk of the population is Negroes, with a very small proportion of them enjoying the franchise."[35] Adolph Edwards observes that "if there had been universal adult suffrage at that time, Garvey would have won. Under the qualified voting system, he stood no chance."[36] Months later, Garvey was still in St. Catherine District prison serving a prison term for discussing publicly the tenth plank of his party's manifesto, which called for the creation of a law "to impeach and imprison Judges who, with disregard for British justice and Constitutional Rights, dealt unfairly."[37]

Garvey was vindicated a month later. While imprisoned, he was elected to fill a vacant seat on the Allman Town Ward of the Kingston and St. Andrew Corporation through a by-election. Vindictive to Garvey to the end, the corporation declared Garvey's seat vacant because he missed three consecutive meetings. Naturally, if he was in jail, he could not attend these meetings. In a stinging rebuke of the council's action, Garvey exploded:

The Municipal Council recorded yesterday, the most atrocious and unprecedented deed of evil doing, yet witnessed in the annals of the colony. To understand the prejudice and the hate, the immorality and the vice, concentrated into this crowning act of a series of criminal efforts to injure a single individual and to destroy the influence of his leadership among the people of his race is to realize the limits of human depravity. . . . It is clear that other influences are at work and have been at work long previous to this, possibly from the very inception of the unholy crusade against Marcus Garvey. There exists no doubt that the hands of the Government are thrust deep in this hostile attempt to shed innocent blood.[38]

The British government in Guyana attempted a similar act of silencing Webber when he criticized a judge's ruling in an offending editorial. As in Webber's case, the chief justice presided over the case. Garvey was fined £100 and given three months in prison. Webber was fined £200 and given two weeks to pay his fine, which he did. Otherwise, he would have spent six months in prison. Webber's followers were able to raise the money to keep him out of jail. The chief justice accepted Webber's apology and was satisfied with giving a fine in lieu of imprisonment. In Garvey's case, imprisonment was the only option. While one member of the court accepted Garvey's apology, "his brother judges would have none of it, and reiterated what a grave offence the accused had committed by imputing dishonesty to His Majesty's judges."[39] The governor refused a petition that sought clemency for Garvey. In Webber's case, the colonial authorities signaled their agreement with the chief justice and recorded their glee at Webber's humiliation. One does not know how they acted behind closed doors in Garvey's case. No one doubted that they felt the same sense of triumph at Garvey's apparent humiliation as they did toward Webber. The colonial authorities were made of the same cloth.[40]

The East Indians had also become alive politically during this period. On the eve of the 1926 general elections, the *Daily Argosy* reported that "a striking feature of the coming elections is the number of East Indians who are coming forward to take an active part in politics, some of them under the auspices of the British Guiana East Indian Association (BGEIA)."[41] Although it did not have a large following, the BGEIA sought to organize its people and demanded a greater voice in shaping the nation's development. Its stated objectives at its Annual General Meeting of April 24, 1929, read as follows: the acquisition of a printing press to publish a newsletter in Hindi, Urdu, and English for the benefit of the East Indian community; vernacular education for the Hindu and Muslim children; cooperation and unity among East Indians; raising funds to clear the association's liabilities and to make additions to the building to accommodate its supporters. Other Indian voices insisted on the teaching of Hindu in the schools "in order that their children should not lose touch with the culture of their Mother land."[42] On October 25 the BGEIA absorbed the Indian National Congress and became one organization. It represented "a memorable event in the history of East Indians in British Guiana."[43]

The activities of some colonial officials in Grenada provided Webber with further evidence of the shortcomings (or what he called the stupidity) of colonial officials and the absolute moribund nature of the Crown Colony system. Given the demand for self-government and the creation of a West Indian Federation, the colonial authorities sough to limit the movement of political activists throughout the region. Therefore, Captain Cipriani's visit to Grenada did not strike them as being in the best interest of Grenadians and/or West Indians, so they tried to place restrictions on his visit. One week after reporting on Cipriani's visit to Grenada, Webber complained about "the littleness of men who must inevitably work for the overthrow of the very system they are entrusted to administer." He observed that Major Peebles, acting administrator of St. Vincent, took upon himself to write to the governor of Grenada, urging that Captain Cipriani should not be allowed to set foot in Grenada, and that in the event of the advice not being taken, it should at least be made obligatory on Cipriani to submit in categorical form, to the governor of Grenada, an outline of the several points on which it was his purpose to address the inhabitants of the island. Webber could not stomach such a proposition. He exclaimed:

> Great God! And that is the type of administrator under Crown Colony Government who we are told are better able to administer our affairs than the elected representatives of the people. One great bird went further than Major Peebles and sent a dispatch to the secretary of state for the colonies in which it was requested that instructions be given for the purpose of making Capt. Cipriani's proposed mission to Grenada abortive! The impertinence of such a dispatch can be best seen in the fact that Capt. Cipriani is better known, personally, to more members of the present British Cabinet than any Governor, or other person in the West Indies.[44]

The colonial authorities were not prepared to accept such agitation on the part of Caribbean leaders and their movement within the area to promote the gospel of liberation. As a result, the British Guiana Legislative Council passed an "Expulsion of Undesirables Ordinance" in 1929. It was based on a Trinidad ordinance of 1922 that prevented the entry of undesirable persons into the colony and the expulsion of such persons from the colony within two years after their arrival. The latter bill was aimed particularly at Marcus Garvey. When the authorities in Guyana sought to enact the bill, Webber fought against it strenuously. He observed: "If

Mr. Garvey wants to come to this Colony tomorrow, I will say: throw the doors open,—the more the people see of him, the more they will understand him and perhaps the less harm he will do. It is the 'forbidden' that is tempting.'" He argued that the bill was political in nature, "the sole purpose for which the Bill was passed was that of political oppression."[45] Although he was not a Garveyite, he believed the government should not be afraid of Garvey. He thought that "a person should be guilty of some moral turpitude before he should be kept out of the colony. If Mr. Gandhi, who was a Saint wanted to come here he should not be prevented because he had served a term of imprisonment."[46] A person, he believed, should be able to express his or her views as freely as possible. It was also important to see how these ideas were circulated around the Caribbean.

Another striking indication of Webber's intelligence was his increasing concerns about the importance of psychology in interpreting people's lives. In February 1921 Webber had lectured to the EIYMS on the "differences in the psychology of the various local communities" in the colony.[47] Later in the year, when he wrote "How I Won the Elections," Webber showed a lively interest in psychology when he observed that he had to know something about "crowd psychology" to be successful in his first election campaign. In 1929 he reflected on the "psychology of the game" as he considered the psychology of the society during an Inter Colonial Cricket Tournament that included teams from Barbados, Guyana, and Trinidad and Tobago. He offered his insightful comments during an exciting cricket match between Barbados and Guyana when, as he says, "The fate of the country hung in the balance, though the chances seemed remote to some, one very weak proof reader asked us in bated breath, what we thought of the game."[48] Barbados needed 69 runs to win the game with six wickets in hand. Apparently, that seemed to be easy pickings for Barbados. Webber recalled:

> The morning after our exchange with the proof reader, and before the match began, a huckster woman accosted us on the street—a privilege exercised by the most humble—and asked:
>
> "Sir, you think we gwine win? Oi, I hope so."
>
> "But who are 'we' anyway," I countered.
>
> "Good dear Sir," she replied, reeking of the truly Barbadian, "Oi is a true born mudhead."[49]
>
> We gave consolation and passed on. Probably that dame did not know how many played in a side, or why the eleventh wicket never fell; but she was true to the land of her adoption. With such a spirit emanating and bubbling over everywhere British Guiana was bound to win. Mass psychology is a wonderful, and sometimes a dangerous thing.
>
> "You see Sir, Everybody wanted them to win so much."[50]

Webber's insight about the psychology of cricket may not have been as profound as that which James displayed in *Beyond a Boundary* (1963). Yet he understood the psychological hold the game had on the ordinary West Indian; a hold that transcended gender, occupation, or geographical region. It is one of the common ties that still holds the West Indies and the international cricketing world together. In November 2005, when Brian Lara scored 224 in Adelaide, Australia, to become the cricketer who has scored the most runs in test cricket in the world, Tony Cozier, a cricket commentator from Barbados, lauded Lara in a way that equaled the tribute paid to an artist in any field. He offered the following paean:

As the familiar figure in the maroon helmet made his way out of the team room and down the steps of the George Giffen Stand to the middle, the members on either side of the aisle rose in long and generous applause.

The ovation spread among those spectators around one of the game's most pleasant venues as Brian Lara stepped onto the field with his West Indies team in its usual bind at 19 for two after both openers were dismissed in the same over by Brett Lee.

It was a heartfelt tribute to a sublime batsman who has lit up the game over a long career with flair and aggression, not least on the same ground, but who, word had it, was on his last tour of Australia.

There have apparently been similar scenes in various Australian cities for the current farewell tour of Luciano Pavarotti, even before the Italian has rendered a note.

In each, quite different case, the assembled crowd was showing its appreciation of greatness and willing one final virtuoso performance.[51]

At this point in his life, Webber began to speak on behalf of the region rather than his country. In a radio address, "British Guiana and Its Resources," which was broadcast throughout Guyana and the West Indies, Webber spoke about the exciting possibilities of Guyanese economic development and the prospect of inviting Caribbean persons to share in the "vast unexplored continental inheritance, in which we all have a common heritage."[52] However, the problem of development lay in a manpower shortage and the vastness of the country. He said:

The problem in this vast territory which is rich in gold and diamonds, rich in platinum and aluminum, rich in timber, rich in vast prairies and grazing savannahs, is obviously one of communications. The Iron Horse must puff its way through 350 miles. Motor traffic may solve the problem of islands 120 miles long, or others no more than 25 miles wide; but distance like ours requires something different. . . . The building of a railway requires imagination and courage; imagination and courage which it seems the entire West Indies will have to scourge to find in sufficient quantities; for it is your heritage no less than ours.[53]

In his address, Webber invoked the Iron Horse as a symbolic image of a new Caribbean age. On November 8, 1929, "old mother" Jane Henry, as she was called, of Good Intent Village and a member of the Congo ethnic group, passed away after having attained the age of 110 years. The *New Daily Chronicle* reported: "The deceased . . . belonged to the Congo tribe and she was brought to the Colony just a little after her girlhood period and indentured to Pin Farm on the East Bank, Demerara. By her demise another link with the days of slavery has been broken."[54] Webber hoped to lead the Caribbean people into a new day of self-government and independence. Jane Henry's death reminded him that the struggle out of slavery and colonialism to self-government, to use the language of Robert Louis Stevenson, was an arduous hill to climb. With strength and patience, he hoped to take his country there one day. The colonial authorities were not making it easy for him to do so.

CHAPTER NINE

THE SUGAR CRISIS, CONSTITUTIONAL REFORM, AND THE WHITE MAN'S BURDEN

Arise! Cry out for the children that hunger and are naked. "Proclaim all these words in the cities of Judah, and in the streets of Jerusalem, saying Hear ye the words of this Covenant and do them" (Jeremiah 11:6).
    —EXTRACT FROM REV. CLAUDE SMITH'S PETITION TO THE GOVERNOR

The Executive Committee of the Labour Union is therefore of the considered opinion that nothing short of adult suffrage and the sweeping away of all qualifications for elections as a member of the Legislature will assure labour significant control of the Legislature to ensure adequate law for the protection of the proletariat.
    —BRITISH GUIANA LABOUR UNION, Memoranda to the British Commonwealth Labour Conference, 1930

THE GREAT SUGAR DEPRESSION OF 1929 took a heavy toll on the Guyanese and West Indian peoples. As the price of sugar fell, so, too, did their wages. As their wages fell, their social conditions deteriorated.[1] In Guyana, the depression brought untold suffering to the working people of the colony, particularly in terms of their health. Malaria had a devastating effect on the population's vitality and took an enormous toll among the East Indians who, as Denis Williams reported, "possessed next to no immunity [to malaria], and suffered throughout life."[2] In his testimony to Lord Olivier's commission, Webber noted that perhaps 50 percent of the deaths recorded as due to other causes were really "super-induced by recurrent attacks of malaria, which weakens the resistance of the people that almost any complaint ends fatally. Had the people sufficient food and sustenance, resistance to malaria itself would be greater."[3] Apart from reducing the birth rate during the first three decades of the twentieth century, malaria "increased the rate of abortions, miscarriages and premature deliveries, resulting in infant deaths from prematurity and congenital debility, which accounted for close on 40% of all infant mortality."[4] Dr. George Giglioli, an Italian physician who arrived in Guyana in

1922 and was responsible for the elimination of malaria from the colony during that early period, supported Webber's observation. He noted: "Malaria intestinal and worm-infections were in fact so wide-spread that they could be regarded as the common background against which all other diseases evolved."[5]

While he worked in Guyana, Dr. Giglioli made major contributions to the scholarship and subsequent treatment of malaria; hookworm infection; black-water fever; chronic nephritis, or Bright's disease; and paratyphoid C, which affected close to 90 percent of the population. In 1935 Dr. Giglioli discovered that *Anopheles darlingi* was the main carrier of malaria, a finding that W. W. C. Komp of the U.S. Public Health Services confirmed when he visited Guyana in 1936. In his autobiography, Giglioli observed "that where malaria occurs in this Colony, *A darlingi* is present; that where malaria is severe, *A darlingi* is abundant; that this species selectively bites man, enters and remains in houses, while it is rarely caught in animal shelters. . . . *A darlingi* [is] by far the most important vector of malaria in British Guiana."[6]

In 1944, through a chance visit to Guyana by Sir Robert Robinson, who was awarded the Nobel Prize in Chemistry in 1947; Sir John Simonson, another distinguished British chemist; and Dr. Alexander King, director of the United Kingdom Scientific Mission in the United States, Dr. Giglioli was introduced to DDT, which, up until that time, was being used under British military secrecy as a larvicide in West Africa and Burma.[7] Having discovered that the *Anopheles* "had habitually rested indoors after blood feeding and so was highly vulnerable to insecticide residues on walls and ceilings of rooms," Dr. Giglioli and his colleagues waged a massive campaign between 1945 and 1947 that virtually eliminated malaria through the indoor spraying of DDT.[8] Christopher Curtis reminds us that because of his "hard-earned knowledge" of all aspects of the malaria problem among the diverse peoples of Guyana, "Dr. Giglioli was able to triumphantly achieve eradication of the disease in the developed coastal areas and near eradication even in the remote inland areas near the frontier of the then highly malarious north-east Brazil."[9]

Dr. Giglioli also made tremendous contributions to the elimination of *Ankylostomiasis*, or hookworm, another parasitic disease that was having devastating consequences among the inhabitants. Between 1914 and 1918, a campaign by the Rockefeller Foundation to treat and eradicate the disease became the first international public health campaign undertaken by the foundation. When Dr. Giglioli arrived in Mackenzie City to work for the Demerara Bauxite Company, the hookworm epidemic was still raging in Guyana. About 80 percent of the population suffered from the disease. Although Dr. Giglioli would become better known for his work in malaria and the use of DDT, the treatment of hookworm was the first public health issue he tackled in Guyana, and it served as a necessary precursor to the public health work that he did in the country. He observed that the hookworm campaign was intended "not only to eliminate a prevalent and debilitating disease, but also to gain the confidence of the population, in respect to the overall public health programme we hoped to develop."[10]

Dr. Giglioli also did important, path-breaking work on blackwater fever, paratyphoid C, and chronic nephritis, diseases closely related to malaria. In 1930 he published *Malarial nephritis: Epidemiological and Clinical Notes on Malaria, Black Water Fever, Albuminuria and Nephritis in the Interior of British Guiana* and read a paper on the subject to the Royal Society of Tropical Medicine and Hygiene of London in 1932 that was not received very well by two of the leading members of the society. It proved to be a very insightful paper from someone who was doing empirical work in the field. In 1969 he reminisced about his success in this area and observed that "blackwater fever has disappeared from Guyana and has become a very rare disease elsewhere: the successful fight against malaria in many countries, the elimination of quinine and the introduction of powerful synthetic antimalarial drugs, effective for both the treatment and prevention of the disease, have revolutionized living conditions in previously deadly areas."[11] Dr. Giglioli's path-breaking work in the area of paratyphoid C also turned out to be important.

Throughout his stay in Guyana, Dr. Giglioli was assisted by Sam Ramjattan, his trained technician, in all of his important work. In talking about his work on the *Anopheles* mosquito, Dr. Giglioli writes: "To ascertain the feeding habits and blood preferences of these two mosquitoes, Ramjattan and I made some experiments, carrying out synchronized captures, on people inside a house, and on a horse tethered close to the front door of the building, only 10 or 12 feet apart. The results remained consistently the same; in the house we caught what we took to be a *A. argyritarsis* and on the horse *A. tarsimaculatus.*"[12] In 1937, when he moved to Georgetown to work on one of the Davsons' sugar estates, he says that "Sam Ramjattan, my technician at MacKenzie and Blairmont, joined me."[13] He makes the following remarks about his experimental work at the Sugar Experimental Station at Sophia: "There is a small cottage occupied by a watchman and his family; it is surrounded by cane and rice lands, and for many years it was my habitual, all-season source of *A. darlingi* supplies for laboratory experimental purposes. All I had to do was dispatch Ramjattan with his capture tube, a cage, and instructions as to the number required."[14] In 1947 Ramjattan was working with Dr. Giglioli in the Rupununi on the first DDT experimental trials with the American Indians. Ramjattan, it seems, should be given more recognition in the story of the work of this great physician.

In 1968 the World Health Organization awarded Dr. Giglioli the Darling Foundation Prize and Medal for his outstanding work in the pathology, etiology, epidemiology, treatment, prevention, and control of malaria. Looking back at his work in the 1970s, he declared: "I still marvel at truly remarkable concatenation of events and chance circumstances in far away 1944, which gave Guyana, its Mosquito Control Service, and its Sugar Industry the opportunity to write so memorable a page in the history of man's long fight against malaria."[15] Despite his major achievement, falciparum malaria reappeared with a vengeance in the 1990s. Today, malaria affects close to 300 to 500 million people each year, while some organizations have called for a total ban on the use of DDT.

Meanwhile the economic situation worsened. By the middle of 1928, over 40,000 persons (out of a population of 307,000 persons) working in the sugar industry had lost their jobs, and the resultant disaster was devastating. Many trading establishments dismissed their workers, and there were recurring deficits in the public finances. In terms of unemployment, the situation deteriorated to such a degree that Governor Edward Denham, in a letter to Lord Passfield, noted that "the number will certainly increase considerably in view of the closing down of estates and reduction in the number of labourers, which are now occurring."[16] Added to all of this, one-fifth of the total expenditure of the country went toward serving the colony's debts.[17] As the situation worsened at the end of 1929, the secretary of state selected Lord Olivier and D. M. Semple to lead a commission (the West Indian Sugar Commission, 1929–30) to inquire into the causes of the depression and to determine what assistance the Colonial Office could render in light of the representations the governors, legislative councils, agricultural societies, and chambers of commerce had made to him about the grim state of affairs in the region.[18]

The members of the commission left England on October 5, 1929, and returned on January 27, 1930. After studying the matter under their charge, they reported that unless some assistance was guaranteed to the sugar producers at an early date, the sugar industry would become extinct. They informed the Colonial Office that if arrangements could be made to assure reasonable prices to the sugar producers throughout the West Indies, then they would be able to obtain the necessary capital to improve their methods. In looking at the factories and the workers' methods of cultivation, the commissioners were convinced that the sugar producers were genuine in their desire to correct matters.[19] Recognizing the plight of the mostly African population of the region, the commission reiterated observations that were made by a West India Royal Commission of 1897, which had visited the Caribbean for similar reasons. The Royal Commission observed that the black population was brought as slaves to the West Indies under conditions that were condoned by the British authorities. The act of emancipation did not divest the British government of its responsibility to the former slaves. It concluded:

> We cannot abandon them, and if economic conditions become such that private enterprise and the profits of trade and cultivation cease to attract white men to the Colonies, or to keep them there, this may render it more difficult for the British Government to discharge its obligations, but will not in any case

diminish the force of them. We have placed the labouring population where it is, and created for it the conditions, moral and material, under which it exists and we cannot divest ourselves of responsibility for its future.[20]

These words were uttered when the "white man's burden" was an all-pervasive force in the minds of European colonizers and Joseph Chamberlain, the quintessential imperialist, was the secretary of state, and they still possessed a resonance in the sensibilities of the English.[21] The English still thought they had an obligation to guide the former slaves to self-government, which, of course, was the battle that Webber and his Caribbean colleagues were fighting: to get away from the whites and their guidance. They believed they could achieve their objectives without the benevolence of whites. The time had come for them to control their affairs and to carve a space in the society to say what they wanted to say.

Needless to say, the conditions of the East Indians who worked in the rice and sugar industries were just as bad as those of the Africans. The sugar planters established a very low standard of housing for these laborers. It was deemed sufficient

that they should be housed in long ranges of single rooms [logies] with floors on the ground. These floors were, no doubt, such as the Indian immigrants had been accustomed to and were dressed by such women as were imported with them, with the traditional compost of cow-dung and clay. West Indian huts elsewhere had often merely hard earthen floors. On many estates on which indentured coolies were settled, the old ranges remained, ruinous, decrepit, and full of dirt, and vermin.[22]

When the East Indians arrived in the colony, the Africans were growing rice "spasmodically . . . in the backlands and swamps as their staff of life."[23] However, the East Indian presence soon made rice a profitable industry, turning a negative economic situation into a positive one. For example, during 1889–93, the average rice imports were 18,735 tons per annum and exports nil. By 1907–8, exports had risen to 6,977,877 pounds. In 1928 rice exports were the highest in the country's history. In 1929 about 64,000 acres were reaped, and 14,091 tons of rice valued at $876,408 were exported. In 1930, 22,480 tons valued at $1,090,431 were exported.[24]

Given this record of success, the commissioners believed that if the rice industry were properly managed, "it may in the course of time, become actually the more important [industry] both as a source of maintenance to the Indian population and as a staple of export."[25] Seechran claims that the development of the rice industry remained "the most important achievement of the Indians in the colony" and "underlined the independence and tenacity of the Indian farmer."[26] In June 1929, writing in the *New Daily Chronicle*, Webber complimented the East Indians once more when he affirmed that there "can be no greater tribute to the inherent powers of self-reliance and initiative of the people than the way the rice industry has survived, despite heart-breaking failures, for which too often the Government has been responsible."[27] Most of the government efforts were devoted to the maintenance of the sugar industry. Rice did not earn as much per acre as sugar, and therein lay the government's attitude toward it.

Country	Persons Directly Employed in the Sugar Industry	Population	Percentage
Barbados	34,157	168,000	20
St. Kitts	6,000	18,000	33
Antigua	9,000	30,000	31
St. Lucia	6,900	57,000	12
British Guiana	50,000	307,000	16
Trinidad	40,000	397,000	10
Jamaica	30,000	975,000	3

The economic depression of the period not only had negative effects among those workers in the sugar, rice, and other industries, but it also affected the family lives of the "labouring poor," particularly those who had to leave the city to work in the interior.[28] Webber, who had worked and lived in the interior and therefore knew it much better than most of his colleagues, who never even ventured beyond Georgetown, was particularly aware of the impact that this condition had on women. The commission reported that over 15,000 males, primarily Afro-Guyanese, were in the interior and, by virtue of that fact, were effectively cut off from their families. The result was calamitous on the women:

> In the Balata Industry these men may remain six or nine months in the Interior. In the Gold and Diamond Industries, men have been known to remain in the Interior three or four years on a stretch. These men, because of the conditions under which they lived, the hardships, the absence of amenities, etc., had not infrequently become a charge upon their woman folk and relatives when they return. In British Guiana then, there is artificially created a surplus of women, which is not unlike that found in Barbados for other reasons. This does not counter balance the shortage of women in the East Indian population [of which Webber had written in *Those That Be in Bondage*], since the two races do not coalesce.[29]

A. V. Crane spoke about the need to develop peasant farming to assist in making the colony more economically independent and deplored the government's policy with regard to small farmers. He declared that the immediate organization of small farmers for the production of exportable crops was the one way to avert "the impending financial ruin of this colony."[30] Like Webber, he called on the government to pay some attention to the interior. He had heard it said that

> the gold and diamond industries had a way of always coming to the rescue when things were getting dull but it seems as though their luck in that direction had become exhausted, possibly due to the failure of government to make the interior of the Colony the success that it should have been and possibly due to the recent controls of those industries (gold and diamond) by large interests which in the opinion of some responsible colonists had had the effect of limiting the production of gold and diamond.[31]

The commissioners were not as sanguine about the possibilities of turning to the interior to solve the crisis the country was undergoing. They reported that outside of a belt averaging about ten miles in width along the coastline, the entire interior might be left out when it came to dealing with its immediate problems of agriculture and the development of the country's economy. Several surveys of the interior by competent authorities had authenticated that position and asserted that "except in certain areas for the production of cattle, the interior of British Guiana nowhere offers any encouraging prospect for agricultural settlement." Timber production was increasing, and there was also "an unreliable source of money in the winning of alluvial gold and diamonds in the bed of some rivers. . . . The industries, however, offer little or no basis for permanent agriculture and development, and their principal effect upon the agricultural economy of the Colony at the present time is to absorb, if not to divert, labour which might otherwise seek employment in the sugar industry."[32] Sugar production must always have first priority in Guyana.

In economic terms, Webber thought that the country had reached its lowest ebb. He believed that the depressed economic condition of the country resulted from several reasons. Apart from the crushing debt that the colony carried and the ill-fortune that befell the sugar and rice industries, the deteriorating economic crisis could be traced, in part, to the failure of government to foster any development schemes in the interior that had been advocated from time to time. The government did not even encourage individual capitalists who were willing to take the necessary risks to invest in the development of the country. The British government reserved the exclusive right to exploit the colony's resources. Such "opposition between government and private investors led to a deadlock in the industry." He believed that the rice industry should be better regulated since bumper yields tended to ruin the industry by pushing prices downward.[33] When he brought his ideas of the rice industry to the attention of the Sugar Commission, S. H. Seymour described his comments as "a compendium of sham smartness, rotary perfervid bunkum and several other kinds of cant and rot."[34] As was consistent with the colonial authorities, the mother country was more concerned with promoting its own interests and did little to protect the interests of its subject peoples.

As the crisis worsened, the working people and the laboring poor took matters into their own hands. In a memorandum to the British Commonwealth Labour Conference, the BGLU expressed its fears about the deteriorating state of affairs in the country. Its major recommendation revolved around saving the sugar industry so that the evils of starvation and unemployment might be stayed. The inability to achieve that objective could result in homes being sold and the homeowners ejected from their homes. The BGLU warned that those persons "who now earn their living as dock labourers, porters, railway men, etc., and who have raised their families to a certain standard of civilization and city life, [will] be driven to swell the ranks of the vicious and unemployed city dwellers, with nowhere to turn in town or country."[35]

The poorer people also began to express their frustrations. Rev. Claude Smith led his Church Army of America in a demonstration against the government to dramatize the frightful toll this crisis was having upon the people. Although the colonial authorities thought he was "sincere in his way, if a little mad," he believed he had a sincere calling from God to intervene in the problems of his people to help to alleviate their starvation.[36] In a preamble and petition to the governor, formulated in eschatological language, he contended that he represented the inhabitants of British Guiana. He believed that the local and imperial governments had breached their commitments, thereby making "the people homeless, destitute, naked and starving and unable to procure work of any sort beside [sic] being compelled to meet heavy taxation in many cases levied against them in spite of universal protest."[37]

A newspaper report described Rev. Smith's followers as carrying banners as they marched in procession to the public buildings, lining up on both sides of the yard to the western end, men and boys being on the northern side, and the women and girls on the southern side. Rev. Smith was carrying a flag with a cross at the head of the pole, while a boy with a bell in his hand walked beside him. Rev. Smith told His Excellency that many "people were being taken to the cemetery daily as a result of starvation and were falling through hunger. . . . He had taken the people there to speak for themselves. They were quiet and law-abiding and if His Excellency asked them to pick pebbles from the ground they would do so. He asked His Excellency to give him a morsel to save them from the cemetery. They were there to support Government and were not inclined to interfere with the Constitution."[38] John Lucie Griffith, a member of the BGLU and Smith's associate, suggested that the government could create jobs for the people by opening up roads in the city and in the interior. They were not concerned with the "tug-o'-war of words" between the Electives and the government. They were asking the government to find them work at once to prevent them from starving. After listening to their pleas, the governor agreed to meet with Rev. Smith and a small delegation the following day to discuss their grievances.

Rev. Smith and his delegation met with the governor and his councilors a day later and outlined their position. His delegation consisted of representatives from the Working Men's and Working Women's Association, the Farmers Association, and Citizens of the Colony.[39] After listening to their presentations, the governor informed them that their proposals involved spending enormous sums of money and noted that the government "can only spend such money as the taxpayers contribute to the revenue. Therefore, if it is necessary to find money, it has in the first instance to come out of the people's pocket. His Excellency said that he wanted that clearly understood and also made clear to the people whom he [Rev. Smith] brought to the Public Buildings yesterday."[40]

Griffith advised the governor about the dire suffering of the people and suggested that if he reconstructed the roads, repaired the government buildings he controlled, and raised some supplementary funds from the legislature, it would go a long way to relieve the suffering of the people by providing them with immediate employment. "Rather than give the people relief in the form of rations, it will be more desirable to give them work. . . . Some of the people were really too weak to walk so as to come and show His Excellency how weak they were. His Excellency has to find some sort of means to give them relief and he would say give them work."[41] He suggested that a road to the interior would not only provide more employment but also prevent the city from becoming overcrowded as inhabitants deserted the districts and came into the city to look for jobs. Griffith stepped on the governor's toes when he assured the governor that "all of that large crowd which came here yesterday would urge His Excellency to construct that road to Tiboku and if he did contemplate doing it His Excellency could count on that crowd supporting him," to which His Excellency responded sharply: "I want to confine myself solely to the question of unemployment, [not politics]."[42] His Excellency did not verbalize the last two words of the quotation. He merely kept them to himself. The members of the delegation understood what he meant. He assured them that the government was doing everything it could to bring relief to this serious situation and "will try to do more to hustle certain things along."[43]

However, in an extraordinary departure from protocol—one may call it a crass political move—the governor asked the delegation, with the exception of Smith and Griffith, to withdraw. He wanted to speak with the two of them in private. It will be remembered that Griffith had chastised the government for not giving "the hardy pioneers of the gold, diamond and rice industries the necessary assistance in the form of roads or railways in the interior and drainage and irrigation on the coast lands for which the industries were prepared to pay." According to a transcript of the meeting, the governor told Rev. Smith that he had been watching his behavior and had reports of his meetings. He assured Smith that he had no objections to the religious meetings he was holding throughout the city but cautioned against his using them for carrying out undesirable propaganda. He warned:

> If anything takes place through any action of yours you will be held responsible. If you lead a procession without the permission of the Inspector of Police through this town or use any inflammatory language at public meetings, proceedings will be taken against you. At the present time, the Government cannot afford to have people stirred up into action they would regret. I will have what I said written out and sent to you.[44]

The transcript does not indicate Smith's reaction, but one can assume that he was taken aback by the governor's intemperate remarks. After all, the governor had invited Smith to meet with him to discuss the gravity of the crisis after he had led a people's march to protest the starvation that had gripped the land. However, the governor used the opportunity to chastise Smith and, by indirection, Griffith. He was well prepared. The day before, W. E. H. Bradburn, the inspector general of police, had sent him a report that described Smith as "a 'Firebrand,' and Inciter to crime and violence and no assurance he may give to Government will alter his attitude."[45] On August 19, 1929, Smith was put on a bond of good behavior for six months for "disorderly conduct." Two months later, he was summoned to court for using "indecent language" for which he was charged $2.96. In November 1929, contrary to police warnings, Smith and his followers let it be known that they would march to Government House to see Lord Olivier, who was in the colony to take testimony on the sugar crisis that was ailing the land. Smith called off his march when Lord Olivier decided to receive his deputation.

Any reasonable critic would have interpreted Rev. Smith's behavior as being within the realm of political and social activism. One could have even viewed Smith as possessing a messianic character with a millenarian zeal for justice. Although he took on the title of reverend and quoted from the Bible constantly, one could have seen Smith's behavior as a form of spiritualism—"a religion with practically no theology, clergy or organization, completely free from any taint of dependency."[46] The governor could not accept Rev. Smith's open defiance of his authority, what he construed to be Smith's lawlessness, and his challenge of the governor's Manichaean worldview that divided the colonizers from the colonized, the good from the bad.

Such a forcible confrontation with the governor in a public place personalized the depth of the social and economic crisis. Little did the governor realize that he was locked in a symbiotic relation with his adversaries from which it would be difficult to escape. Although the governor and other officials believed that

Rev. Smith possessed a touch of madness, his advocacy and that of others drama-tized the plight of the people and made the authorities take it much more seriously than they were inclined to do initially. Rev. Smith and his army never let up. He remained a thorn in the government's side until he was imprisoned a year later.

At the beginning of 1930, the governor set up a five-member Economic Investigation Committee that was chaired by W. Bain Gray, the director of edu-cation, "to investigate and report on the extent of unemployment and to advise as to any measure by which it might be possible to find employment for those seeking it."[47] Webber was made a member of that committee. On June 18 the com-mittee presented its findings to the governor, who in turn transmitted them to the secretary of state for the colonies. Throughout their deliberations, the colonial authorities feared "a racial tinge will probably be given to the discontent which must arise, as unemployment, owing to the degeneration of the sugar position, increases."[48] The crisis had the potential to create social havoc and the division of the society along racial lines.

The threat of civil disruption made the Colonial Office more concerned about the unemployment situation and its negative effect on the population. Seeing the tremendous suffering in the Caribbean, George Grindle, a senior civil ser-vant, proposed financial assistance to the islands until the economy had restored itself.[49] He was refuted. However, one of the officials at the Colonial Office rec-ognized that "relief works must be authorized at once by telegram if a dangerous situation is to be averted. Money has got to be provided from some source and I am inclined to think that we should telegraph at once telling the governor to start relief works on macadamized roads and sea defences and drainage of agricultural areas . . . in view of the seriousness of the situation as disclosed."[50] On April 7 the secretary of state approved a loan of £12,000 and a grant of £3,000 to build a road into the interior along the Bartica-Karburi trail. Although the acting governor was at pains to point out that the decision to build the road "had nothing to do with the immediate problem of employment," the British officials were becoming nervous.[51] This project would employ approximately 300 persons. Even as they announced their employment relief program, another company was announcing plans to dismiss 200 workers. The net gain in jobs was only 100 persons. The government had decided to deal with its economic problems by granting loans to Guyana.

The leaders of the people were happy with the government's decision to go ahead with this road-building project in the interior. However, they were only too aware of the "callous indifference of 'our Masters' at Downing Street towards the fate of Caribbean Colonies."[52] The editors of the newspapers resented the attitude of the colonial masters. An editorial in the *Daily Chronicle* announced that as "the studied indifference becomes more apparent, the exasperation of our people grows greater. The sneers of Mr. Snowden, and the smiling placidity of Lord Passfield's 'jam and smiles' attitude are too mixed a diet for the digestive organs of the hungry people of these Colonies to assimilate."[53] It's not too presumptuous to believe that these lordly men were not listening to the cries of the people. Their cynicism could have been inferred from newspaper reports. Lord Snowden, for one, possessed firm views on the matter. "He saw 'sound' money as the bedrock of social progress. He fully accepted the aim of driving down prices until the £1 had reached a level at which the Gold Standard could be restored.... His policy, naturally, was the traditional Treasury one of fighting the spending departments with a view to avoiding extravagance and cutting down costs. He carried it out with a zest that delighted his officials.... Snowden took a thoroughly Treasury point of view."[54] Under such circumstances, Snowden could not be disturbed unduly by the plight of a few colored persons in Guyana. When he became chancellor of the exchequer in 1929, he was equally emphatic: "unremunerative public works were self-defeating; the extra employment provided by them would be offset by a corresponding fall in the volume of private employment."[55] John Maynard Keynes would take a different approach to the matter.

Things continued to deteriorate in Guyana. On August 8 an unsmiling Lord Passfield reminded a sneering Lord Snowden of the urgency of the situation and begged him "to expedite Treasury decision on this correspondence, and to open a little the spigot of your cash! I have held back as long as I could the demands for money (and help to the sugar industry). But unemployment is now at last there, and in a negro population without any Poor Law it is a very short step to firing the canes and looting the stores. We must let the Governors [of British Guiana and Antigua] start their Relief Works."[56] Concerned about the deteriorating situation and its possibility for leading to violence, the governor sent the following telegram to the secretary of state: "Unemployment Situation daily becoming more serious and estate population inflamed generally only partially employed. Urgent to start relief work and request earliest authorization."[57] Given such an inflammable situation, the Colonial Office had to act quickly. As in all things, Governor Denham urged the secretary of state to respond to his request as quickly as possible and reminded him that "September 8th is nomination day and attempts to arouse ill feeling will likely be endeavoured during the election campaign on account of the delay and unemployment excited [sic]. Opposition to Constitution is, at the present moment, slight, but it would be dangerous to create one."[58] When the governor received authorization to commence relief work programs in early September, he telegraphed the secretary of state to thank him for the assistance he had rendered "in the relief of unemployment by these grants. Work now commenced as approved, and further communication awaited re[garding] other work proposed."[59]

Such an order was a triumph over Lord Snowden's philosophy of balanced budgets and his favoring the business sector over the government as an engine of growth. Cross noted that Snowden was "the most autocratic Chancellor the twentieth century had ever seen."[60] He was always "a *clear* thinker rather than a *deep* thinker, and as he grew older his clarity hardened into prejudice. . . . He ran into the danger of confusing the mechanical tools of economics with the moral principles of thrift and frugality on which from childhood he lived his own life. The maxims of nineteenth-century economics became moral laws in his mind."[61] Under him, the unemployed people of the Caribbean, or even Great Britain for that matter, could not hope to receive much relief.

The British government did not care about the Caribbean particularly. Given the economic problems the British were facing at home (in 1929 over 300,000 British citizens were unemployed; by July 1930 over 2 million were unemployed) and the worldwide depression, they were more concerned about putting their house in order than they were with some colonials overseas. The Great Depression had engulfed almost every country, "whether free trade or protectionist, agricultural or manufacturing, backward or forward. . . .' It formed the crucial background to the generalization of Keynes's theory from the 'open' to the 'closed' economy, as well as his radical re-evaluation of the prospects of unmanaged capitalism."[62] Although Webber lived in a backward country and possessed neither the education nor the exposure of Snowden, as we will see in chapter 12, he evinced a more advanced understanding of economic development than Snowden, who was a prisoner of the economic maxims of the nineteenth century. Webber was firmly located in the twentieth century and was among the forerunners of liberal-progressive twentieth-century economic thought.

As the governor saw all too clearly, the economic crisis was tied up with the political crisis, especially when the people were fighting to retain aspects of a new constitution that gave them some control over their affairs. Necessarily, the issue of constitutional reform took a prominent place in this crisis since, as Lenin reminds us, economics is nothing but politics taken to its highest level. It was not coincidental that the economic crisis was gripping the country at the same time that the 1928 constitution took away the power of financial control from the Electives. Sir Cecil Clementi, a former colonial secretary of Guyana, argued that the constitution of Guyana, "as it existed for more than a century prior to 1928, was, in the words of Mr. E. F. L. Wood (now Lord Halifax), 'unique in the Empire.' It was a freakish by-product of the Napoleonic Wars and the creature of pure mischance [in that it involved] . . . the premature grant of representative institutions and in the control of finance by elected legislators not charged with administrative responsibility." Hence the desire on the part of the Colonial Office to allow the governor to alter and amend the constitution any time he saw fit.[63] Such a change brought Guyana's constitution into line with the other Crown colonies in the region by eliminating the elective assembly and vesting executive and legislative power in the governor, subject only to the overriding authority of the imperial government.[64] This action represented retrogression in the constitutional arrangements of Guyana. It was necessary that the people show their opposition to such a move.

In November 1929 Webber protested the government's directive that required employers to accompany new voters to register and to swear that they were in receipt of a certain salary. He thought that "this was a gratuitous insult which tended to disenfranchise three fourths of the employees of the country.... He saw no reason why registrars of births and deaths and postmasters and Justices of the Peace could not be called upon to receive them."[65] Such restrictions impeded the registration of new voters. This was evident in the new voters' registration list, which showed 10,000 voters inclusive of women who were granted the franchise for the first time; 14,000 persons were registered on the old registration list, although it did not include women. Undoubtedly, something was wrong. To rectify this matter, Webber moved a motion in the Legislative Council to extend the registration period. This motion was accepted; the registration period was extended to January 16, 1930, and the regulation requesting a statutory declaration from employees in support of an application for the registration of voters was withdrawn.

On December 11, 1929, the BGLU held a meeting in which its members requested the support of the British Labour Party and the International Federation of Trade Unions Congress to secure universal adult suffrage for the colony and carried another resolution that drew the secretary of state's attention to the fact that "not even one of the five Nominated Members of the Legislative Council was a person identified with Labour and urging that Labour should be adequately represented."[66] The BGLU also demanded that the income qualifications requiring each voter to have an annual income of $300 be reduced "in the interest of the large number of workers who had been thrown out of employment, as well as those who although regularly or casually employed could not earn $300 per annum."[67] In his address to the meeting, Critchlow quoted Captain Cipriani, who thought that everyone must be educated to take part in the political process, and declared:

> In the colonies the great majority of the population are cultured and intelligent people, who are quite able to exercise that suffrage, and there can be no good argument whatever to deprive them of it. . . . We feel like all the other West Indian islands that the time has come when we should be afforded the privileges of universal suffrage and until good cause can be made out as to why we should be deprived of this privilege, I shall always find myself on the side of those who advance and support it.[68]

The BGLU and other working-class organizations also called for the enlargement of the franchise. In a memorandum to the British Commonwealth Labour Conference, the BGLU made it clear that the 1928 constitution had disenfranchised the voters of the colony by piling up far more onerous qualifications on voters and on those who wanted to be candidates. The capitalist class, the union said, had complete control of the economy, and so the BGLU resolved "that nothing short of adult suffrage and the sweeping away of all qualifications for elections as a member of the Legislature will assure to labour sufficient control of the Legislature to ensure adequate laws for the protection of the proletariat."[69] Along with Critchlow and Griffith, H. Bartan (secretary of the BGEIA), Victor C. Ransarran, and delegates from other organizations endorsed the position. This progressive position became law seventeen years later in the British Caribbean and Guyana. Jamaica received universal adult suffrage in 1944, Trinidad in 1946, and Guyana in 1953.

The *Daily Chronicle* believed that "the time was not ripe for universal suffrage," even though it thought the income qualification should be reduced in light of the unparalleled economic crisis that gripped the island. The newspaper also believed that the BGLU was too disunited to warrant representation in the Legislative Council and reminded the union "to take a leaf out of the book of the working men of Trinidad [who] not only have an accredited labour representative in the Legislative Council of that colony, but also a labour organ of their own."[70]

On December 21 the BGLU sent copies of its resolutions to the British Labour Conference seeking support of its positions on universal adult suffrage and its desire to have a labor presence among the unofficial members of the Legislative Council. Such a resolution was apropos. The All-India Trades Union Congress raised a similar question at the British Commonwealth Conference about the "preparation of subject people for self-government." The memorandum from the British labor union to the conference had insisted that self-government demanded by the inhabitants of these territories should be granted.[71] In an accompanying letter to Williams Gilies, the union declared that only 1,000 men and women had been enrolled in the city of Georgetown, while the old registrar for the city contained the names of over 5,000 men alone. Although the government had extended the time for registration by one month, "no one after this could have the slightest doubt that Labour would almost be disenfranchised owing to the inability of the ordinary working men and women to earn $300 (£662:10/-) per annum. I [Critchlow] leave it to your judgment to decide whether you will recommend to the British Government Universal Suffrage for us or a reduction of the income qualification."[72] The income qualification was not only a matter of placing more persons on the voting rolls. Given the economic crisis, it also entailed the survival of the union as a viable working-class organization.

The Colonial Office offered mixed responses to the BGLU's resolutions. One official observed that British Guiana was practically bankrupt, so that one could not alter the constitution at that time. He averred: "Under the present constitution it will be difficult enough to run B.G. as a grant-in-aid Colony with more popular control it would be well nigh impossible. But, if there is a suitable person to be found, the nomination of the representative of labour under the present constitution might well be considered." Another official thought that however desirable this position may be in principle, there were two practical difficulties: "One is that labour is divided on racial lines into East Indians and Negro. Probably no single representation would be acceptable to both races. The other is to find suitable individuals."[73]

The Colonial Office might have been putting its fingers on a fissure in the political culture. In an act of racial solidarity, Victor Ramsaran, of the BGEIA, declared that his organization would support East Indians, whom they considered worthy representatives of the East Indian community and the people as a whole. The BGEIA was also prepared to support certain "Negro" candidates who were a credit to their race and the colony. In fact, the BGEIA wanted to support the best candidates irrespective of race.[74] Ramsaran's proposal seemed an honorable one. However, it ran into problems when Webber and the other Electives asked that the general election be postponed for one year so that they could lead a united struggle to obtain a new constitution. At a meeting called by the BGEIA and attended by the BGLU, the Workers League Farmers Conference, and the New Amsterdam Progressive Association, a resolution was passed that condemned a pact that was made by the elective members of the Legislative Council to see themselves returned en bloc to the Legislative Council at the general election. Together with several organizations, they declared their strong disapproval of any such pact and pledged themselves to defeat such action.[75] The East Indians were not prepared to be denied greater representation in the Legislative Council, especially when they constituted 42 percent of the population.

On Christmas Day, 1929, almost as "an afterthought," as an editorial in the *Daily Chronicle* termed it,[76] the Electives released their General Manifesto, requesting that each elective member be returned to his seat "without a contest, at the forthcoming General Elections, and with one mandate."[77] The Electives pledged to press for an amendment to the constitution to provide for universal suffrage based on a literary test; the rearrangement of the electoral districts so as to accommodate sixteen rather than fourteen Electives; an elective majority in the Legislative Council, with the retention of the nominated unofficial members and the reserve power of the secretary of state; and an increased proportion of Electives on the Executive Council. They promised that as soon as an Order-in-Council was granted to achieve these ends, there would an immediate dissolution of the council, and an open general election would be held where the Electives would account for their stewardship in every constituency.[78]

On December 27 the Electives clarified their position through an editorial in the *New Daily Chronicle* that was written presumably by Webber. They defined their case as one of national importance, an issue of the entire colony "for or against the perpetuation of the present constitution, through new instruments or through old. The man or woman who stands aside and pleads disgust with either side is frankly a traitor to the country and is silently stabbing in the back those who would wrestle with the problems of the country."[79] As to the BGEIA's charge about their insidious "pact," the Electives responded that the BGEIA's comment was premature and was made without the association having all of the necessary information. Assuring the BGEAI that they had no intention to hold on to office in perpetuity, the Electives pledged that as soon as the Order-in-Council was changed, they would dissolve themselves and submit to a new general election. Their seeking two additional seats for Electives "should satisfy certain persons, even though all the fourteen electives were again returned for the second time, which is not conceivable."[80]

According to Webber, such a plan would leave room for more persons to be elected, and that should satisfy the demands of the East Indians. E. F. Fredericks, one of the Electives who signed the General Manifesto, also responded directly to the charge that the Electives were participating in an ignoble "pact." In a letter to the "Loyal Toast," a dinner of the Electives that was held on December 23, he asserted that "the present Constitution created by the Order-in-Council is so unsuited to the country that it would be poor judgment if under it there should be contested elections of one kind or another." He saw the Electives' position as an unselfish act "to secure to the colony a better Constitution than the present one. [It] is the worthiest political plan that any such body constitutionally hampered as we are could carry out to an electorate as ours is."[81]

Griffith also objected to the Electives "pact" and saw it as a backward step that would have afforded excellent amusement if the measure and the men could have been regarded lightly. He believed that the pact was a menace "of the first magnitude which demands the gravest consideration. The people of the Colony are threatened with the deprivation of their most fundamental constitutional rights and privileges for the Electives have constituted themselves the Electorate, and declared that none but themselves shall be elected to the Legislative Council." Interpreting the action of the Electives as a bold grab for power, he called on the citizens of Guyana to vigorously object to what he considered the "tyranny of the Electives."[82]

A reader of the *Daily Chronicle* who styled himself "Torchlight" saw the financial crisis that the country was passing through as being more important than the constitutional crisis to which the Electives' proposal addressed itself. He noted that the "matter calls for very stern reprisals from the electorate, which I hope would not fail to record the strongest disapproval of the declarations of a conclave of men which passeth man's understanding."[83] The *Daily Chronicle* voiced its objections in a different manner. It did not believe that new men in the next legislature would oppose the majority of Electives on the question of constitutional reform or that after a "Short Parliament" the Electives would amend the constitution.

It suggested that every candidate for the next election should be committed to "Constitutional reform and to work on those broad lines of policy defined in the electives memorandum."[84] The newspaper could not countenance the electorate being denied the right to select their representatives and men of "sterling character . . . good judgment, sound commonsense and honor" being denied an opportunity to serve in the legislature and therefore objected to the Electives' pact.

The East Indians seemed most aggrieved. The BGEIA supported all efforts to defeat the pact and decided to "broadcast" Griffith's article against the pact.[85] Its objections were not without merit. In seeking to extend the franchise on the basis of a literacy test, a disproportionate number of East Indians as well as American Indians stood to be disenfranchised. Webber made it clear in his editorial that the literacy test was "the safeguard that was adopted in the case of Brazil where there was an enormous illiterate aborigine population, to extend the vote to whom would be a great danger in the hands of unscrupulous persons; the same applies here to our aborigine [American Indian] population as well as to large sections of immigrants."[86] One is not too sure who those "unscrupulous persons" might have been. Just as the BGLU interpreted the $300 eligibility requirement as an obstacle to its members taking part in national affairs, it is entirely possible that the East Indians saw the literacy test as an obstacle to their having greater representation in the Legislative Council. Such a test would have instituted a form of legal inequality, setting severe limits on freedom and equality through the franchise. For those who seek perfection in their heroes, this was not the best moment for Webber, although his intention was noble and his demand for a more democratic constitution a worthy and honorable end. A franchise open to all citizens over the age of twenty-one was the more progressive way to proceed. In this context, the BGLU's position was the most enlightened and, if accepted, would have solved all these problems. Its memorandum to the British Commonwealth Labour Conference called the secretary of state to craft a constitution in which the nominated "employer" members of the legislature would never be able to "combine" with the nominated officials, "always strongly pro-employer in sentiment, to defeat any measure designed for the protection of the masses. That cannot be achieved unless the elected members are in a permanent majority over all classes of the nominated members."[87]

After much national discussion, the Electives called a conference on February 1, 1930, in which they invited representatives of local organizations to discuss their General Manifesto. At the end of the conference, Critchlow moved and N. Duke of the British Guiana National Trades Union seconded a resolution that called on the government to postpone the elections "to allow the present members of the Legislative Council in collaboration with colonial organizations and supported by the masses of the people, to commence development work at once, to give relief to the starving masses."[88]

When Rev. Smith and his followers met with the governor on the morning of February 5, they presented him with a petition in which they demanded that the election be held as the law required.[89] Later that day, Webber moved in the Legislative Council that the general election scheduled for 1930 be postponed for a year so that voters would have more time to register. The Executive Committee voted against Webber, which meant that general elections would be held in 1930 on the basis of the existing constitution.

This is one move in which Webber might have stubbed his political toe. According to the *Daily Chronicle*, the Electives' position was "universally condemned as [well as] universally criticized in local political circles."[90] Many saw it as an unabashed political grab for power. However, in spite of their disappointment, Webber and the Electives urged their constituents to return them to their seats in the forthcoming elections and pledged that in the event of their being reelected, they would press for the amendment to the constitution.

CHAPTER TEN

EXPLORING NEW WORLDS

Sugar, sugar, everywhere,
But ne'er a crystal to spare;
Sugar, sugar, everywhere,
Its sweetness none can share.

Sugar, sugar, everywhere,
Its rancidity is tasted all around;
Sugar, sugar, everywhere,
Yet starvation and deprivation abound.
—SELWYN R. CUDJOE, "Rime from an Ancient County"

Let me tell any boys and girls, or boys alone, or girls alone, who are anxious to spend a wonderful Easter holiday, to make the trip. See a country that is a hidden book to nearly everybody, and come back missionaries for a Greater Guiana.
—A. R. F. WEBBER, *Exploring Unbroken British Guiana*

AT THE END OF 1929, EVERYWHERE THEY LOOKED, any way they turned, the people of Guyana saw the effects of a sugar economy gone sour, leaving ruination; devastated plantations; starving, desperate people; and a helpless, inept government. Diseases had increased, unemployment had jumped, schools began to close down, head teachers were being laid off, and families began to break up. Viewing the predicament the people faced, one could not help but think of a Guyana variant of Samuel Taylor Coleridge's *Rime of the Ancient Mariner*, "Rime from an Ancient County."

The sugar industry, the largest employer of skilled and unskilled labor, was always the backbone of Guyana's economy. According to Denis Williams, "For better or worse, ours has been a sugar psychology . . . whilst robbing us of some of the most unalienable of rights, [it] has nevertheless . . . kept us alive. . . . In 1922, despite at times crippling ups-and-downs, sugar remained the sheet-anchor of our economy—and our psychology."[1] Given this reality, like so many of his compatriots, Webber was exasperated by the reluctance of the colonial authorities to assist the Guyanese people during their hour of need and felt devastated by the utter helplessness of his people. As 1929 came to a close, he, too, seemed to have been overcome momentarily by the depression that inundated the people of the land. It was as though an albatross was placed around his neck. He wrote a prescient, melancholy poem, "The Great Dissolve," in which he seemed to challenge fate. He wrote:

> *No Sunset and evening star for me,*
> *Nor twilight and vesper bell.*
> *Let me fall on the raging battle field*
> *With banners gaily flying,*
> *In full throated battle cry*
> *With drums a'throb and bugles calling.*
>
> *Give me not a forgotten soldier's fate*
> *To lie like a log in a stagnant pool.*
> *'Tis better to fall with ideals high,*
> *Tossing buckler and pennon bright*
> *To those that will seize with exultant cheers,*
> *For the crowds onrush to final victory.*
>
> *Though I go with work undone*
> *The world's work is never complete*
> *'Tis better to leave the fields aglow,*
> *And a following with falchions flashing bright,*
> *Than to wait and watch the fires grow dim,*
> *And steal away in the still and darkening night.*[2]

At that point of his life, Webber could not have known that he only had two and a half more years to live. His brother George Isaac died two months later, at the same age and from precisely the same disease from which Allie died (Webber was sometimes called Allie, a shortened form of his first name). Sensing the melancholia that lay beneath the poem's surface, a reader, J.R., in defiant optimism and inspiration, castigated Webber's seeming to despair:

> *Why talk at all of the Great Dissolve,*
> *Of going while work remaineth undone?*
> *Hast thou lost heart in the raging fray,*
> *Or see'st thou a shadow dark'ning thy Sun?*

Fear not, but press on with might and main,
The Country needs men still of valiant heart
Though thou'rt leading a forlorn-hope,
Victory is thine if thou'lt play well thy part.

Not always doth Might prevail over Right,
Not always the struggle will nought avail
Legions may sink in the thickening dust,
But the faith that endurerth is bound to prevail.[3]

Although Webber was discouraged by what he saw around him, he had lost neither heart nor hope about the future. At the beginning of 1930, he was still wearing freedom's flag and leading his troops into battle. He and his colleagues held large public meetings throughout the country to encourage those who were eligible to register and vote. On January 7 Webber, Arnold Seeram (an elected member of the Legislative Council) and Victor Ramsaran (a political activist) shared a platform in which both East Indian and African leaders came together to encourage their fellow citizens to vote. Seeram pointed out that "the man who did not register was an enemy of the man who registered. He regretted the absence of women who for the first time in the history of the colony were given the right [to vote] on the same grounds as men." Ramsaran thought that citizens ought to register "to show they had an interest in the welfare of the colony."[4]

On the same day that the *New Daily Chronicle* reported the East Coast meeting, a notice in the newspaper urged its readers to register to vote, arguing that "every claim filed is a brick or a pebble brought to the great superstructure of a reformed constitution, to secure the real progress of British Guiana." To counter the various stratagems that commissioners of oaths were using to prevent prospective voters from registering, the notice reminded readers: "All a Commissioner of Oaths has to do, is to enquire of the person declaring, whether it is his signature; whether he has read the document; and whether what he is declaring is true and correct; and the Commissioner certifies accordingly, that the person has made those declarations."[5] In this way, Webber and his men were educating voters about their rights and how they could enforce them.

By March 1930, Webber felt betrayed by the inability of the Labour government to support the falling prices of Guyana sugar. Sensing an ally in H. B. Morgan, the Labour M.P. for Paddington who was born in Grenada, Webber sent him a telegram in which he reminded him of the colony's amazement "at the Labour Government's callous refusal to save the sugar industry in its fight for existence or [to] protect local labour from unemployment while for the protection of English capitalists maintaining a beet bounty equal to our entire cost of sugar production and granting that industry further customs protection in Home markets while denying our industry even equivalent preference with English beet."[6]

Webber also strongly objected to the colonial government preventing locals from exploring reports of oil discoveries in Guyana. Given the government's reluctance to act, segments of the population began to question the usefulness of the colony's political connection to Britain, whether it was yielding the anticipated benefits, and whether, under the circumstances, a political union with the United States or even Canada was not in their better interest. Particularly because Morgan was a West Indian by "birth and early training," at the end of his telegram Webber quoted an unsettling warning that appeared in one of the daily newspapers: "Though no responsible section of opinion is as yet advocating annexation to the United States, nearly all classes are beginning to examine the British connexion and ask whether loyalty may not be bought at too high a price."[7]

The severity of the crisis again brought the discussion about the formation of a West Indian Federation to the forefront of the political debate and allowed for a more urgent consideration of the matter. On April 2 the *Daily Chronicle* observed that one of the most unexpected results of the distressing condition of affairs that was agitating the minds of West Indians and Guyanese was likely to be the closer relationship between the colonies that the present threat was slowly but surely bringing about. "Hitherto the West Indian Colonies had been too individualistic in attacking their problems. Each colony sought to deal with its own little problem from its individual point of view, and did not interest itself, save from an academical point of view, with the worries of its neighbors."[8] Politically and administratively, the newspaper concluded that the solution to the West Indian problem lay in the formation of a West Indian Federation.

On April 5 the *Daily Chronicle* editorialized about the issue again and complained that notwithstanding the repeated representations that had been made on behalf of West Indian sugar during the past few months, the attitude of the imperial government was still befogged in uncertainty due largely to the desire to play up to popular tradition, and to refrain from giving a definite indication of the government's fiscal policy before the budget speech had been delivered.[9] The only person who seemed to be agitating for the West Indian cause in London was Lord Olivier. Lord Snowden, who was directing the Colonial Office's policy toward the West Indies, favored free trade at the expense of any preference or subsidy on West Indian sugar. He was of the view that because West Indian planters had not put aside adequate resources during the years of prosperity, they could not expect any assistance from the Colonial Office during the crisis. In response to Lord Snowden's criticism, the *Daily Chronicle* averred that "a few individuals benefited from the war prosperity of sugar, and most of these saw to it that they were rid of the incubus of sugar long before the lean years came, so that the people now saddled with the necessity of carrying on the industry are, in the majority of instances, not those who profited from its prosperity in the happy war days."[10]

Amid all of this suffering, George Webber, Allie's only brother in Guyana, died on February 20, 1930. It caused Webber to reflect on his life. Like Allie, George also favored red roses, "undoubtedly due to their significance of life."[11] On March 2 Allie placed a lovely bouquet of roses at the front of the pulpit in Kingston Wesleyan Methodist Chapel, where George's funeral service was conducted. To the strains of Cecil Alexander's hymn "There Is a Green Hill Far Away" and St. Paul's admonition to Timothy, George was ushered into what Allie called in another context, "the long loneliness of the Forever."[12] Yet Allie must have derived much courage from St. Paul's charge:

I charge *thee* therefore before God, and the Lord Jesus Christ, who shall judge the quick and the dead at his appearing and his kingdom;

Preach the word; be instant in season, out of season; reprove, rebuke, exhort with all longsuffering and doctrine....

I have fought a good fight, I have finished *my* course, I have kept the faith:

Henceforth there is laid up for me a crown of righteousness, which the Lord, the righteous judge, shall give me at that day: and not to me only, but unto all them also that love his appearing (2 Timothy, 4:1–8).

Rev. J. England Underwood, who conducted the service, reminded the mourners that "God's work must continue despite the fact that a leader had dropped out. A worker leaves the ranks but there must be no gap as Canaan remained still to be occupied."[13] Although Webber may not have professed his Christianity openly, there were too many parallels in Underwood's sermon with the sentiments he echoed in "The Great Dissolve." In his own way, Webber was determined to fight the good fight and to finish his course upon "the raging battle field with banners gaily flying." He might have been more imbued if he had perused Paul's sentiments contained in his first epistle to Timothy: "Neither give heed to fables and endless genealogies, which minister questions, rather than godly edifying which is in faith: *so do*" (1 Timothy 4:4). It was so much in keeping with the activist posture Webber advocated in "The Great Dissolve." If only for his brother's sake, he would continue to devote his energies to building British Guiana.

From March 22 through March 27, having said farewell to his brother and having offered a memorandum to his fellow Electives about the construction of a road from Bethany to Moreni Island, Rockstone (an alternative to the government's proposal to build a road from Bartica to Kangaruma),[14] Webber traveled up the Araby River and explored the unknown Berbice savannas, a part of the country he always wanted to know. Out of that experience came "Exploring Unbroken British Guiana," a series of six articles that appeared in the *New Daily Chronicle* between March 29 and May 2, 1930, that demonstrated Webber's great love for the outdoors and his fascination with Guyana's vast forested territory. These articles allowed Webber to reflect on several issues that engaged him throughout his life. It was the last sustained nonfictional piece (with the exception of *Centenary History*) that he wrote before his untimely death.

Although Webber is the narrator of the tale, he says little about himself except that the Electives, of which he was a part, were blamed unnecessarily by the government for the backwardness of the society. Instead, he exposes the unrivaled beauty of the interior; the abundance of animal and bird life; the adventurous nature of the trip; the economic possibilities of the land; and his sympathy for a dying American Indian civilization, remnants of which he found along the river. Webber also draws upon the English poets (John Keats and Sir Walter Scott) and uses biblical references to inform poignant moments of his experiences. He even demonstrates his acquaintance with some of the latest scientific discussions when he alludes to the theory of evolution and the work of Sir Oliver Lodge.[15] Just as important, this travelogue allows Webber a measure of philosophical reflection and a chance to defend the Electives from the government's libelous charges that they were responsible for the economic backwardness of the land.

Webber begins "Exploring Unbroken British Guiana" with the premise that those who have not ventured outside of Georgetown, a strip on the coastland of the colony, cannot possibly know the country's richness, its beauty, and its possibilities. On Saturday, March 22, Webber and two other companions (Henry and McDonald) left Georgetown and traveled along the East Coast Road to the Abary Bridge, where they boarded their boat, "the old faithful Johnson motor," for a trip up "the wonderful wind-tossed Abary [River]," which led into the Demerara River. Although he had explored every important river in Guyana previously—at least, that was his boast—he had never been up the Abary, one of the smaller rivers that served as a means of communication for inhabitants who lived along its bank. He was stunned by what he saw. It literally teemed with life. "No other river that I have been on is like the Abary: either in scenery or the life that abounds on it. . . . Bush fowl and sea fowl rise in swarms. Alligators, big, medium and small swarm on every bank. High overhead I observed a predatory hawk with a fish gripped tight in his talons."[16] Webber was overwhelmed. The Abary was famous for its waterfowl, ducks, and snipe. *The British Guiana Handbook* (1922) described the region as follows:

> The vicissi duck (*Dendrocygna discolor*) is often seen in flocks of thousands, and the wonderful white Cranes (*Ardea cocoi*) and the Egrets (*Ardea Egretta*), so

valuable to the milliner for their plumes, are one of the sights of the coast-lands. Other birds which may be noted are the Negro-cop (*Mycteria Americana*), the Heri (*Euxenura Maguari*), the Curlew (*Numenius Hudsonicus*), the Pika (*Totanus melanoleucus*), the Flamingo (*Phaenicopterus ruber*) and the Long-leg (*Totanus flavipes*).

The Golden plover (*Charadrius dominicus*) and the Muscovy Duck (*Cauruna moschata*), the Powis (*Crax alector*) and the Marudi (*Penelope marail*) are common enough to afford excellent sport up the Abary Creek. Of the "bush birds" the "maams" (*Tinamus* and *Crpyturus* spp.) are plump-breasted and make capital eating.[17]

The coming together of these three different personalities made for an interesting trip. In fact, their "complete contrariness" made their exploration an exiting affair. Webber called the group the three musketeers. Henry was "ebullient, garrulous and amusing with many castles in the air"; McDonald, or McD, was always "cynical and bored, with his nose among the fleshpots, and both his feet upon the ground"; and Webber's moods varied from being "stoic and philosopher to savage and fool, ever ready to tune in on the mood of either of the other two musketeers."[18] It is no wonder that when Webber observed the initial scene of his adventure he became philosophical. He rejects the adjective "predatory," which he thinks is misleading when applied to animals. He asks: Is the predatory beast "any more predatory than man? We call hawks predatory, tigers cruel, and sharks voracious; indeed so persistently until 'hawk,' 'tiger,' 'shark' have become synonymous for describing certain types of men." He believed that it was more accurate to describe certain species "as man-brutes, for men are more predatory, more cruel, and more voracious—without the half excuses—than either hawk or tiger and shark. They, at least only kill from sheer necessity or hunger, and would avoid a conflict or seek peace whenever they can. Man, on the other hand, provokes a conflict, too often, only for sport."[19]

After this philosophical interlude, Webber and his companions came upon a colony of Canje pheasants, "sober hued, yet in a measure gorgeous." This picturesque scene prepares us for the abundance of plant and animal life that Webber encounters along the river:

Everywhere the brighter hued spurwings flew in vast clouds: white clothed cranes spotted the landscape everywhere. . . . The scenery on both banks of the river . . . was smoothing and subdued; a regular pastoral idyl, with cattle brousing gently, or the more frisky juvenile of their kind gamboling over the green swart. It was quite a novel sensation, almost eerie, to be steaming up a mighty river, deep enough to take ocean-going craft cut in dead level lands. It was forever like a canal dug through wide prairie lands. On either side spread thousands and thousands of acres of grass lands. Sometimes on one side devoted to rice lands; at others studded with herds upon herds of cattle. Regular clouds of ducks—vicissi as well as muscovy—rose upon the wing as we approached; always beyond gun shot, fortunately for them.[20]

Aghast at this avian feast, Henry and McDonald tried to get ashore to stalk a flock of birds of the savanna but the cattle would have none of it. Perhaps the cattle saw them as invaders trespassing upon sacred territory, hence their response: "Led by a great roar—or whatever is equivalent in oxdom—the herd advanced in mass formation, bellowing lustily, and both McDonald and Henry beat a rapid retreat to the boat."[21]

On Sunday Webber and his colleagues left the Blairmont pumping station and steamed up the river to gain deeper entry into the Upper Berbice and to reach Duckpond, where they hoped to stay for the night. Such a destination seemed foreboding. "The house," as he says, "following the scriptural injunction against the times when the flood cometh, was built upon a hill."[22] They had to reach that house in a time of mud and rising water. As they steamed up the river, the country opened up, to their great wonderment. "The water-fowl visibly increased. Veritable clouds of ducklas, clouds of ducks, and clouds of spurwings, rose on the wing as we turned every bend. It was a veritable naturalist's paradise."[23] This enormous, unpopulated region forced Webber to question "why all these magnificent lands should be empty of population, with Jamaica anxious to unload some 50–60,000 [persons] and the lesser West India islands ready to offer a gentle 10,000? Something is radically wrong with our machinery somewhere. And that is, it seems to me, because our administrators think they know Guiana who only Georgetown know."[24] Such a question brought him back to his original injunction: "Had I the will I would see that every new Governor [of the colony] did trips like these, out of the beaten tracks, and where they can gather enthusiasm for what British Guiana means, and inspiration how to accomplish it."[25] Webber was correct since this remote part of Guyana was unknown even to native Guyanese, and regular contact with this part of Guyana only took place in 1950 with the establishment of air services to the region. Dr. Giglioli observed: "Until 1950, the number of Government officials who had any personal and direct knowledge of the Rupununi might been counted easily on the fingers of one hand. To this day [1969], if one is to be guided by some recent official and other statements regarding the Rupununi, it is evident that ignorance and misconception still prevail."[26]

In a section entitled "Mudlarking in the Dark," Webber describes the scenic changes that took place as they traveled upriver. "From the magnificent wind swept river—the thing is a river, not a creek—and rolling savannas, we come to an uprising of the foliage. Trees threw their branches high overhead. Lovely homesteads were to be observed here and there. The Abary now changed to the familiar landscape of the upper reaches of other rivers of the colony."[27] Farther up the river, the landscape changed again. To pass the time away, they shot at ducks and alligators until they reached Duckpond, where they encamped for the night. Getting to the house, on a hill, 300 or 400 yards from where they had landed, constituted the real drama of the evening. Their tramp in the dark commenced. Their torches were of little value amid the high grasses that abounded. Webber, an old bushman, rued his decision to carry his hammock and his blanket with him. Mud was all around them. He describes what it means to be in the bush, in unforgiving territory:

> We splishsplashed in the mud: sometimes ankle deep, sometimes knee deep— but we never reached Fredericks' waist deep. It was the first time I ever met a bush man who understand the difficulties. Usually it's, "just over there," for five miles: "a little climb," for a soul distressing mountain. "A little water," for floods up to your neck, etc. . . . One struggled through high grass to go from a bit of high mound, down into a slough or trough knee deep. Then, sometimes profanity took the place of laughter. All the while I was holding in dread con-templation the possibility of my [be]coming a dead cropper, with my hammock and blanket splashing in the muddy waters." Eventually, they gained Mt. Ararat and "slept the sleep of peace."[28]

Next morning, they awoke to the glorious vista of Mt. Ararat, where "luscious grasses abounded." At 7 A.M. they returned to their boat to continue their jour-ney up the Araby River through "winding channels and under overhead branches which had to be sometimes backed away as we got to the higher reaches of the river." Thence they came upon "the regular two mouths" of the Mahaicony and Araby rivers, "which must have confused the geographers as to which was par-ent stream and which tributary." Following the right bank, Webber and his party proceeded to the upper reaches of the Berbice, where the scenery continued to change to "another kind of country altogether" and where "homesteads and bush camps peep from the undergrowth. Coconut trees tell of long habitation: and eve-rywhere we gave a friendly salutation before passing on."[29] At noon they reached Crabwood camp, the bridgehead to the Upper Berbice, which brought their river journey to an end.

That afternoon, they lazed around and bathed in the Araby. They broke camp early the following day, loaded their horses, and moved on. The ride through that part of the country "was a sheer delight. First, through the almost twilight of the early morning in a forest glade, and then through the giant ferns, to emerge into comparative open spaces, produced by the fierce forest fires which ravaged all our forests in the last drought."[30] The large expanse of open savannas so far away from Georgetown fascinated Webber. He says, "Always my travels away from the coast had been in high forests, with giant trees; just a clearing here or there made for some camp or the other. To be on an open savannah, mounted on horseback, with freedom to give rein and gallop any where was an entirely novel sensation."[31]

To gallop a horse in that manner was quite a different matter. Twenty years has passed since Webber had sat on a horse for that purpose. Initially, he almost came to a disastrous end when, failing to adjust his stirrups, his horse, Pluto, led him on the "wildest ride" of his life. Pluto "galloped fiercely up to the landing entrance to the house at Friendship and there halted on his own volition. Further would have been disaster for man and beast, for that house is built on top of a cliff 200 feet down to the river. My chief scare was that I was thundering into unknown territory without knowledge of whither to guide."[32] When his frenzied ride had come to an end, his bones shrieked with pain, and he was "palsied with rigid rheumatism."[33] He could not move a finger or dismount from his horse. Sitting countless minutes to recoup his composure, Webber quickly got off the mound, lay upon the boards of the log cabin, and congratulated himself upon having made the journey on horseback to the Upper Berbice.

The bone-racking nature of Webber's journey paid off handsomely. From his house atop the hill, he gazed delightedly upon the placid waters of the Upper Berbice River. The feelings of discovery and elation that this sight evoked reminded him of similar feelings of discovery that enraptured Balboa when he gazed upon the Pacific after his arduous trek through the jungles of Panama in 1513 and which John Keats captured in the liquid freedom of his sonnet "On First Looking into Chapman's Homer," with which Webber opened the third installment of his essay "The Wonder Savannahs of the Great Divide."[34] Reflecting on his near disastrous moment, Webber drew upon Walter Scott's sentiments to express his feelings: "As I lay in that blessed hammock, I recall that only McD's sudden dash off had stopped me, when he had ordered a thunder forward, from repeating that famous line from Scott: 'Charge, Chester, Charge! On, Stanley, on!' Then I remember that Scott adds that those 'were the last words of Marmion.' I had escaped; they would not be recalled as my last words!"[35] After recalling the thrill at seeing a wild horse being lassoed, Webber and his colleagues reinvigorated themselves in "the cool, invigorating and refreshing waters of the upper Berbice."[36] After his bath, Webber mixed with the inhabitants of the area and even tried a new fruit or nut that could not be boiled with salt. "If anyone were to cook it with salt, all the fruits (or nuts whichever you will) on the trees, would contain nothing but water the next season. Mr. Patoir assured me that the superstition was very deeply rooted among the river folk."[37]

The next morning (Tuesday), the three musketeers continued on their journey. Although the two other musketeers questioned Webber's ability to handle his saddle after the previous day's mishap, he assured them that he had no fear at all. McD offered a change of horses, but Webber would have nothing of that. He resolved:

"Better bear the ills we know, than mount another strange steed. I knew how to urge Pluto and how to stop him."[38] Once they were into the little savanna, they encountered convoys of quail, the real game birds. After galloping for a couple thousand yards, they came upon the bank of Kateribisci Creek, where they encountered what at first appeared to be a natural escarpment. However, Kateribisci was once an important center of Dutch culture and achievement. The early Dutch inhabitants mastered the great obstruction that the valley of the Kateribisci imposed by rallying their slaves to undertake this challenge. They "decided to build this great escarpment by combined effort. That work, according to local tradition was accomplished some 250 years ago. The giant forest growth shows that it was no accomplishment of yesterday while the engravings on the tombstone took us to interments of 1733."[39] Webber's journey had taken him back in time long before the various countries of Guyana became a political unit.

After they cleared the forest, the great savanna came into view. Webber was so impressed with this vista that he compared it to the English countryside of Kent and Surrey in springtime. Such a sight allowed him to revel in the beauty of his country: "What a country is this vast British Guiana that could really within a day's journey of Georgetown unfold at every turn such magnificent spectacles; such gorgeous opportunities for wealth and endeavour!" Enamored by the economic possibilities of the land, Webber reiterates his observation that every governor should be made to see this part of the land: "After seeing this country, I certainly would compel him to spend a week with half of his official advisers with him." He believed that the area contained oil deposits and averred: "The great oil fields of Texas are in the centre of the wide open grazing areas of the prairies."[40] Webber spent his day exploring the plains. Later that month, he would continue his discussions with the colonial secretary with regards to the oil-producing capacity of the colony and the hydroelectric plant he was working on establishing.

Ever with an eye for the economic development of the country, Webber also saw the possibilities of developing "home industries" in the area to relieve Georgetown's overpopulation. He gives a glimpse of the people who live in these forgotten areas of the country and their economic activities, particularly in light of the severe economic problems of the country. They produced rice and a sauce called *casareep*, which he believed could be exported to the "great sauce making houses of Lea and Perrins of Worcestershire fame of equally well known sauces and condiments."[41] Hammock making was also a possibility. He thought it was quickly becoming a lost art. Cotton weaving could be encouraged to relieve the movement of young people from the country to the town. He acknowledges that many of the people who practiced cotton weaving had come from Africa. It was "an art hundreds of years old" that they had brought with them to their new land. In speaking of the importance of the area, he observed:

It is all these little up river and up country settlements which are bringing up bright, intelligent boys and girls, with no home industries, that are filling the city and towns with a growing army of youths of no occupation, and just sufficient education to unfit them for one thing and not equip them for another. They flee from opportunity, competence and even wealth, to fields in which not one in 10,000 succeed; and all because there is no machinery for mobilizing, in their own districts, the talent and intelligence which are native in these people.[42]

Webber also spoke of the menace of tigers, "these rogues," as he calls them, to the inhabitants' livelihood and the toll they took on their stock. "Herds of pigs numbering 1,000 in one month may number no more than a few score some months later. Cattle are not decimated to quite such an extent. Indeed, the average tiger would pass by an ox, and stalk a pig instead. Calves suffer more. But cattle suffer enough to make the matter serious." Drawing on the example of Zululand, Natal, where the government paid inhabitants to kill menacing crocodiles, and India, where bounties were offered for the destruction of snakes, Webber believed that the British Guiana government could pay inhabitants to perform a similar function in British Guiana—that is, to eliminate the tigers. It would mean a lot for the people there. He could not but feel sorry for the people who lived there. After speaking to the villagers, Webber opined: "A prosperous people means a prosperous Government, and vice versa. I could not help thinking, as I talked to these people, heard their woes, and saw opportunities going a begging how people were like Government, and Government like people. Ichabod seems written over the doors of them both."[43] Webber tried to give a sense of the inglorious fate of these people by alluding to Ichabod, a biblical character whose name seemed to suggest that "the glory is gone." Webber's journey demonstrated how much more work was left to be done.

Webber demonstrated his scientific knowledge and his acquaintance with the theory of evolution. Observing the activity of the quatta (*Ateles paniscus*), or black spider monkey, Webber claimed that this New World primate "grows to quite respectable sizes, and develops a snow white face to their black bodies. They can be trained to almost human usefulness in the field. They can be taught to sow as well as to reap."[44] While they did not approach the "pithecanthropus erectus . . . it is a pity that all over the world these wonderful reminders of a common ancestry to all creation are being allowed to die out. Perhaps in less than a hundred years every ape would have disappeared from the earth, as completely as the ape man of Java . . . and to many of the intermediate links between different species, from microorganisms to man."[45] He might have been well on the mark. Although the quatta monkey is not among the endangered species, habitat destruction and overhunting can lead to a decrease in its population.

Early on Wednesday morning, Webber set out to visit the tombs and pyramids of the ancient Dutch settlement. Although it was a very important cemetery when it was built, it had fallen to neglect. Webber wanted to decipher what was written on the tombstones, while Henry, the Intrepid, wanted to take one of the headstones back to camp. Bourne, a veritable roughneck, was more insistent. He wanted to take back a skull to Georgetown. He declared: " 'Boss, I want to dig down, maybe we will find a skull!!' He was taking me beyond my depth into directions that I did not care to wander."[46] In his quest for historical relics, Henry wanted to search for a sword and other regalia that were buried with one of the governors of the ancient territory. While there was no time for excavations, "a la Tutankhamen," they were able to observe the tomb of no less a person than "an ex-President of the Legislative Council, who doubtless, as was the fashion of his day, discharged on occasion the duties of Officer Administering the Government [acting governor]."[47]

The health of these inhabitants and the decimation of the American Indians also troubled Webber. Mr. Patoir lost six of his twelve children, although he had an "ordered house." Nonetheless, his sympathies lay with the American Indians, who were decimated by various diseases. "First of all, it was small pox of the last century; then came influenza, and now comes measles; not to say anything of the incidental and endemic diseases like malaria and syphilis."[48] However, all was not sorrow. While these "goodly country folks have their sorrows they also have their divergences," which is one reason why Webber ended his travelogue with the following bit of gossip about

how A had eloped into Brazil with Miss B, in defiance of the laws of consanguinity. How Miss B had subsequently returned to the patriarchal roof tree and formed new liaison with Mr. C. But, mercy on us, it appears that Mr. C was not himself free from other entanglements as his morganic [sic] wife from the other side and with the aid of her relatives carried fire and sword, very literarily, into the camp of her faithless swain. B and C escaped with their lives and have since fled the district."[49]

This was the humorous side of Webber to which his daughter Edith referred.

The marauding tigers fascinated Webber, particularly during the last days of his trip. They took a heavy toll upon the stock and the hunting dogs, the training of which involved a "tiresome and weary process." However, it was not beyond him to take home a tiger skin as a trophy of his triumphant journey, which remained a pest to his wife's life since "it positively refuses to cure—and its bouquet is not relished in a lady's boudoir." Taking leave of his readers and hoping that they enjoyed "their imaginary journey as much as we did the actual one," he asked his readers to forgive him if at times he wandered from his story or grew ribald. "I ask them to remember that 'the greatest of all of these [virtues] is Charity!'"[50]

Although the savanna lands are close to Georgetown, they appeared so far away to the people on the coast. In 1930 the area seemed outside their consciousness. "Exploring Unbroken British Guiana" opens up that world and makes it accessible to them. As far as Webber was concerned, this part of Guyana represented a new world that needed to be explored and utilized for the benefit of the people. It also needed to become a part of their mental landscape and a reality in the minds of the governor and his aides who were responsible for developing the colony. When he drew upon Keats and sought inspiration from his sonnet, he hoped to kindle that awe and breathlessness of discovery that was so important if a people were to develop their mental horizons. In the process, he used the probative dimension of poetry and science to discover the familiar and unfamiliar to come to grips with the unknown. Were he so inclined, he could have drawn upon Milton to capture that world of surprise and imaginative encounter that Milton displayed in *Paradise Lost* when he observed:

> Satan from hence now on the lower stair
> That scal'd by steps of Gold to Heav'n Gate
> Looks down with wonder at the sudden view
> Of all this World at once. As when a Scout
> Through dark and desert wayes with peril gone
> All night; at last by break of chearful dawne
> Obtains the brow of some high-climbing Hill,
> Which to his eye discovers unaware
> The goodly prospect of some foreign land
> First-seen, or some renown'd Metropolis
> With glistering Spires and Pinnacles adorn'd,
> Which now the Rising Sun guilds with his beams.[51]

In 1969, when he wrote *Demerara Doctor*, Dr. Giglioli reflected on the Araby and the savannas he saw in 1927 and their subsequent despolation. In those days, there were few settlements along the Araby, and cattle occupied the savannas. Rice cultivation and a rise in the use of motor cars and speedboats made the lonely savannas "accessible to scores of trigger-happy weekend sportsmen from Georgetown, and have suffered great disruption of wild life; on Sunday nights they return to the city with their trophies, leaving behind them a trail of floating alligator corpses to drift up and down with the tides for several days, polluting the air and the water."[52] In the 1930s, at the very place that Webber had visited, the number of ducks on the Araby had been very much reduced. The savannas had been opened up to a new population.

When Webber's trip ended, he, too, took his trophy back to Georgetown. The area still remained a naturalist's paradise, a wonder to behold. In the debate on the reopening of the Bartica-Kaburi road that took place just before Webber undertook his exploration, the Hon. R. E. Brassington observed: "I know nothing about this road and I am going to display my ignorance by speaking here. I am afraid that a lot of ignorance has been displayed by members in regard to the interior of the Colony. I know nothing about, but I am certainly not going support the road going to Butukari." On the contrary, Webber could exclaim with confidence: "If any other Member of this Council has gone over that road it is the speaker [meaning Webber]. I have gone over that road."[53] It was that knowledge of the physical country that made Webber such an effective representative of his people. He had explored his country. He knew it more intimately than most and possessed the oratorical skill to express his views coherently, convincingly and with aplomb.

CHAPTER ELEVEN

PATRIOT AND BUSINESSMAN

In every representative assembly in the world there is usually one man who stands out as the Tribune of the People. Such a man will make a mistake but such a man is vitally necessary. Mr. Webber has filled the role of Tribune with distinction. An orator who can move his hearers to laughter and to tears, Mr. Webber is the man you need to be ever vigilant in your cause, but ever ready to encourage Government in any measure which will benefit you. . . . An electoral district would be proud to have Mr. Webber as its own representative.
　　—"A POLLING-DAY LETTER TO THE VOTERS," *Daily Chronicle*, September 18, 1930

Verily man has been given dominion over all things, and the last enemy to be underfoot is death. I ponder as I fly. If death is conquered, then there must be no more births. The theme is not attractive. There are worse things than death which is, after all, only a manifestation of life, and probably just as good.
　　—A. R. F. WEBBER, "Hors D'Oeuvre of the Ocean Passage"

AFTER WEBBER RETURNED FROM THE IDYLLIC ARABY AND RUPUNUNI, he still had to face the rough and tumble of elections. At that point of his career, he was well liked and respected by the electorate, although he remained a thorn in the government's side. Penning an election biography on Webber, Reno Rohini observed that "having done much traveling in British Guiana, especially in the interior and being an observant and well-read man, he made good use of his opportunity to study the country's problems. He acquired a first-hand knowledge of things and was well-informant [*sic*] on the various topics and discussion of the times."[1] And well might he be. Webber needed such knowledge as he traversed the country, advocated on the people's behalf, and sought to make the government reverse itself on the constitution as well as on its economic policy. Rohini noted that "his adherents were the masses in the majority, while his detractors were quite a few of the 'classes.'"[2]

As the new elections loomed (they were scheduled for September 18), the Electives fanned out into the community to present their views about the defects of the 1928 constitution and the need to adopt one that reflected the views of the people more accurately. On March 15, 1930, in his contribution to the debate on a loan of £12,000 to the government from the Colonial Development Fund to build the Bartica-Kaburi Road and its extension to Butukari on the Essequebo, Webber made it clear that from the time the constitution was changed, "this colony has been cursed with the most powerful Administration and the most incompetent in the history of the country from the time when it came under the British flag."[3] Therefore, his main task was to make the government more responsive to the needs of the people and to allow the elected members to participate in the governance of their land. As far as Webber was concerned, constitutional and economic reforms were the most important issues that faced his people. A week and a half earlier at Danielstown on the Essequebo coast and "amidst loud applause," Webber "explained that the Constitution question was a most important one [issue] at the present time."[4] He urged his listeners to reelect the fourteen Electives so that they could work to change the constitution. Acknowledging that R. E. Brassington and S. M. de Freitas, two of the Electives, were good men, he advised his audience: "Get your constitution changed first and then change your representatives—every day, if you like."[5]

Even as he prepared for the elections, Webber found time to make a radio address to the members of the International Shortwave Club in Canada and the United States on the possibilities of investing in Guyana. In "one of the most interesting and enjoyable programmes ever broadcast locally," Webber argued that Guyana provided an "opportunity for a man of genius and inspiration to plan and execute a great railway venture from Georgetown, the capital of British Guiana to Manaos, the capital of the state of Amazonas."[6] That was his dream. It was also his uncle's dream. Such an endeavor would open up the South American continent to world trade and bring it closer to the developed-nation status that one saw in the United States and Canada. With great prescience, Webber exclaimed: "In the great upland and unexplored territory, the present products are diamonds, gold, timber and bauxite, the native ore of aluminum. In this last ore will yet be traced the future greatness of British Guiana. In the nineteenth century every country which grew great was the one in which iron and coal were found.... In aluminum is a metal which will prove, in the twentieth century, what iron and steel were to the nineteenth: it will replace steel, copper and bronze."[7] He also extolled the scenic beauty of the country in his address.

On June 28, on the eve of his departure to attend the British Commonwealth Labour Conference in London, Webber made yet another radio broadcast in which he sought to draw pioneers to his country. He drew on the example of Sir Walter Raleigh, who "believed in the destiny of Manaos and the golden city. He it was that threw his coat in the pathway of Queen Elizabeth, rather than that the Virgin Queen should have soiled her dainty slippers. Such are the men nursed in chivalry and steeped in adventure. Hundreds of years afterwards we, the inheritors of their imagination realize that Raleigh's dreams were based on something solid and something true." Webber was bent on proclaiming the oil-producing potentials of Guyana, declaring that "geologists and others have assured us that British Guiana must share the prosperity of Venezuela and be one of the great oil producing countries of the world of the 20th century." He also extolled the possibilities inherent in Guyana forests, its gold and diamond deposits, and its mighty waterfalls, "which offer all the necessary power for converting those vast woods into first class wood pulp and even into manufacturing paper."[8]

The next day Webber left British Guiana to attend the British Commonwealth Labour Conference that commenced on July 21. A few days later, his colleagues left Guyana to attend the same conference. At that conference, Webber raised questions about support for the sugar industry and the introduction of a workmen's compensation act. Webber and his colleagues hoped to get the Labour movement to use its influence to assist them in these areas. In their memorandum, Webber and his colleagues raised several important points vis-à-vis what they called "Embargo by Capitalistic Government against exploitation of natural resources of [the] Colony in oil, water power and bauxite." First, they insisted that since the Labour Party affirmed, as an article of faith, that the British colonial sugar industry was "not entitled to protection in the Home Markets, . . . we cannot discover by what process of reason it should be demanded that British capital should be protected in the markets of an impoverished country like British Guiana. The British Government while insisting on Free Trade in England preaches and practices protection in British Guiana though the country can ill afford it."[9]

Second, the delegation chastised the British government for refusing to explore the oil deposits in the country even as it prevented other countries from investing in such activities. Third, they demanded that they be allowed to look for capital in other areas and from other sources. They noted that there were men in British Guiana who had friends in Holland, in the United States, in Brazil, and even in France and Germany, who were prepared to put millions of dollars into the development of the oil resources of British Guiana, but they were forbidden to do so by the Colonial Office that was acting on behalf of capitalistic groups in England. Granting that the Colonial Office might not want to have such important resources in the hands of foreigners, particularly in a time of a national emergency, the delegates were willing to concede that they would be wiling to stipulate "in the licenses or leases of occupancy that the Crown reserved to itself the right at any period of national emergency, to commandeer and sequestrate the produce from all oil wells on given terms, or even to assume possession and operation of lands and wells on terms stipulated beforehand."[10]

In keeping with their thrust for political and economic independence (or certainly self-government), the Guyanese delegates demanded the right "to exploit its natural resources with equal freedom as Canada, Australia, New Zealand or South Africa." They regretted that "under its form of Government it has not the same liberty of action as the Dominions named."[11] In other words, Webber and his colleagues wanted British Guiana to be put on the same political footing as the other Commonwealth countries that enjoyed dominion status within the empire. It did not hurt that most of the people who lived in those countries were white, a form of "kit and kin" policy. The delegates affirmed that while those embargoes lasted, the country could never develop to its potential.

In terms of strengthening the social fabric, the members of the executive of the BGLU wanted to introduce a workmen's compensation act and a workmen's compensation court, and to establish a minimum wage in the country. They also urged the Labour Party to assist them to establish an eight-hour workday (some workers worked as long as twelve and fifteen hours a day) in the colony. They ended their memorandum on "Industrial and Social Legislation with Special Reference to Workmen's Compensation Act" with the following admonition: "Social legislation is urgently demanded in British Guiana if its labouring girls and women are not to be utterly ruined and shamelessly exploited."[12] They were determined that the conditions of the working people in Guyana should be brought up to twentieth-century standards.

Although Webber had devoted a considerable portion of his adult life to politics, publishing, and writing, he also showed an interest in business. As he said in the debate of the Essequebo Land Settlement scheme, when the government acquired Plantation Anna Regina for the purpose of maintaining sugar cultivation in the district and settling the labor population permanently on the land, "I am not a sugar planter or an agriculturalist."[13] Yet Webber had invested "90 percent of his capital in that undertaking."[14] In 1929 he obtained a lease of approximately 115 square miles of forestland within the Bartica-Kaburi Forest Reserve, with an option to use the timber on another 76 square miles for the purpose of manufacturing pulp paper. He was also granted a timber lease under the condition that he took no more than one year to raise the necessary capital for his company.

On February 19 Webber wrote to the commissioner of mines for a concession to erect a hydroelectric plant on the Essequebo River or on one of its tributaries to operate "wood pulp mills, saw mills, and general logging operations [that] . . . will probably be constructed to develop upwards to 50,000 horse power." Additionally, he wanted the right "to distribute and to sell power to any consumer who may be disposed to buy that and for that purpose be allowed to construct transmission lines over any available Crown or Government lands." Once the plant was approved and erected, he requested that "no other concession would be granted to any other party to erect a similar plant within a prescribed radius, and within a given number of years."[15]

When Webber made his request, there was no legislation on the books regarding this particular endeavor, so the governor or the government had no statutory power to grant Webber such a concession. Additionally, the Colonial Office did not trust Webber. To get over its dilemma, the governor requested that Webber draft a bill "embodying the various points raised by him in connection with this application."[16] Subsequently, the Hon. Alfred Crane, a solicitor and colleague in the Legislative Council, formulated a draft bill that he submitted to the governor as a means of offering guidance in the matter.

Once Webber's request reached the Colonial Office, the authorities began to stake out their positions. It was decided that

> no concession should be given, and no preliminary agreement should be entered into, until reasonable precise information as to the scope of the project, its estimated cost, and its possibilities, has been supplied.... When such details have been supplied, the local administration, aided by expert advice, will be in a position to consider the advisability of entering into a preliminary agreement, a time limit, reasonable with regard to all the circumstances, should be fixed. One year might possibly be suitable. It is important that a time limit of a reasonable character should be fixed, otherwise the way would be blocked for others.[17]

It was not so much that the officials were unalterably opposed to such a scheme. Lord Passfield, in his capacity as secretary of state for the colonies, wanted to be certain that Webber's scheme fitted into British colonial policy, that Webber and his business associates had sufficient capital to sustain their operation if a concession was granted, and that the government could control the rate that would be charged for electricity. To protect British interests, he also demanded that any company formed for the purpose of carrying out the concession should be a British concern with a majority of British directors on the board and should stipulate, if possible, that the plant, machinery, and equipment should be of British manufacture.[18] An unnamed official in the Colonial Office thought that Webber should ask a British company to do the work even if Americans controlled the project. All colonial development had to be in Britain's interests. It was in keeping with the Melchett-Tillett Report, which encouraged that any scheme of development within the Crown colonies involving considerable expenditure should use equipment manufactured in Britain.[19]

Webber found himself in a catch-22 situation. The Colonial Office wanted to see a draft of any proposed legislation before it was brought to the Legislative Council. Yet it was unwilling to grant him a license for the plant until he had determined where the plant would be located, which, as Webber acknowledged, would incur great expenditure. Webber was not ready to incur such an expenditure until he was in possession of a "definite undertaking by Government however guarded that undertaking may be, that when Government was finally satisfied on the result of such examinations and surveys, that a concession would be granted on such terms as may have been decided beforehand, or as may be decided would be mutually beneficial."[20] According to his estimates, such a plant would have cost him and his associates approximately $5 million. To make things easier, the government would have had to grant him a prospecting license to undertake the preliminary surveys, which would have led to a preliminary agreement and finally to exclusive rights "for the sale and distribution of power on terms that may be mutually agreeable."[21] However, the Colonial Office tried to make things even more difficult for him by wanting to know the financial standing of the other promoters of the undertaking. This incensed Webber. He wrote to the colonial secretary:

Names, brokers and underwriters mean nothing. I consider I am a sufficiently responsible member of the local community to be given full consideration in any such propositions. My friends and associates say they will put up the money when they see the nature of the concession and terms available from Government. The Government on the other hand is apparently inclined to give nothing until the capitalists put up the money, and thus we reach the perpetual deadlock. Unfortunately, the Colony is more in need of capital to finance such undertakings, than is capital in need of the opportunities in British Guiana, and I fear that the Colony will remain forever stagnant, while this policy of cat and mouse continues.[22]

Webber's next difficulty with the Colonial Office derived from the suggestion that his company should be "a British concern with a majority of British directors on the Board." In his letter, he reminded the secretary of state that the report on the hydroelectric possibilities of Guyana was published in 1919 and was available for all (including engineers in the United Kingdom and Canada) to see. Yet no one seemed willing to invest in or explore the opportunities the report suggested. In exasperation, he declaimed: "Writing as a Legislator, it seems gratuitously harassing and detrimental to the progress of the Colony that any measures of development should be held up for the protection of British investors who show no inclination to take advantage of the opportunities offered."[23]

On April 24 the colonial secretary wrote to Webber reiterating most of the points that had been made in Lord Passfield's memorandum. On April 28 Webber asked the secretary of state to cable his general approval "as to whether Government may in the first place pass an ordinance to enable it to grant me the necessary locating and survey license, and thereafter to grant power to generate current for my own use. The wider subject of a franchise to develop power for distribution and sale could then be reserved for future correspondence."[24] The next month Webber traveled to London to pursue his scheme and to raise capital for his operations. Governor Edward Denham had looked upon Webber's proposal favorably and had advised Lord Passfield that "Mr. Webber has shown keen interest in the development of the interior both in and out of the Legislative Council and deserves encouragement in his effort to attract capital to the Colony."[25] After all, Webber had begun his career in Bartica, knew the interior better than many Guyanese, and was related to one of the most distinguished families of that township.

In August 1930 Webber was in London for the British Commonwealth Labour Conference. While he was there, he looked out for his own interests. He had several interviews with the officials from the Colonial Office. On August 15 he met with E. R. Darnley, head of the West Indian Department, and observed that the secretary of state was inclined to grant him a concession for his hydroelectric scheme. Webber agreed that he needed to get a qualified engineer to examine the site, was prepared to buy British machinery, and set up a board of directors with a majority of British directors. Since he had to return to Guyana for the forthcoming election, he needed a letter authorizing a survey and the assurance that when he completed the survey and formed a company as the government had requested, the government would grant him a concession. Once he had fulfilled those conditions, he would receive a concession to take water power, a position that Darnley's letter to Webber on August 16 reiterated.

On September 12, six days after Webber returned from London to fight the general election, the colonial officials were still trying to determine if they should give him a concession to erect his hydroelectric plant. In a letter to the governor, Lord Passfield submitted that an agreement made by the governor of Nigeria and Northern Rhodesia Tin Mines Limited and an ordinance enacted in Palestine by the Palestine Electric Corporation could serve as guides to the sort of legislation that might be useful in Webber's case. However, the matter kept dragging on, and Webber never got the necessary permission to construct his hydroelectric plant, although he was in a position to raise the necessary capital and certainly do a good job in carrying out his project. The last word we hear on this project was a telegram the governor sent to the secretary of state for the colonies: "Your dispatch of the 19th August, No. 225. Wood pulp industry. In view of the importance and development which am desirous of encouraging shall be glad if Wood, Conservator of Forest, can be instructed to study possibilities as fully as possible before he leaves. He should see the big pulping machinery manufacturers. Walmsley has been mentioned."

Webber was not successful in his endeavor to establish a hydroelectric power plant in Guyana, but it was not for the lack of trying. He did not get a license because his company was not controlled by the British, even though in the end he was prepared to make such a concession. Although some Labourites supported his efforts to change the constitution and encouraged him to exact a certain amount of labor unity at home, they were not ready to assist him on the economic front. He could not know that even the Fabians had accepted the right of Europeans to occupy the tropics "by rejecting the notion that the natives of a territory had any natural right to its potential wealth."[26] Lord Passfield, the secretary of state, was a Fabian socialist. Even a progressive socialist such as Lord Olivier argued that there "can be no reasonable question of locking up these sources of wealth because certain barbarous tribes, as the result of migration of centuries, are found in this day and age sparsely inhabiting countries which can produce them."[27] This, of course, may have been a version of the "Black Man's Burden."[28]

The same day Webber left for England he was unceremoniously fired from the *New Daily Chronicle* and replaced by Wilson Marshall, an Englishman, who joined the newspaper as a cartoonist in 1927. There was no hint of trouble, and no explanation was given for his dismissal. It may have been that the insiders knew something the outsiders did not know. According to the *Daily Chronicle*, although Webber's dismissal "came as a great shock to the general public but in journalistic circles, it was not wholly unexpected. In fact, it was known several days."[29] Webber, it seems, had fallen out of favor with Cannon, with whom he had formed the Popular Party and founded the *New Daily Chronicle*.[30] In a magnificent cartoon, "A Lover's Quarrel, Or, The Tragedy of a Shattered Romance," published in the *Daily Chronicle* on July 6, Webber is seen in tears as he sits on the arm of a couch entitled *New Daily Chronicle*. In his right hand he holds a handkerchief with which he dries his eyes, while his left hand is outstretched to Cannon, who commiserates with his sorrow. Cannon, in his turn, stands erect. He has his right hand in his pocket; his left hand is raised to his eyes, though he is not as teary eyed as Webber, as he holds his hat with his free fingers. The following dialogue appears at the bottom of the cartoon:

> Love-Sick Artie: And must it end like this? Is the great love we bear each other to count for naught? Why should we part when parting gives us pain?
>
> Miss Nell: I am sorry dear, so sor-ry dear, b-b-but we must, no matter how it hurts.
>
> N.B.—There was mild sensation in local journalistic and political circles during the week when it became known that there was a breach between the Hons. Cannon and A. R. F. Webber, the David and Jonathan of local politics, which had resulted in Mr. Webber severing his connection with the New Daily Chronicle of Events, a paper which he founded in 1926.

When Webber left for London at the beginning of July, he was sure he would be back in the country before the elections in September. Under the new constitution, a candidate could be nominated and elected in his absence, although there seemed to be some confusion on this point.[31] However, Webber had not even arrived in London before the jockeying started for his legislative position. On July 9 a West Coast Berbice voter bewailed that Webber had "left the Colony in the interest of the Colony, yet somebody is essaying to usurp his place as representative for West Berbice." He observed: "It would be a calamity if this great statesman, debater, orator, and journalist is not elected. He is a terror to the enemy of the masses, and a doughty guardian of the inherent rights of the inhabitants of British Guiana. The seats of Sir John Sion and the members of the Indian Commission were held inviolate during their absence from Great Britain by the Conservatives, Labour and Liberal alike, because these parties admitted they were serving the Empire."[32] He urged his fellow voters to remember Webber's services and to support him enthusiastically during the next election.

Although Webber was out of the country, he campaigned for his new seat, Western Berbice, his old district having been divided into three separate constituencies (Western Berbice, Eastern Berbice, and Berbice River District). In a letter to his constituents, he informed them that he was conducting the public's business and reminded them that he might not be present on nomination day (September 8); he left his fate in their hands with this reminder:

> I am in your service today though I am 4,000 miles away, and, just as I have never betrayed you during 10 years of such service, so I fear no betrayal at your hands on Nomination Day.
> Voters, Friends and Co-Workers
> YOUR FRIEND WEBBER
> Appeals to you that there should be
> NO OPPOSITION
> Let that be your slogan—NO OPPOSITION![33]

Such a gallant call from abroad and the enthusiastic letter from the West Coast Berbice voter did not dampen the determination of Peer Bacchus, successful rice and cattle farmer and a friend of Webber, to challenge Webber's candidacy. Bacchus argued that he was not opposed to Webber but felt betrayed by Webber's decision to fight for the Western Berbice seat rather than the Eastern Berbice seat. Bacchus claimed that on various occasions, Webber gave him "every encouragement to seek political honours. It was only four days before he left the colony that he informed me he was going to stand for Western Berbice and he assured me in the same breath that he would like me to win a seat in the Legislative Council."[34] Bacchus claimed that he and Webber had reached an agreement, which Webber felt compelled to break because of the Electives' pact. Bacchus essayed that the contest between them would be a friendly one because of their friendship. He stated that after Webber tried to dissuade him from running against him, they arrived at the following agreement:

> [Webber:] If I am in the colony, I would go on your platform and tell the people I would like to see you elected a member of the Legislative Council but of course I won't like you to win me. The only thing I ask you is to give me your word that there would be no election petition whoever wins.
>
> [Bacchus:] I promised him our fight would be as clean as possible and we parted the best friends.[35]

Webber, of course, had his defenders. In an immediate response, Charles Bristol, a fervent supporter of Webber, disagreed sharply with Bacchus's interpretation of events and declared publicly that Bacchus had asked him to use his influence "to get Mr. Webber to accept the call from Corentyne, because he, Mr. Bacchus, intended to stand for West Berbice. I asked him whether he would also oppose his friend Mr. Luckoo and why he did not try the electorate of the Corentyne. He said that he would oppose all comers, excluding Mr. Webber whom he thought was the only person to defeat him at the polls in West Berbice."[36] Prior to his reported conversation with Webber, Bacchus had asked other constituents to intervene with Webber to dissuade him from running for the West Berbice seat. Webber, it is reported, "bluntly refused to do so." Bristol concluded that he would not have written his letter to the editor except for "the half veiled innuendoes made against Mr. Webber who is absent and who had proved himself publicly a friend of Mr. Bacchus." Under the circumstances, he had no choice but to oppose Bacchus's candidacy because he thought that Bacchus was not equipped sufficiently to fill the role of representative in the Legislative Council, "and what is more, he stands opposed to one of the keenest legislators that ever graced a legislative hall."[37] The *Daily Chronicle* also supported Webber. In spite of Bacchus's many outstanding qualities, the newspaper thought it unfortunate that "he should be opposed to a man who is undoubtedly the ablest and best informed publicist and politician in the country; and moreover a man who has rendered yeoman service, not only to the particular division, but to the colony as a whole."[38]

After the close of the Commonwealth Labour Conference, Webber returned to Guyana on September 6 via Trinidad to be home in time for nomination day. In Guyana, the battle royal had begun. The Webber-Bacchus contest turned out to be the most spirited. The *Daily Chronicle* called it a "Homeric struggle," one of the keenest contests among the fourteen seats that were being contested. Bacchus was wealthier than Webber, and some of Webber's friends assisted Bacchus. However, Webber remained his defiant self and defined himself as the defender of the working people.

The first thing Webber did upon returning to British Guiana was to report about his trip to England at a BGLU public meeting. He explained that his delegation held out for the improved conditions of the workers and greater political and legislative privileges for the people. He believed that the working people of Guyana could achieve their goals only if they were better organized. Citing his leftward-leaning position, he said: "It might be asked why it was that he had identified himself with the Labour movement. It was because the success or development of every country must rise from something, therefore progress and development of every country was determined on what it was based upon." He saw Trinidad as the model: "When Capt. Cipriani spoke of their movement, he spoke of a working membership of 70,000 [persons]."[39] He was happy to report that their demand for a workmen's compensation act was well received, and every effort was made to strengthen the educational system in the country. Children should not be thrown out of school at an early age, more schools should be kept open, and everything must be done to retain their head teachers, who were being dismissed because of the worsening conditions in the sugar industry.

Although Bacchus had promised a clean fight, his campaign sought to depict Webber as a "stranger" and Bacchus as one of their own. S. W. Dolphin, a speaker at one of Bacchus's rallies, reminded the audience that it would be an inspiration to their children to know that "*one of their own* had the supreme honor to sit with representatives of His Majesty the King and plead their own cause. Let them consider the great moral effect on their children to know that after they had done their best in making themselves competent their activities would not be restricted to the Village Council."[40] In fact, an editorial in the *Daily Chronicle* accused Bacchus of being more concerned with local problems than he was with the colonial problem and suggested that since the future prosperity depended on how well one treated the latter problem, West Berbice "will be well advised to eschew such a representative."[41] Hence, the newspaper had no problem in endorsing Webber. Although he may have made some mistakes in the past and might have neglected some of the local problems of West Berbice in favor of wider colonial issues, "in assessing his value to the body politic consideration should be given to the fact, that he paid attention to the colonial problems, thus treating first things first and leaving secondary matters for future adjustment."[42]

At one of Bacchus's campaign meetings, he accused Webber of doing nothing for West Berbice; he read a letter that suggested Webber was more interested in his own financial well-being than he was with his constituents' financial problems; and he intimated that Webber had gone to London to feather his own financial nest. Lucie Smith, a BGLU comrade of Webber, endorsed Bacchus and also accused Webber of doing very little for West Berbice. He intoned: "Look at the rotten state of the villages; consider how their standard of living had got reduced! What was the use of a representative who after talking for ten years had got not a single thing done for their improvement? Why, if merely to talk while they were dying out was what they chiefly wanted a representative to do, he should say, go on choosing any talker they pleased."[43]

Initially, Webber was losing ground against this onslaught since he was not in the country to defend himself. Once he returned to the campaign trail, things began to turn around. In its editorial the day before the election, the *Daily Chronicle* reported that Webber's presence on the "battlefield" had wrought a complete metamorphosis. It averred that "the extraordinary personality of the man Webber, his persuasiveness, his eloquence—the self-same qualities which he employs to sway Government in his advocacy of any cause on behalf of the people—are assisting him in breaking down the barriers of an unwarranted and unjustified opposition, and bringing under his banner men and women voters who had previously been seduced by the parrot cry 'give the local man a chance.'"[44]

Meanwhile, Webber was making a mas' of his own in the short time he was on the campaign trail. In spite of his eloquence and oratorical skills, Webber also possessed a dramatic touch, a characteristic that his daughter remembered well. At a "monster meeting" held in his support, T. T. Thompson described Webber as "an old war horse" who knew "the ins and outs of every phase of public life" and who should be returned to office "in gratitude for and appreciation of services rendered not only to Berbice [his former constituency] but also to the whole Colony."[45] Of course, Webber's supporter had to refute the allegation that Webber had done nothing for his local constituents, the most trenchant charge that was made against him. Bristol, who had written in support of Webber previously, observed that although Bacchus was one of them, "Mr. Bacchus never gave any help to his people, and it would be base ingratitude to elect him instead of Mr. A. R. F. Webber."[46] Although Webber denied he had ever encouraged Bacchus to seek public office, the best line came from Ramnarine, a supporter of Webber who urged the voters to stick with Webber and concluded: "Since Mr. Bacchus was already a 'Peer' and was welcomed to the House of Lords, he may well leave the 'Hon.' of the L[egislative] C[ouncil] to poor Mr. Webber, the true and tried."[47]

Webber's supporters did not disappoint him. When the battle was over, Webber had won by 29 votes, his having received 146 votes as opposed to Bacchus's 117 votes. When the newly elected members of the Legislative Council reconvened, Webber was elected as the whip of the Electives once more, and Cannon and John D'Aguiar were appointed to examine the Customs' Tariff and to report on what steps could be taken with regard to the British Preferential Tariff. Given the love affair that went on between Webber and the *Daily Chronicle*, on October 18 Webber became a columnist and a consultant with the editorial department of the newspaper.

As was his custom, Webber wrote about his trip back to the West Indies. Having always admired the opposite sex and not being afraid of adventure, his trip provided opportunities to exercise these tendencies. The first leg of his trip from London aboard the S.S. *Crijnssen* brought him into contact with a beautiful senorita from Venezuela, whom he could not stop admiring. He was fifty years old; she was nineteen or twenty years old and was returning from her honeymoon in Europe. That did not stop him from plunging into rapturous delight and admiration. Lyrically, he sounded like a contemporary rap artist. According to Webber, she had eyes "that could make a train jump its tracks. I had long before always thought the women of Caracas the most beautiful in the world, but then I had never been to Merida." She was a brunette but, as he rhapsodized, "If she from Caracas [she] could make a train jump its tracks, [if] she from Merida [she] would make it stand up on end."[48]

Not satisfied with expressing such admiration, he had to gain her attention. He could not speak a word of Spanish; she could not speak a word of English. But she danced like a sylph, and he had to dance with her: "Dancing with her, and not being able to exchange a word, made me know what hell Tantalus was in. But she had eyes that could talk; so the trip could not end in the Gulf of Paria."[49] One would remember that Tantalus was the son of Zeus who was invited to share in the food of the gods. He abused his privilege and was punished (or tantalized) with hunger and thirst in Tartarus, the deepest portion of the underworld. Webber was intent on seeing how far he could go with this young woman. Stuck overnight in Trinidad, he was determined to meet "the honeymooning couple." He was not afraid of being plunged underfoot.

They were all staying at the Hotel de Paris in Port of Spain. He passed his time there as he waited for his airplane ride, which was scheduled to leave for Georgetown the following morning. He became distracted as he drank white wine in the hotel lobby. The white wine began to taste like vinegar when the "Maid from Merida" noticed his distraction. Desperation overcame him, and he threw caution to the wind:

A hurried inquiry through her husband-interpreter, a wonderful smile, glistening teeth, and Richard was himself again. I confessed preoccupation at the chances of feeding the fishes in the Caribbean. Oh no, she assured me, I was born lucky and so would die happy. Then and there I decided on the flight, after turning what compliments I could. It is very embarrassing paying compliments to a radiantly beautiful woman through a husband-interpreter but in Latin America that is allowed. [It] flatters husband and pleases wife. And I am a Roman.[50]

And he lived to tell the story.

British Guiana awaited, and Webber had to return to Georgetown to file his nomination papers for election. The next morning he was off to Cocorite, Port of Spain, to engage in his other nail-biting adventure: his flight to Georgetown aboard a Pan-American airplane, the second airplane ride he would undertake in his life. Although he liked adventure, he was not the bravest of passengers. He had to summon all of his courage to make this airborne journey. As he said: "I had already flown once and emerged with safety; but flying for minutes and for hours are two different things."[51] And then the plane he was about to board was not as large as the twenty-seat plane he had flown in at Croydon, England. This was a little thing that carried four passengers, including the wireless operator. In addition, there was a pilot and his assistant.

Webber thought that the takeoff, perhaps the scariest part of the flight, was not so bad. "It was more like racing a surf boat, but the waves seemed to follow and threaten and engulf from behind; but in a trice we were skimming the surface, and then rising gracefully into the air. . . . Gradually, she rose higher and higher over the Gulf of Paria with the ships growing smaller and smaller below." He describes the town of San Fernando from the air. The well-kept cane fields interspersed with roads or roadways looked "like bits of thread from the air. Palms swaying gracefully, hillsides sloping with perfect abandon. Yes, everything was beautiful but I wished the pilot would clear the land and come back to a decent elevation over the water."[52]

Webber felt more comfortable after he was in the air for about half an hour. At the end of two hours he had regained control over his nervousness. Thereafter, he relaxed and slept for an hour. When he woke up, he began to see familiar sights. The water below began to change back to "mud green." As he got closer to Georgetown, he saw all the familiar places, some hardly out of their slumbers. "Queenstown, Zorg, Suddie, with Hampton Court punt dragging its weary self down to bring us back unsaleable sugar. Then that gorgeous sight, the mouth of the Essequebo, spreading nearly as far as the eye can reach." Then, miracle of miracles, while they were way above the clouds, the wireless operator spoke to Port of Spain and Georgetown, which led Webber to observe: "Verily man has been given dominion over all things, and the last enemy to be under foot is death. I ponder as I fly. If death is conquered, then there must be no more births. The theme is not attractive. There are worse things than death; which is, after all, only a manifestation of life, and probably just as good."[53] Webber, it seems, was preoccupied with death. He certainly voiced his concerns about it a lot, but then he took so much pleasure in living and in his adventures. Such was his temperament. Even as he lived he was in death. In fact, death was just another phase of life, which meant that one really had no reason to fear it.

The trip from Trinidad and Tobago, his former home, had taken four hours. He was happy to be home. He had appropriated British Guiana as his own. "The Demerara River was mine. Put me in it, was my mental comment, anyhow, head or tail foremost, but I would make the bank."[54] He had sent no word to his family in British Guiana that he would be returning by airplane or at what time he would arrive. But "Henry the Intrepid," his dear friend from their trip up the Araby, was there on a tug to meet him. Webber was happy to see him there, hence his exclamation: "His faith had made him whole. It is good to have friends like those."[55] It was good, also, to be home where one was loved and accepted.

CHAPTER TWELVE

WEBBER: A KEYNESIAN

British Guiana alone cannot right the world's under consumption; but it can see to it that it does not aggravate under consumption within its own borders. Let us stretch our vision. Let us look beyond the immediate horizon. Away with cringing fear which bids us shiver. The night must pass. Panic helps nobody. Let us greet the unseen with cheer.
—A. R. F. WEBBER, "I Am an Economic Heretic"

Look after unemployment and the Budget will look after itself. . . . We must save if spending is to be healthy, and we must spend if savings is to be healthy.
—JOHN MAYNARD KEYNES, quoted in Robert Skidelsky, *John Maynard Keynes*

Woman must have a high estimation of her sex and she must want the best of everything for her sex and the only way for that to be attained in British Guiana is for each woman in her own sphere to endeavour to do her best always remembering the brilliant members of her sex past and present who have striven and won. . . . We want British Guiana to be better, happier and godlier. Do you my sisters take each your part in the work?
—GERTIE WOOD, "An Ideal Womanhood in British Guiana"

WHEN THE NEW LEGISLATIVE TERM RESUMED, several issues about the social responsibility of the state were placed on the agenda for discussion. Webber, an acknowledged "student of constitutional practices" and the magnetic glue that held the Electives together, was reelected whip of the House.[1] The Electives were determined to examine the Customs Tariff, to see "what steps could best be taken with regard to the British Preferential Tariff,"[2] and to introduce measures such as old-age pension and workmen's compensation. On October 23 Webber gave notice to the Legislative Council that he would introduce a workmen's compensation act.[3] The BGLU also wanted legislation for an eight-hour workday and better protection for sewing girls and shop assistants.[4] In all of this, the Electives had not forgotten the oppressive nature of the constitution, a fight they would continue during the next year and which will be the subject of chapter 14.

Webber's concern also extended to the nation's prisoners. It was a sign that he realized that a society is judged sometimes by how well it treats its prisoners. On November 7, 1930, prison reform was debated in the Legislative Council. Prior to the debate, he had visited Georgetown Prison. He observed that the prisoners' meals were not nutritious and urged that they be provided with local products. Webber objected to the conditions under which the prisoners were accommodated and noted that the prison was run more like a penal settlement. It was a demoralizing and debasing place. Prisoners slept on the floor and were not even provided with a box to sit on. "There was poor ventilation and no light in the cells. Prisoners were locked up in their cells in solitary confinement from 2 P.M. on Saturday until Monday morning with nothing to read and all they do was to brood over their crime." He recommended that every cell be lit so that the prisoners could "read the Bible in their cells; it was a forbidden book."[5] The governor intervened to say that he had given instructions to install lights in the cells, and the prisoners would be able to read until 10:30 P.M. The colonial secretary added that "all the prisoners were now supplied with cots and they were now making stools" to accommodate them.[6] Webber's intervention had helped even the most demeaned (some would call them "the dregs") of the society.

Webber's last symbolic act by way of postelection maneuvers revolved around a simple question that he raised in the Legislative Council in the dying days of 1930. He wanted to know if the government had received any communication from the West Indian Press Association with regard to the Newspaper Ordinance of 1839, "which still encumbers the Statute Books of the Colony,"[7] and if the government would appoint a committee to look into the matter. The acting colonial secretary said he did not believe that the ordinance was archaic (Webber had called it archaic) or that it encumbered the statute books of the colony. He assured Webber that it "occupies but six and a half pages of the Statute Book and compares favorably with similar legislation in other colonies. In recent proceedings for contempt of Court certain provisions were found to be useful. . . . The Government does not consider that the appointment of a Committee as suggested is necessary or that it would serve any useful purpose."[8]

This exchange highlighted the reactionary nature of the colonial government. To argue that an ordinance that was passed five years after slavery had been abolished (one year after the slaves were finally freed) was neither archaic nor in need of amendment was simply too extraordinary a position to accept. It almost seemed as though the colonial government was stuck in a bygone era from which it was afraid to emerge. Webber, a victim of this archaic law, knew how much the government had used it to intimidate its adversaries. The government even tried to imprison him and those who threatened the system. He realized that although much may have changed for black folks during the century after slavery, many things had remained the same. The government was still ready to use its laws to achieve its unworthy ends.

One month after he was elected to the legislature, Webber tackled the economic situation of his people head on by writing an important article, "I Am an Economic Heretic," in which he lambasted the government for cutting its spending in the midst of rising unemployment and misery among the people. Contrary to the popular view, hence an "Economic Heretic," Webber urged the government to increase its spending to deal with the economic depression that was gripping the country. The article declared in its four-decked headline: "I Am an Economic Heretic," "Drastic Administrative Economies Cannot Save Us," "Will Aggravate Depression and Unemployment," and "Courageous Forward Policy Only Remedy," all of which conveyed how Webber felt about the economy and demonstrated how his travel abroad had influenced his education generally and his economic knowledge particularly.

In his article, Webber responded to Lord Snowden's rigid orthodox financial measures, his belief in balanced budgets, and his favoring the advice of businessmen over that of economists, none of which was able to stem the growing economic depression that was talking place in Great Britain and in British Guiana. Snowden, "the crippled prophet" of the Independent Labour Party, was a Christian socialist who believed that taxes and budgets (fiscal policy) should be used "to remedy the grosser injustices of capitalism, and also slowly produce that social context of equality in which the eventual transition to Socialism would be painless and inevitable."[9] He did not believe that the budget could be used to stimulate the economy during a depression and restrain it when there was inflation. According to Colin Cross, his biographer,

> The Keynesian notion of a Chancellor of the Exchequer regulating a mixed economy so as to eliminate unemployment and to provide a rising standard of living for workers would have appeared to him for most of his life as utterly fantastic, although in his powerless old age he did show signs of moving towards it. . . . All of his active life he believed that unemployment was an inevitable consequence of the capitalistic system and that it could not be abolished without abolishing capitalism. As for fiddling with the value of money, the idea would have filled him with horror.[10]

During this period, there was little accumulation of capital in British Guiana, and most of the country's profits were sent to England. Although the productivity in the sugar industry was very high and the output per acre increased, the benefit accrued "chiefly to industrial purchasers in the form of lower prices for sugar."[11] The depression in Great Britain reached its lowest ebb during the autumn of 1932. Since British Guiana's economy depended so centrally on the British economy, the depression in Great Britain affected British Guiana, whose accumulated debt was $24,000,000, which included an annual charge of $1,444,000 at the end of 1929. During the first half of the 1930s, high taxation and cutbacks in public expenditures were two of the policies that exacerbated the Guyanese situation. A commentator noted:

> The continued depression in primary product prices and the completion of the capital works programme aggravated an already serious unemployment situation. . . . The main features of this bleak situation, notably low wages, poverty and unemployment, were reproduced throughout the West Indies, and it is not surprising that after 1935 the area was swept by a wave of unrest, strikes, and disturbances leading to violence and loss of life, from which British Guiana was not excepted.[12]

Webber was totally immersed in the plight of his people. He began "I Am an Economic Heretic" by declaring that on every hand one heard the cry: "Government expenditure must be reduced." After outlining the problems, he offered his position on economic theory: "It is generally believed that if Government were forced to reduce its expenditure, dock salaries, and dismiss a swarm of officials, the Colony would be placed upon the high road to prosperity. I do not share those views. If that be orthodox faith, then I am an economic heretic." Then he goes on to state his objections:

> Drastic administrative economies, in the present state of local trade and commerce, would but aggravate the evils from which we are presently suffering. Sir Gordon Guggisberg [the governor of the colony] hit Water Street [the financial district] to the tune of $300,000, in his ill advised scheme of administrative economies. When the Government budget was reduced by that amount, it forthwith constricted the spending power of the community by that sum. Trade was depressed, and commercial employees were dismissed all round who all went to swell the ranks of the unemployed, and compete for what jobs were going with the small army of retainers who were thrown out of Government employment.[13]

In castigating the government's reckless economic policy, Webber made it clear that what was being saved apparently in "one direction is more than lost in another. Pensions have to be found for these men out of the pockets of an already overtaxed and impoverished community."[14]

Webber also wanted to show the shortsightedness of trying to balance the budget on the backs of workers, particularly when it resulted in greater unemployment. Like Keynes, he believed that in the long run, they would all be dead. He wrote:

> I shudder at the thought of some administrative wizard catching hold of the Annual Estimates, and reducing them by $750,000 per annum; since there is one item of expenditure that cannot be touched, viz., the appropriation for debt charges, which amount to some $1,200,000 per annum. It therefore means that the $750,000 would have to be saved from votes [savings] of local services. [That is,] cuts in salary here, and cuts in salary there; dismissals where the fancy speeds; reduction in services votes, such as food in hospitals and prisons, fuel for railways and colonial steamers, etc. etc. But mark we, when all these drastic economies have been accomplished, not one penny of taxation will be reduced; for Government would be left with just about a balanced current budget, with nothing to pay off the previous deficits.[15]

With all these savings, he asked, "What will be the results?" He answered the question with great acuity and foresight:

> The officials whose salaries have been reduced, or those who have been dismissed, must restrict their individual spendings accordingly. The service, food and fuel bills reduced must likewise restrict the expenditures of the contractors and purveyors everywhere. In a word, spending capacity, though I prefer to say, buying capacity, of the community would be reduced by $750,000 per annum, plus Sir Gordon Guggisberg's $300,000. Expressed in another way $1,000,000 would have been withdrawn from circulation at its source. Shops must therefore be closed and employees dismissed in keeping with the trade available.[16]

In addition to the government withdrawing monies from circulation, a cutback in spending by the capitalists would only make matters worse:

> The sugar estates have been compelled to withdraw $2,500,000 from circulation, because they are not receiving it from their sales. The slump in diamonds has withdrawn another $2,500,000 from circulation. Rice, copra and coffee have added their withdrawals, easily amounting to another $1,000,000. I cannot therefore regard with anything like equanimity Government joining the ranks of destroyers by adding another $1,000,000 to trade restriction, without the vestige of a visible hope of taxation being reduced by an equivalent sum; or even by the paltry sum of $100,000.[17]

According to Webber, cutbacks were not the best ways to restore economic growth and take the country out of its depression. He believed that government policy should stimulate spending and, through it, employment. In putting forward his theory, he reminded his audience of a conversation he once had with Arthur Jack Cook, who was the national secretary of the Miners' Federation of Great Britain (MFGB) from 1924 to 1931:

> What is required in British Guiana is *increased earning power* in the community rather than *restricting buying capacity*. Arthur J. Cook (Emperor Cook) said to me in London, "Webber, my boy, the world is NOT suffering from over production. It is suffering from under consumption." This might sound like a foolish euphonism [*sic*]; but it is as sound as a bell. The present sugar situation is due to restricted consumption, dating from the shilling a pound days, which sent the stocks accumulating. So in other commodities.[18]

After the collapse of the postwar boom (around 1921), when unemployment had reached record levels, labor leaders attempted to "link it with underconsumption and recommend[ed] public works as a contracyclical device and certain measures of redistribution along the lines of their earlier memoranda to the Ministry of Reconstruction, which would raise the floor of effective demand."[19] As a trade unionist and self-avowed Marxist, Cook would have been aware of these discussions. Having studied and subsequently taught economics at the Central Labour College in London, he devoted his entire life to the working class. At the end of 1928, he was concerned about "the plague of poverty, unemployment [and] underemployment" that had ravaged the mining community. He called "for a programme of public works, early retirement at sixty for miners, and the raising of the school-leaving age."[20] His secretary's review identified terrible conditions of the coalfields, with unemployment and poverty growing worse every day. Those, he said, "must be the first claim upon any leader's services. There should be no division in regard to the necessity for immediate steps to save the mining community from starvation. To that task, with others, I have set my hand."[21]

After an initial stormy relationship with the Labour Party, Cook began to align himself with the party, which he saw as the only way through which he could achieve any relief for his workers. He affirmed: "It is the bounden duty of all of us to put on one side disagreements or personal differences and work for a majority of Labour government."[22] Both Webber and the BGLU saw the Labour Party as a panacea for the problems of unemployment, starvation, and the achievement of voting rights in Guyana. Although it is possible that Webber might have met Cook during his earlier visit to London, he certainly met him when he attended the British Labour Party Conference in July 1930. He was also acquainted with Cook's writings that appeared in the *Miner* and other working-class publications. Webber and Cook agreed that the government possessed the ability to address the persistent poverty and unemployment in the economy. It could spend more money, reduce taxes, or manipulate the interest rates, or it could rely on the classical approach of doing nothing and hoping that the economy returned to equilibrium. But as Keynes showed, an economy could be in full and stable equilibrium and still remain below full employment. Both Webber and Cook believed that the Labour Party should initiate policies to deliver the workers out of their misery. When Webber bemoaned the disinvestment (or the pulling out) of millions of dollars from the economy without the simultaneous reduction of taxes, he was demonstrating Keynes's macroeconomic way of looking at the world.[23]

In 1923 Oswald Mosley, a British MP from Harrow and a supporter of Indian self-government, read Keynes's *Tract on Monetary Reform* after he returned from India where he met Mahatma Gandhi. In 1925, with the assistance of John Strachey, he published *Revolution by Reason*, "a complete scheme for the restructuring of Britain's industrial base which aimed greatly to reduce the reliance on exports."[24] It "was the first political attempt to apply Keynes's ideas to economic policy. Mosley squarely blamed unemployment on the lack of 'effective demand.'"[25] In 1926 Keynes responded to the Independent Labour Party's pamphlet, *The Living Wage*, with its proposal "to increase working class purchasing power through redistributive taxation and credit expansion."[26] In a letter to one of the pamphlet's authors, Keynes wrote:

> I don't think I quite subscribe to [J. A.] Hobson's doctrine of underconsumption. But I do agree with a notion, which is perhaps kindred to his, to the effect that prosperity is cumulative. If in existing circumstances we could do something, orthodox or unorthodox, to stimulate demand, from whatever quarter, that demand would call forth an increased supply, which in turn would maintain and intensify the demand, and so on. But all the same it is not quite what Hobson has in mind I think.[27]

In 1928 and 1929 Keynes helped to draft the Liberal Party's proposal that called "for expenditure of £251 million over two years on what were then called 'public works.'"[28] However, his ideas did not "permeate the whole Liberal Party [since] a substantial portion of it remained wedded to older doctrines."[29] Treasury officials were not convinced either and persuaded the chancellor, Neville Chamberlain, that "the only prudent course was to continue to aim at a balanced budget, albeit with a smaller sinking fund to repay the national debt than hitherto."[30] The Conservatives and Labour members who believed in running a "sound" fiscal policy rejected Keynes's proposals. In 1931 Mosley was the only person in the House of Commons who supported Keynes and pleaded with the government to intervene into the economy. He tried to get the Labour Party to support his proposals on public expenditure, but he failed to convince his colleagues. He affirmed that it was "vastly more important to deal, and deal quickly, with the industrial situation than it is to deal with the Budget. And for this reason: the continual decline and collapse of the industries of this country makes completely illusory any attempt to balance the Budget."[31]

Keynes published *Tract on Monetary Reform* in 1923 and *Treatise on Money* in 1929, two of his major works on economics. In 1931 he began to write *The General Theory of Employment, Interest, and Money* (1936), a "study of the forces which determine changes in the scale of output and employment as a whole."[32] In it, Keynes noted that "the volume of employment in equilibrium depends on (i) the aggregate supply function, (ii), the propensity to consume, and (iii), the volume of investment. This is the essence of the *General Theory of Employment*."[33] Robert Skidelsky observes that in this book, Keynes offered "a systematic way of thinking not just about the behavior of contemporary economies, but about the pitfalls in the quest for greater wealth at all times. . . . Keynes was the first economist to visualize the economy as an aggregate quantity of output resulting from an aggregate stream of expenditure. This new way of seeing the architecture of an economy is the *General Theory*'s most enduring legacy."[34] In large measure, Keynes's life work was an attempt to explain the determinants of total national output, or gross domestic product (GDP). The level of GDP quite directly determines the level of employment and the level of household income. An economy could be in a stable equilibrium at the level of GDP and still fall way below full employment. In Guyana in 1930, in spite of all attempts to balance the budget and increase taxes, unemployment continued to rise.

Keynes also argued that it was possible to increase or decrease the level of GDP by acting to increase or decrease the level of aggregate expenditure using tax and expenditure policy (fiscal policy) or by central bank control of the money supply and interest rates (monetary policy). In the Keynesian model, sustained increases in government spending or sustained tax reduction raised the level of GDP and increased employment. Harry Landreth observed: "Keynes maintained that the level of income and employment depended upon the level of aggregate effective demand. The fault of previous theor[ies], as he saw it, was that they assumed that supply creates its own demand. There could never be a deficiency of aggregate demand, since, in the process of producing goods, sufficient purchasing power was necessarily created to take these goods off the market at satisfactory prices."[35]

Webber's analysis and orientation reflected a Keynesian approach to economics. Webber believed that the government could halt the depression that was taking place by increasing spending and cutting taxes. His analysis and prescription went against orthodox economic theory, which held that "depressions were self-correcting and that the proper policy for the government was to refrain from intervention in the market, to follow sound cannons of public finance, and to balance its budget."[36] Webber did not accept this traditional way of looking at the economy, which is why he declared himself "an economic heretic." Like Keynes, he believed that when unemployment was high, the government should spend (that is, invest in the economy) when the private sector was afraid to do so. Keynes noted in *General Theory*: "I expect to see the State, which is in a position to calculate the marginal efficiency of capital-goods on long views and on the basis of the general social advantage, taking an ever greater responsibility for directly organizing investment."[37] Government, he believed, had the capacity to ease the economy into full employment.

This is what Webber intended when he argued that the government had to adopt a "courageous forward policy" if it wanted to attend to the depression that was gripping the colony; hence his comment: "I can only say that is beyond the scope of the present article whose sole purpose is to show the folly of drastic administrative economies, which would leave our debt charges untouched, and taxation at its present strangling level." Webber concluded his article by placing Guyana in the larger international capitalist economy: "Of course, British Guiana alone cannot right the world's under consumption; but it can see to it that it does not aggravate under consumption within its own borders."[38] He understood that British Guiana could not solve its economic problems alone. Its economy was tied into the larger international economic order.

How did Webber arrive at an approach that was so far in advance of his time or not well known in his part of the world? Eric St. Cyr has suggested that while the economists were theorizing, the political practitioners were dealing with "real" problems that confronted their society.[39] Karl Case wrote: "Webber clearly spent time in London. If he was writing this stuff, my bet is that he had contact with Keynes or his friends. He either anticipated Keynes or he was one of the first practitioners."[40] Webber did not meet Keynes, although he was acquainted with the fierce debate that was taking place in Britain during the spring of 1930 around the "Mosley Memorandum" (a document that Keynes approved) and the work of the Fabian Society who were a part of the British Labour Party. Keynes promoted his ideas through his active participation in public debates about economic policy with academicians, civil servants, and businessmen and made his views known in the newspapers. Shelton Nicholls has suggested that "since the West Indian colonies were experiencing economic hardship during the 1920s and 1930s it is quite possible that Webber may have come into contact with the revolutionary ideas being proposed by Keynes in his debates with the colonial office."[41]

When Webber visited London in July 1930, Cook was engaged in a struggle with the Labour Party over the coal miners' bill that became law on August 1, 1930. Although Webber spoke enthusiastically about other persons he met during the conference, he did not mention Cook, except for his short reference to Cook's advice in "I Am an Economic Heretic." Such a reference, however, suggests that Webber may have come to know Cook very well and that they spent some time together. Cook's greeting, "Webber, my boy," certainly shows a familiarity, which suggests that Webber had built up quite a friendship with Cook, who was an ardent admirer of Mosley. In the process, Webber became familiar with Cook's ideas and those of Mosley and the Fabians, adopted them, and used them when he returned to Guyana.[42]

Webber's political and economic development pushed him more and more into accepting a socialist interpretation of his world. Such a position can be gleaned from an interview he granted to the *Trinidad Guardian* on September 6, 1930, after he returned to the Caribbean, when he used the term "proletariat" for the first time in his public discourse. Webber was impressed by the introduction of universal adult suffrage in Ceylon (Sri Lanka), irrespective of property, income, education attainment, and its advancement toward dominion status. It was the first colony in the British Empire to gain adult suffrage. Webber recalled his conversation with Drummond Shiels, undersecretary of state for the colonies, who informed him that the Labour government was not prepared to hand over the destinies of these colonies to any form of oligarchy, whether it arose from the planters, the merchants, the lawyers, the clergy, or any privileged class. When the Labour government demits its powers and its privileges, "it will always be of the proletariat rather than the oligarchy. And that is the whole keynote of the Ceylon Constitution when the elections roll was increased from a couple of hundred thousands to a couple of millions."[43]

Shiels, "an advocate of labour reform in the Caribbean colonies," was also a member of the Fabian Colonial Bureau, whose purpose was "to formulate, in practical terms, that part of 'War Aims' which dealt with dependent Empires—British, for the most part—their liberation and transformation into self-governing states, as laid down time and again in the declarations and programmes of Socialist and Labour parties the world over."[44] He was also sympathetic to the rising demands of self-government for which the colonial territories were clamoring and was brave enough to meet with Jomo Kenyatta, the leader of the Kikuyu Central Association, in London in January 1930 (just about the time that he would have met Webber), in spite of the disapproval of the leading officials in the Colonial Office. In 1947, speaking about constitutional developments in Ceylon in 1931, he recalled the two main constitutional principles that were laid down: "(1) that the use of the vote can only be learned by exercising it, and (2) that power without equivalent responsibility leads to irresponsible, unconstructive, and persistent Oppositions. Unofficial majorities without corresponding responsibility are, therefore, not necessarily a mark of progress."[45] Webber, it seems, was correct in his prescription of and insistence upon the self-government of Guyana. It was in keeping with the sentiments of the more progressive members of the British Labour Party and the labor movement of Great Britain.

When Webber reported back to the BGLU on his participation in the British Commonwealth Conference, he also described the workers as the proletariat. He declared that the Labour government "adopted the attitude that they did not want to hear the opinion of a single individual but the organized opinion of the proletariat of British Guiana."[46] Such descriptions suggest he had immersed himself into the cause of labor and had picked up the ideas (and the language) of the Fabian socialists. He believed that the development of British Guiana could be based only upon the organized action of the Guyanese proletariat and that labor solidarity was the key to the country's future development. Then he took a major step:

> He thought it was outrageous to give a man 50 cents per day and particularly when he could only work three days a week. Mr. Critchlow had given them a budget of how 50 cents was to be spent but he was wrong because it was three days pay but it would have to be spent for a week. They should get a deputation to go to the Governor and ask why labour should be asked to make all the sacrifice to enable the money to go further. If that money was not sufficient, they must get more. He believed in measures of persuasion and did not advocate violence because violence only defeated its object. The men who succeeded were those who adopted the constitution and businesslike methods. A resolution would be submitted to them and it was for them to support it. They were not getting relief but were oppressed and it was "worse than the first wife time."[47]

Webber was alluding to several things here. He thought that the economic crisis was taking a heavy toll on the working people of the country and that under the circumstances, persuasion, one of the central principles of Fabianism, was more effective than violence to achieve the aims of the working people. In this sense, violence was not necessarily coterminous with socialism, and he harked back to his preference for the ballot rather than the bullet.[48] He also believed that the private sector (that is, the sugar barons) was using unemployment to bring down wages, rejected the notion that reduced sales countered by short-time working hours would lead to prosperity, and saw the lack of effective demand as a major cause of unemployment. As a businessman, he believed that business had its part to play in getting the economy out of recession. A businessman himself, he was one with Keynes, who noted: "If you believe in the capitalist system, you must give businessmen more confidence in your policies. Otherwise you won't get a proper recovery going."[49] Keynes embraced the *state of mind* one achieves in the pursuit of money. He spurned "the money making motives as it is commonly understood (the desire for money for its own sake) and embraces something more complex: the enjoyment obtained in using one's talents to pursue an end."[50] Although one may describe Webber as a Fabian socialist, he saw a businesslike, working-class socialism as the solution to the problems of Guyanese workers.

In 1936 W. Arthur Lewis, a graduate student at the London School of Economics and the recipient of the Nobel Prize in Economics (1979), wrote "The Evolution of the Peasantry in the West Indies," the first "general economic history of the period [1838–1936]," in which he argued that "the sugar depression has called in question the foundations of West Indian society." He believed that the salvation of the West Indies lay in the transformation of the entire economy "from plantation to peasant production."[51] When Lewis wrote this essay, there existed no formal economic theorizing in the Caribbean. Prior to Lewis's essay, St. Cyr identified two strands of economic thinking: "a mixture of mercantilist thought and nineteenth century liberalism, with a smattering of Keynesianism later in the day." He notes that "Lewis' unlimited supplies model is clearly the first attempt at theory construction for a specific West Indian economic problem."[52] Lloyd Best suggests that Lewis's great insight "was to understand stagnation in the poor producing countries in terms of the surplus of the one productive factor. Keynes's *General Theory* had been emphatic: underemployment and the low level of economic activity involved abundance—an involuntary idleness—of the whole range of factors."[53]

Unlike Lewis, Webber did not possess any academic training in economics that would have allowed him to offer a detailed analysis of the West Indian economy. However, his practical immersion in the field gave him a first-class understanding of how economics functioned and the role that the government should play in stimulating aggregate demand. Like Lewis, Webber was a member of the "transitional" generation who was concerned about the devastating effects that the depression was having on society. Webber could only see dimly what Keynes, a professional economist, saw more clearly and which would take Lewis a longer time to see.[54] Thirty years into his work, Lewis was more explicit about the activist role of government in economic development. In 1983, in his presidential address to the American Economic Association, he argued for "a theory of government" that changed from "viewing government as autonomous and an exogenous factor in any development analysis to making government endogenous."[55]

Yet Webber and Lewis were in agreement on two things. Just as Webber saw Guyana's problem as being a subset of a larger international problem ("British Guiana cannot right the world's under consumption"), as a development economist Lewis's major strength was that he "never considered the problems of the LDC's [Lesser Developed Countries] in isolation but always in the context of a world economy as a single interdependent system."[56] He also saw the strengthening of peasant production and a transformation of the political situation as two of the ways to solve the chronic unemployment that faced the working people of the Caribbean. He suggested that if "the state ceases to be dominated by the plantocracy, if, for instance, a change in the franchise brings political power within the range of labourers and peasants, the prospects of the peasantry will become much brighter. Whether or not such a change is probable within the near future, we cannot say."[57] Lewis, too, was close to the Fabian Society. It was responsible for the publication of *Labour in the West Indies*, subtitled *The Birth of a Workers' Movement*. He realized that part of the transformation of the Caribbean lay in the political control of the state.

"I Am an Economic Heretic" represented a culmination of Webber's lifelong thinking about economics, a process that had begun when he wrote "The Rise and Wane of the Colony's Industries" (1915) and which continued in his discussion of monetary policy at the West Indian Conference (1926), his constant debates at the Legislative Council on fiscal matters, and his masterful discussion of Guyana's economic development in *Centenary History and Handbook of British Guiana* (1931). In Webber, the Caribbean possessed an activist-intellectual thinking in the Keynesian manner long before it became acceptable in Britain or in the Caribbean and long before Lewis advanced his theories that would lead to his winning the Nobel Prize in Economics. Webber was one of the earliest Caribbean thinkers and working-class leaders to adapt the economic wisdom at his disposal to understand "the complex of institutions and activities through which . . . [his people] sought to meet their material needs."[58] Skidelsky observes: "As Keynes's respect for orthodox economists waned, his respect for 'economic heretics' increased."[59] Keynes would have accepted Webber's practical knowledge of how economies in his part of the world functioned and welcomed him into the club of economic heretics. At a time when Lewis was hardly thinking about economics (Lewis says that in 1933, when he went to the London School of Economics, he had "no idea what economics was"[60]), Webber was willing to assess where his country had gone wrong and to think new, radical thoughts about how one ought to reorganize the economy to satisfy the people's needs. In 1930 no other Caribbean thinker was as advanced as Webber as far as economic theorizing was concerned.

Just as the economic situation in British Guiana was influenced by what was happening in Great Britain and other parts of the world, the same thing was happening with the BGLU, which deepened its links with the international trade union movement as its leaders came into contact with progressive trade union leaders attached to the British Labour Party and the International Federation of Trade Unions (IFTU). This was not particularly new. Rodney notes that Guyana "had long been part of the international division of labor—ever since slavery—and the working class of the nineteenth century was in a position to recognize its affinities with labor elsewhere."[61] The economic depression in Europe and the United States also affected the workers in Guyana. Therefore, the labor leaders of Guyana began to draw on the tactics and strategies that their counterparts in the advanced capitalist countries were using to deal with their problems. They also looked abroad to see what assistance they could get. In 1920 the BGLU turned to the British Trades Union Congress to assist it in gaining recognition by the government. The Hon. Arthur Henderson, a Labour minister and a leading member of the Fabian Society, used his influence to pressure the local administration "to pass legislation for the registration and supervision of trade unions."[62]

With the depression, the BGLU heightened its activities among the workers. On December 5, 1930, when the workers learned that the Chamber of Commerce was suggesting that their wages should be reduced, the union called the workers together to hear their opinions.[63] At a meeting held at Lacytown, Critchlow addressed these concerns by referring to a press report he had received from the IFTU that blamed capitalism for the economic crisis that had ruined millions of workers throughout the world and which was threatening the entire foundation of the working class. It also warned against the evil of the capitalist economic system that

> produces new crises at intervals, the instability of peace, the attacks of Fascism and other political disturbances.... The ruling classes are not only doing nothing to temper the consequences of the crisis for the workers, but are helping to aggravate the distress still further by a futile policy of protective tariffs, by economic nationalism and by numerous other measures. The employing class, failing to appreciate the responsibilities, is attempting to represent high wages as the cause of the crisis.[64]

It was natural that the BGLU would rely on the advice of the IFTU, although George Padmore, a founder of Pan-Africanism and a Trinidadian, referred to the IFTU as "a white chauvinist international ... [that] reflects the interests of the upper strata of the working class in the imperialist countries, and looks down upon the trade union movement of the colonial and coloured peoples." He also contended that "the struggle against Garveyism represents one of the major tasks of Negro toilers in America and the African and West Indian colonies."[65] The IFTU was formed in 1919. Between 1920 and 1925, the IFTU had established relations with several trade unions in Trinidad and Tobago, Jamaica, and islands in the French West Indies.[66] By 1930 its membership had grown to 13.5 million, with branches in twenty-five countries. In *Forty-five Years, 1901–1945: International Federation of Trade Unions,* Walther Schevenels, former general secretary of the IFTU, did not mention his union's association with British Guiana, although there was a relationship, no matter how minimal. Indeed, the IFTU sent fraternal greetings to the BGLU in May 1931 on the occasion of its May Day celebration.[67] The IFTU called upon workers internationally to resist any attempts to reduce their wages and warned that "any lessening of the purchasing power of the masses must result in an increase of unemployment." It opposed any "measures adopted by the capitalistic economic organizations, which prevent the adjustments of prices and finished goods to the fall in the prices of raw material."[68] It also called for "an international programme of public works ... to relieve unemployment."[69] Critchlow endorsed the IFTU's statement and concluded that "a reduction in wages would make a greater amount of work and workers would not be in a better position."[70] The only way workers could hold their own was to organize and resist any further reduction of their wages. He called upon the unorganized workers to organize themselves, "as a band of disorganized people would never succeed."[71]

Critchlow had attended the Commonwealth Labour Conference in London and was influenced by some of the same voices that Webber had heard there. He was also influenced by the ideas of the IFTU and viewed his union's cooperation with the IFTU as an essential element of his struggle for survival. Both Ramsay MacDonald, Britain's prime minister from 1929 to 1931, and Snowden, his chancellor of the exchequer, had urged (or were certainly sympathetic to) the cutting of wages as a means of solving industry's ills. Even the British government at the time indulged in this behavior.[72] Andrew Thorpe has observed that "wage cuts offended the whole Labour ethos: the idea of solving capitalism's problems in this way was opposed by hard-headed trade unionists and ethical socialists alike."[73] They believed that wage cuts reduced purchasing power and thereby depressed industries even further. When the representatives of the BGLU, with Webber as a member of the Advisory Committee, met with the visiting financial commissioners from England on March 25, 1931, they made some of the same recommendations Webber had advanced in "I Am an Economic Heretic."[74]

At this point, the struggle of the Guyanese working people had become internationalized. Not only were they working in cohesion with their comrades in Britain, they also began to think of their problems in similar ways. Like Cook, both Webber and Critchlow began to feel a deep sense of allegiance to their comrades. In 1931 Critchlow went to Germany to attend a conference that was hosted by the IFTU and visited Russia afterward. When he returned from Russia, "Critchlow brought back the term 'Comrade,' which was at once accepted by the entire Caribbean [trade union movement] to emphasize equality and fraternity among workers."[75] Like Cook, Webber and Critchlow had arrived at the point where they could say: "To hell with everybody bar my class. To me, the hand of the German and Austrian is the same as the hand of my follow workman at home." In advancing his cause of a minimum wage in 1925, Cook declared: "I am more concerned with the Labour Movement than I am with the Labour Party."[76] At this point in their careers, both Webber and Critchlow could have agreed with Cook's sentiments, although Webber continued to work at the parliamentary level. He might have been enamored by the Fabians' notion of "the inevitability of gradualness" as far as the achievement of socialism was concerned.[77] Webber and Critchlow were more concerned with the interests of their class than they were with the colonial-capitalist class that ruled their society. Webber had moved a long way from the appellation "planters' candidate," with which his opponents tagged him when he fought his first election in 1921.

The deepening world crisis had brought tremendous economic hardship to the people of Guyana. During that period, the trade unions had to fight against the employers to maintain the wage levels and the purchasing power of the workers. They also had to put up a desperate fight to prevent their social rights from being taken away.[78] To make the state responsible for the welfare of all of its citizens, the BGLU called for the passage of an old-age pension scheme, a recognition that a well-defined class of people "was to be allowed, as of right, to draw a fixed allowance from the rest of the community." As early as 1908, Snowden had given a rationale for this important social benefit when he submitted that "any man with a knowledge of working-class conditions will agree with me, that it is utterly impossible for any working man with the average working man's responsibilities, out of the average working man's wages, to provide his family and himself with the necessaries of life, let alone the comforts of civilized existence, and at the same time lay by anything at all as a provision for the future."[79]

Throughout the period, the BGLU had to agitate for the social rights of its workers. At a public meeting at Lacytown in December, Critchlow continued to call for an old-age pension scheme, one of the demands his union had made of Lord Olivier when he visited Guyana a year earlier.[80] In his speech, Critchlow referred to the "many old Water Street workers who were too old to work and had to depend on begging their brothers who could scarcely earn sufficient to maintain themselves and their families."[81] Internationally, workers were making some of the same demands. The IFTU's "Guiding Principles of Social Policy" (1931) called for sickness insurance, old-age and survivors' insurance, death insurance, unemployment insurance, maternity insurance, and family insurance. Suffice it to say that BGLU demands were in keeping with the most progressive impulses of the workers in the developed world.

The progressive nature of the BGLU was manifested also in its quest for women's equality by creating a women's section within the union in 1925. Necessarily, unemployment and underemployment affected women more severely than it did men. As wives and mothers having to care for their families, these women had to fight for themselves and their families. However, this working-class consciousness on the part of women went back to their involvement in the Portuguese riots of 1889 and the Ruimveldt Riot of 1905. In 1930, when Percy C. Wight, mayor of the city of Georgetown and one of the wealthier men of the community, recognized the hardships the women of the country were undergoing, he did not think there was anywhere in the world "where the female section of the community had to put up with such a lot as those in British Guiana. He sympathized with his servants and did his best for them. He kept business going because he did not want to throw people out of employment."[82] His servants, more than likely, were women.

As women's participation grew in the movement, they began to demand that their voices be heard and that they participate purposefully in shaping their economic and social destiny. Gertie Wood, a community activist, saw the unions, clubs, associations, and leagues as part of the best training ground for women to participate in all of the activities of the society. Women, she believed, should participate actively in politics. They should form a woman's political union "admitting as members every woman who is a registered voter either for the Town Council or the Legislative Council." She noted that the economic situation "weighs as heavily on woman as on man, if not more so, because she has to invent ways and means to feed and clothe the same number of people and generally keep house on less money. The great unemployment question affects woman from several angles, be she mother, wife or daughter and also if she is endeavoring to be self-supporting.... The excessive taxation in vogue here also affects woman." Women must be "militant" in their views because men did not represent their views sufficiently. They must send capable members of their own sex "to sit around the horse-shoe table and voice woman's opinions and fight woman's cause fearlessly for her.... Woman must be heard, but the great thing is for her to be so trained that she will know what she wants, the best way to express those needs, to whom to express her wants, and to be consistent in her demands."[83]

Wood also had specific views about employment for women during the depression. On March 1, 1931, she raised the question of the inequality of women in the workplace in a way in which only a woman could. Pointing out the need "for a very strong and representative womanhood in British Guiana," she delineated the special hardships that women faced, especially as they related to their men:

First—the unemployment of men—this phase of the situation bears very heavily on women, for in this case, when all the ready cash is spent to provide the necessaries of life, one by one the woman's few pieces of jewels, acquired by self-denial and thrift, go to the pawn shop. Every woman worth her salt loves her home, and yet in these days she has to sit quietly by, while piece by piece, her household treasures go to the poorman's shop, and what may be left of them go to the saleroom in exchange for the rent due to the landlord.

When it comes to daily bread, the man out of employment is always on the move around the town, he gets a drink here, and a smoke there, and perhaps a part of a bread or a cake, but he never or seldom gets anything worth while to carry home to his wife and children, or his womanfolk on the whole, but the woman (his wife) has to remain at home washing and doing other household work, and has to be satisfied with the one substantial meal per day which may be got, and she has added to this the sorrow of hearing her poor little children complaining of hunger which she is unable to appease. Therefore I say, fearlessly, that even putting aside a woman's natural sympathy with her unemployed man, his being unemployed is a very hard drag on her.[84]

Never in the history of the colony were such sentiments put on public display. Although women had played a major part in the 1889 and 1905 riots, they had never verbalized their aspirations in such a public manner. In fact, the inequality of women in the workplace struck Wood as an even greater evil. "Several women," she said, "work for their living under very adverse and unfair conditions, but there are no avenues in which women can earn a decent livelihood. There is no organized industry carried on for the purpose of finding employment for the womanhood of Georgetown."[85]

The conditions of work and the indignities to which women were subjected were other causes of anguish for Wood, hence her demand of equal pay for equal work. She asked, "Why should a woman be expected to get less pay for any job, only because she is a woman—given equal proficiency and if required to work the same number of hours—why not the same pay? Then, even when a woman is forced to accept less pay than a man in the same job, she has to subject herself to many indignities to keep her job."[86] She was thinking of the sexual abuse to which women were subjected in the workplace. In doing so, she was advancing a cry for female equality that was raised much earlier when an Indian woman sued for wages equal to that of her male workers. Magistrate Hasting Huggins ruled: "I know of no principle of law or of equality which would justify me in awarding to a female—forsooth she happens to be a woman—for the *same* amount of work, a *less* amount of wages." Walter Rodney observed: "Understandably, this progressive sentiment earned general acceptance neither in colonial Guiana nor in the colonizing society."[87] Suffice it to say that Wood was calling upon the capitalist class to open up the economy to absorb a new category of workers.

Wood was also concerned with "sweated labour" (women who worked as seamstresses at ridiculously low wages) that ruined women "physically and morally," hence her plea that Guyanese women "throw off the shackles that bind you. There must be something you want to say for yourself." She called upon them to throw off their man-made shackles and make a bold stand for their liberation. She implored: "It is high time for British Guiana women to stop following men and taking whatever they say for granted—step out from behind and lead out somewhere, somehow, over rough and thorny places perhaps, it matters not so long as the goal is reached."[88]

In spite of their hardships (or perhaps because of them), the women were giving vent to their feelings and creating a sense of working class solidarity. Not only were they demanding their own space, they were beginning to call for equality in the workplace and greater participation in the public sphere. Wood insisted that a woman was "tired being called a child and [seen] as an ornament."[89] Webber and the BGLU were astute enough to recognize that one could not carry off a liberation struggle while women remained enchained and "in their place." This was an insightful, progressive realization of the part of these leaders. Women would become the pivotal players in Trinidad during the labor disturbances of 1937. As leaders such as Webber, Critchlow, and Wood moved forward, they realized that they could not leave such an important reservoir of labor idle and unfocused.

In 1954, when Lewis wrote his magisterial work, *The Theory of Economic Growth* (much of the book paid attention to the LDCs), two values were paramount in his thinking. He recognized that "the benefit of economic growth is *not* that it increases happiness, since there is no evidence at all for this, but that it increases the scope for choice by giving man greater control over his environment, thereby increasing his freedom."[90] The liberation of women was his second concern. He wrote: "It is open to men to debate whether economic progress is good for men or not, but for women to debate the desirability of economic growth is to debate whether women should have the chance to cease to be beasts of burden, and to join the human race."[91] Lewis was concerned about freedom (he chose his career because of the British color bar in the Caribbean) and the women's question as much as Webber and his colleagues were in 1931 and 1932.[92] C. L. R. James wrote *The Life of Captain Cipriani* (1932) and *The Case for West Indian Self-Government* (1933) because he was concerned about the pervasive white rule in the English-speaking Caribbean.[93]

Webber, James, and Lewis were a part of a magnificent triumvirate of the period. Their works sowed the seeds for Caribbean intellectual development and advanced a vision of what a liberated Caribbean should be. Although these societies took a long time before they gained self-government and independence, these freedom fighters were bravely reinforcing the terrain over which others had trod and building new bridges to advance the journey to its next stage of social development. Theirs was one of the many legs in a relay in the people's liberation.

CHAPTER THIRTEEN

COLONIES IN SEARCH OF A NATION

Guiana is a country that hath her maiden head, never sacked, turned nor wrought. The face of the earth hath not been torn, nor the virtue and salt of the soil spent by manurance, the graves have not been opened for gold, the mines not broken with sledges.

—WALTER RALEIGH, *The Discovery of Guiana*

Nations inspire love, and often profoundly self-sacrificing love. The cultural products of nationalism—poetry, prose fiction, music, plastic arts—show this love very clearly in thousands of different forms and styles.

—BENEDICT ANDERSON, *Imagined Communities*

HAVING PARTED COMPANY WITH THE *New Daily Chronicle* rather unceremoniously, Webber returned to the *Daily Chronicle*, his old home as it were, to continue his literary pursuits. On October 19 the *Daily Chronicle* announced that its editorial staff would be strengthened "since the Hon. A. R. F. Webber, publicist and journalist, will be associated with the editorial department and contribute to the literary columns of the paper." In that issue Webber "announced that pending the maturity of the agreement, my literary and journalistic activities will be, in the meantime, freely devoted to the interests of this paper."[1] He would spend the last two years of his life at the *Daily Chronicle*, the newspaper where he started his journalistic career.

Always a man of action, Webber turned his attention to the celebration of the centenary of the union of Guyana's three former colonies, Berbice, Demerara, and Essequebo, in 1831.[2] The celebration was particularly important for the country. Having held together as a country for a century, it was fitting to celebrate that historic union. Webber proposed that the country mark its centenary with a special issue of stamps that "would serve the very useful purpose first of all of marking the great historical event and also of providing mementos for those who desired to keep them."[3] The governor supported the suggestion. "He thought the stamps would be useful not only in bringing revenue but also from the point of view of advertising the colony."[4] Webber threw "all his weight behind the [centenary] movement as a whole."[5] It was a cause in which Webber could invest himself, an expression of an incipient nationalism that he welcomed.

In light of his new interest, Webber was made a member of the Colonial Tourist Committee, which the governor empowered to make the necessary arrangements for the centenary celebrations that were scheduled initially for July 19–25, 1931, but were postponed to October 13–17 of that year. On January 15, 1931, Webber shared his thoughts about the celebrations with the press. Conscious of the economic depression that gripped the land, he was aware that some persons might see the celebrations as blasphemous acts "tempting Providence." Yet he thought that nothing could be gained by "moaning and groaning and bewailing our fate and going about in sackcloth and ashes. Celebrations such as these may in themselves help to cure our industrial evils by bringing the Colony and its resources more to the forefront."[6] Like Keynes, he understood that "what was really necessary for prosperity was not public works projects and government budget deficits [alone], but hope and optimism on the part of capitalists [and the people]."[7] At that juncture of their history, it was important to promote the psychology of hope.

Webber was enthusiastic about the psychological uplift such an event would generate. As a student of Guyanese history, he was aware of the perilous journey that these three colonies had undertaken and the tenacity it took to keep them together. He could not have been unaware of the conclusion, drawn by the British Foreign Office, that there was "no other territory in the world where the settled inhabitants contained a greater variety of races divided from one another by history, tradition, and colour, all living side by side on terms of friendly co-operation, and without any of the bitterness or strife arising from class or caste distinctions."[8] To create a nation, the society had to tap into its inner domain (history, culture, religion, and so forth), which was outside the colonizer's control. Webber recognized that the anticolonist struggle consisted in an endeavor to recover and to create a culture and selfhood that had been eroded systematically during colonialism and that "nations, like other communities, are not transhistorical in their contours or appeal, but are continually being re-imagined."[9]

Webber envisioned a joyous celebration in which the North American and West Indian naval squadrons would synchronize their activities, while the former would rendezvous with Dutch and French ships in the colony's waters. If he had his way, he would invite "the Governors of Dutch and French Guiana to pay us an official visit during the celebrations."[10] To make the celebrations more enchanting, all the activities would take place during the month of July, when the full moon was likely to be at its most entrancing beauty. On second thought, the possibility of rain in July and the difficulty of planning so many events so quickly led to the postponement of the celebration to September 1931.

Several persons endorsed the idea of the centenary. J.R., writing in the *Daily Chronicle*, agreed with Webber's suggestions, and thought that the centenary should be celebrated in a manner "worthy of its historical significance, and in a manner also that would, at the same time, serve to make better known to Britishers themselves and to the outside world generally, the existence of a British possession in South America, and one of enormous area, vast resources, and of almost infinite possibilities."[11] He might have been describing a new El Dorado. The supporters of the event wanted to keep the promise of British Guiana's greatness alive and to recapture the promise of its Edenic past. They had in mind the difficulties inherent in transforming a Dutch territory (with its laws and customs) to a British country and the task of constructing a nation. The centenary celebrations would consist of races and sporting events, agricultural and industrial exhibitions, a governor's ball, and similar receptions. There would be a regatta on the Demerara River, and even "a few airships, circulating over the Colony, would not be out of place."[12] Exhibits representing the various racial groups—American Indians, Europeans, Africans, Chinese, East Indians—that inhabited the country would demonstrate how "this variety of races, work[ing] together in perfect amity, presents one of the most interesting and striking features in the life of the Colony, and has few counterparts in other countries of the world." Such events would impress upon the public the interracial aspects of the society and the tremendous difficulties their leaders experienced in keeping the society together. The events would also remind the nation's schoolchildren and the general population "of the potential greatness of their country" and make them realize that "upon themselves in a large measure depends the realization of this greatness."[13] Like other commentators, J.R. believed that any centenary scheme that lessened unemployment would provide an additional blessing.

About three weeks after Webber's first announcement, the Colonial Tourist Committee members sent an interim report of their deliberations to the governor "to adopt or to reject as many of their proposals as was deemed advisable." Webber regarded the celebrations as "a real God-send." Although some segments of the society and the press were reluctant to celebrate the centenary, Webber opined that not celebrating the centenary "would not provide a solitary breakfast for one of the starving unemployed—not a month's rent more would be paid and not an eviction stayed by sitting down and folding our hands and crying 'starvation! starvation!'" This was Webber's response to those whom he claimed "were trying to throw cold water and cheap sneers upon the idea of the Centenary celebrations this year because of the dire poverty now facing the colony."[14]

Always the economist, Webber thought about how much money the celebrations would bring in, how they would stimulate the economy and provide jobs to the unemployed. He noted:

It is safe to say that at least 500 visitors will come to the colony during that week and spend not less than £10 each which of course means £24,000 being put into circulation. Then half a dozen warships in the harbour during the week would mean a spending from a personnel of say 1,000 men, each of whom, on the average, would spend no less than £5. Here then is another £5,000 or $24,000 and from these two items alone—visitors and warships—we have $48,000 being put into circulation in the city, for the improvement of trade in general.[15]

Such a venture, he believed, would place Guyana on the map and bring "its opportunities to the notice of the world." He insisted that the present state of economic depression and want could not last forever and that it was "not a part of constructive statesmanship to sit and wait until the clouds disperse. It is the business of representatives of the people to assist in dispersing these clouds."[16] The Guyanese people had a right to do things for themselves to alleviate their conditions, to stimulate demand, as it were. The centenary celebrations fitted nicely into that frame of reference. Hence his use of a local adage, "When worms are scarce, hens must scratch the harder."

All Guyanese people were not enthusiastic about the celebrations. The *Daily Argosy*, the mouthpiece of the planters, raised strong objections to the celebrations, saying it could not participate for the simple reason that it could not discover a necessity for them.[17] The newspaper thought that the British government had neglected British Guiana and taken scant interest in its progress. It berated the governors who had been sent to administer the affairs of the colony, suggesting they were "either men of no particular high caliber, however courteous and amiable, or men who were past their prime and could do little else than hold things together while they qualified for their perhaps well-earned pensions."[18] This was a familiar complaint. Since its union, forty-three governors had been sent to administer the country's affairs. It was "farcical" to celebrate a union that was characterized by neglect by the mother country.

The enthusiasm that the centenary generated caused many Guyanese to reflect upon national beginnings and to recall the country's achievements. If 1831 represented the throwing together of three communities for administrative convenience, 1931 revealed a nascent national self-consciousness.[19] This was reflected in a need to rewrite and to reinscribe the society into its time and space. Indeed, 1931 represented a moment in British Guiana's history when a significant number of people in the community considered themselves or behaved as if they were forming one country.[20] It was a period of an evolving nationalist consciousness in which local interests were beginning to predominate and greater local representation in government was being emphasized. Even in the midst of an economic crisis, the centenary celebrations provided an opportunity for the Guyanese people to look back on their history. Important historical documents were republished that told of the nation's founding, allowing citizens to reflect on their history and to contemplate their contemporary circumstances.

And so the Guyanese began their national celebration by reprinting articles that had appeared in the nation's newspapers 100 years earlier and by publishing articles that traced the history of British Guiana. The *Daily Chronicle* carried the Articles of Capitulation that were taken from the only existing copy of the original document at the Georgetown Museum.[21] To show how "the newspapers of a century ago report[ed] the Union of the three counties," the *New Daily Chronicle* published a paragraph from the *Royal Gazette* of July 21, 1831, and the proclamation of the new colony that was made by Charles Wilday, colonial secretary. Not to be outdone, the *Daily Argosy* also carried a copy of the proclamation, the editorial, and the leading articles that were published in the *Royal Gazette*.[22]

The *New Daily Chronicle* also carried Constance Theobald's "The Empire of Guiana of the Century," a long article subtitled "A Mysterious Land," in which she rhapsodized over the romance of British Guiana, the only continental possession of the British Empire in South America and which its admirers called "the Magnificent Province." Although she was not sure of the origin of the country's name, she believed that it was derived from the root word "winna," meaning water, or watery country. She elaborated on the origins of British Guiana:

> This is the place which unknown till the latter part of the fifteenth century, was looked upon during the sixteenth century, as a mysterious land, and it was said that Guiana was an Empire not inferior to that of Mexico and Peru; and that gold was found there and collected without the trouble of digging. It was supposed that there were untold treasures to be found in a city called Manoa or sometimes El Dorado, the capital of the Empire of Guiana. The rumor attracted a host of adventurers and an expedition was organized by Sir Walter Raleigh, who was released from prison by James I in 1616 to search for this El Dorado. The expedition came to grief and Raleigh on his return to England was executed on a charge of treason in 1618.[23]

Theobald then recalled the significant events in Guyana's history, paying attention to the various European groups that explored Guyana after Raleigh stumbled (the British, Spaniards, Portuguese, French, and English and which was held successively by the Dutch, French, and English); the struggle against slavery that was followed by abolition in 1838; the coming of the East Indians (1838); the introduction of trial by jury (1847); the discovery of gold (1863); the creation of botanical gardens, "unsurpassed for beauty and utility in the West Indies" (1878); the discovery of diamonds (1890) with the height of production in 1923; the introduction of a sewerage scheme into Georgetown during the governorship of Sir

Wilfred Collett (1917–23); the demand for more responsible government (1927); and the ugly economic depression in 1931. Although the Colonial Office had claimed that a new constitution would draw financiers into the country, poverty still "stalked" the land. Although the governor had shown that he was the one who governed, "the financiers are yet to be found who are willing to invest money in the Colony."[24]

Another writer, signing himself "Colonist," also wrote of the early history of British Guiana. He took a different tact: he depicted Guyana as a tract of land that was "inhabited by three tribes of Indians—Caribs, Arawaks, and the Warrows" before their encounter with the Europeans. Thereafter, he charts the changing ownership patterns of these lands until the beginning of the eighteenth century, when enslaved Africans laid the foundation of Berbice and Essequebo, emphasizing that in 1740 Governor Gravesande opened up Essequebo to all with freedom of taxation for ten years to all nations.[25] "Colonist" introduces the role of international events in the shaping of Guyana. He notes that the slogan of the French Revolution, "Liberty Equality Fraternity," became an integral part of Guyana's early development and speaks of a time, May 1795, when the Prince of Orange, who had fled Holland and resided in England, issued a dispatch to the governor of all Dutch colonies requesting them to consider the British as allies. After speaking of how the colonies went from one European power to another, "Colonist" concludes his article by juxtaposing the union with the emancipation of the slaves.[26]

In his article, "Colonist" suggests that the coming together of the union had much to do with the resistance of the slaves in the colonies. In this context, the influence of Victor Hugues, the Negro commissioner for the West Indies appointed by the government of France, was also instrumental in forcing the union of the colonies that eventually became British Guiana. Hugues planned to arm the slaves and rouse them to rebellion in the British colonies, the result of which was evident in British Guiana. Henry Bolingbroke, an English merchant in British Guiana, wrote: "The dread of being consigned to the mercy of such a band of lawless miscreants as composed Victor Hugues' army, determined the inhabitants to apply for advice and protection to the island of Barbados, where some considerable proprietors resided, who had also estates in Guiana."[27] Hugues's directives led eventually to a maroon uprising by "Bush Negroes," the suppression of which was very costly to the Demerara-Essequebo administration. Because of this uprising, the Court of Policy resolved "that four Keizer's, two from Demerara and two from Essequebo, should join the four unofficial members of the Court of Policy to supervise the raising of the Colony Fund and its expenditure. This Combined Council . . . develop[ed] into the Combined Court, which was the most distinctive and important feature of our nineteenth century constitution."[28] In fact, the Combined Court lasted into the first quarter of the twentieth century, until the British rendered it powerless in 1928.

The influx of slaves into the Demerara-Essequebo county after the end of the slave trade in 1807 also helped to speed up the union. Between 1815 and 1825 there was a net inflow of 7,000 slaves, "mainly from Berbice, the Bahamas and Dominica. Others were brought in as domestics and a few may have been smuggled in."²⁹ In 1823, under the leadership of Quamina, an enslaved African, the slaves rebelled. Believing the king had set them free (he had only ruled that female slaves should not be whipped), these slaves struck another blow for freedom. Rev. John Smith, a Methodist missionary who was associated with this rebellion, was arrested and placed in prison. He died in prison in February 1824.³⁰ As a result of this rebellion and Rev. Smith's death, the British government pressured the Court of Policy to pass an ordinance that ameliorated the condition of slaves by limiting their working hours, appointed a protector of slaves, and allowed the slaves to marry, to hold property, and to purchase manumission.³¹ These provisions infuriated the British Guiana planters, who were bitterly hostile to this interference "from the other side of the water" and who also thought "their humanity insulted, their authority enfeebled and their properties and lives consequently endangered."³² In spite of their objections, the British government saw that it was in its best interest to bring the colonies together to ensure that they were administered better.

Yet it was the intransigence of the slaves and their desire to be free that kept up the pressures on the planters to ameliorate their conditions. In 1824 Governor Benjamin D'Urban wrote to Lord Bathurst: "The spirit of discontent is anything but extinct. It is alive as it were under its ashes, and the Negro mind although giving forth no marked indications of mischief to those not accustomed to observe it, is still agitated, jealous and suspicious."³³ A declining slave population led to an increase in the trading of slaves and thereby the continued prosperity of the colonies.³⁴ Williams notes that "the slave trade was certainly essential to the further progress of British Guiana, but the Negro has his own opinion about its value to his race."³⁵ Such a prospect did not bode well for the future of the colonies and their prosperity.

Under pressure from the antislavery movement, the British had to curtail the slave trade. The Dutch, who were under no such compunction, kept on the trade (and the smuggling) in slaves. In 1825 Governor D'Urban wrote of "the convenience and advantage of both colonies if they might be declared as one, as far as [it] relates to the intercourse and transfer of slaves."³⁶ Three years later, he sought to convince the British government about the need for a "free intercourse and transfer of slaves, between the colonies of Demerara and Berbice."³⁷ It was hoped that a union of the three colonies "would lead to greater freedom of transfer of slaves from Berbice to Demerara-Essequebo."³⁸ This pressure for labor led to the speeding up of the union. Undoubtedly, the British were listening to the advice of D'Urban. He was appointed governor of British Guiana on March 4, 1831, when the three colonies became a political unit.

The coming together of this political unit led Webber and other celebrants of British Guiana's centenary to offer narratives to comprehend (or "imagine," as Benedict Anderson puts it) the Guyanese society.[39] During the centenary year (and even immediately before that), several histories about the society were either written or reprinted. In their attempts to include the indigenous or "first peoples" into the national story, both the *Daily Chronicle* and the *New Daily Chronicle* published informed articles on Walter Roth, the leading anthropologist in Guyana and the English-speaking world at that time, who went to Guyana in 1906.[40] William Gomes describes Roth as "the father of Ethnology in British Guiana, . . . the greatest living authority on the Aboriginals of British Guiana . . . and one of the few really great men in our midst."[41] Most of his studies were published in the *Bulletin of North Queensland Ethnography* (Australia) and the Smithsonian Institution's publications in the United States. In 1922, when Webber, in his capacity as manager of the *Daily Chronicle,* won the right to publish Roth's translation of Richard Schomburgk's *Travels in British Guiana, 1840–1844*, he exclaimed: "[This] book will sell like hell."[42] The Combined Court had paid $4,000 to have the book published. After the book was published, an English journal observed that Richard Schomburgk had found "a capable and sympathetic translator in Mr. Walter E. Roth, who appears now to have established himself very much on the same plane as the Schomburgks and [Everard] im Thurn as an observer of Indian manners and customs in British Guiana."[43] In 1929 the *Daily Chronicle* published Roth's translation of P. M. Netscher's *History of the Colonies: Essequebo, Demerary and Berbice from the Dutch Establishment to the Present Day*, with an attractive map of British Guiana. Intended for the layperson, this translation left out the author's preface and appendixes, which the translator anticipated "would only be required by the advanced student."[44] The Smithsonian published yet another of his translations of Richard Schomburgk's *Travels in Guiana and the Orinoco during the Years 1835–1837* in celebration of the centenary and Roth's seventieth birthday.

On June 7, 1931, the *Daily Chronicle* ran an interview with Roth that sought to explain the American Indians' belief in Kanaima, the vengeful spirit of the Guiana Forest. During that week, an aboriginal Indian was acquitted of murdering his wife after he claimed that he had been drinking a native Indian drink called Casiri. After killing his wife, he had remarked that "Kanaima killed my wife." In his book *Animism and Folklore of the Guiana Indians*, Roth investigated this practice of the Arawaks and reported that "Kanaima is said to be the name of a certain tree growing in the savannahs, of which the sap has remarkable properties. After rubbing himself with it a man will go mad and become changed into some animal as a tiger or a snake, and do people harm. The sap can also be thrown over other folk with similar results."[45] Although the occasion for this interview revolved around a killing under the influence of the Kanaima, in the construction of this new nation, even the beliefs of the indigenous peoples had to be included in the national narrative. Roth's anthropological work and translations of classical studies on Guyana's ethnography had also become a part of the national story.

On July 21, the actual date of the centenary, thanksgiving services were held throughout the country. The official service was held at the Cathedral Church of St. George, where the governor, Sir Edward Denham, "attended in state." Members of the Executive and Legislative councils, members of the judiciary, heads of the government departments, and members of the general public attended. The service began with a prayer for the country in which the officiating pastor thanked God for having made "of one blood all nations of men to dwell upon the face of the whole earth."[46] Rev. O. H. Parry set the tone for the centenary celebrations when he took Psalm 90, verses 16 and 17, as the text for his sermon: "Shew Thy Servants Thy Work and Children Thy Story." Drawing on Joseph B. Lightfoot, an English theologian and bishop of Durham in the nineteenth century, Bishop Parry declared: "He was fond of saying, 'the best cordial for drooping spirits is the study of history,' and one of the best fruits of the celebration of that day's centenary would be the study of the Colony's history for the last hundred years."[47]

In his sermon, Bishop Parry sketched what he called "the spiritual history" of the colony and reminded his audience that the first services for "the Negroes" were held "in spite of much opposition from and padlocking of pews but with the loyal support of the Vestry." He indicated that the Anglicans supported the London missionaries at Rev. Smith's trial "for which he was deprived of his chaplaincy."[48] Bishop Parry also sketched the origins of the various religions in the country, such as the Lutherans, the English and Scottish churches, the Roman Catholic church, the Wesleyans, and the independent missions of the Moravian, Congregational, and Methodist churches. He acknowledged the work that the Moravians and Wesleyans did among the Africans and said that to the former "belonged the honour of first preaching the gospel to the Negroes and Aboriginals. They arrived in Berbice in 1738. Driven thence by jealousy of the Dutch and insurrection of the Negroes they established Missions on the Corentyne, but the work ended with disaster in 1808, and was not renewed until 1878 with the help of Mr. Quentin Hogg."[49]

Returning to the present, he asked, rhetorically, if the high endeavor and hopes of a hundred years ago had fulfilled themselves. He answered that "nowhere on earth was religion more professed than in this colony." He observed that profession of Christianity was easy, and in British Guiana practically everyone did it. However, he warned that self-satisfaction, indifference, and selfishness "met like moth and rust among us" and counseled:

> These three evils that eat away our religious, moral and civic life are due not so
> much to bad will or intention as—if I may say without offence—to ignorance

of the religion we profess, and I believe it to be a fact that the better educated man is in secular affairs, the more likely he is to be ignorant of the vital truths of Christianity. It was our Lord who said they are hidden from the wise and prudent, and revealed to children, that is to the poor and simple, not because the former cannot, but because they do not care to learn.

He recognized how wonderful it was that "in this country six nations have been welded into a common life under Christian influence. Surely this is a pledge of a future inspired with the thought of a great common heritage, and the call to use it for a great purpose."[50]

E. Sievewright Stoby's *British Guiana Centenary Year Book, 1831–1931* was also of signal importance in imagining the society. Stoby thought that his book should give pleasure to those who read it and should "serve to make them more conscious of a pride in their country." However, it was targeted primarily to the younger generation, whom he wished would "emulate the deeds of some of our famous men [and women] and, in some small measure, point the way to a Greater Guiana in the century which we are now entering."[51] A civic and cultural inventory of the society's resources, as it were, *British Guiana Centenary History Year Book* chronicled the achievements that had contributed to the construction of Guyanese society over its 100 years of existence. Graced with a foreword by Sir Edward Denham, the book contains articles by some of the leaders of the society and short histories of the three counties that made up the country. It also contains histories of the various ethnic groups and their religions, and narratives of the industries of the original counties and of the six greatest men of the society. Unfortunately, Guy de Weever, the author of this last article, does not include any indigenous Guyanese on his list. They are all Europeans.[52] The biographical sketches of eighteen notables of the century include eight persons who were born in Guyana. There is one East Indian, but no Portuguese or Chinese are included.[53] The book ends with a wonderful essay—actually, it is the second-to-last article in the book—on Guiana orchids that reflect Guiana's uniqueness.[54]

When the book came out, a reviewer with the initials C. A. R. called it "a well edited compilation; attractively arranged and pleasantly discursive."[55] He believed the book made an important contribution to British Guiana's history because most Guyanese were "ignorant" of their history, not necessarily because they did not want to know it but because no one taught it to them. He reminded his readers that the Guyanese educational system taught its students more about the development of Great Britain and other parts of the empire than their own homeland. "It is for this reason, therefore, that the idea of a Centenary Celebration has been so welcome, since it gives a chance of delving into our past." In an astute insight, he noted that "the present tendency in all branches of history is to generalize, to look into cause and effect, conditions and their results, rather than to memorize the dates certain kings lived or died or killed each other."[56] He uttered this idea long before E. H. Carr's *What Is History*.[57]

On the first day of November, the *Daily Argosy* announced the publication of Webber's *Centenary History and Handbook of British Guiana* and remarked that it aimed to bring the history of the colony up to date and, at the same time, to correct a number of historical errors committed by earlier historians and perpetuated by their successors. The person who wrote the report thought that Webber's work would complement the other handbooks and historical publications that were issued in connection with the celebrations.[58] Webber spent most of 1931 working on his book, which he completed around September of that year. Edith, his daughter, said that *Centenary History* "took more out of him—the brain work. To really work on it, he had to monitor and correct all of this information his friend was picking out from these old history books."[59]

Once the book was finished, he set out to have it reach the public. From August to October, the book was publicized almost daily in the *Daily Argosy*. From November 1, when it became available to the public, it was advertised each day to the end of the year. Each advertisement was approximately half a page. The newspaper announced the book as "The Romance of Your Country . . . a picture gallery of living pages . . . [containing] six enchanting water colours by R. G. Sharples." It proclaimed that the book told of the "four broad changing periods" of British Guiana, "each period recording a milestone in the march of time" and offering "a masterful marshalling of events; great governors; stirring periods; spectacular events; chronological records." Such descriptions positioned the work more as a romantic account of the country's history than a formal, antiseptic narrative of events. If Webber wanted to reach a majority of the reading public, he had to present his (hi)story as though it were a replay of fabulous events rather than the dry recording of events that had taken place in a distant past.

Webber's work challenged how British Guiana presented its story previously. Written in the same easy, conversational style of his earlier works, Webber brought to this project all the skills he had learned as a journalist, novelist, and travel writer. It summed up his previous works and contributed significantly to the national reimagining of the society. In conception and design, he had to craft a story that was consistent with his enterprise and to create a mood and feeling of the place he wanted to bring to the attention of his readers. In a way, he had to elicit meaning from the immediate geographical space around them and the inner spaces of his people's consciousness. Like all other conscientious Guyanese artists and writers, Webber had "to use time to feel mentally and physically comfortable in the terrestrial and human space around him instead of over-emphasizing time lost by colonial servitude, and contaminated by historical injustice."[60]

In order to grapple with this problem visually, on the cover of the book Webber placed an American Indian woman in bronze with a goblet on her head with an inscription that reads "Land of Perennial Summer and Many Rivers," which suggests the eternal youth of the country, brimful of possibilities, but exceedingly sexualized. Such a depiction also reminds us of a tradition in which America was represented as a woman (remember Stradanus's famous sixteenth-century picture of America, half-naked and rising out of her hammock to be discovered/deflowered by Vespucci) but who, by the time of Webber, may have lost her maidenhead. Sharples's watercolors captured the vastness and natural beauty of the territory, a partial response to Roberts's challenge when he observed that in Guyana, "Space is all around us. It is in our minds. It is not an idea that originated with Space Capsules, Satellites or UFOs." He believed that "every artist has to solve the problem of space, or how to act upon the blank space of paper, canvas, stone, wood, steel, book page, roll of film or musical instrument. . . . How an artist arranges paint, wood, sentences, phrases, musical notes, filmed scenes, etc. constitutes the existence of his or her art. It is not the inspiration, inherent necessity, or inner compulsion which drives one to make art."[61] Since Sharples was the first Guyanese painter to isolate the subject matter of space as an important aspect of Guyanese landscape and consciousness, his achievement parallels Webber's endeavor in the field of history.[62]

Centenary History draws upon and completes earlier histories of British Guiana. Henry B. Dalton wrote a two-volume history of the colony in 1855.[63] Netscher and James Rodway had already written two major histories of British Guiana (Webber described Rodway's history as being "always entertaining but sometimes inaccurate").[64] Webber included information not available to earlier historians but which was revealed when British Guiana's border dispute with Venezuela erupted at the end of the nineteenth century. This additional information made Webber's study more comprehensive and authoritative than those written previously.[65] Written at a time when the seeds of self-determination were becoming deeply entrenched among the colored middle and the laboring classes—the author himself was an actor in the political drama unfolding at the time—Webber's history turned out to be the most nationalistic history of British Guiana published up until 1931.

Dalton's history reads like an apologia for the imperialist class. He saw those who participated in colonial expansion as contributing "their mite [*sic*] towards relieving this country from the evils of a too thickly populated soil, and at the same time assist[ing] in the diffusion of population over countries where fruitful nature pines for help of industry and skills." To Dalton, "the voice of tradition was silent, or incoherent" among the original inhabitants. It was a place in which there was "no monument of man's fabrication to mark the grandeur or barbarity, the happiness or the misery, of his progenitors; there was no vestige of a higher, or of a more debased state of existence."[66] These values existed in England. Their apparent absence in America signified the barbarity of its inhabitants. Moreover, Dalton likened the West Indians to animals who followed the dreary tract of ages of oblivion and were utterly destitute of energy and excitement. "Such," he argues, "have been the unvaried course of generation after generation. The fulfillment of an instinct, the gratification of a passion, summed up the sluggish round of existence. Like the animals which for centuries had trodden the soil feeding and dying, so the untutored child of this land grew on to manhood, and was returned to the dust without leaving any inheritance but the instinct of his kind."[67]

Dalton's comments about Africans were equally harsh. Even though he lamented the evil nature of slavery, he did not flinch from advancing the dominant intellectual position of the age. Africans, bereft of the civilizing influences of Christianity, were the most debased human beings on the face of the earth and, like American Indians, were perceived to be analogous to animals. As a consequence, servitude was their only vocation.[68] It did not matter that his own evidence of the Berbice Rebellion of 1763 dramatically disproved his thesis about the innate inferiority of Africans or that servitude in the New World testified to their enduring strength. His English, colonial-imperialist eyes prevented him from seeing the inaccuracy of his portrayal, nor could he adequately reflect the activities of a people who were colonized by the British.

Needless to say, Webber's portrayal of the slaves' conditions and the factors that led to the Berbice Rebellion was quite different from Dalton's. As far as Webber was concerned, "slaves in Guinea, however, experienced none of the atrocities or outrages suffered in Guiana or the West Indies from masters of a strange race; alien in colour, language and sympathy. . . . No African owner debauched the wives and daughters of his slaves. Breaking on the rack, amputating a leg and plunging the stump into boiling tar, burning to death over slow fires, even branding, were all practically unknown atrocities practiced in Africa."[69] Webber offered a far more balanced picture than Dalton. He emphasized the cruelty of the British by describing the treatment meted out to the slaves: "In February 100 prisoners were selected for trial, 47 were pardoned and 53 sentenced to death. The sentences were carried out with the brutal atrocities of the day."[70]

Centenary History went back into the mythic beginnings of Guyana's history (Sir Walter Raleigh and the myth of El Dorado) and takes the reader up to the centenary of the coming together of "Demerary-Essequebo with Berbice in 1831" (*CH*, 2),[71] although it does not examine the early period of Guyana's history or the slave trade as extensively as does Dalton's history. Dividing the history of the society into four periods (1581–1831, 1831–51, 1851–91, 1891–1931) that reflect the "industrial progress, social evolution, or political development" of the society (*CH*, 1), the text examines these various periods and their relative importance to the growth and development of Guyana. Webber interprets the history as involving the central conflict between the planter class and the growing power of the "proletariat" (his word), the subsidiary conflicts between the planter class and the governor, and the rising importance of the "coloured intelligentsia."[72] He examines

the hardships the colonizers encountered in founding the colony and their difficulty in keeping the society together; the difficulty of the Africans in moving from
slave to nonslave status, and thus the need for strong administrators; the formation
of free villages among the freed Africans, and the problems encountered in finding
immigrants to people the society; the movement toward constitutional government; and the right of the dispossessed to participate in governing themselves.

Compared with the histories written prior to 1931, *Centenary History* makes
the most eloquent statement against slavery and articulates a convincing case for
the political autonomy of the colony. He repeats an argument that he made in
Those That Be in Bondage that the constant moving of the foreign administrators
to better jobs in different parts of the British Empire did not conduce to the social and economic development of the society. The experience they gained while
residing in the colony was of little benefit to the society, since they were not committed to the development of the society, and so an indigenous colonial stratum
never really developed. This tendency kept the society in a backward state since
there was not indigenous labor, indigenous planters, or indigenous thought in the
country. In frustration, he observed: where there is no thought, there can be no
vision. Likewise, it is written, where there is no vision, the people perish. Webber
could not excuse the British. They had done little to develop the resources of the
colony, hence his conclusion:

> After 100 years of immigration—whether slave bound, indenture bound, or
> free—there was no labour. The local Planter was an exotic. Those who acquired
> a competence retired to another country, to rejoin the females of their kind;
> and their offspring were reared in another climate.
>
> The higher officials were for the most part but birds of passage, going as
> hastily as they came; ever on the alert for the sudden call of promotion. Ere one
> could sense the essentials of colonial economics, and reach to the point where
> his counsels would be listened to with respect or patience, he was transported
> to another field; to learn anew his lessons. Governors were sent to the colony
> to balance budgets, maintain law and order, and prevent the colony from trou-
> bling [*sic*]. The siren voice of promotion brought them, the wander lust of fur-
> ther promotion, or the senility of old age sent them hither. (*CH*, 233–34)

As a historian and politician, Webber realized that the society could not construct
a solid foundation without some stability at the administrative level and the cultivation of leaders who were committed to the society's development. Two years
later, C. L. R. James echoed similar sentiments in *The Case for West-Indian Self
Government.*[73]

The last part of *Centenary History* tells of the attempts by the colonial powers
to negate the popular will and the various disguises they used to defeat the will of

the people. He noted that the act that gave the British king the power to amend British Guiana's constitution by an Order-in-Council, and which was accepted by Parliament on March 13, 1928, reduced the number of Electives to less than 50 percent of the Legislative Council, thereby preventing British Guiana from being a "Representative Legislature" (*CH*, 359). Throughout his book, he tries to dissuade his readers about having any illusions about the governor or his council's capacity to change things in the society. He wanted them to recognize that their problems were systematic and that it was left to the country's educational system to change things: "Without this work of education and the understanding of its problems, it is to be feared that British Guiana will ever be haunted by the ghosts of strangled opportunities, and the cry of what might have been" (*CH*, 363).

Centenary History is an original work that interpreted the history of Guyana through the activities of its people. It preceded Daly's *A Short History of the Guyanese People* (1975) and Walter Rodney's *A History of the Guyanese Working People* (1981) in depicting the history of the Guyanese people as a struggle between the plantocracy and the working people, with the colored intelligentsia playing an important role in supporting the aspirations of the latter. This emphasis is especially important not only because Webber introduced an extremely modern and progressive approach to historical analysis but also because he depicted the history of the society as that of an oppressed group that was trying to come to terms with its dispossession and demanding at each turn the right to be recognized as human beings. Indeed, he presents his story as the adventure of three colonies in search of creating a nation.

A pioneer in Caribbean historiography and an important contributor to Caribbean literature, Webber was "fluent and forceful with his pen as he was of speech." At the time of his death, he was "regarded as an authority on the political and economic life of British Guiana and perhaps the West Indies."[74] Daly called *Centenary History* Webber's "most notable contribution to Guianese [*sic*] literature," whereas Tommy Payne, a former archivist of the Guyanese Museum, called it "the most authoritative history written about Guyana up until that time and many years afterward."[75] Given its political edge, it interpreted Guyanese people in a new light, encouraged them to challenge their subordinate position, and gave them a new sense of self. Thereafter, it remained a part of the curriculum of the Guyanese schools.

Prior to Webber, no indigenous historian in the Caribbean located his or her work in the bowels of his or her people. In an interesting twist of history, on October 25, just six days before the publication of *Centenary History*, the *Daily Argosy* announced that "E. E. Williams, son of Mr. Harry Williams of the General Post Office" in the island of Trinidad and Tobago, had won an island scholarship to study at a university abroad.[76] In 1944 Williams published *Capitalism and Slavery*, a work that emphasized the economic aspects of the abolition of the slave trade and slavery. Although it may be no more than coincidence, one might argue that part of Williams's mission was to extend Webber's work. In larger cosmological terms, one can read this coincidence in much the same way that Walter Isaacson read the relationship between Galileo's death and Newton's birth: "Just as Newton had been born the year that Galileo died, so Einstein was born the year that [James Clerk] Maxwell died, and saw it as a part of his mission to extend the work of the Scotsman."[77] Although it may not have been a conscious intent on Williams's part—he probably did not know of Webber beyond his work—it is still true that in their academic pursuits, James, Williams, and Rodney extended the work Webber had begun.

In the same year that Webber published *Centenary History*, George Padmore published *The Life and Struggles of Negro Toilers*, in which he examined the exploitation of Africans in Africa, the United States, the Caribbean, and Latin America. Just as Webber was fighting for the overthrow of Crown Colony government in Guyana and the other Caribbean territories, Padmore was urging "Negro toilers" (workers) that their alternative was "to fight for the overthrow of imperialism or to starve. The toilers are beginning to follow the road of struggle which we will describe elsewhere." Padmore, a Trinidadian by birth, recognized that the "Negro masses in the West Indies are just as viciously exploited as the natives of Africa or the black toilers in the southern parts of the United States of America" and therefore needed to fight for their liberation as well.[78] The work that Webber and Critchlow were doing in British Guiana was a part of the international struggle against the exploitation of African and American Indian workers. Although Padmore was more radical than Webber (he was a Marxist), he certainly would have agreed with Webber's conclusion in *Centenary History* that little progress was made in British Guiana during Europe's long reign over the country.

Centenary History anticipated James's *The Life of Captain Cipriani* (1932) and Cipriani's struggle for self-government in the West Indies;[79] *Centenary History* also anticipated James's *The Black Jacobins* (1938) and Lewis's *Labour in the West Indies* (1938). Williams's *The Negro in the Caribbean* (1942) continued in a similar vein of examining the response of black workers to their oppression in the Caribbean. Of all of these writers, only Williams would mine *Centenary History* when he wrote "The Historical Background of British Guiana's Problems," published in the *Journal of Negro History* in 1945. While Webber's writings may not have embodied the radical socialism of Padmore, they certainly reflected a commitment to the working people and laid the groundwork for those thinkers, Marxist and otherwise, who came after him.

CHAPTER FOURTEEN

GOING DOWN WITH HIS COLORS FLYING

The Colonial Office regards a reformer in any of these islands as an agitator.
—H. B. MORGAN, "West Indian Rule"

Nothing in Hindu scriptures prohibits the education of girls.
—AKBAR SHAH, "News and Views of Indian Interest"

One finger can't catch a flea.
—A. R. F. WEBBER, "Hon. A. R. F. Webber Defeated by 29 Votes"

ALTHOUGH WEBBER TOOK MOST OF 1931 to complete *Centenary History*, he still found time to continue his legislative duties and to make a living since the elective members of the Legislative Council were not paid a salary, nor were they given "out-of-pocket expenses" for their services.[1] Legislatively, Webber and his colleagues were still pressing on with their opposition to the 1928 constitution. On May 29, as the chief whip of the Electives, Webber requested that the legislature accept his resolution that called on the governor "to invite His Majesty's Government to dispatch a mission to this Colony to review the whole constitution situation to the end of introducing universal suffrage on a literacy test, a restoration of an elected majority in the Legislative Council, fuller representation of the Electives in the Executive Council, and some greater measure of responsibility of the Electives thereon to the Legislative Council."[2] This led to a full-scale debate in the Legislative Council.

In his motion, Webber sought to bring to the attention of the government and the British Parliament that the people of British Guiana were dissatisfied with their constitutional arrangements. He thought he had an obligation to his colleagues throughout the British West Indies "to bring to the notice of His Majesty's Government the fact that in general, British Guiana and the West Indies were not satisfied with the Constitutions under which they laboured and suffered."[3] He had discussed self-government in London previously, and certain elements in the House of Commons and elsewhere were very much disposed to a favorable reception of a movement of this kind. Drummond Shiels urged Webber to move the motion, although he thought that the government would use its majority to defeat it.[4] Webber could count on Shiels, a trade union MP with whom he had a good relationship. Shiels had sent out the first dispatch from the Colonial Office that permitted trade unions to be registered legally and welcomed Jomo Kenyatta, the young freedom fighter and representative of the Kikuyu Central Association, when he visited Britain in the summer of 1929.

Perhaps the most disturbing feature of the 1928 constitution was its complete disenfranchisement of the people. In his contribution to the debate, Webber referred to Order 59 of the Order-in-Council, which prevented the elected members from having any input in their affairs.[5] He interpreted the order to mean: "Not a single Elected Member could move a reduction of a dog tax by a penny nor could he move an increase of Customs duty by a fraction of a cent, except by the Governor's express approval." Given such humiliation, he wondered, "What self-respecting body in any part of the world could consent to or could live under such a threat of, and in the house of such a danger? The order, which descended upon them from the blue, was a menace to progress and the well-being of the Colony."[6]

Webber made many suggestions to correct the constitutional imbalances. First, he asked that His Majesty's government send a delegation to British Guiana to examine the situation, a principle that Cannon supported, and the Electives accepted this friendly amendment.[7] Second, Webber asked that an elected majority be restored to the Legislative Council, something that could be accomplished by increasing the number of elected members on the Executive Committee. Third, he wanted to see the franchise widened to include more persons and a reduction of the financial qualifications for membership of the legislature. He also called for the introduction of a literacy test for the voters, but this was rejected by the colonial secretary, who believed that "if they had literacy test a great number of people in the Colony would be unable to become voters, especially with the female franchise and its effect on the East Indian population."[8] Needless to say, many members of the East Indian community had opposed the literacy test as a requirement to vote.

In supporting Webber's motion, the Hon. A. V. Crane observed that the "the local Government for fully eighty years had been endeavoring to grasp more power without responsibility." He believed that the "Constitution under which they operated was imposed on the Colony without a fair deal being given the people of the Colony to decide what they wanted." The committee that recommended the changes to the 1928 constitution could not have that "consummate interest in the development of this colony which those who were born here, live here and must die here would have. There were thousands and thousands of people in the colony who were capable of giving an opinion as to what form the Constitution should take and what changes should be carried. All except two of the members of the committee were strangers in their midst."[9]

On the other hand, the government officials thought the people were not ready to represent themselves, although the colonial secretary discerned a desire on the part of the people to change the constitution and assured them that "as soon as this Colony could show itself capable and financially able, without any assistance from His Majesty's Government, to control its own affairs, then and then only would Parliament give this Colony responsible government."[10] This was a typical colonial response, although some of the members of parliament thought that the islands of the Caribbean should be given some form of self-government. The governor took the position that there was no need to add more elected members to the Executive Committee and that it was the "opportune moment for the Elected Members as well as the Officials to show their mettle and prove their worth to assist generally in relieving the present situation."[11] He did not see how the visit of a commission could accomplish anything or, for that matter, did not see the constitution as an obstacle to progress.

Faced with the certain defeat, the governor asked Webber to withdraw his motion and assured him that a full account of the debate would be sent to the secretary of state for his purview. Webber did not conduct business that way. He refused and offered a full-throated cry: "I always prefer to go down with my colours flying." One and a half years earlier, he had pronounced:

> No sunset and evening star for me,
> Nor twilight and vesper bell.
> Let me fall on the raging battle field
> With banners gaily flying,
> In full throated battle cry
> With drums a throb and bugles calling.[12]

The members on the government side voted against the motion, while the elected members supported Webber's motion and Cannon's amendment. This willingness to take on the powerful and to accept the consequences of his actions always characterized Webber's behavior. Although he had lost his motion, Webber had the support of progressive elements in the Labour Party, and that boded well for his future relations with the Colonial Office. His untimely death prevented him from exploring that possibility.

The movement to revise the constitution gradually picked up momentum among all sections of the community. An editorial published in the *New Daily Chronicle* argued that although the world crisis had damaged the country's economy, it was the "Constitutional vandals who shackled this colony with Crown

Colony administration—a system of Government which has made popular representation a hollow sham and left the colony at the mercy of transient officials who hardly stay here long enough to discover their own mistakes." The editorial also castigated the government for "riding roughshod" over the elected members. "The 'permanent Opposition' which the Wilson-Snell Commission deplored under the old Constitution is now more solid than ever, though unfortunately, as conditions are today, absolutely powerless in the Legislature."[13]

The *New Daily Chronicle* decided to take its own initiative. It announced that when the government ruthlessly rejected the Electives' motion for reform of the constitution and even boasted that the people of the colony were satisfied with Crown Colony administration, means must be found to circumvent or break through such "high-handed and impudent opposition. Today we are able to show what steps have been taken and what action is proposed to achieve that end." The newspaper called for a fully representative conference of all the elected members of the Legislative Council to consider a memorial to the king, "which, in the final form, will answer to the local Government's despotism." It ended by reminding "every loyal citizen" that the future of the country lay in his or her hands and the kind of action he or she should take to ensure it remained so.[14]

This revolt against the despotism of the colonial government was not confined to British Guiana alone. The *Union Messenger*, a newspaper originating in St. Kitts-Nevis, came out against Crown Colony government, arguing that the government should be a "servant" to the people, "a conception which is foreign to the very nature of a Crown Colony Constitution."[15] On July 4 the *New Daily Chronicle* carried the entire article beneath a four-decked headline:

KILLING BY "OFFICIAL MAJORITY" THE SPIRIT OF A NEW MANHOOD

Silent Revolution Against Crown Colony Government

GOVERNORS NO LONGER CONSIDERED SPECIAL DISPENSATIONS FROM HEAVEN

Mere Men From Whom West Indies Expect Simple Merit

Fifteen or even ten years ago, the privilege of being a Nominated Unofficial Member of Council was felt to be the high water mark of personal preferment, in the Colonies.

Today, the feeling has been entirely changed, the men of the present generation regarding their nomination to a seat on the Council as the opportunity to give expression to the views of the people. In those olden days, a Governor was considered a special dispensation from "Heaven," a sort of superman, whose exclusive privilege it was to receive the homage of men. Today, that too has gone by the board, and a Governor is considered just one of us men, who have had a fortunate turn of good luck in the Civil Service and with the removal from our conception of the folly of the divine right to rule the people, we expect and look for simple merit in their conduct and behavior.

More than these changes have taken place. The people have come to regard the Colonies as home, and Governors, not as ministering angels, but as well paid birds of passage.[16]

The newspaper called this reconceptualization of government "a silent revolution" that had been taking place while the imperial authorities had buried their heads in the proverbial sand. It called on the imperial authorities to revise the constitution of the colonies and to recognize the "manhood rights" of what it called "a new generation."[17]

In Trinidad and Tobago, a similar cry against official despotism was being reported. Sydney Harland, an Englishman and professor at the Imperial College of Tropical Agriculture, observed that there was "no mechanism in Trinidad whereby the desires of the thinking part of the community can be translated into action."[18] When the Trinidad government passed a resolution that allocated $25,000 for the relief of the British government, the four elected members voted against the resolution, in spite of the governor's plea for a unanimous vote. Tito Achong, a member of the Port of Spain City Council and vice president of the Trinidad Labor Party, averred:

Every man in a Crown Colony and with any degree of intelligence knows that the primary function of a British Crown Colony is to pay tribute to Great Britain. Had the Government not been very generous with other people's money the unofficial syncophants [sic] would have dreamed of loyalty . . . ? In matters affecting the people as a whole, some commonsense should be exercised even by nominated members of the Council. Political balderdash, tempered by the boot-licking propensity, should have no place.[19]

Lillian Cooze, an Englishwoman, speaking of the hardships of the Trinidadian people even as the government offered this huge sum of money to Britain, observed:

They turned a deaf ear to the call of humanity and while personally they are making no sacrifice thousands of people are suffering untold hardships. . . . As I rode along the roads of the outlying districts (in Trinidad) all sense of pleasure vanished at the sight of poor people carrying for miles cans and buckets of water, each drop of which is more precious than the choicest wines at the rich man's banquet. . . . When Legislative action and public opinion work together more valuable effects are achieved than when these two forces pull in opposite directions.[20]

In British Guiana, as in Trinidad, St. Kitts-Nevis, and Grenada, these two forces were undoubtedly working against each other. The strikes and riots that took place later in the decade confirmed this position.

In Guyana, the people continued their revolt against the imposition of Crown Colony government as the Electives continued to push for the repeal of the 1928 constitution. After the Electives held public meetings in Georgetown, New Amsterdam, and Anna Regina (that is, in the three counties of the union), they ratified and adopted the final text of a memorial to the king at a conference of representative bodies at the Georgetown Town Hall on July 27. Outlining their grievances in a long and detailed memorial, they stated that "the 1928 Constitution as provided by the British Guiana (Constitution) Order in Council, 1928, is unsuited to the needs, status and aspirations of the people of British Guiana and has given general dissatisfaction."[21] In support of their conclusion, they noted that on twenty-eight occasions since the 1928 constitution was enacted, the government overruled or defeated the unanimous votes of the elected members. As a sign of protest, the elected members boycotted or walked out of the chambers to make their feelings known.

The memorialists also took exception to the colonial secretary's comment that the 1928 constitution was satisfactory "and that the government has no evidence whatever that the people are dissatisfied with the present Constitution." They believed such a statement was "unsympathetic towards the people of the Colony and ignorant of their desires."[22] They insisted on the "moral right" of people to control their own affairs and reminded His Majesty of his government's argument that it needed to change the constitution to control the economy so as to ensure the prosperity of the colony. That did not happen. The country, they said, was less satisfactory in 1931 than it was in 1928 when the new constitution went into effect. They concluded that the colony "can best be governed by men who, from personal experience and abiding interest, know its needs, means and potentialities."[23] In fact, the bureaucratic apparatus that the government had put in place only made things worse.

By far the most egregious blunder of the new system was its mismanagement of the educational system. The memorialists argued that the government sought to "depress the standard of education in the colony" and failed to educate the citizenry because government officials were unaware of "local conditions, the ambitions, tendencies and prejudices and traditional training of the people. . . . It is impossible for a Governor, a Director of Education or any other official from another country to be thoroughly conversant with these conditions." Their "bird of passage" status prevented them from "fully appreciate[ing] the needs of the people in education or correctly interpret[ing] their feelings. By placing greater responsibilities for education policy on the elected members of the Legislative Council the root cause of many public grievances would be speedily and easily removed."[24] The government had failed the Guyanese people most of all in the field of education.

The memorialists saw the appointment of unofficial nominated members as being responsible for "the farcical proceedings in the Legislative Council." They recommended that the Electives, rather than the governor, choose the elected members to the Executive Committee and that the franchise qualification, "especially with regard to the ownership of land," be reduced. They assured His Majesty that they submitted their memorial not because they had lost faith in him but because they distrusted "a system of government which is unsuited to the needs, aspirations and status of Your Majesty's subjects in this colony." They hoped that His Majesty would be "graciously pleased to amend the British Guiana (Constitutional) Order-in-Council, 1928, as respectfully suggested" in their memorial.[25]

In Britain, this cry for self-government was taken up by H. B. Morgan, their major supporter of Caribbean affairs in the House of Commons and the legislator to whom Webber had written previously. In an extended address to the House, Morgan warned that the cries for self-government coming out of the West Indies should be treated seriously. Taking up Shiels's contention that there was "more or less autonomy" in the various Crown colonies in the West Indies, Morgan observed that apart from Barbados, the Bahamas, and British Honduras, there was "an official and nominated majority as against the elected members" in all of the territories.[26] Noting that World War I, the opening of the Panama Canal, and the introduction of wireless, the cinema, and the airplane had changed the intellectual and political contours of the Caribbean landscape, Morgan argued that the British should examine their outmoded system and send out a parliamentary commission to inquire into the state of affairs in the West Indies. Rejecting the Colonial Office's contention that West Indians were not ready for self-government, Morgan challenged the undersecretary of state to demonstrate differently:

> They say that if you do not think that they are fit for self-government that we should send out a Parliamentary Commission, not a piecemeal commission, not a sugar commission or a commission for Trinidad or a commission for Barbados, but a commission representing the three parties in this country to inquire into the whole position of their economic conditions and their need for social legislation, and also their ability to exercise the functions of Government in a way which will ultimately lead to self-government under a federal system leading to Dominion status.[27]

For almost two years, at the behest of local leaders, Morgan had tried to speak about this issue in the House but was prevented from doing so. Given this opportunity, he also raised the color question that was plaguing West Indians at home and abroad: "The inhabitants have come to Great Britain for higher education, and they say that immediately the color bar is put up against them. They suffer under various other disabilities. All the plums in the civil service in the island are retained for Britishers. Once a man is appointed to the island he is never able to leave it."[28] Although the British believed that "the inhabitants of distant colonies are all illiterate or ill-educated," Morgan assured them that West Indians were highly educated and were thirsting for education.[29] All they asked was that Parliament "give them the opportunity and the scope to develop gradually if you like towards the ideal of self-determination. Even though they are a negroid population on an African basis, they ask you to remember that their civilization is British and not American."[30]

The people of the West Indies believed that they were conducting their political business within the same political orbit as the British people and that their association with British institutions had made them fit for self-government.[31] There was a corresponding feeling among the labor movement in Britain that suggested some colonial peoples were better suited for self-government than others. In a memorandum to the Commonwealth Labour Conference, the British Labour Party made a threefold division of the dependencies into areas of European, Oriental, and "primitive" cultures. The members of the labor movement believed that the first two groups should be granted self-government, the West Indies being included in the European area. Most of Africa was included among the "primitive" cultures and deemed not worthy of self-government.[32] In 1932, in *The Case for West-Indian Self-Government*, C. L. R. James echoed similar sentiments when he played up the uniqueness of the West Indies: "Cut off from all contact with Africa for a century and a quarter, they [the West Indian people] present to-day the extraordinary spectacle of a people who, in language and social custom, religion, education and outlook, are essentially Western and, indeed, far more advanced in Western culture than many a European Community."[33] Like Morgan, he believed that West Indians were essentially a Westernized people who had more in common with Europeans than Americans. Gupta, however, offers a necessary corrective when he observes that this description

of the pre-colonial regime in the so-called "primitive" group was not true of many peoples in West, or for that matter, in parts of East Africa. Not only did this analysis ignore the vitality and adaptability of native agriculturalists in the Gold Coast or Buganda but it wrongly assumed that elsewhere in the "Oriental" and "European" colonies—in Malaya, Ceylon and the West Indies for example—the degree of the natives' economic dependency on foreigners was significantly less. Yet in such territories responsible government or even complete independence was contemplated, while all of Africa were to be subject to paternalism.[34]

In his response to Morgan, Shiels acknowledged that many of the laws and customs among the West Indians had developed "during many generations, and that the process of dealing with them must be a long and complicated one. But we are making a start."[35] He assured Morgan that the secretary of state had set up a special committee to look into issues such as workmen's compensation, the relations of employers and the employed, and minimum wages. He conceded that the West Indies may have been ready for some form of a federation—an idea that was in the wind—although "local patriotism" or the distances between the islands may have made such a proposition difficult. He said that some work was being done on the issues that Morgan raised and assured him that "these conditions will not last long and that there will be a possibility of making social and constitutional progress in the West Indies which I am sure we all wish to see made."[36]

Almost as if to show their gratitude, Webber and other West Indian progressives began to raise monies to ensure Morgan's reelection to the House of Commons. At a meeting at the BGLU headquarters, Webber remarked that although times were hard, "Marryshow had written stating that Grenada and Trinidad were subscribing to the Morgan Fund. British Guiana should do their best.... Webber then referred to the Labour Conference held in 1925 and the advice of Mr. William Gallies that there should be two or more West Indian representatives in Parliament."[37] The president of the union also read the speech that Morgan had made to the House of Commons and asked his members to contribute six cents to the effort. It was probably the first time that West Indians had contributed financially to the reelection efforts of someone who supported their interest in the British Parliament.

Given its inability to control the Electives, the British Guiana government decided to impose a form of district and village governance upon the people. Although the Electives did not agree with every aspect of "The Report on Local Government and District Association," the proposed plan for village governance, they believed that it offered the village councils an opportunity to prepare themselves for self-government. Under the scheme, districts that did not have an operational village council would be required to create one. Webber thought it was his duty to educate and to prepare the people for this process of self-government. "Government," he said, "had a scheme of subjugation, to take away all the rights of the people but his scheme was to educate the people in self-government. Government would not be able to carry their scheme except over his dead political body."[38] Webber held several meetings throughout the country to explain his position. At one of these meetings, he drew an analogy with India in which he said:

There was a big controversy raging in India over the question of self-government and one of the strongest and bitterest arguments made by the British Government against granting self-government to India was that the people of India—the Indian princes and others—had no training in self-government. They had not learnt the rudiments, wealthy and educated though they were. That argument had also been advanced by the Colonial Office when the change of the colony's Constitution was being considered. It had been put to him both publicly and privately while in England and as a result of that he had decided that one of his first battles in the cause of self-government for British Guiana was to assist in training the people in the art of self-government through the Village Councils, on to the County Councils, and finally up to the Legislative Council.[39]

Many of the villagers, particularly the chairpersons of these councils, objected to strengthening the village councils, fearing that they would lose some power in the process. Some believed that the consolidation of village councils would increase the cost of administering them. Others feared that the district administration officer would be a "Czar" in his district "who would stand between them [the villagers] and the Governor and make it difficult for them to make representations to Government."[40] Some thought that a merger would result in some of the villages losing their identity. Webber collapsed the tension between village identity and the interests of the larger society by locating the problem within the ongoing struggle that had always existed in British Guiana: a federation of the village councils as opposed to individualism and local pride. Webber believed that the strengthening of the local government was in the interest of all of the working people of the country.

There was much opposition to the proposal. Some community leaders thought that Webber was fighting against their interests. He reminded them that he was on their side and had given his life to the struggle for self-government. "I do not come to you to betray you. . . . I come to you with a great forward movement for self-government in British Government. I have come to stage a fight to educate my people."[41] He explained that he had met with many of the officials in England, including Ramsay MacDonald and Lord Snowden, to discuss the future of the country. Their responses were always the same: "It was never said that we were incompetent but that we lacked training and experience."[42]

Webber was aware of the Colonial Office's objections to self-government (although some members of the Labour Party were supportive) and was trying to prepare his people to deal with them. He thought that the press exploited the recommendations of the elected members while it endorsed the government's recommendations. He was convinced that the introduction of the district administration scheme was an important "stepping stone" along the road to self-government in that it empowered more individuals and added to their dignity. If such a scheme were adopted, no one would owe his or her job to the governor's smile. Webber could not understand how any progressive could object to such a scheme when it meant greater democratization of the society.

A brooding resentment against Webber's response to the "The Report on Local Government and District Association" may have led to his defeat when he contested a by-election to become a councilor on the Georgetown Town Council, on which he had served previously. The colonial secretary sent out a damaging letter on the eve of the election that also contributed to his defeat. Wilson Minshall, a protégé who had replaced Webber as the editor of the *New Daily Chronicle*, led a surrogate fight for Cannon, with whom Webber had his differences. It was Minshall's first election campaign and Webber's first election defeat. The *Daily Chronicle* opined: "Mr. Minshall, in the view of citizens, would be merely his employer's echo. He would be entering political life with an unfair handicap."[43] Minshall, however, was pleased with his performance.

Webber took his defeat in good stead, proclaiming: "I am a seasoned campaigner accustomed to victory and not daunted by defeat." He complained that some of the press had misrepresented his views and that one of the voters had tried to malign him by ascribing "sinister motives and nefarious practices forming the reasons why he had been seeking re-election."[44] This was a victory of the 1,200 taxpayers of Georgetown, the wealthy few, who did not want to pay any more taxes to take care of the social amenities they received. Minshall's apparent reliance on the goodwill of the Lords Commissioners of the Treasury to implement a sewerage system in Georgetown—it was the major issue of the campaign—and his desire to make the matter a colonial question did not bode well for the city. He needed the goodwill of all his burghers. Webber warned: "One finger can't catch a flea,"[45] or as is said in other parts of the Caribbean, "One hand can't clap."

The last three measures that Webber brought to the legislature had to do with a tax that the government proposed on wireless sets, a fee for outpatients at the hospitals, and the education of Hindu girls. In the first instance, the government wanted to impose a $3 tax on the ninety-five wireless sets in the country, which Webber was against. "People in the bush [meaning the interior]," he said, "were utterly cut off from civilization and were chiefly kept in contact by means of wireless receiving sets, and he did not think it was a proper thing for Government to suppress the use of such sets. He knew Government was hurting for cash but they were going a little too far with those petty licences."[46] In one of his famous asides, he chided the government when he observed that there was a registration tax in England for the support of broadcasting stations. "In the U.S.A. the air was free but in British Guiana, it was felt that the air they breathed and listened to must not be free."[47]

Webber took a much harder line on a proposal that required outpatients to pay a fee for their medical treatment. Unfortunately, the Hon. P. James Kelly, the surgeon general, ended his contribution to the Legislative Council by arguing: "If the procedure proposed is adopted, it would result in the Hospital staff being less exploited and it would also control to some extent, the system which, in recent times, has become somewhat of a nuisance to the Hospital staff."[48] Never one to miss a beat, Webber was on his feet to reject the surgeon general's contention that his constituents were a nuisance to the hospital staff and had no business seeking help there. "It was an enormous statement to make: that the taxpayers who paid the wages of the staff every day in the month, had no business in the Public Hospital. . . . Was the hospital to be administered for the convenience and amusement of the doctors?"[49]

The surgeon general tried to amend his language by conceding that he might have used "a happier word than 'nuisance.'"[50] But the damage was done. He had exposed his disdain for the ordinary people of the country. Although Webber believed that patients should pay for some of their care, he could not understand why there should be "that halo of fascines and barbed wire strung around the Surgeon Specialist, whose skill they were paying to obtain. It is unkind, unjust and particularly unwise. The skill of the highest paid man on the staff should be available as long as they were able to pay for it."[51] Whether the surgeon general liked it or not, he had to be more amenable to his public.

Webber was most forceful in his advocacy of the education of East Indian girls whose parents, out of respect for their religion, did not send them to school. He believed that the noneducation of East Indian girls was "the greatest blot in the literacy statistics of the Colony."[52] He also believed that more boys should be encouraged to attend school. Out of a total of 1,455 teachers, only 104 were East Indians; of the 864 female teachers, only 13 were East Indians. Rev. C. F. Andrews observed: "The lack of East Indian girls in the schools and the lack of East Indian female teachers are correlated. He suggested that the situation here must be speedily remedied if the whole community is not to suffer badly."[53] Three days after Webber's death, Akbar Shah acknowledged that his sudden demise

> robbed the Indian community of a doughty champion in the cause of Indian girls' education. . . . All must realize that his last ten years of unceasing political activity reacted beneficially upon the Indian community—he waked it from its 80 years of slumber. It is therefore satisfying in a sense that this strong advocate of equality and justice should only a short while before his death have propounded before the legislature the immorality and inhumanity of keeping Indian womanhood in the bondage of illiteracy.[54]

Even those persons who did not care much for Webber were forced to honor him after his death.

Webber ended his career as he began it: in open support of East Indian women and children and their right to an education. Like their fellow Africans, they, too, ought never to be kept in bondage. Little did he know that within two weeks after his vibrant support of these women, he would be transported to "the deep and underground" without any warning, without any fanfare. Although the Colonial Office saw him as an agitator, the people of Guyana and the Caribbean viewed him as a visionary, a statesman, and one of the most erudite citizens of his day. It would take almost ninety years before one could evaluate his legacy.

CHAPTER FIFTEEN

IDEOLOGY, RACE, CELEBRITY

While rivers run into the sea, while on the mountain shadows move over the slopes, while heaven feeds the stars, ever shall thy honor, thy name, and thy praises endure.
—VIRGIL, quoted in P. H. Daly, *Stories of the Heroes*

What is the end of Fame? 'tis but to fill
A certain portion of uncertain paper.
—LORD BYRON, quoted in the *New Daily Chronicle*, June 30, 1932

I will cut myself a path through the world or perish in the attempt. Others have begun life with nothing and ended greatly. And shall I, who have a competent if not a large fortune, remain idle? No, I will carve myself the passage to Grandeur, but never with Dishonour.
—LORD BYRON to his mother, 1805

WHEN WEBBER ENTERED THE PUBLIC ARENA IN 1916, he brought a complex legacy to his social and political persona. It should be remembered that after Webber left his uncle's firm, he became the secretary of the British Guiana Sugar Planters' Association and publicity secretary for the Georgetown Chamber of Commerce, the mouthpiece of the planters. In 1921, when he fought his first election, he was offended by the canard (his word) that he was "bound to obey the lawful and unlawful requests of the Planters" and that he could be dismissed as editor of the *Daily Chronicle* if he did not do the planters' bidding.[1] R. E. Brassington, the chairman of the *Daily Chronicle*, had also supported Webber's candidacy for the election. As soon as he won the election, Webber wanted to distance himself from those connections, declaring: "I have fought for the black man's place in the sun both in and out of the columns of the *Daily Chronicle*." Webber also made it clear that he was "on the side of the people and an avowed champion of their legitimate aspirations."[2] Whatever concerns there might have been about his identity or commitment to the poorer classes, Webber made it clear that his sympathies lay with the African and East Indian peoples. However, no reasonable person could dismiss the work he had done for the Planters' Association and the Chamber of Commerce and the apparent conflict of those endeavors with the interests of black people.

Webber came from an interesting past. His uncle, S. E. R. Forbes, was a prominent member of the Bartica community and identified with the more progressive members of the black and colored middle class. In 1897, when the West India Royal Commission held its hearing on the sugar and other industries in Guyana, Forbes sent a memorandum to Patrick Dargan, a prominent member of the People's Association, and D. M. Hutson, a former chairman of the Reform Association and a member of the Executive Council and of the Court of Policy, who were testifying at the hearings, which he wanted them to transmit to the commissioners. As "a large Owner of Property at Bartica" (the commission's description of his prominence) and a civic leader of the township, he was interested in seeing the area developed. Convinced of the "natural advantages of Bartica as a port of call," Forbes argued that if a railway were constructed from Bartica into the Upper Amazon, it would open up the interior and generate enormous trade with the Amazon valley. Apart from the revenue that would accrue from that venture, "such a railway would pass through the present gold diggings at Omai Comaka, etc. and in close proximity to those of the Potaro and Conawarook and would more than any other route that could be suggested serve to develop the gold districts of the colony and the opening up of the Savannah regions of the interior."[3] He thought that a new road that was being built from Kartaboo Point on the Massuruni River, about six miles from Bartica, would cripple the township further.

Forbes was part of a progressive element of the British Guiana middle class that spoke on behalf of the black working class and the laboring poor. In his memorandum, he objected to the secretary of state's indifference to the construction of the railway and said that the building of a new road would not be in the best interest of the township. On this, like other matters, Forbes had thrown in his lot with the radical element of society, who were not afraid to take on the planter class. In fact, the gold industry developed in spite of the objections of the planters, who thought that it took workers away from the estates. Although prospecting for gold was more dangerous than working on the estates, it offered them better rewards for their labor. Hutson reminded the commissioners that the gold industry had "reared its head without the slightest aid from the Government. I know that in its infancy it met with considerable opposition from the hands of the planters. . . . Happily, the production of gold has increased."[4]

Forbes was among those leaders who "had won the respect of the broad masses through their roles in the People's Association" and the work they did on behalf of the people in the colony.[5] That Forbes was able to telegraph his memorandum to Dargan and Hutson, two of the leaders of this radical middle-class group, and have it submitted to the commissioners, suggests that he was very much a part of that progressive element of society. Although the commissioners would have preferred to question Forbes about his memorandum ("there is always a disadvantage attaching to papers which are put in and upon which the Commissioners have not an opportunity of asking the witness questions"), they accepted his statement and made it a part of the record.[6]

When Webber arrived in Guyana, he entered into a tradition of resistance to planter domination and the subaltern's struggle for self-realization. That Webber adopted Forbes's name, signed himself as his uncle did (his uncle was S. E. R. Forbes; Webber became A. R. F.), and include the name Forbes in each of his daughters' names reflected the pride he took in his uncle's work and the respect he had for the man who introduced him into Guyanese society. In spite of the progressive work that Forbes did in Bartica, the question of color—his being a colored person in a society where there was a rigid demarcation between coloreds and blacks—structured his relationship with this segment of the community in a particular way. He could not be indifferent to the biases of the coloreds or to the sense of distrust that the blacks felt toward the coloreds.

There is no doubt that the progressive members of this colored middle class supported the black workers. Hutson, for example, objected strenuously to G. H. Richter's (he was a planter) assertion to the commissioners that "the black man is lazy." Conceding that "the black man" may be lazy if one looked at it in relative terms, "absolutely, it is untrue. . . . Naturally, the enervating influence of the climate has its effect upon him more or less, but to say absolutely that he is lazy I beg to differ. He is no more lazy than the German mechanic who refuses to work on Monday, or any other tradesman who exercises the free right of manhood to say whether he will work or not."[7] Views such as those of Richter tended to devalue the intrinsic worth of black people. Dargan, Hutson, and Forbes stood up for black people and their dignity.

When Webber entered the political arena, he brought much of this legacy into his work, even though he may have wavered along the way. Once he became a legislator, he spent much of his time trying to eradicate the perception that he favored the ruling class. The more he became involved in his legislative work, the more he associated with working people and identified with their aspirations. In 1926, when he addressed a branch of the BGTU that was being established in New Amsterdam, unconsciously he drew on the refrain from Stephen Foster's "Poor Ole Joe" that celebrated the passing of slavery,[8] as he affirmed:

Gone are the days when our fellow creatures will accept with a calm stoicism the severest buffets of an unkind fortune without murmuring; gone are the days when our fellow creatures will submit to be led along paths which their eye of reasoning cannot discern; now, instead, they contest against Fate every inch of her onward march and will only be content to bear with adversity when not necessity, but expediency and calm counsel warrant such a course. Thanks to this union, the hitherto "disorderly rabble," the prey of the plans of well-ordered and mischievous minds, has now been converted into the semblance at least of orderliness, and, however feeble, their voices can now and must now be heard.[9]

On February 26, 1926, in an editorial, Webber acknowledged the important role Critchlow had played in bringing working people together, his achievement in teaching them to unite for a common cause and to use their brains to think for themselves, and how he guided them in the far more important function of acting "to secure the measure which should be meted out to them."[10] He insisted that it was an age of democracy in which people and institutions had to change to accommodate the aspirations of working people. During this period, the trade union embraced the struggle both for social reforms and political advancement, which is why Webber and Critchlow worked so well together.[11]

Given his enthusiasm for the important work Critchlow was performing, it was only natural that Webber became the spokesman for working people in the legislature, since no one represented their interests in that body, and few colored men cared enough to speak out in support of poor black people. Necessarily, the requirements to be a member of the Legislative Council allowed for few, if any, working-class persons to join that august body. More important, Webber's association with the trade union movement led his antagonists, particularly those from the white colonialist class, to refer to him as a socialist, which to them was a term of derision, or as an agitator. He spoke out continuously in the interest of the colored middle stratum, the working classes, and the laboring poor, all of whom remained loyal to him. At his death, the *New Daily Chronicle* remarked: "He was one of the greatest critics of Government at times."[12]

Webber could not help but be influenced by socialist ideas, particularly after he began to travel back and forth to London and came into contact with many members of the Labour Party, saw the heightened labor activities taking place in London, and read socialist materials. He was also influenced by the activities of other union leaders or nationalist figures in countries such as India, Ceylon, and Kenya, all of whom were going to London to present their case to the Colonial Office and to seek the assistance of the British Labour movement. Webber's speeches were laden with references to these activities.

Webber's meetings with members of the Fabian Society—many of whom were members of the Labour Party—also influenced his politics. His relationships with Arthur Henderson, Drummond Shiels, Ramsay MacDonald, A. J. Cook, and others were instrumental in influencing his views on socialism. The Labour Party (then known as the Labour Representation Committee), which was formed in 1900 and which consisted of a relatively loose federation of trade unions and some socialist societies such as the Independent Labour Party (ILP), the Social Democratic Federation (SDF), and the Fabian Society, by 1920 had fused together a "popular working class consciousness with socialist attitudes."[13] Moreover, he could not have been unaware of the desire of the Fabian Society to "to bring back, somehow, into the Labour movement a sense of socialist purpose and programme of Socialist action."[14] Although he never declared himself a scientific socialist, he adopted many socialist principles in terms of workers' rights, the need to create a state in which the workers got their just due, and the need for a system that enhanced the well-being of the people. Webber's conception of socialism may not have been as advanced as that which Norman Manley advocated in Jamaica in 1940.[15] Had he lived, he might have arrived at a similar position.

Webber could have taken the people in any direction he chose. He bonded with his people in a way that no other politician of his generation did. On June 30 the *Daily Argosy*, the most conservative of Guyana's three leading newspapers and one of his major detractors, acknowledged that Webber was "undoubtedly one of the best known figures in the colony [and led] . . . one of the most colourful lives within contemporary local history." It elaborated on this theme:

> Few persons in the society possessed the extensive knowledge of the psychology of the masses which enabled him to mould them to his will and to impose upon them his views even in the face of their skepticism. Few persons possessed, as he did, the flair of language which could sweep hundreds under his banner to prove the motive power for the achievement of his aims. . . .
>
> His rank Radicalism, his utter defiance of the conventions, his vitriolic attacks upon Government methods and Government officials made him the idol of the masses and the accredited champion of this, if of no other, section of the community. At a later period they all but repudiated him but to the end he continued to exercise, even though in a diminished degree, a peculiar influence over the lower classes.[16]

On the morning after his death, the *New Daily Chronicle* offered its sympathy to his family and called him "a most versatile man" who could "adapt himself to any surroundings or circumstances. He had his ups and downs like any one else in public life. When he was up he did not lose the common touch; when he was down he was not downhearted."[17] He made friends easily, and bore no ill will toward anyone. Even those who differed with him in the field of politics liked and respected him as a person. At least this is what the *New Daily Chronicle* claimed. C. D. Douglas-Jones, the acting governor, in a moment of generosity stated that the attacks that Webber made against the government and "the losses which he inflicted never left any bad blood between us. There was never the slightest desire on his part to carry anything in the nature of a feud with a particular member or with the Government in general."[18]

Against this background we can examine an allegation that Webber identified and associated himself primarily with the colored middle stratum of his society, even as he struggled for the rights of the oppressed. Clarence David Kirton (1909–), a freelance journalist who edited *Guyana Business*, the journal of the Georgetown Chamber of Commerce and Industry, worked as a journalist for the *Daily Argosy* beginning in 1928 and became the editor of the paper in 1954. Thus he practiced his profession at the same time Webber did, although he worked for a rival paper. He was seventy-eight years old when I interviewed him in 1987, and he had a decided opinion about Webber:

> Webber never recognized himself as a black man. He identified as a mulatto. In thinking, he was a mulatto and identified with the cause of the mulattoes. All of his children, his wife and associates were all colored people. In those days Webber recognized that color had both a social and economic value and therefore he kept within it. If a black man had approached Webber for the hand in marriage to any of his daughters, he would have rejected him. The people whom they married were people from the colored middle class who were members of the colored people's club—the very light-colored clubs—namely the British Guiana Cricket Club.[19]

There is a deep sense of personal antagonism buried within this statement—a sense of resentment that Kirton, a black man, may have felt toward Webber—although he praised Webber for being a fearless journalist. After all, a person who was adored by the black masses, fitted in with them so easily, and articulated their grievances with such passion could not have had as much animosity toward them. However, there is no doubt that Webber's color proved to be an advantage in a color-conscious society and was instrumental in "the deference which was extended to him."[20] Webber's wife also came from the colored middle class. Webber could not have been exempted entirely from these powerful social attitudes.

Color prejudice in Guyanese society was more complex than Kirton made it out to be. Bernard Matthews, a surveyor and protector of records who was a contemporary of Webber and Kirton, argues that the black (he used the word "Negro") and the colored worlds were deeply intertwined and that Webber was a major catalyst in bringing these worlds together. Webber also "stimulated" the forward movement of the progressive elements in each group.[21] In "We Are Moving Along," Rodney's last lecture before he was assassinated in Guyana in 1980, he cites the revolutionary activities of Louis de Souza, a Portuguese lawyer and one of the more popular men in the country at the time, to underscore the progressive tendencies of some of the members of the middle-class stratum of which the colored group was a part.[22] Rodney cites de Souza's challenges against the corruption of the colonial courts (he was charged with contempt of court for criticizing a judgment rendered by the court) and reminds his audience that black people could accept that de Souza was Portuguese because "when he challenged the corruption of the chief justice and the courts, he was really striking a blow that they themselves wished to strike."[23]

In other words, the black masses willingly rallied behind anyone who supported their quest for liberty, regardless of his or her color or social status. Black people's response to Webber can be interpreted in a similar manner. In supporting him, they advanced their own class interest and thereby continued the struggle for their own advancement. In the process, they grew to love and worship him. Nothing else can explain the outpouring of grief from that segment of the community when he died. Subjected to the same social limitations of his time, Webber must have displayed some elements of class preference. However, this does not mean that Webber did not associate with the black masses that he represented and of whom he was a part.

Webber transcended the limitation of his color and his class and became one with his people. Each morning he would go into his office, chat with his staff, leave the office, and then walk down High Street, Georgetown, where he would meet the common people to have discussions and drinks with them. (Both Kirton and Edith acknowledged that Webber drank a lot. Edith remarked: "He loved his rum and water.") "Very often, when he returned from his walks he brought back many leads to stories."[24] This was Kirton's testimony. Webber embodied the psychology of his people and literally understood where they were coming from.

Webber was acutely aware of this problem of color. When he had the opportunity to witness race mixing or certainly race acceptance in New York City, he recognized how much Guyana's colonial situation had cemented the racial barriers. He noted that while there were grades of color in the West Indies, in New York a person was either "white or Negro." Webber took exception to the fact that in Guyana one was boxed in by one's color status. Viewing the level of race mixing in New York, he exclaimed: "On this race question New York is producing a wonderful experiment, and other great cities in a lesser extent, in annealing all the races of the earth into one. Incidentally, it is in New York that the greater barriers of color prejudice will become submerged—25, 50 years hence. At the present it is the great melting pot of the earth."[25] This insight came some thirty-five years before Nathan Glazer and Patrick Moynihan's famous study *Beyond the Melting Pot*, which examined the impact of mass immigration of various groups into New York City and the city's capacity to assimilate them.[26] Webber was much more aware of the complexity of the color problem than even Kirton suspected.

Webber's other social commitments brought him in touch with diverse segments of the population and demonstrated his concern for their welfare. He was the honorary president of the Georgetown Shorthand Writers Association and a member of the Young Men's Christian Association (YMCA), the Young Men's Improvement Association, and the Young Women's Mutual Improvement Association. In 1929 he was elected a fellow of the Royal Geographical Society. In 1930 he became a member of the Institute of Journalists and a member of the British Guiana Literary Society, founded by N. E. Cameron.

When he died, he was in poor straits financially. In 1930 he was fired from the *New Daily Chronicle* and was not paid a salary for his legislative duties, so he had to make a living through other means. Generally, legislators would be appointed to various government bodies, be awarded government contracts, and be able to generate more fees in their professional careers. However, some governors were vindictive. They would remove some of these representatives from various government bodies when they did not agree with the representatives' political stance. Since Webber was not a professional man, he did not receive those benefits.

In 1930 Webber joined R. Evan Wong's stone-quarrying business. In fact, he was traveling to the goldfields of Bartica to conduct a business transaction on behalf of Wong's quarry when he collapsed on board the S.S. *Basra* between Parika and Fort Island. He also acquired the Demerara Leather and Boot Factory and the Demerara Meat Company. However, when his will was probated on July 22, 1932, his assets included 5,000 shares in the Colonial Tanning and Refrigeration Company, some shares in the Rupunini Development Company, and two insurance policies with the Demerara Life and Manufacturers Life of Canada.[27] His shares in the companies did not seem to be worth much. Edith's only recollection of her father's financial worth was an insurance policy of little value that he left for his family.

But then Webber was not much concerned about money, although it was important to him. His vocational concerns were more akin to the Fabians, who championed the "elimination of Laissez-faire capitalism in the colonies . . . and a fair deal for the native worker."[28] He advocated the scientific development of national resources within the framework of a West Indian Federation and would not have been adverse to the nationalization of the economy for the benefit of the workers. His temperament was more people focused. He loved people, made friends easily, and took a special delight in literature. Lord Byron was one of his favorite authors. An editorial by the *New Daily Chronicle* best captured Webber's rumination on his life when it noted that "with a characteristic shrug in a moment of good-humoured resignation," he might have chosen his epitaph from *Don Juan*.

> *What is the end of fame? 'Tis but to fill*
> *A certain portion of uncertain paper.*
> *Some liken it to climbing up a hill,*
> *Whose summit, like all hills, is lost in vapour.*

> *For this men write, speak, preach, and heroes kill,*
> *And bards burn what they call their midnight taper,*
> *To have, when the original is dust,*
> *A name, a wretched picture, and worse bust.*[29]

When Ernest Forbes brought his nephew to Guyana, he was not thinking about the contributions that Webber may have made to the country and how he would end his life in his adopted country. When he wrote to the West India Royal Commission via Peter Dargan about the prospects of economic development for Bartica, he could not have anticipated that his nephew's impending fame would rival that of Dargan, who, in death, was honored by his people and consecrated a national hero. Think of the coincidence, then, when, on Friday, July 1, 1932, the *Daily Chronicle* carried a four-decked headline that read:

THOUSANDS PAY LAST RESPECT
TO DEAD LEGISLATOR

Crowds Line Route of Hon.
A. R. F. Webber's Funeral

MEMORIES OF PATRICK DARGAN'S
PASSING RECALLED

Laid to Rest Under Shade of
Eucalyptus Trees

and observed: "Memories of the funeral of the late Hon. Patrick Dargan whose political career resembled in many respects that of Mr. Webber came vividly to old colonists with the same sad but imposing spectacle and many there were among them who claimed that yesterday's public demonstration of sympathy was the greatest accorded a public man in this country within living memory." Webber's life not only bridged a gap between generations, it also bridged a gap between him and his uncle and pushed the dream toward self-government one step farther toward its fulfillment.

Perhaps it was only ironic that Webber eulogized Dargan in his *Centenary History* in very much the same way in which the *Daily Chronicle* eulogized Webber and compared his funeral and his contributions to society with those of Dargan. Both Webber and Dargan died when they were relatively young (Dargan was forty-eight years old when he, too, died suddenly). Each left an indelible mark upon his society. Such is fate. Webber may have been writing his own eulogy when he wrote of Dargan's contribution to Guyana:

On the 21st February, 1908, Patrick Dargan, a creole of mixed race of outstanding political genius, and known to the present generation as the greatest champion of the people, died somewhat suddenly. Dargan, was a barrister-at-law, who, without influence and without means, had fought his way up to the topmost rung of his profession. Fighting under a constitution that gave scope for little except obstruction and criticism, he found them his only weapons. For the fourteen years he spent in the Legislature he was the outstanding figure of the day and overshadowed everyone else in the imagination of the people.[30]

When Webber ruminated upon Lord Byron and his approach to life, he may have been thinking specifically of the fame and celebrity that Byron came to represent in his lifetime. Like the Risorgimento leader Giuseppe Mazzini, Webber may have come to recognize that there was not a more beautiful symbol than "the holy alliance of poetry with the cause of the peoples; the union—still so rare—of thought and action which alone completes the human Word."[31] Such ruminations informed Webber's politics, his attitude toward life, and his commitment to his people. Ernest Forbes brought him to Guyana and imbued him with a love of his adopted country, whereas his travel to the Caribbean generated a love of the people of the region. His color may have been a source of ambivalence, but in the end his commitment to his people and his deep concern for their welfare earned him a place in their hearts and their grateful recognition of all that he had done to serve them.

CHAPTER SIXTEEN

A DEVOTED WEST INDIAN SON

Death moves with its majestic sway
And sweeps us to the deep and underground
But I do wonder, if red roses bloom in vain,
If children's laughter finds no echo
In the far and far, and then again,
I do no more than wonder: I do not know.
—A. R. F. WEBBER, "When I Depart"

Albert Raymond Forbes Webber is dead. Is it true? Everyone was asking this yesterday.... Let us leave Allie Webber with God his Creator who I am sure having regard to his humanity and kindliness of heart with all men, will undoubtedly find for him a place of happiness condign to his service. In this belief I pray God rest for his soul.
—E. F. FREDERICKS, *Daily Chronicle*, July 2, 1932

WEDNESDAY, JUNE 29, 1932, dawned as any other day in Guyana. A bright and sunny day, it was untroubled by any clouds. On the morning of that fateful day, before the sun began to display its luminance, Webber left his home and boarded the S.S. *Basra* to go on a business trip to Bartica, the first place where he had settled after he arrived in Guyana in 1899. At about 12.35 p.m., shortly after he and C. S. Ridley, government land surveyor, sat down for a late breakfast, Webber collapsed and died ten minutes later. He was only fifty-two years old. Although he had complained of a slight headache, there was no need for alarm. He seemed to be in the pink of health. He was not aware of his family's history of hypertension. An hour after his death, his body was placed on a tent boat and taken back to Georgetown. It arrived at 7.30 p.m. A grieving throng of family, friends, and fellow legislators, along with a large group of anxious citizens, met the boat when it arrived. An even larger crowd stood in silence when Webber's body arrived at his residence at 173 Charlotte Street in Lacytown.

When Edith, his younger daughter, heard the news, she worried about how her mother would accept her husband's death. On the morning of that fateful day, Edith had gone to town to visit McIntosh, a family friend, who had had a stroke. Fearing that McIntosh would not survive, she stopped at a dress shop on her way home "to try on a dress to wear for a little mourning, a little white dress with trimmings."[1] As she was arriving at her house, the family cook, who lived opposite, rushed out of her gate and exclaimed:

"Miss Edith, yo' hear the news. Yo' father dead!" to which Edith responded: "What father?"

Edith thought the cook was referring to a Roman Catholic priest or some other such personage. It never occurred to her that the cook was talking about her father. The cook replied: "No, yo' father! The news just come and dey say dey bringing him home now. Dey bringing him down. Dey had to stop the steamer in mid-river and bring him back down."

Taken aback, Edith rushed into the house. She could only think: "My God, my mother had gone to see these people who lived in Kingston. Who is going to tell her, what am I going to tell her?"

Edith knew that her mother did not take death well. If anyone died who was close to her, she would cry unceasingly. Edith pondered again: "How am I going to tell her this news?" Eventually, she arrived at a solution: "I am going to tell Aunt Milly [Wilson Harris's mother]. She will have to do the job."

With that resolution, Edith walked to her aunt's house and told her what had happened. Her aunt agreed to be the bearer of the bad news. Taking a taxi, they went to meet Beatrice, Webber's wife. She was in the company of Nora Jones, Webber's sister. They were returning home to Charlotte Street. Aunt Milly took Beatrice inside the house to tell her what had happened.

"As I stood outside wondering how my mother was going to take the news, I heard a loud scream. I said, 'O Lord! We in trouble now!' My mother could not believe it. Her husband had left her in all of his strength and health. He broke down over the breakfast table on the boat. They just see him put his hand to his head and he collapsed. And that was that! He was dead already. So it was a worse death even for my mother." Edith could not know how much her mother would suffer later in life because of this sudden death of her husband.

Thursday, June 30, pandemonium almost broke out in Georgetown as Webber was laid to rest in a tomb at Le Repentir Cemetery. A massive crowd of sympathizers of all shades of color and from every class of society had gathered. Guyanese with long memories of these public demonstrations claimed that it "was the greatest [demonstration] accorded a public man in this country within memory.

Indeed, so large was the attendance that ere half the vehicles forming the procession had entered the cemetery, the body had been interred and the last graveside scenes closed."[2]

Then there were the flowers and the tributes. Red was the color of the day. Webber never went anywhere without a red rose that adorned the lapel of his coat. The red rose had become his talisman. The hearse that took his corpse to the cemetery was covered with wreaths of red roses and any other red flowers that the mourners could find. Even the members of the BGLU had attached a red flag to the back of the hearse. The women members of the union, wearing the union's red rosette, walked immediately behind the hearse. It was a sight to behold. Two years before his death, Webber had composed a poem, "When I Depart," that marveled about death and his response to it:

> Death moves with its majestic sway
> And sweeps us to the deep and underground
> But I wonder, if red roses bloom in vain,
> If children's laughter finds no echo
> In the far and far, and then again,
> I do no more than wonder—I do not know.
>
> That no rose's fragrance ever ends:
> That no baby's laughter, bright and clear
> But does ever soften hearts, and mould them:
> Then, when I die, throw red roses on my bier
> Toss me red ones when you feel me near.
> I shall hear the children's laughter.
>
> When you throw them—never fear!
> And I shall tell the angels
> These did make me, built me—
> Rising on the morning bright and clear,
> Never faltering—nor forgetting—
> Roses red, and children's laughter!!![3]

Tributes in verse and prose poured into the newspaper offices in Georgetown from all parts of Guyana, the Caribbean, and London. Everyone was constrained to honor this "noble and fearless representative" of the people.[4] These tributes demonstrated how much Webber had touched the lives of Guyanese and West Indians alike. The secretary of state for the colonies wrote to Beatrice Webber to convey his expression of sympathy.[5] The *Daily Chronicle* noted that his "ready wit" and "genuine sense of humour" endeared him to his supporters and protected him even from those who differed from him in the field of politics. It recognized him "as the ablest contemporary journalist in the colony" and described him as "an astute politician and an orator of no mean order."[6]

The Hon. E. F. Fredericks, his legislative colleague from Essequebo River, marveled at Webber's sudden death. To him, the news of Webber's death seemed so strange. He had seen Webber move through the streets of Georgetown a few days earlier, "but few realized or imagined or dreamt that he was to be a dead man ere yesterday had fled. His loss is a distinct void in the community that he has served so well. His career here can be easily placed in several compartments of time and events, but I need not now category [sic] them. I regret his death but I must be pardoned to say that I rejoice that he has died as he died, for who can deny that he went down in the midst of the fight."[7]

The *Tribune* of Guyana praised Webber's contributions to his society in its Sunday editorial and opined that when the history of the men who had fought for the liberty of Guyana was written, the name of Albert Raymond Forbes Webber, historian, journalist, publicist, politician, and businessman, will "verily be prominent." It continued:

> [He] died in the prime of his life. He had not reached the point on life's highway that marks its highest point: but being weary he lay down to rest and taking his burden for a pillow sank into a dreamless sleep that kisses his eyelids still. We cannot honour him now; we can only mourn our loss. The work he has done for the benefit of his fellowmen in this colony still lives in our memory. Let us unite in this hour of grief and resolve that the unfinished work he had begun in this our fight for freedom from political and economic slavery shall not suffer extinction by his death but that it will instill in us fresh determination to carry on the struggle with the feeling that he still lives and leads us on to that victory which we wish that he had lived to enjoy.[8]

The *Daily Chronicle* staff correspondent from New Amsterdam emphasized the sadness Webber's constituents of West Berbice felt over his death and noted that he was a devoted political worker who "never spared himself in the cause of the masses." He was an ardent and enthusiastic supporter of any measure that was calculated to promote their welfare and "an uncompromising opponent of any unjust or retrograde policy." The correspondent recalled Webber's "powerful resistance" to the change in the 1928 constitution and his "tremendous faith in the economic possibilities of the county."[9]

The Legislative Council also convened to convey its sympathy to Webber's widow and family. W. Bain Gray, acting colonial secretary, recognized Webber's towering stature in British Guiana's public life and recalled that as a delegate to the

1926 West Indian Conference in London, Webber proved to be "one of the [most] outstanding figures of the Conference." When Gray returned to London after the delegation had left for the colony, he was informed by a high authority who had followed the work of the conference very closely that Webber "had created in the minds of many who heard him an impression that he was capable of taking a high place in the political life of the United Kingdom itself."[10] That Webber could hold his own with politicians from the mother country was one of the highest accolades that could be showered on a colonial politician. Gray considered *Centennial History* "a useful history of the colony, which will keep its place for a long time to come as the only complete review of the history of the colony within the compass of a single volume."[11]

E. G. Woolford, Webber's political colleague from New Amsterdam, reiterated Webber's strong advocacy for the "underdog" and reminded the council that Webber was opposed "to autocratic government in any shape or form." Six months before he died, Webber noted that he was in "the evening of his days" and that "his sun was westering." Picking up on that analogy, Woolford concluded that Webber's sun had "dipped below the horizon; but I know, sir, that I interpret the sentiments of everyone present when I express the hope that from below there will radiate such a twilight of his memory as the efforts of time will not readily efface from the recollection of each and every one of us."[12]

In winding up the tributes, C. D. Douglas-Jones, governor of the colony, observed that Webber's demise was a great loss to the colony. He praised him for the services he rendered to the country, especially during the terrible depression, and acknowledged that he "contributed more than his share [to the colony]. He had always been of great assistance to the Government in the difficult problems government had had to decide." Douglas-Jones described Webber as "a severe critic of Government" and asked the members of the legislature to accept Crane's motion for an adjournment to honor the memory of "our late friend."[13] In death, Webber had become a friend to all.

Of all his comrades, Theophilus Albert Marryshow seems to have taken Webber's death in the worst possible way. He remembered the many struggles they had gone through and Webber's tremendous devotion to the cause of West Indian freedom. He described him as a "trusted, bosom friend" and a "comrade" in arms. In death, Webber stood at the pinnacle of his career, and the tragedy of his death touched many persons throughout the Caribbean. Upon hearing of his death, Marryshow went to pieces: his limbs hung loosely, his brain became dulled, and he could not prevent his tears from pouring out. In his grief, he exclaimed: "Webber dead? Then the cause of West Indian freedom has lost a finished fighter. Taken all in all, he was a devoted son of Mother West India."[14]

Beatrice Webber did not accept Webber's death well. Edith recalled that she used to cry day and night and call out his name as soon as she awoke. "Sometimes she did not know where she was. She used to say, 'Allie, Allie, Allie!'" Asked if her mother went insane after her husband's death, Edith responded that her mother "just had a mental breakdown. She used to cry morning, noon, and night. She also cried like that over his brother, who had died some months earlier with a stroke. She would not let us come out of mourning for a year. She made us mourn for him."

Beatrice adored her husband and measured all men by his standard. She never remarried after Webber died. Mentally and psychologically, she died with him. As the months passed, she lost a lot of weight and continued to wear black clothes. She never came out of black. Her children tried to persuade her to wear lighter colors so as to remove that halo of sadness and mourning that surrounded her visage. In her grief, she pretended that Allie was still with her by leaving things exactly as they were while he lived. Jennifer Welshman, Edith's daughter, who lived with her grandmother during her last years, recalled that she "grew up in the presence of this person-like figure. Grandma kept his top hat and had a little drawer with his clothes in it. Nobody touched his top hat; nobody touched his tails. She had a press [drawer] with everything he had ever written to her. Ever since I can remember I was aware of his presence although I was born long after he died."[15]

In 1926 Webber attended a wedding in England at which he observed that there is more cause for sorrow and misgiving at a wedding than at a funeral. "At the latter," he said,

> you can but reveal past mistakes, and forgive or forget them as you will: still there is some satisfaction left in that they can make no more, and all is over. At the beginning, however, of this Great Adventure there is so much to dread, and so much to fear. Even the advent of the Grim Reaper himself may not be far off to bring disaster where we have but roses strewn.[16]

To Beatrice, the Great Adventure—marriage—and the Grim Reaper called death merged into one reality. Webber married Beatrice when she was only nineteen years old. She never stopped loving him, nor, for that matter, did she ever stop mourning him. She paid great reverence to him, and he remained a god to her. He only died truly when Beatrice died in 1962. By then Guyana had gone in a new direction, and new gods were arising to chart its destiny. Even one of these new gods, Forbes Burnham, had been named after Webber.[17] His father, James Ethelbert Burnham, was an admirer and follower of Webber.

Webber lived a noble life, rooted in an honorable tradition of West Indian freedom and located "in the dynamics of self-liberating acts and the desire of the human spirit to be free."[18] Daly observed that the struggle for West Indian freedom must be seen "as fundamentally a people's revolutionary movement, going back to the slave rebellions on the plantations, and coming forward to the rebellion against the present governments West Indian legislatures."[19] Webber was a part of that tradition. Although he never declared himself a socialist, he adopted many socialist principles and may be described as a Fabian socialist, the main characteristic of which was eclecticism. He followed no particular leader but took ideas where he found them, and adapted and developed them to the conditions of his country. He felt great indignation at the exploitation of his fellow human beings and believed that the industries of the society should be organized to benefit the many rather than the few. He was committed to the freedom of the press, which he organized; the freedom of speech, which he practiced vigorously and for which he got into trouble frequently; the freedom of the individual to strive for liberation from colonial domination; and the necessity of the state to provide for basic human needs. Nettleford observed that "Fabian socialism accommodated to, while claiming to mitigate, the evils of capitalism at home and abroad. Fabiansim and responsible trade unionism came to be embodied by many leaders of the Caribbean labour movement, Grantley Adams and Norman Manley being two of the most influential leaders." Such a description would have fitted Webber's career as well. His political ideology could be called a kind of socialism through parliamentarianism.

On July 3, 2007, I set out to find Webber's tomb at Le Repentir Cemetery. The section in which Webber was buried was located at the side of a canal. The grave was covered with shady jamoon (jamun) trees, Wiruni downs, and razor blade grass, a typical West Indian plant with sharp edges. The eucalyptus tree under which he was buried had long disappeared. When I finally discovered his tomb, I saw that the original marble headstone had been removed. All that was left was a deep scar where the inscription recording Webber's death should have been. An etching on the side of the tomb read: "B. E. W. 5-6-62," indicating, as the ledger at the sexton's house confirmed, that Beatrice had been buried in Webber's tomb on June 5, 1962. Derek Whitehead, Webber's grandson, was also buried in Webber's tomb on January 3, 2002. I had met Derek on the second day that I visited Guyana in 1987 in my search to recover Webber, and he had given me a photograph of Webber's family.

Locating Webber's tomb brought an end to my journey, even as I cleared away the trees and plants that had overtaken his final resting place. It was certainly an appropriate way to end. Not only did I have to reconstruct his life, I also had to liberate his tomb from the overwhelming forces of nature that had threatened to erase his memory. But then he could not have been entirely forgotten since Webber's family had returned to bury his grandson in the same tomb. I asked Gairy Moore, a Guyanese photographer, to take a photograph of Jainarine Parahu, the assistant foreman in charge of the cemetery; Wayne Forbes, a driver from President Bharrat Jagdeo's office; and myself as we looked over Webber's grave. As I viewed the grave, I felt that after I departed, the plants and the grasses would once again overtake the grave. Apart from the sheer neglect on the part of the authorities, the weather in this part of the world would be unrelenting in claiming its victims and its space. It seemed a lonely, losing battle to keep up with the intransigence of nature.

To have laid my eyes on Webber's tomb gave this intellectual journey a sense of closure. I had done enough to reclaim Webber for the peoples of Guyana, Trinidad and Tobago, and the Caribbean. After he had given so much of his life to and for his people, it seemed a shame that he should lay in Le Repentir Cemetery so forgotten and alone. His life embodied the best within us and the insistent desire of a people to be free. In that tomb lay the remains of one of the most distinguished politicians, orators, journalist, and literary men of Guyana and the Caribbean.

As I left the cemetery, all I could think of were the haunting words of Alice Walker as she rediscovered the power and beauty of Zora Neale Hurston: "*We are a people. A people do not throw their geniuses away.* And if they are thrown away, it is our duty *as artists* and *as witnesses for the future* to collect them again for the sake of our children, and, if necessary, bone by bone."[20] Webber remains a Caribbean genius. He deserves our deepest respect and admiration.

NOTES

INTRODUCTION

1. Z, "A. R. F. Webber," *Daily Argosy*, July 1, 1932. The line "the fame fight he made" was taken from Charles Wolfe, "The Burial of Sir John Moore," in which he remarked: "Slowly and Sadly we laid him down, / From the field of his fame fresh and gory." The analogy with Moore refers to Webber's patriotism and the pride he took in the defense of his nation.

2. While the newspapers accounts at the time of his death gave Webber's birth year as 1879, his birth certificate gives his birth year as 1880. The mistake is replicated on his "Certificate of Death," which notes his age as fifty-three (he was in his fifty-third year when he died) and the cause of death as "cerebral hemorrhage."

3. Around 1890, James and Sarah Webber (nee Hope) separated, and James immigrated to Guyana, where he joined his two half-brothers who had immigrated to Guyana previously. Ernest, Percival, and James had the same mother. Along with Ernest, Percival, and James, there were three other sisters, Lena, Edith, and Lucille, the last of whom became mentally ill.

4. See *Report of the West India Royal Commission*, Vol. 2, Appendix C (London: Her Majesty's Stationery Office, 1897).

5. Interview with Louis Ross, January 1989.

6. A. R. F. Webber, *Centenary History and Handbook of British Guiana* (Georgetown, British Guiana: Argosy, 1931), 335.

7. *Daily Chronicle*, June 30, 1932.

8. See Leach Reade Rosenberg, *Nationalism and the Formation of Caribbean Literature* (New York: Palgrave Macmillan, 2007), chap. 3, for a discussion of the novels of de Lisser.

9. See Morley Ayearst, *The British West Indies* (Washington Square: New York University Press, 1960), for a description of this search for self-government.

10. Ibid., 111.

11. Reno Rohini, "The Hon. A. R. F. Webber," *Daily Chronicle*, May 4, 1930.

12. C. L. R. James, *The Life of Captain Cipriani* (Nelson, Lancashire: Coulton, 1932), 5.

13. W. Arthur Lewis, *Labour in the West Indies* (1938; reprint London: New Beacon, 1977), 38.

14. *New Daily Chronicle*, February 1929.

15. Private communication, January 2, 2007.

16. Private conversation, August 2007.

17. C. A. R., "History and General Knowledge Attractively Served," *Daily Chronicle*, July 5, 1931.

18. Denis Benn, *The Growth and Development of Political Ideas in the Caribbean, 1774–1987* (Mona: Institute of Social and Economic Research, University of the West Indies, 1987), 113.

19. This is an excerpt of a poem that Webber wrote to his daughter Ivy on December 1, 1920. It is in the collection of Barbara Cox (nee Whitehead); a copy was sent to this author on May 15, 1989. Barbara married Joe Cox.

20. See my Note on Nomenclature.

21. Rohini, "Hon. A. R. F. Webber."

22. Harold Perkin, *The Origins of Modern English Society, 1788–1880* (London: Routledge, 2002), 216.

23. See Cheddi Jagan, *The West On Trial* (New York: International, 1972), chaps. 4 and 5, for a good account of the political development of Guyana during that period.

24. Benn, *Growth and Development of Political Ideas*, 60. Benn says that *Froudacity* "not only constitutes an important element in the development of a nationalistic consciousness but may also be said to mark the tentative starting point of a systematic intellectual tradition of nationalist protest in the region." Ibid., 60–61.

25. Quoted in Nicole King, *C. L. R. James and Creolization: Circles of Influence* (Jackson: University Press of Mississippi, 2001), 31.

26. Franklin Knight, "Introduction." In *Richard B. Moore: Caribbean Militant in Harlem: Collected Writings, 1920–1972*, ed. W. Burghardt Turner and Joyce Moore Turner (Bloomington: Indiana University Press, 1988), 7.

27. Ibid., 8.

28. See Kenneth Ramchand, *The West Indian Novel and Its Background* (London: Heinemann, 1980); and Anthony Boxhill, "The Beginnings to 1929," in *West Indian Literature*, ed. Bruce King (London: Macmillan, 1979), 42.

29. See Harold Lutchman, *From Colonialism to Co-operative Republic: Aspects of Political Development in Guyana* (Rio Piedras, Puerto Rico: Institute of Caribbean Studies, 1974); and Harold Lutchman, "Middle Class Colonial Politics: A Study of Guyana with Special Reference to the Period 1920–1931" (Ph.D. diss., University of Manchester, 1967).

30. Clem Seecharan, *Tiger in the Stars: The Anatomy of Indian Achievement in British Guiana, 1919–29* (London: Macmillan Education, 1997), 152–53.

31. See Jagan, *West on Trial*, 64–65.

32. Ayearst, *British West Indies*, 111.

33. See Roy Arthur Glasgow, *Guyana: Race and Politics among Africans and East Indians* (The Hague: Martinus Nijhoff, 1970); and Peter Simms, *Trouble in Guyana* (London: George Allen and Unwin, 1966).

34. See Nigel Westmaas, "1905: Guyana's Rebellion," http//www.solidarity-us.org/act/114Westmaas.html.

35. Seecheran, *Tiger in the Stars*, 80.

36. See the *New Daily Chronicle*, June 18, 1930, for an account of a special meeting of the BGLU.

37. Quoted in Frank Birbalsingh, *The People's Progressive Party of Guyana, 1950–1992: An Oral History* (London: Hansib, 2007), 30, my emphasis.

38. In 1937 Ayube Edun, an official of the British Guiana East Indian Association (BGEIA), formed the Man Power Citizen Association (MPCA), a sugar union, to represent Indians, most of whom worked in the sugar industry. In 1943 Critchlow and Edun were nominated, and subsequently became nominated members, by the governor to represent workers in the Legislative Council. The MPCA also worked assiduously to elect Jagan to the Legislative Council.

39. "Against the Grain," *Stabroek News*, March 5, 2006.

40. Cary Fraser, "The PPP on Trial: British Guiana in 1953," *Small Axe* 15 (March 2004): 22.

41. According to Jagan, "Plantation life in British Guiana was hard. At a very early age, my parents had to join their mothers in the canefields, my father at Albion and my mother at Port Mourant. They both worked in the Creole gangs. . . . She often recalls how difficult those days were: 'Bhaiya, ahwee proper punish' (Brother, we really suffered). My mother has a way of calling me by the all-inclusive term 'brother,' a common practice among Indians." Jagan, *West on Trial*, 12. Jagan's grandparents came to Guyana as indentured laborers and settled in Berbice, the county that Webber represented.

42. Manley understood the relevance of Garvey's "Back to Africa" message but saw "the destiny of Jamaica as being tied up with the future of Jamaica. He could not reconcile black nationalism with plural demo-cratic nationalism and he acted on the belief that race, though important to Jamaicans, was not suffi-cient to provide the *force vitale* for change and development." Rex Nettleford, ed., *Norman Washington Manley and the New Jamaica: Selected Speeches and Writings, 1938–68* (Trinidad: Longman Caribbean, 1971), lxvii.

43. Jean-Paul Sartre, *Colonialism and Neocolonialism*, trans. Azzedine Haddour, Steve Brewer, and Terry McWilliams (London: Routledge, 2001), xii.

44. Paul Davies, *A. J. Cook* (Manchester: Manchester University Press, 1987), 74–75.

45. "Grenada Tribute to Late Hon. A. R. F. Webber," quoted in the *New Daily Chronicle*, July 5, 1932.

46. Michel-Rolph Trouillot, *Silencing the Past: Power and the Production of History* (Boston: Beacon Press, 1995), 6, 27.

47. Selwyn R. Cudjoe, *V. S. Naipaul: A Materialist Reading* (Amherst: University of Massachusetts Press, 1988).

CHAPTER 1. THOSE THAT BE IN BONDAGE

1. *New Daily Chronicle*, April 3, 1930. A bushman is one who is acquainted with and loves to be in the bush; in Webber's case, that was the vast forests of Guyana.

2. "Finding the Road," *Daily Chronicle*, March 13, 1931.

3. "What of a Night," "Wisdom Cometh in the Morning," and "The Jealous Scribe" appeared on January 1, January 9, and February 1, 1916, respectively.

4. "The Rise and Wane of the Colony's Industries," *Chronicle*, Holiday Number (August 1916), 58.

5. Eric Williams, "The Historical Background of British Guiana's Problems," *Journal of Negro History* 30, no. 4 (October 1945): 360, 361.

6. "Rise and Wane of the Colony's Industries," 60.

7. Ibid., 58.

8. Ibid.

9. "Rev. Andrews Discusses Immigration with Chamber of Commerce," *Daily Chronicle*, May 24, 1929.

10. In 1897 Bechu, an indentured Bengali, testified to the Royal West India Commission that the overseers exploited East Indian women and noted that it was "another ground for discontent and sometimes leads to riots, yet immigration agents close their eyes to the matter." This practice continued throughout indentureship. In 1929 C. W. H. Collier, acting for the protector of the Indians, investigated allegations of sexual misconduct on the part of G. W. Sutherland, deputy manager of Plantation Rose Hall, and concluded that the latter "had immoral relations with Sookari. It is apparent that her children's father was a white man." The governor saw such behavior as having the potential to threaten the "peace and quiet" of the colony and wrote the following to the secretary of state for the colonies: "In view of the fact that there still exists a disproportion of sexes among East Indians in this Colony, the withdrawal of even a single woman from the Immigrant's dwelling to the Overseer's quarters is likely to lead to discontent, the unfolding of discipline on the Estate, and possible serious disturbances." "Copy of a letter from the Immigration Agent to the Honorable Colonial Secretary dated 10th April 1930," Public Record Office, CO 111/688/5, 1930.

11. A. R. F. Webber, *Those That Be in Bondage: A Tale of Indian Indentures and Sunlit Western Waters* (Georgetown, British Guiana: Daily Chronicle, 1917), 6 (hereafter cited in the text as *Bondage*).

12. Jeremy Poynting sees such depictions as continuing what he calls "the prurient estate stereotype" that are found in these early kinds of novels. See Jeremy Poynting, "East Indian Women in the Caribbean: Experience, Image, and Voice," *Journal of South Asian Literature* 21, no. 1 (Winter, Spring 1986): 141.

13. C. L. R. James takes this up in his book *The Case for West Indian Self-Government* (London: Hogarth Press, 1933), a point that Webber continued to make throughout his career. Suffice it to say that Webber preceded James by almost fifteen years in his concerns of the West Indianization of these jobs. Wint made a similar point for the education profession in Jamaica.

14. See a rather dramatic account of this fire in the *Daily Chronicle*, March 1917. Some of the reports of the fire are also republished in the *New Daily Chronicle* on March 8, 1932.

15. See A. J. Seymour, "The Literary Adventure of the West Indies," *Kyk-Over-Al* 2, no. 10 (April 1950): 36. Webber inserts this actual historical event into his text. In *Those That Be in Bondage*, he notes: "Friday, the 7th of March, 1913, dawned in all the intense loveliness of the tropics; not the most confirmed pessimist could claim to have had [a] premonition of the ghastly tragedy at hand; and the heavens seemed to smile down peace and benediction" (210). In *Centenary History and Handbook of British Guiana*, a report of the same incident reads as follows: "Friday, the 7th March, 1913, proved a day of great sacrifice to the Catholic community and indeed to the whole colony, with the total destruction on that day by fire of the beautiful Cathedral of the Immaculate Conception" (337).

16. Wilson Harris, "Afterword." In *Those That Be in Bondage: A Tale of Indian Indentures and Sunlit Western Waters*, by A. R. F. Webber (Wellesley: Calaloux, 1988), 239–40.

17. A. R. F. Webber, *An Innocent's Pilgrimage: Being Pen Pictures of a Tender-foot Who Visited London for the First Time* (Georgetown, British Guiana: New Daily Chronicle Printing, 1927), 36.

18. Ibid. 92.

19. Harris, "Afterword," 238–39.

20. Ibid., 239.

21. Seymour, "Literary Adventure," 38.

22. See ibid.

23. Harris, "Afterword," 237.

24. Ibid.

CHAPTER 2. THE PRIVATE THOUGHTS OF A POLITICAL MAN: THE MAKING OF A. R. F. WEBBER, 1917–19

1. A. J. P. Taylor, *The First World War* (New York: Capricorn Books, 1972), 165.

2. C. L. R. James, "The Making of the Caribbean People," *Radical America* 4, no. 4, Special Issue (May 1970): 46.

3. Ibid., 47.

4. Ibid., 48.

5. Ibid.

6. Vere T. Daly, *A Short History of the Guyanese People* (Georgetown, Guyana: Vere T. Daly, 1966), 310.

7. Report by Hon. E. L. F. Wood, M.P., on his visit to the West Indies and British Guiana, December 1921–February 1922, London, 1922, 556 (hereafter cited as "Visit to the West Indies").

8. Wood was accompanied and assisted in his inquiries by W. Ormsby-Gore, M.P., and R. A. Wiseman of the Colonial Office.

9. "Visit to the West Indies," 6. Lord Moyne made the same derogatory comments about Africans in the Caribbean in his report in 1938. Much of what James says about Moyne's comments about the nontransfer "of any important traces of their [African] traditions and customs" to the Caribbean is applicable to Wood's comments in his report on this question. See James's response to Moyne's comments in "Making of the Caribbean People."

10. "Visit to the West Indies," 65.

11. See Ron Ramdin, *From Chattel Slave to Wage Earner: A History of Trade Unionism in Trinidad and Tobago* (London: M. Brian and O'Keeffe, 1982).

12. See "Visit to the West Indies," 85-87. British Guiana seems to be the only territory to have suffered a decrease in population during the period 1913–18. According to Wood, the mortality figures "have been decreased, but the influenza epidemic in 1918, during which year the death-rate rose from 30 to 40 thousand, falling in 1920 to 25.6. Even this latter figure is sufficiently large to show that health conditions are very far from satisfactory." Ibid., 85.

13. Webber, *Centenary History*, 340.

14. The Allies actually happened upon the principle of "national self-determination" as they sought to win U.S. support of their efforts. Taylor notes: "The Germans were only concerned to keep the United States neutral. The Allies however wished to win America to their side. They had to give a more positive reply—to define the moral superiority, which they really felt, in such a way as to satisfy American idealism. The British and French governments had hastily to discover what they were fighting for. They came out with an answer on 10 January 1917. It was easy to demand the evacuation of all territory occupied by Germany, its restoration at German expense—Belgium, Serbia, Rumania, western Russia, and northern France. Beyond this they had no idea what to do with Germany except to defeat her. They therefore spoke vaguely of 'full security and international settlements such as to guarantee land and sea frontiers against unjustified attack.' This was not enough as an appeal to American sentiments. The Allies has also to display some great principle. They found it in 'national self-determination.'" Taylor, *First World War*, 161.

15. See Ayearst, *British West Indies*, 111.

16. Taylor, *First World War*, 173.

17. The title page of the printer's copy of *Glints from an Anvil* states that these poems were "reprinted from the columns of the *Daily Chronicle* and *Chronicle Annuals*, together with some hitherto unpublished lines." It was published by the Daily Chronicle Press (Printers) as "our 'two minute contribution' to the British Guiana Red Cross Fund." It is clear that Webber was doing a lot of writing during this period. He also listed the fact that he wrote "How I Found the Giant Sloth" and an "Imaginary Interview with Santa Claus." I have not been able to locate these works.

18. Taylor, *First World War*, 65. During the war, "Gott strafe England" (May God punish England!) was a slogan of the German army. Some commentators suggest that this "Christmas truce" lasted as long as a week.

19. See "The Dilemma," in J. C. Squire, *The Survival of the Fittest and Other Poems* (London: George Allen and Unwin), 1916.

20. Ovid Edgar Leland Sharples studied law at Oxford and returned to Guyana as a qualified attorney in 1900. Wayne McWatt, a cousin of Sharples, notes that Sharples's legal future in Guyana "was somewhat limited to the extent that there was not much prospect of him, as a coloured man, becoming a judge. Having grown up in England [he immigrated to there when he was seven years old] he found it difficult to adjust to life in Guyana." Private correspondence, August 20, 2006.

21. *New Daily Chronicle*, February 20, December 1929.

22. Norman E. Cameron, *Guianese Poetry* (Georgetown, British Guyana: Argosy, 1931), 169.

CHAPTER 3. WEBBER'S ENTRANCE TO THE POLITICAL ARENA, 1919–21

1. See A. R. F. Webber, "How I Won My Election," *Daily Chronicle*, November 5, 1921.

2. Lutchman, *From Colonialism to Co-operative Republic*, 58.

3. Peter Ruhomon was the leading East Indian intellectual of the period. He was secretary of the EIYMS from its formation in October 1919 to the late 1930s. According to Ruhomon, the objective of the

EIYMS was "to afford an opportunity, so much needed in the colony, to young Indians to improve their minds and character to profitable advantage to themselves and for the good of the community to which they belong." Quoted in Seecharan, *Tiger in the Stars*, 304.

4. *Daily Chronicle*, July 24, 1921.

5. "The Wail of the Submerged Tenth," *Daily Chronicle*, July 15, 1921.

6. Ibid.

7. "The General Elections and Ourselves," *Daily Chronicle*, August 31, 1921.

8. See "Mr. Webber's Chances Roseate," *Daily Chronicle*, September 29, 1921.

9. Ibid.

10. *Daily Chronicle*, October 9, 1921.

11. "Mr. Webber's Candidature," *Daily Chronicle*, October 11, 1921.

12. "Berbice F. R. Seat," *Daily Chronicle*, October 13, 1921.

13. "Vote for Webber," *Daily Chronicle*, October 18, 1921.

14. *Daily Chronicle*, October 20, 1921.

15. *Daily Chronicle*, October 21, 1921. In this context, the term "black man" is used to include both Africans (or Afro-Guyanese) and East Indians.

16. Webber, "How I Won My Election," *Daily Chronicle*, November 19, 1921.

17. Webber, "How I Won My Election," *Daily Chronicle*, November 5, 1921.

18. See Webber, "How I Won My Election," *Daily Chronicle*, November 5, 12, 19, and 26, 1921.

19. See Webber, "How I Won My Election," November 5, 1921.

20. Webber, "How I Won My Election," November 26, 1921.

21. Ibid.

22. Webber, "How I Won My Election," November 19, 1921.

23. Ibid. In the introduction, I compare Webber's platform style with that of A. J. Cook, which Herbert Smith describes as follows: "With coat off and sleeves rolled up Mr. Cook addressed them. As he proceeded waistcoat would be shed, then collar and tie, until he stood, with shirt neck open, sweeping a vast crowd of people with emotion, as few speakers have ever done." Smith, *A. J. Cook*, 110. Webber may not have gone as far as Cook did, but he understood the importance of the dramatic gesture when one addressed a crowd.

24. Webber, "How I Won My Election," November 19, 1921.

CHAPTER 4. WEBBER'S POLITICAL ASCENDANCY, 1921–25

1. The British Guiana legislature consisted of the Court of Policy (the governor, seven officials, and eight elected unofficial members) and the Combined Court (the six Financial Representatives). The latter body possessed the power of imposing taxes and in particular the right to control the appropriation of public monies. It could reduce or reject any item on the annual estimates that were prepared by the governor in Executive Council.

2. *Daily Chronicle*, August 26, 1921.

3. *Daily Chronicle*, October 27, 1921.

4. Webber, *Centenary History*, 347–48.

5. Ibid., 352. "Crosby" was the immigrant agent general to whom the East Indians appealed for relief from their sufferings.

6. Ravi Dev, "State and Societal Violence against Indians in Guyana: The Ethnic Security Dilemmas," *Kaieteur News Column*, October 29, 2006. In 1917 indentureship ended. However, the planters still desired Indian immigrants to work in the colony. Therefore, in 1919 they proposed a colonization scheme

that would involve the settling of large amounts of East Indians in the colony as independent farmers. J. A. Luchoo and Dr. Hewley, who were authorized by the British Guiana East Indian Association to travel to India to convince the British authorities in India about this scheme, offered that its aim was "to induce more Indians from the motherland to join our ranks, increase our numbers and so help us to make British Guiana an Indian Colony." This scheme drew the ire of African leaders, who took an aggressive stand against it; they saw it as an act of discrimination and argued that it "would tend to rob [blacks] of their potentialities, as they would be in the minority in any voting contest—the Indian vote would become more than or equal to the votes of any two of the other sections of the community; it would be detrimental to good government and the preservation of the peace." In 1921 Indians were 42 percent of the population, Africans were 39 percent, whereas the Coloured were 10 percent. Needless to say, such an idea created tensions between the two major ethnic groups. Both of these quotations are taken from Dev, "State and Societal Violence against Indians in Guyana."

7. Seecharan, *Tiger in the Stars*, 365.
8. Walter Rodney, *A History of the Guyanese Working People, 1881–1905* (Baltimore: Johns Hopkins University Press, 1981), 186.
9. Lutchman, *From Colonialism to Co-operative Republic*, 83–84.
10. Ibid., 145.
11. "Graeme Thomson to L.C.M.S. Amery, P.C.," May 26, 1925, Public Record Office, CO111/657, 1–2.
12. Ibid., 2.
13. Ibid., 4–5.
14. Ibid., 6.
15. Webber, *Centenary History*, 350, my emphasis.
16. "Removal of Ammunition Magazine at Camp Road to Constabulary Depot, $1,200," May 6, 1925, Public Record Office, CO111/657.
17. "Graeme Thomson to L.C.M.S. Amery, P.C.," May 26, 1925, 13.
18. "Combined Court," *Hansard*, May 5, 1925.
19. "Encouragement of Cotton Growing," *Hansard*, May 8, 1925.
20. Ibid., my emphasis.
21. Ibid.
22. *Report of the West India Royal Commission*, Vol. 2, Appendix C, 90.
23. "Combined Court," *Hansard*, May 14, 1925.
24. Ibid.
25. James, *Case for West-Indian Self Government*, 23–24.
26. See "The Stifling of Debate," *Daily Chronicle*, May 16, 1925; and "Recklessness of a Legislator," *Outlook*, May 16, 1925.
27. E. Sievewright Stoby, ed., *British Guiana Centenary Year Book: 1831–1931* (Georgetown, British Guiana: Daily Chronicle, 1931), 138.
28. Quoted in Seecharan, *Tiger in the Stars*, 190–91.
29. "Minutes by the Inspector-General of Police forwarding a report by District Inspector Matthey on Mr. Dodds," May 11, 1925, Public Record Office, CO111/657.
30. "Webber to Amery," May 26, 1925, Public Record Office, CO111/657.
31. Ibid.
32. "Amery Notes," September 22, 1925, Public Record Office, CO111/659.
33. Ibid.
34. "Thomson to Amery," May 26, 1925, 15–16.
35. Thomson's worst fears turned out to be correct. A report by G. D. Bayley, commissioner of lands and mines, July 6, 1925, showed that within a period of four years (1921–25) the electorate increased by 85

percent (from 4,967 to 9,215 voters), "due almost entirely," as Bayley noted, "to the political activities of Mr. A. R. F. Webber." "Copy of minutes by the Honourable G. D. Bayley, C.B.E., Commissioner of Lands and Mines," May 6, 1925, Public Record Office, CO111/658.

36. "Reginald Popham Lobb to L.C.M.S. Amery," July 27, 1925, Public Record Office, CO111/658.

37. Ibid., 17.

38. Ibid., 21.

39. "Playing to the Gallery," *Daily Argosy*, May 14, 1925.

40. "Thomson to Amery," May 26, 1925, 8.

41. "Note prepared on interview between Sir G. Thomson & S/S/," July 25, 1925, Public Record Office, CO111/659.

42. Ibid.

43. "Copy of letter from Acting Colonial Secretary King to Mr. A. R. F. Webber, F. R.," August 12, 1925, Public Record Office, CO111/658.

44. "Note prepared on interview between Sir G. Thomson & S/S/," July 25, 1925.

45. Naiva Tasya, "Entre Nous," *Tribune*, July 26, 1925.

CHAPTER 5. THE CONSTITUTIONAL CRISIS: THE BULLET OR THE BALLOT

1. Seecharan, *Tiger in the Stars*, xxiv, 185. See chapter 14 of *Tiger in the Stars* for an account of Robertson's advocacy in support of the East Indians. It helped that he was also a rice farmer.

2. Ibid., 107.

3. Jagan, *West on Trial*, 292.

4. "R. J. Craig to L. S. Amery," June 31, 1926, Public Record Office, CO111/661.

5. "Lobb to Amery," July 27, 1925. Up to 1835 the qualification for a voter in Guyana was the ownership of twenty-five slaves.

6. Jagan, *West on Trial*, 292–93. On this point of workers' unity, Jagan seems to contradict himself in his 1984 interview with Frank Birbalsingh. He notes that the work he did while he was in Parliament (1947–53) led "to the formation of the People's Progressive Party and to the victory of the party in 1953. More importantly, it was a foundation that united the working people who were divided until that time." Birbalsingh, *People's Progressive Party*, 30. Although Critchlow's name does not appear prominently in Guyana's labor history until the second decade of the twentieth century, as a dockworker in 1905, he took part in the 1905 riots where he "persuaded the 'boys' to strike as soon as their bargaining position was improved by the presence of six ships in harbour. Critchlow was arrested but released without being charged, so that his name does not appear on the court records." Rodney, *History of the Guyanese Working People*, 208.

7. *Report of the British Guiana Commission* (London: Her Majesty's Stationery Office, 1927), 49. Up to 1795 the Dutch ruled the colony (Demerara and Essequebo). The Court of Policy, the only legislative body of the colony, was composed of four officials (including the governor) and four planters elected by the College of the Kaisers or Electors. In 1795, when a British invasion threatened the colony, the governor summoned four members of the College of Kaisers to the council chambers for the express purpose of giving him financial advice. This was the beginning of the Combined Court. When the British captured the colony in 1796, the British agreed that six of these Financial Representatives should be elected by certain plantation owners. When Berbice was ceded to the British in 1803 (Berbice, Demerara, and Essequebo became British Guiana in 1831), the same constitutional formula was retained in accordance with the Articles of Capitulation. When Amery tried to remove the powers of the Financial Representatives in the 1928 constitution, Webber relied on the identical language of the British agreement of 1796.

8. "Note Prepared by Order of the Secretary of State," (n.d.), Public Record Office, CO111/659.

9. Ibid.

10 Ibid.

11. Dev, "State and Social Violence against Indians in Guyana."

12. Ibid.

13. *Proceedings of the West Indian Conference, London, May–June 1926* (London: Colonial Office, 1926), 3.

14. The recommendation brought forward for discussion read as follows: "As soon as the conditions in Great Britain change and it is possible to absorb the British silver now current in the West Indian colonies then, if those Colonies favour the sterling dollar scheme and the establishment of a Currency Board of their own, on the lines set out above, we recommend your taking the necessary action to effect such change." Ibid., 3.

15. Ibid., 37.

16 Ibid., 39.

17. Ibid., 40.

18. "Trinbagonian" is a shortened name for a citizen of Trinidad and Tobago.

19. *Proceedings of the West Indian Conference*, 41–42.

20. Ibid., 41.

21. "Note on the discussion of the railway question between the secretary of state and the British Guiana delegates," June 26, 1926, Public Record Office, CO111/660.

22. Ibid.

23. Ibid.

24. "Making British Guiana One of [the] World's Highways," Public Record Office, CO111/663.

25. *Proceedings of the West Indian Conference*, 69.

26. Ibid., 3.

27. There seems to be some confusion here. In "From an Editorial View-Point" (1928), Webber's next travelogue, he says that he first went to England in the winter of 1917–18. It might be that he had not been to London during his first visit to England or that this was the first time he was visiting London in his capacity as a journalist.

28. See Webber, *Innocent's Pilgrimage*. All quotations are taken from this book.

29. Although I differentiate between Webber being colored and his relationship to blackness in chapter 15, for purposes of this analysis, unless stated otherwise, we can characterize Webber as a black person.

30. In his trip to Europe and the Holy Land, which *The Innocents Abroad* depicts, Twain suggests that the major purpose of his writing this book is "to suggest to the reader how *he* would be likely to see Europe and the East if he looked at them with his own eyes instead of the eyes of those who traveled in those countries before him." Mark Twain, *The Innocents Abroad* (New York: Grosset and Dunlap, 1911), preface. Like Webber, Twain was a newspaper correspondent and feature writer. His trip to Europe and the Holy Land was paid for by the *San Francisco Daily Alta Californian*. Perhaps it is in this context of seeing England in "his own eyes" rather than the eyes of those who traveled there previously that allowed Webber to describe himself in the subtitle of his book as a "tender-foot who visited London for the first time." It also might have been that he had not really seen London before he undertook the writing of it.

31. Webber, *Innocent's Pilgrimage*, 49 (hereafter cited in the text as *IP*).

32. The pagination in this text is off somewhat. The first installment of the series (eight pages) is numbered in roman numerals, whereas the last eighteen pages are numbered in Arabic numerals and begin on page 4. I retain the pagination of the original text.

33. Henry Mayhew was an English journalist who ventured directly into the poorest parts of London to interview pickpockets, petty criminals, sweatshop workers, prostitutes, and others. His articles were collected together in book form in three volumes under the title *London Labour and the London Poor* (1861). The fourth volume examined the lives of prostitutes, thieves, and beggars. His work had a lot of influence on Christian socialists such as Thomas Hughes and Charles Kingsley. Harold Perkin notes

that the objective of his work "was not just to describe and moralize, but to 'cause those who are in 'high places' and those of whom much is expected, to bestir themselves to improve the condition of a class of people whose misery, ignorance and vice, amidst all the immense wealth and great knowledge of 'the first city of the world' is, to say the very least, a national disgrace to us." Perkin, *Origins of Modern English Society*, 167.

34. Ibid., 162.

35. Ibid., 168–69.

36. Feminist scholars may take issue with the analogy that Webber makes between London and "a certain type of professional lady." The characterization deals with the society in which he lived. We are told by his daughter that although he was a protective father against whom she had to rebel, Webber adored his daughters and loved his wife immensely. After he died in 1932, his wife wore black until her death in 1952. It also needs to be added that the Popular Party, of which Webber was one of the leaders, called for the franchise of women as early as 1926.

37. Advertisement, *New Daily Chronicle*, October 13, 1929.

CHAPTER 6. WEBBER'S LEADERSHIP, THE POPULAR PARTY, AND THE CONSTITUTIONAL CRISIS, 1926–27

1. Rodney reminds us that in 1901, the People's Party, or what he calls a "proto-party with well defined positions," was formed in Guyana. See Rodney, *History of the Guyanese Working People*, 173.

2. Lutchman, "Middle Class Colonial Politics," 110.

3. Ibid., 76, 114.

4. Lutchman, *From Colonialism to Co-operative Republic*, 84.

5. Quoted in the *New Daily Chronicle*, July 13, 1927.

6. See letter from R. A. Wiseman to J. B. Cassels, September 25, 1926, Public Record Office, CO111/663.

7. *Report of the British Guiana Commission*, 3. The personnel of the commission were R. Roy Wilson, M.P., chairman; H. Snell, M.P.; and R. R. Sedgwick, secretary. All other references to this report are noted in the text as *BGC*.

8. My emphasis. At that time only males could vote. The designation "black and coloured population" excluded Indo-Guyanese, although their numbers were very small.

9. Quoted in Lutchman, "Middle Class Colonial Politics," 118.

10. *Report of the British Guiana Commission*, 1927. The members of this commission were C. Douglas Jones, chairman; Hector Josephs; J. Hampton King; Williams M. B. Shields; W. Bain Gray; Eustace G. Woolford; and R. E. Brassington. In 1976 Frank Brassington claimed that his father, R. E. Brassington, "led the British Guiana delegation to England in 1929 when the then mainland territory was seeking Constitution Reform and a wider measure of representation for the people in State affairs." The record does not seem to bear him out on this point. However, he is correct when he says that "in consort with his colleagues, [he] even sought Dominion status for his country." As chapter 12 shows, he joined the Electives as they struggled to overthrow the 1928 constitution that introduced Crown Colony government to the country. In a move reminiscent of Webber, Frank Brassington immigrated to Trinidad in 1946 and became the honorary secretary of the Democratic Labour Party of the West Indies, one of the two major parties that contested the federal elections in 1958. See Frank Brassington, *The Politics of Opposition* (Diego Martin, Trinidad: West Indian Publishing, 1976), 2.

11. Portuguese, East Indian, Negro, colored, and whites were the appellations that were used during the period.

12. Lutchman, "Middle Class Colonial Politics," 118.

13. Ayearst, *British West Indies*, 111.

14. Quoted in Lutchman, "Middle Class Colonial Politics," 117.

15. Ibid.

16. *Daily Argosy*, November 5, 1926.

17. *Daily Argosy*, October 17, 1926.

18. *Daily Argosy*, November 3, 1927.

19. Lutchman, "Middle Class Colonial Politics," 120.

20. Ayearst, *British West Indies*, 111.

21. Quoted in Lutchman, "Middle Class Colonial Politics," 121.

22. *Daily Argosy*, October 20, 1926.

23. Lutchman, "Middle Class Colonial Politics," 125.

24. Ibid., 123.

25. Ibid., 135.

26. "Inquiry into the Administration of Justice in the Colony," *New Daily Chronicle*, December 19, 1926.

27. "A Judicial Scandal," *New Daily Chronicle*, December 19, 1926.

28. Public Record Office, CO 111/665/4, 1927. The chief justice ruled as follows: "Any act done or writing published that might bring a Court or a judge of the Court into contempt or lower his authority is a contempt of Court. The article contains much personal scurrilous abuse of a judge, abuse in reference to his conduct while sitting as a judge.... That which is called 'the liberty of the Press' is no greater than the liberty of every subject of the king." Ibid.

29. In 1888 Louis de Souza, a prominent attorney of Guyana, was charged with contempt of court for a letter he had written in the *Royal Gazette* that criticized a judgment of the court. He was found guilty for bringing the administration of justice and the judges into disrepute and sentenced to six months in prison. He died in prison while he was serving his sentence. See P. H. Daly, *West Indian Freedom and West Indian Literature: Stories of the Heroes, Book 3* (Georgetown, British Guiana: Daily Chronicle, 1943), 267–93, for an account of this case.

30. "Proceeding Against A. R. F. Webber and R. A. Small for Contempt of Court in Publishing in 'The New Daily Chronicle of Events' an article entitled 'A Judicial Scandal,'" Public Record Office, CO111/665, April 22, 1926.

31. Rohini, "Hon. A. R. F. Webber."

32. Governor C. H. Rodwell to L. S. Amery, April 27, 1927, Public Record Office, CO 111/665/4.

33. Public Record Office, CO 111/665/4, June 21, 1927.

34. In a letter by Grace Thomas (b. 1905 in Tobago), a cousin of Webber, to Dolores Thompson, another cousin of Webber, in August 1986, Thomas remembers kidding Webber about his relationship to British Guiana when he visited Trinidad in 1928: "I asked him why he was fooling the BG people making them believe that he was one of them. He got serious and said: 'My dear girl, never you believe that.'" I am not sure if Webber meant Thomas should not believe that he was fooling the Guyanese people or that he had not relinquished his Tobagonian origin. At any rate, from Thomas's recollections, Webber seemed to have had a wonderful time with his cousins in Trinidad when he passed through the country as they reminisced about the past. See Grace Thomas's undated letter to Dolores Thompson, in private collection of Dolores Thompson.

35. Lutchman, *From Colonialism to Co-operative Republic*, 30.

36. Quoted in ibid.

37. *New Daily Chronicle*, July 13, 1927.

38. *New Daily Chronicle*, August 11, 1927.

39. John Smith of Guyana and William Gordon of Jamaica are well-known freedom fighters of the Caribbean who lost their lives at the hands of the colonizing powers because they defended their people's rights.

40. *New Daily Chronicle*, August 11, 1927.

41. Kim Blake, "T. E. S. Scholes: The Unknown Pan Africanist," *Race and Class* 49, no. 1 (July–September 2007): 64.

42. Eric Williams, in his castigation of those who were opposed to self-government, offered his famous "Massa Day Done" speech years later in Trinidad and Tobago. See "Massa Day Done," in Selwyn R. Cudjoe, ed., *Eric E. Williams Speaks* (Amherst: University of Massachusetts Press, 1990), 237–64. Colin Palmer says that Williams's "Massa Day Done" speech will go down in the historical annals as one of the strongest indictments of the psychological impact of colonial rule made by a head of government anywhere." Colin Palmer, *Eric Williams and the Making of the Modern Caribbean* (Chapel Hill: University of North Carolina Press, 2006), 23.

43. *New Daily Chronicle*, August 11, 1927.

44. Ibid.

45. See, for example, "Mr. J. A. Luckhoo Raises Hornet's Nest in New Amsterdam," *New Daily Chronicle*, August 16, 1927; "Editorial," *New Daily Chronicle*, August 18, 1927; and Luckhoo's letter to the *New Daily Chronicle*, August 18, 1927.

46. Quoted in Dev, "State and Societal Violence against Indians in Guyana."

47. See *Timehri*, vol. 5 (1891).

48. See Lutchman, "Middle Class Colonial Politics," 130–35, for an explanation of what he called "the temporary nature of the Popular Party." I am indebted to this work for my analysis of the rise and fall of the Popular Party.

49. Lutchman, *From Colonialism to Co-operative Republic*, 131.

50. Daly, *Short History of the Guyanese People*, 312.

CHAPTER 7. WEBBER: A TRAVELING MAN

1. See "By the Editor," *New Daily Chronicle*, April 20, 1928; and "Gathering Up the Ashes," *New Daily Chronicle*, April 29, 1928.

2. *New Daily Chronicle*, April 29, 1928.

3. Ibid.

4. *New Daily Chronicle*, June 29, 1928.

5. *Jamaica Mail*, April 12, 1928, quoted in *New Daily Chronicle*, April 13, 1928.

6. *New Daily Chronicle*, June 20, 1928.

7. Ibid.

8. *New Daily Chronicle*, December 9, 1928.

9. Ibid.

10. A. R. F. Webber, "New York versus London," *New Daily Chronicle*, January 30, 1929. In his handwritten notes in his notebooks, Webber appended "I" as if to suggest that this piece was the first of a five-part series. The other parts are numbered two through five.

11. Ibid.

12. Ibid.

13. Ibid.

14. Ibid.

15. See V. S. Naipaul, "Jasmine," in *The Overcrowded Barracoon and Other Articles* (London: Deutsch, 1972).

16. A. R. F. Webber, "The Women and Worries of New York," *New Daily Chronicle*, February 7, 1929. These sentiments echoed those of Mary Seacole, a Jamaican Creole woman—her description—who made it clear in her travel book "that it was confidence in my own powers, and not at all from necessity, that I remained an unprotected female. Indeed, I do not mind confessing to my reader, in a friendly confidential way, that one of the hardest struggles of my life in Kingston was to resist the pressing candidates

for the late Mr. Seacole's shoes." This can be read as an example of early "womanism" in the Caribbean. Mary Seacole, *Wonderful Adventures of Mrs. Seacole in Many Lands* (1857; reprint, New York: Oxford University Press, 1988), 8.

17. Ibid.

18. Ibid.

19. Ibid.

20. A. R. F. Webber, "New York Facts and Fancies," *New Daily Chronicle*, March 14, 1929.

21. Ibid.

22. A. R. F. Webber, "New York Pen Pictures," *New Daily Chronicle*, April 4, 1929.

23. Ibid.

24. A. R. F. Webber, "Pen Pictures of New York—Fleeing from the Wrath to Come," *New Daily Chronicle*, May 2, 1929.

25. Ibid.

26. Ibid.

27. Ibid.

28. Ibid.

29. *New Daily Chronicle*, July 14, 1927.

30. *Daily Chronicle*, February 2, 1929.

31. *New Daily Chronicle*, January 24, 1929.

32. "Report on the West Indian Press and Rules of the Association," *Daily Chronicle*, February 5, 1929.

33. The delegates to the conference consisted of D. T. Wint, *Jamaica Critic*; N. A. Parker, *Jamaica Mail*; T. A. Marryshow, *Grenada West Indian*; A. P. Ambard, *Port of Spain Gazette*; W. H. Bishop, *Labour Leader*, Trinidad; H. Philips, *Daily Chronicle*, Guyana; P. Gordon, *St. Lucia Voice*; H. T. Williams, *Antigua Magnet*; Mr. Spurling, *Gazette*, Bermuda; C. L. Gale, *Advocate*, Barbados; G. H. Adams, *Agricultural Reporter*, Barbados; and C. W. Wickham, *Barbados Herald*. Delegates from the Congress of the Associated West Indian Chambers of Commerce, several delegates to the West Indian Conference, and members of the general public attended the conference. Mr. Partridge, editor of the *Trinidad Guardian*, did not attend because he was sick. The editors of *Sports Weekly* and the *Sporting Chronicle* of Trinidad, Grenada *Guardian*, the *St. Vincent Sentry*, the *Vincentian*, the *St. Vincent Times*, the *Demerara Tribune*, Belize *Clarion*, and the *Monitor* of Trinidad did not attend but sent their best wishes.

34. *Daily Chronicle*, February 2, 1928.

35. Ibid.

36. *Port of Spain Gazette*, January 24, 1927, reprinted in *New Daily Chronicle*, February 6, 1929; *Port of Spain Chronicle*, reprinted in *New Daily Chronicle*, February 6, 1929.

37. *Daily Chronicle*, February 2, 1929.

38. *New Daily Chronicle*, February 19, 1929.

39. *New Daily Chronicle*, February 1929.

40. *Daily Chronicle*, March 9, 1929.

41. Lutchman, "Middle Class Colonial Politics," 67, 68.

42. See Immanuel Geiss, *The Pan-African Movement: A History of Pan-Africanism in America, Europe and Africa*, trans. Ann Keep (New York: Africana Publishing, 1974), part 1.

43. C. R. L. Fletcher and Rudyard Kipling, *A School History of England* (Oxford: Clarendon Press, 1911), 240, quoted in the *Daily Chronicle*, March 10, 1929.

44. See J. J. Thomas, *Froudacity* (1889); T. E. H. Scholes, *British Empire and Alliances or Britain's Duty to her Colonies and Subject Races* (1899); T. E. H. Scholes, *Glimpses of the Ages or the "Superior" and "Inferior" Races, So-Called, Discussed in the Light of Science and History* (1908); Owen Mathurin, *Henry Sylvester Williams and the Origins of the Pan African Movement* (1976); C. L. R. James, introduction to J. J. Thomas, *Froudacity* (1969); and C. L. R. James, *Black Jacobins* (1938).

45. Geiss, *Pan-African Movement*, 96.

46. The text of the NPC letter to Bain Gray, the director of education, reads as follows: "Whereas there appeared in the *New Daily Chronicle* of March 3, 1929, an extract from *A School History of England* at present in use at Queen's College by C. R. L. Fletcher and Rudyard Kipling, which is a contemptuous and malicious libel against the Negro Race in this colony and other parts of the West Indies; Be it resolved that the Director of Education of the Colony of British Guiana be asked to receive a deputation reasonably to discuss this objectionable feature of the book with the hope of getting it withdrawn, and if the Director cannot see his way to do something about the matter, he be asked to accompany a deputation to the Governor for his due consideration." *Daily Chronicle*, March 27, 1929.

47. *Daily Chronicle*, March 27, 1929.

CHAPTER 8. THE QUEST FOR SELF-GOVERNMENT

1. Fletcher and Kipling, *School History of England*, 222, my emphasis.

2. *Daily Chronicle*, July 12, 1929.

3. Ibid.

4. *Daily Chronicle*, June 11, 1929.

5. "De Omnibus Rebus," *New Daily Chronicle*, May 19, 1929.

6. *New Daily Chronicle*, May 19, 1929.

7. "A Call for Combined Action," *New Daily Chronicle*, May 19, 1929.

8. *Daily Chronicle*, June 13, 1929.

9. Jagan, *West on Trial*, 65.

10. *New Daily Chronicle*, July 28, 1929.

11. Ibid.

12. *New Daily Chronicle*, July 29, 1929.

13. "Government Charges Electives with Obstruction," *New Daily Chronicle*," December 5, 1929.

14. See "Respectable Man Says Daily Argosy Incited Him," *New Daily Chronicle*, November 30, 1929.

15. "Hon. A. R. F. Webber Apologizes to Mr. P. N. Brown, K.C.," *New Daily Chronicle*, December 12, 1929.

16. "West Indian Federation Delegates for Labour Party Conference in 1930," *New Daily Chronicle*, September 29, 1929.

17. Ibid.

18. Ibid.

19. Quoted in Lutchman, *From Colonialism to Co-operative Republic*," 51.

20. Quoted in ibid., 42–43.

21. Letter to the Secretary, the Colonial Office, London, May 8, 1933, Public Record Office, CO 111/711/14.

22. Seecharan, *Tiger in the Stars*, 153.

23. Several years after the emancipation of slaves in the British colonies in 1834, American abolitionists such as Nancy Prince celebrated August 1 as the true date of emancipation. According to Ronald Walters, "For years afterward [the British emancipation of their slaves], some of their number celebrated August 1, rather than July 4, as the true birthday of freedom in the New World." Ronald Walters, introduction to *A Black Woman's Odyssey through Russia and Jamaica: The Narrative of Nancy Prince* (1799; reprint, New York: Marcus Wiener, 1990), xviii.

24. Letter to the Secretary, the Colonial Office, London, May 8 1933.

25. Quoted in ibid., 42.

26. See Norman E. Cameron, *The Evolution of the Negro*, vol. 2 (Georgetown, Demerara: Argosy, 1934).

27. Geiss, *Pan-African Movement*, 96.

28. See N. E. Cameron, *The Evolution of the Negro*, vol. 1 (Georgetown, Demerara: Argosy, 1929), vii. Cameron realized that the use of the word "Negro" was objectionable, but not for the reason we may suspect. He says: "I was rather surprised when I read a book written by an Englishman, Francis Moore, in 1734 that the Senegalese (or West Africa) took great offence in being called 'Negroes' by Europeans. Nor were they the only African people to object thus to the word. Their argument seems to have been that from time immemorial they used national names or place names. Thus, the people of Manding called themselves Mandingoes; those of Nubia, Nubians.... Why should they be all labeled under one name 'Negro' as if the use of national names was not intended to signify differences (among things)? These Africans believed that the word was intended for slaves who had no country.... There is another objection to the word and that is, that it can be spelt with a common letter without the writer being accused of bad spelling. Then again the word is loosely applied when the question of race arises. Thus some writers say that the Bantus (advanced tribes of South and Central Africa) are 'not of the Negro race.' ... Everything depends on what they mean by the word 'negro,' and indeed the question hardly concerns me.... Thus we see by applying the term 'Negro' to certain African peoples and not to others, misunderstanding may arise when the Americans are included. I am an advocate of place names and venture to suggest that when persons of African descent in the Americas are to be spoken of, the term Afro-Americans or Afreur-Americans be applied to them all, and when those of any particular island or country are referred to that the name of the place be used, e.g., a Trinidadian, or if greater definiteness is required, an Afro-American Trinidadian, or a Trinidadian Afro-American, just as we speak of Trinidad East Indian." Ibid., vi–vii. In this, Cameron seemed to be ahead of his time.

29. Ibid., xv.

30. *Daily Chronicle*, November 10, 1929.

31. "The Evolution of the Negro," *New Daily Chronicle*, January 29, 1930.

32. See *Daily Chronicle*, July 28, 1929. Amy Ashwood Garvey was married to Marcus Garvey on December 25, 1919. Their marriage was terminated on March 6, 1920. According to Tony Martin, "Most of her very fruitful life thereafter was spent under the shadow of a grievance. She considered herself the wronged party in an eternal triangle in which she was the spectacular loser." See Tony Martin, *Amy Ashwood Garvey* (Dover, Mass.: Majority Press, 2007), 123–25 for an account of Amy Ashwood Garvey's visit to Guyana.

33. In 1929 Garvey formed the People's Political Party to contest Jamaica's national elections. Among the fourteen planks of his party manifesto were: to secure representation in the Imperial Parliament for a larger modicum of self-government in Jamaica; a minimum wage for the laboring and working classes of Jamaica; the expansion and improvement of town and urban areas without the encumbrances or restraints of private proprietorship; a Jamaican University and Polytechnic; and the creation of a legal aid department to assist those persons who could not represent themselves. See Adolph Edwards, *Marcus Garvey: 1887–1910* (London: New Beacon Books, 1967), 27–28.

34. *New Daily Chronicle*, February 2, 1930.

35. Quoted in Tony Martin, *The Pan-African Connection: From Slavery to Garvey and Beyond* (Cambridge, Mass.: Schekman, 1983), 124.

36. Edwards, *Marcus Garvey*, 31.

37. See "Garvey and the Beginnings of Mass-Based Party Politics in Jamaica," in Martin, *Pan-African Connection*, 111–31.

38. Quoted in Edwards, *Marcus Garvey*, 29–30.

39. Edwards, *Marcus Garvey*, 29.

40. See chapter 6 for a description of the Webber case.

41. *Daily Argosy*, September 3, 1926.

42. Ibid.

43. *Daily Chronicle*, October 27, 1929.

44. "De Omnibus Rebus," *New Daily Chronicle*, September 29, 1929.
45. "Undesirable Persons Bill Passed," *Daily Argosy*, December 20, 1929.
46. *Daily Argosy*, December 20, 1929.
47. Seecharan, *Tiger in the Stars*, 301.
48. "De Omnibus Rebus," *New Daily Chronicle*, October 13, 1929.
49. "Mudhead" is a nickname given to Guyanese people. Sometimes Guyana is called "a land of mud." The *Daily Chronicle*, March 15, 1929, asserts: "That is the first impression of British Guiana. Miles and miles of it, and muddy Atlantic waves beating upon the northern shores of South America."
50. "De Omnibus Rebus."
51. Tony Cozier, "Lara's New World Record," *Trinidad Express*, November 26, 2005.
52. "Ideal Settlement for West Indians with Grit and Muscle," *New Daily Chronicle*, October 23, 1929.
53. Ibid.
54. "Death of Woman Who Had Been Slave in Colony," *New Daily Chronicle*, November 8, 1929.

CHAPTER 9. THE SUGAR CRISIS, CONSTITUTIONAL REFORM, AND THE WHITE MAN'S BURDEN

1. In the 1920s there were violent fluctuations in the sugar prices. From £50.16s per ton in 1920, sugar prices declined to £14.16s and £12.6s per ton in 1928 and 1929, respectively. In 1920 sugar and its exports yielded about 80 percent of export earnings; by 1929, they yielded about 55 percent of the export earnings.
2. Denis Williams, *Giglioli in Guyana 1922–1972* (Georgetown, British Guiana: National History and Arts Council, 1973), 41. Rice production, to which the East Indians devoted much of their labor, needed thousands of acres of swamps in which to grow. Unfortunately, these swamps were the ideal breeding ground for mosquitoes of every kind, which had devastating effects on the East Indians. On his second assignment to Guyana in the 1930s, Dr. George Giglioli observed that "the conditions of housing, sewage disposal and water supply were of themselves more than sufficient to explain the high incidence of respiratory and intestinal complaints I had found in the hospital wards and in the estate death registers; it was surprising, in fact, that only some, and not everybody, were affected." George Giglioli, *Demerara Doctor: The Autobiography of a Self-Taught Physician*, ed. with a foreword by Chris Curtis (London: Smith-Gordon, 2006), 135. Interestingly enough, whereas East Indians demonstrated a tremendous susceptibility to malaria, the Africans, Chinese, and American Indians showed considerable susceptibility to tuberculosis. East Indians, on the other hand, showed considerable resistance to tuberculosis.
3. Quoted in Seecharan, *Tiger in the Stars*, 76.
4. Giglioli, *Demerara Doctor*, 66.
5. Ibid., 54. Much original work on the study of malaria occurred in Guyana. Although Lancisi, a physician to Pope Clement XI, was the first person to make a systematic study of the environment in which these fevers occurred and the first person to use the term "malaria," in 1717, the modern study of malaria began with Alphonse Laveran's studies in Algeria that began in 1878. Thirteen years later, in 1891, Dr. Ferguson carried out important work on malaria and hookworm in Guyana and published a long paper on the pathology of material cachexia in the *British Guiana Medical Annual*, the first medical journal published in the British colonial territories. Between 1893 and 1896, C. W. Daniels conducted important anatomo-pathological studies in a series of over 2,500 autopsies he performed at the Georgetown Hospital. Dr. Giglioli notes: "His careful observations are recognized as classic; they threw new light on the varying reaction to malaria infection in the different races constitution the Guyanese population." Ibid., 62. In 1899 Grassi, Bignami, and Bastiamelli, working in Rome, published "a complete description of the development of the three known malaria parasites of man, in the *Anopheles* mosquito. The centuries-old mystery of the cause and transmission of intermittent marsh fevers was at last completely

unravelled." Ibid., 63. It is not too far-fetched to argue that these important discoveries had much to do with the aims of colonialism: the desire of Europeans to acclimatize to the tropics and a desire to increase the profitability of their operations. Nothing, however, can take away from the dedication of some of these physicians and the enormous contributions of these path-breaking discoveries. The life and work of Dr. Giglioli are emblematic of the latter consideration.

6. Ibid., 142.

7. Looking at the secret manner in which these DDT experiments were carried out by the British in Burma and West Africa, it is easy to see how experiments related to AIDS could have been carried out secretly by scientists from the developed countries, leading to consequences that no one could foresee. See ibid., chapter 22, for an interesting discussion of this secret experimental work.

8. Ibid., ix.

9. Ibid.

10. Ibid., 56.

11. Ibid., 88.

12. Ibid., 140.

13. Ibid., 157.

14. Ibid., 160.

15. Ibid., 217.

16. Governor Denham to Lord Passfield, July 3, 1930, Public Record Office, CO 111/688/8.

17. Ibid. According to Governor Denham, "British Guiana . . . has to carry annual interest charges of over one and a quarter million dollars, or over one fifth of the total expenditure of the Colony and over three times the provision made for all public works expenditure. Of the local commitments—which total 22 million dollars of which 70% has been expended on sea defences, drainage and water supplies—9 millions spend on sea defences may be regarded as entirely protective and unproductive expenditure. The annual burden now falling on the Colony in respect of the Salvage works, taking interest at 5% and sinking fund charges at 1% amounts therefore to approximately just short of 900,000 dollars, being nearly 3 dollars (12/6) per head of population." Ibid.

18. See *Report of the Sugar Industry of the West Indies and British Guiana, West Indian Sugar Commission, 1929–1930* (London: Her Majesty's Stationery Office, March 1930), 3–4 (hereafter cited as Report of the West Indian Sugar Commission).

19. Ibid., 24.

20. Ibid.

21. In 1899 Rudyard Kipling, the poet of European imperialism, alluded to this burden in his poem, "The White Man's Burden." The first stanza reads as follows: "Take up the White Man's burden. / Send forth the best ye breed. / Go bind your sons to exile, / To serve your captive's need. / To wait in heavy's harness / On fluttered folk and wild— / Your new-caught, sullen peoples, / Half-devil and half child."

22. Report of the West Indian Sugar Commission, 52.

23. Stoby, *British Guiana Centenary Year Book*, 81.

24. Ibid., 82.

25. Report of the West Indian Sugar Commission, 101.

26. Seecharan, *Tiger in the Stars*, 148, 149.

27. *New Daily Chronicle*, June 3, 1928.

28. The "labouring poor" is a phrase taken from Harold Perkin. It refers to a much narrower group than the working class. It includes casual laborers, villagers, paupers, beggars, and so forth, people with "no property or skill to shield them from the pressures of the daily struggle for existence." Perkin, *Origins of Modern English Society*, 19.

29. Report of the West India Sugar Commission.

30. *Daily Chronicle*, December 5, 1929.

31. Ibid.

32. Report of the West Indian Sugar Commission, 98.

33. *Daily Chronicle*, December 1, 1929.

34. *Daily Chronicle*, December 7, 1929.

35. British Labour Conference, 1930, Public Record Office, CO 111/687/4, 1930.

36. Public Record Office, CO 111/686/17, 1930.

37. Ibid.

38. *Daily Chronicle*, February 5, 1930.

39. The persons present at the interview consisted of the governor; the colonial secretary; the inspector-general of police; Rev. Smith; E. B. Barker, chaplain and working men's deputy; John Richard Moore and William Thomas Phillips, people's deputies; John Lucie Griffith; Pundit Gharbharan Doobay; Ellis Van Rossum; and Adjutant Virgina Latour.

40. "Report of Interview Accorded to Mr. Claude Smith by His Excellency the Officer Administering the Government," Public Record Office, CO 111/686/17, 1930.

41. Ibid.

42. Ibid.

43. Ibid.

44. Ibid. I have taken the liberty of transcribing this part of the document from the third to the first person.

45. "Inspector General of Police to the Colonial Secretary," February 4, 1930, Public Record Office.

46. Perkin, *Origins of Modern English Society*, 206.

47. Public Record Office, CO 111/686/17, May 13,1930.

48. Public Record Office, CO 111/686/17, May 8, 1930.

49. Grindle sent the following note to Lord Snowden, Lord Passfield, and A. V. Alexander: "Whether Indian or Negro, these people have been brought voluntarily from their homes and transplanted to islands too small to support them by any other form of cultivation and this is in order to grow sugar for this country. The black and colored populations of the sugar colonies have a claim on us such as no other colonial producers have." Quoted in Partha Sarathi Gupta, *Imperialism and the British Labour Movement, 1914-1964* (1975; reprint, New Delphi: Sage, 2002), 138.

50. J. B. Sidebotham, Public Record Office, CO 111/688/8, 1930.

51. "The Economic Crisis," *Daily Chronicle*, April 8, 1930.

52. Ibid.

53. Ibid.

54. Colin Cross, *Philip Snowden* (London: Barrie and Rockliff, 1966), 202–3.

55. Ibid., 236.

56. Lord Passfield to Lord Snowden, Public Record Office, CO 111/688/8, August 28, 1930.

57. Ibid.

58. Governor of British Guiana to the Secretary of State for the Colonies, Public Record Office, CO 111/688/8, August 26, 1930.

59. Telegram from the Governor of British Guiana to the Secretary of State for the Colonies, Public Record Office, CO 111/688/8, September 9, 1930. Initially, they were granted £35,000. After that, they were granted £125,000 for a program of works:

Roads	£32,000
Sea defences	£11,000
Buildings	£7,500
Improvement works on sugar estates	£40,000
Drainage	£35,000
Irrigation	£125,000

60. Cross, *Philip Snowden*, 207.

61. Ibid., 84, my emphasis.

62. Robert Skidelsky, *John Maynard Keynes, 1883–1946* (New York: Penguin, 2003), 436–37.

63. See "British Guiana Constitutions 1891 and 1928," Public Record Office, CO 111/703/1, 1932.

64. See Benn, *Growth and Development of Political Ideas*, 31, 53.

65. *Daily Chronicle*, November 8, 1929.

66. *Daily Chronicle*, December 15, 1929.

67. Ibid. Of the six qualifications, the three major ones were ownership of six acres of land, whether culti- vated or not; ownership of property worth not less than $500; and income or wages of $6 per week, of $300 per annum.

68. Ibid.

69. "Political Reform with Special Reference to Adult Suffrage," British Commonwealth Labour Conference, 1930.

70. *Daily Chronicle*, December 19, 1929.

71. Gupta, *Imperialism and the British Labour Movement*, 124, 129.

72. Public Record Office, CO 111/787/4, April 15, 1930.

73. Public Record Office, CO 111/787/4, April 1930.

74. *Daily Chronicle*, December 21, 1929.

75. Ibid.

76. "Specious Arguments," *Daily Chronicle*, January 7, 1930.

77. *New Daily Chronicle*, December 27, 1929.

78. Ibid.

79. "The Electives' Manifesto," *New Daily Chronicle*, December 27, 1929.

80. Ibid.

81. *Daily Argosy*, December 23, 1929.

82. J. Lucie Griffith, "A Vigorous Protest," *Daily Chronicle*, January 5, 1930.

83. *Daily Chronicle*, January 5, 1930.

84. "Specious Arguments."

85. See "Anti-Pact Political Association," *Daily Chronicle*, January 11, 1930.

86. "Electives' Manifesto."

87. "Political Reform with Special Reference to Adult Suffrage," CO 111/687/4, 1930.

88. *Daily Chronicle*, February 2, 1930.

89. "Report of Interview Accorded Mr. Claude Smith."

90. *Daily Chronicle*, January 7, 1930.

CHAPTER 10. EXPLORING NEW WORLDS

1. Williams, *Giglioli in Guyana*, 27.

2. A. R. F. Webber, "The Great Dissolve," *New Daily Chronicle*, December 20, 1929.

3. "Nil Desperandum," *New Daily Chronicle*, December 24, 1929.

4. "The Enemy of the Registered Voters," *New Daily Chronicle*, January 9, 1930.

5. *New Daily Chronicle*, January 9, 1930.

6. "Colonial Opinion Is Exasperated Beyond Endurance," *Daily Chronicle*, April 1, 1930.

7. Ibid.

8. "West Indian Federation," *Daily Chronicle*, April 2, 1930.

9. "Help for W. I. Sugar," *Daily Chronicle*, April 5, 1930.

10. Ibid.

11. "Memorial Service to Late Mr. G. I. V. Webber," *New Daily Chronicle*, March 5, 1930.

12. A. R. F. Webber, "Among the Tombs and the Pyramids," *New Daily Chronicle*, April 18, 1930.

13. "Memorial Service to Late Mr. G. I. V. Webber."

14. See "Mr. Webber's Memorandum," *New Daily Chronicle*, March 2, 1930.

15. Sir Oliver Lodge (1851–1940), world-famous British physicist, was awarded the Albert Medal of the Royal Society of the Arts for his pioneering work in wireless telegraphy. He was well known for his research in radio and his belief that death is not the end of life.

16. A. R. F. Webber, "Exploring Unbroken British Guiana," *New Daily Chronicle*, March 29, 1930. In 1927 Dr. Giglioli visited the Abary and offered an equally idyllic description of the area. He noted: "I had visited the Abary during a brief hunting trip in 1927; these swampy savannahs used to be a real paradise for the naturalist; particularly notable for the number and variety of waders of all sizes and kinds, from the great black-headed storks to the smallest sandpiper. Snipe abounded in the boggy areas, and great flocks of 'visissi' tree-ducks rose from the ponds, when disturbed, circling noisily around to settle again on another pond only a short distance away. Clumsy, crested hoatzins, or Canje pheasants, a primitive bird species, floundered and flapped in the groves of tall Moka-Moka arums, which bordered the river and the ponds scattered across the savannah; their low-placed nests overhang the water, and the young, featherless chicks deliberately drop overboard when alarmed, swimming around in between the spiny stems of the arums and finally climbing back to the nest, helping themselves effectively with the fully-developed claw which arms a rudimentary finger on the last joint of their wings. The river was exceptionally rich in fish, and teemed with alligators; of these I have counted 30 or more within sight at the same time. Riding along a dam in this area was always exciting, as they lay motionless in the high grass along the canal bank till one was nearly on them, and then plunged into the water with a mighty splash; the horses' reactions were equally sudden and unpredictable!" Giglioli, *Demerara Doctor*, 155.

17. William Francis and John Mullin, eds., *The British Guiana Handbook, 1922* (Georgetown, British Guiana: Argosy, 1923), 84–85.

18. "Not a Star," *New Daily Chronicle*, April 25, 1930.

19. Webber, "Exploring Unbroken British Guiana."

20. Ibid.

21. Ibid.

22. A. R. F. Webber, "On Horseback to the Upper Berbice," *New Daily Chronicle*, April 4, 1930.

23. Webber, "Exploring Unbroken British Guiana."

24. Webber, "On Horseback to the Upper Berbice." One is reminded of the words of C. L. R. James's preface to *Beyond a Boundary* (1963; reprint, New York: Pantheon, 1983): "What do they know of cricket who only cricket know?"

25. Webber, "Exploring Unbroken British Guiana."

26. Giglioli, *Demerara Doctor*, 225–26.

27. Webber, "On Horseback to the Upper Berbice."

28. Ibid.

29. Ibid.

30. Ibid.

31. Ibid.

32. Ibid.

33. Ibid.

34. Webber opened this section of his travels with the following lines from Keats: "[Or] like stout Cotez, with eagle eyes / He stared at the Pacific—and all his men / Look'd at each other with a wild surmise-- / Silent, upon a peak in Darien." He takes exception to Keats's reference to "Cotez" and re-

minded him that Vasco Nunez de Balboa was the first European to see the eastern shore of the Pacific Ocean.

35. A. R. F. Webber, "The Wonder Savannahs of the Great Divide," *New Daily Chronicle*, April 11, 1930. Webber's quotation is taken from Sir Walter Scott, *Marmion*, ed. with notes by William J. Rolfe (Boston: Ticknor, 1885), 20.

36. Webber, "Wonder Savannahs of the Great Divide."

37. Ibid.

38. Ibid.

39. Ibid.

40. Ibid.

41. Webber, "Among the Tombs and the Pyramids." Casareep, sometimes spelled cassareep, a sauce made by boiling down the juice of the bitter cassava, was first made by the Indians of South America, and is used as a preservative in a dish that can be kept for months.

42. Ibid.

43. Ibid.

44. Ibid. Quatta is an American Indian appellation for the black spider monkey.

45. Ibid.

46. Ibid.

47. Ibid.

48. A. R. F. Webber, "Hope, Faith and Charity," *New Daily Chronicle*, May 3, 1930.

49. Ibid.

50. Ibid.

51. John Milton, *Paradise Lost*, ed. Barbara Lewalski (Malden, Mass.: Blackwell, 2007), 84.

52. Giglioli, *Demerara Doctor*, 155.

53. "Alternative Transport Route to Polaro District," Public Record Office, CO 111/684/3, March 1930.

CHAPTER 11. PATRIOT AND BUSINESSMAN

1. Rohini, "Hon. A. R. F. Webber."

2. Ibid.

3. "Alternative Transport Route to Potaro District."

4. "Constituents Promise Support," *Daily Chronicle*, March 7, 1930.

5. Ibid.

6. "A First Radio Broadcast," *Daily Chronicle*, May 19, 1930.

7. Ibid.

8. "Boundless Capacities for Fortune in British Guiana," *New Daily Chronicle*, July 1, 1930.

9. Public Record Office, CO 11/687/4, 1930.

10. Ibid.

11. Ibid.

12. Ibid.

13. *Hansard*, February 24, 1927.

14. Public Record Office, CO 111/167/11, 1927.

15. All these quotations are taken from "Copy of letter from the Hon. A. R. F. Webber to Commissioner of Lands and Mines," Public Record Office, CO 111/685/8, 1930.

16. C. Douglas-Jones to Rt. Hon. Lord Passfield, January 6, 1930, ibid.

17. "Memorandum," February 25, 1930, ibid.

18. Note, March 21, 1930, ibid.
19. See Gupta, *Imperialism and the British Labour Movement*, 83.
20. Webber to the colonial secretary, Public Record Office, CO 111/685/8, April 28, 1930.
21. Ibid.
22. Ibid.
23. Ibid.
24. Ibid.
25. Governor Denham to Lord Passfield, July 14, 1930, ibid.
26. Gupta, *Imperialism and the British Labour Movement*, 30–31.
27. Quoted in ibid., 31.
28. E. D. Morel's, *The Black Man's Burden* seeks "to convey a clear notion of the atrocious wrongs which the white people's [*sic*] have inflicted upon the black . . . [and] to lay down the fundamental principles of a humane and practical policy in the government of Africa by white men." E. D. Morel, *The Black Man's Burden* (London: National Labour Press, 1920), vii. According to Gupta, Morel puts forward "an ideal of African peasant proprietors growing cash crops for export and using that income to spend on European goods. Morel was thus opposing one particular type of capitalist penetration in the colonies and in its place putting forward an alternative pattern of capitalist relationship, reminiscent of mid-Victorian free trade imperialism." Gupta, *Imperialism and the British Labour Movement*, 31.
29. "Mr. Webber Leaves the *New Daily Chronicle*," *Daily Chronicle*, July 2, 1930.
30. See the Reno Rohini political biography of Cannon, *Daily Chronicle*, March 16, 1930.
31. See the editorial of the *Daily Chronicle*, August 7, 1930.
32. "Call by West Coast Berbice Voter," *New Daily Chronicle*, July 9, 1930.
33. "Mr. Webber Due in Trinidad on September 6," *Daily Chronicle*, August 26, 1930.
34. "The West Berbice Seat: Mr. Peer Bacchus States His Case," *Daily Chronicle*, August 27, 1930.
35. Ibid.
36. "The West Berbice Division," *Daily Chronicle*, September 2, 1930.
37. Ibid.
38. "The Stage Is Set," *Daily Chronicle*, September 7, 1930.
39. "The B.G. Labour Union: Welcome to Delegates at British Commonwealth Conference," *Daily Chronicle*, September 10, 1930.
40. "The West Berbice Contest," *Daily Chronicle*, September 14, 1930, my emphasis.
41. "Webber, Wong & Crane," *Daily Chronicle*, September 17, 1930.
42. Ibid.
43. "West Berbice Contest."
44. "Webber, Wong & Crane."
45. "Vote for Webber," *Daily Chronicle*, September 17, 1930.
46. Ibid.
47. Ibid.
48. A. R. F. Webber, "Hors D'Oeuvre of the Ocean Passage," *Daily Chronicle*, October 19, 1930.
49. Ibid.
50. Ibid.
51. Ibid.
52. Ibid.
53. Ibid.
54. Ibid.
55. Ibid.

CHAPTER 12. WEBBER: A KEYNESIAN

1. "Regulations Misunderstood," *Daily Chronicle*, September 20, 1930.
2. *New Daily Chronicle*, September 25, 1930.
3. See "Introduction of Workmen's Compensation Act," *Daily Chronicle*, October 24, 1930.
4. See "B.G. Labour Union," *Daily Chronicle*, November 5, 1930.
5. "Prison Reform," *New Daily Chronicle*, November 8, 1930.
6. Ibid.
7. "1839 Newspaper Ordinance to Remain," *New Daily Chronicle*, December 14, 1930.
8. Ibid.
9. Cross, *Philip Snowden*, 83.
10. Ibid.
11. W. Arthur Lewis, "Economic Development with Unlimited Supplies of Labour," *Manchester School of Economic and Social Studies* 22, no. 1 (January 1954): 183.
12. Daly, *Short History of the Guyanese People*, 294.
13. A. R. F. Webber, "I Am an Economic Heretic," *Daily Chronicle*, October 12, 1930.
14. Ibid.
15. Ibid.
16. Ibid.
17. Ibid.
18. Ibid. Drawing on Marx's position that says "It is purely a tautology to say that crises are caused by the scarcity of solvent consumers, or of a paying consumption," Paul Sweezy concluded: "This statement flows naturally from the discussion of crises in Volume 1, and it is directed against the kind of crude trade underconsumption theory which has always enjoyed considerable popularity, particularly among trade unionists." However, he is quick to add: "There could be nothing more absurd, however, than to cite this passage as 'proof' that Marx regarded the magnitude of consumption as of no consequence in the causation of crises." Paul Sweezy, *The Theory of Capitalist Development* (New York: Monthly Review Press, 1970), 150–51.
19. Gupta, *Imperialism and the British Labour Movement*, 27–28.
20. Davies, *A. J. Cook*, 162.
21. Ibid.
22. Ibid., 163.
23. I am indebted to Karl Case's assistance for this understanding of Keynes.
24. Andrew Thorpe, "The Industrial Meaning of 'Gradualism': The Labour Party and Industry, 1918–1931," *Journal of British Studies* 35, no. 1 (1996): 95.
25. Skidelsky, *John Maynard Keynes*, 378.
26. Ibid.
27. Quoted in ibid.
28. George Peden, "Keynes and British Economic Policy," in *The Cambridge Companion to Keynes*, ed. Roger Blackhouse and Bradley Bateman (Cambridge: Cambridge University Press, 2006), 105.
29. Cross, *Philip Snowden*, 219.
30. Ibid., 107.
31. Quoted in Skidelsky, *John Maynard Keynes*, 448.
32. John Maynard Keynes, *The General Theory of Employment, Interest, and Money* (San Diego, Calif.: First Harvest, 1964), vii.
33. Ibid., 29.
34. Skidelsky, *John Maynard Keynes*, 528.

35. Harry Landreth, *History of Economic Thought* (Boston: Houghton Mifflin, 1976), 445.
36. Ibid.
37. Keynes, *General Theory*, 164.
38. Webber, "I Am an Economic Heretic."
39. Private conversation with Eric St. Cyr, August 2, 2007.
40. Private correspondence, January 2, 2007.
41. Note to the author, September 21, 2007.
42. At the beginning of 1930 the economic outlook for England was gloomy. In January 1930 Mosley presented his memorandum to Ramsay MacDonald, prime minister of England. It was rejected by the British Cabinet on May 19. The following day Mosley resigned from the Cabinet. On March 1, 1931, Mosley launched his political party to deal with the economic crisis. On March 10 he was expelled from the Labour party for "his act of gross disloyalty" in launching a party. H. P. Morgan, the Labour M.P. to whom Webber had written to support British Guiana's constitutional initiatives became the chief whip of Mosley's new party. This information was carried in the daily newspapers of British Guiana. See "Labour Party Expels Sir Oswald Mosley," *Daily Chronicle*, April 12, 1931; "West Indian MP is Chief Whip in Mosley's Party," *Daily Chronicle*, July 16, 1931; and Nigel Jones, *Mosley* (London: Haus Publishing, 2004).
43. "Dawn of Better Representative of Government Has Come," *New Daily Chronicle*, September 12, 1930.
44. Margaret Cole, *The Story of Fabian Socialism* (Stanford, Calif.: Stanford University Press, 1961), 282.
45. Drummond Shiels, *The Colonies Today and Tomorrow* (London: Longmans Green, 1947), 30.
46. "The B.G. Labour Union," *Daily Chronicle*, September 10, 1930.
47. Ibid.
48. In this context, it is instructive to note Norman Manley's notion of the role of violence in the construction of socialism in the early days of the People's National Party (PNP) in Jamaica. Manley and the PNP also subscribed to principles of Fabian socialism. Sir Stafford Cripps, M.P. an official of the Fabian Party, addressed the inaugural meeting of the PNP in September 1938. See "The PNP declares Itself a Socialist Organization" in Nettleford, *Norman Washington Manley*, 59–64.
49. Interview with Lord Skidelsky, *Commanding Heights* (PBS program), 18.
50. Backhouse and Bateman, *Cambridge Companion to Keynes*, 2.
51. W. Arthur Lewis, "The Evolution of the Peasantry in the British West Indies" (London, 1936), 36, 43.
52. Eric St. Cyr, "The Theory of Caribbean Economics: Its Origins and Current Status," 2, 3, Occasional Paper 4, Institute of International Affairs, University of the West Indies, St. Augustine, Trinidad, 1983.
53. Lloyd Best, "Economic Theory and Economic Policy in the Twentieth Century West Indies: The Lewis Tradition of Town and Gown," in *Economic Theory and Development Options for the Caribbean* (Kingston, Jamaica: Ian Randle, 2007), 58.
54. In 1936 Lewis's position was clear: "The 'increased settlement of labourers on the land as peasant proprietors offers the best prospect of establishing a stable and prosperous economy in the West Indian colonies.' For not only is there a possibility that, if land were made available, it would increase the total output of the colonies, but it is also certain that in securing a more equitable distribution of the social product, it could not fail to raise the general standard of living." Lewis, "Evolution of the Peasantry," 41.
55. Gerald Meier, "Sir Arthur Lewis and Development Economics: Fifty Years On," in *Economic Theory and Development Options*, 140.
56. Ronald Findlay, "On W. Arthur Lewis's Contribution to Economics," *Scandinavian Journal of Economics* 82, no. 1 (1980): 62.
57. Lewis, "Evolution of the Peasantry," 42.
58. Ibid., 2.
59. Skidelsky, *John Maynard Keynes*, 462.

60. Lewis's autobiographical note in Assar Lindbeck, ed., *Nobel Lectures in Economic Sciences, 1969–1980* (Singapore: World Scientific, 1992), 395.

61. Rodney, *History of the Guyanese Working People*, 165.

62. Carlyle Harry, *Hubert Nathaniel Critchlow*, rev. ed. (Georgetown, Guyana: Guyana National Service Publishing Center, 1977), 19.

63. "Labour Union Discusses Economic Crisis," *Daily Chronicle*, December 5, 1930.

64. Ibid.

65. George Padmore, *The Life and Struggles of Negro Toilers* (1931; reprint, Hollywood, Calif.: Sun Dance Press, 1971), 121, 125.

66. See Walther Schevenels, *Forty-five Years, 1901–1945: A Historical Précis* (Brussels: IFTU Board of Trustees, 1956), 167.

67. "B.G. Labour Union Celebrates May Day," *Daily Chronicle*, May 3, 1931.

68. "Labour Union Discusses Economic Crisis."

69. Schevenels, *Historical Précis*, 176.

70. "Labour Union Discusses Economic Crisis."

71. Ibid.

72. The election of MacDonald and the Labour Party in 1929 coincided with the growing problem of unemployment in Britain. MacDonald asked Sir George May to examine this problem. When May and his committee produced its report, it suggested that the government should reduce its expenditure by £97,000, including £67,000 to be cut from the funds that were provided for employment. MacDonald and Snowden accepted the report, but when it was discussed by the cabinet, the majority voted against the measures proposed by Sir George May. See http://www.spartacus.schoolnet.co.uk/PRmacdonald .htm.

73. Thorpe, "Industrial Meaning of 'Gradualism,'" 102.

74. See "The Only Means of Making Government Solvent," *Daily Chronicle*, March 26, 1931.

75. Harry, *Hubert Nathaniel Critchlow*, 38–39.

76. Davies, *A. J. Cook*, 28, 66.

77. This phrase is taken from the Labour Party's program, *Labour and the New Social Order*. Margaret Cole suggests that it bears "the unmistakable [Sidney] Webb trademark." See Cole, *Story of Fabian Socialism*, 172–76.

78. Schevenels, *Historical Précis*, 169–70.

79. Cross, *Philip Snowden*, 95.

80. In 1929, in a memorandum to Lord Oliver's commission, Critchlow and the BGLU called for the implementation of workmen's compensation, health insurance, old-age pensions, a juvenile court, land settlement schemes, and technical training schools.

81. "Labour Union Discusses Economic Crisis," *Daily Chronicle*, December 5, 1930.

82. "The Unemployment Question," *Daily Chronicle*, October 29, 1930.

83. Gertie Wood, "A Call to British Guiana Women to Be Militant in Local Politics," *Daily Chronicle*, November 23, 1930.

84. Gertie Wood, "To Guianese Women," *Daily Chronicle*, March 1, 1931.

85. Ibid.

86. Ibid.

87. Rodney, *History of the Guyanese Working People*, 41–42.

88. Wood, "To Guianese Women."

89. Ibid. See also Wood's address to the sixth anniversary celebration of the women's section of the British Guiana Labour Party, *Daily Chronicle*, March 11, 1931.

90. Findlay, "On W. Arthur Lewis' Contributions to Economics," 63.

91. Quoted in ibid.

92. Lewis wanted to be an engineer, but this seemed pointless to him "since neither the government nor the white firms would employ a black engineer. Eventually, I decided to study business administration, planning to return to St. Lucia for a job in the municipal service or in private trade." Lindbeck, *Nobel Lectures in Economic Sciences*, 395.

93. It is remarkable how Lewis's concerns cohered with those of James and Webber. In *Labour in the West Indies*, Lewis averred: "The white element dominates every aspect of West Indian life. Economically and politically the white man is supreme, he owns the biggest plantations, stores and banks, controlling directly or indirectly the entire economic life of the community. It is he whom the Governor most often nominates to his councils, and for his sons that the best Government jobs are reserved. Socially, the whites in general constitute the aristocracy." Lewis, *Labour in the West Indies*, 11–12.

CHAPTER 13. COLONIES IN SEARCH OF A NATION

1. *Daily Chronicle*, October 19, 1930.

2. Prior to the union of the colonies in 1831, Demerara-Essequebo was one colony, while Berbice was another. In 1838 the colony was divided into three counties—Demerara, Essequebo, and Berbice—for economic and administrative reasons. Vere Daly points out: "This led Guianese to speak of Demerara and Essequebo as though they were two colonies prior to the union. Hence the misconception prevailed that in 1831 the three colonies of Demerara, Essequebo, and Berbice were united, whereas in fact the union was between two colonies, Demerara-Essequebo, which had been effectively united under one Court of Policy, since 1789, and Berbice." Daly, *Short History of the Guyanese People*, 127. Webber makes a similar point in *Centenary History*, 189.

3. "Union of B.G. Colonies to Be Commemorated," *Daily Chronicle*, November 6, 1930.

4. Ibid. When the centenary stamps were issued in July 1931, F. Birkitt, the postmaster general, sent Webber the following letter: "I am directed by His Excellency the Governor to send you herewith a complimentary set of the British Guiana Centenary postage and revenue stamps, and to convey to you His Excellency's congratulations in having made the suggestion in the Legislative Council on the 5th November last that such stamps should be issued. His Excellency feels sure that it will be as gratifying to you as to His Excellency that it has been possible to carry out your suggestion." "Governor Congratulates Hon. A. R. F. Webber," *New Daily Chronicle*, July 23, 1931.

5. "How Celebrations Will Put Money into Circulation," *Daily Chronicle*, February 7, 1931.

6. "Mr. A. R. F. Webber Outlines a Grand Scheme," *Daily Chronicle*, January 15, 1931.

7. Backhouse and Bateman, *Cambridge Companion to Keynes*, 10.

8. G. W. Prothero, "British Guiana," in *Handbooks Prepared under the Direction of the Historical Section of the Foreign Office*, No. 135 (London: Her Majesty's Stationery Office, 1920), 34.

9. Ania Loomba. *Colonialism/Postcolonialism* (London: Routledge, 1998), 203.

10. Ibid.

11. J.R. "Centenary of the Union," *Daily Chronicle*, February 3, 1931.

12. Ibid.

13. "Magnificent Wealthy Country—Hopes for the Future," *New Daily Chronicle*, July 21, 1931.

14. "How Celebrations Will Put Money into Circulation."

15. Ibid.

16. Ibid.

17. "After One Hundred Years," *Daily Argosy*, October 13, 1931.

18. Ibid.

19. Eric Williams writes: "Where fifty years before [1805], West Indian colonies would have been annexed [to Britain] with glee and rejoicing, in 1814 the Earl of Lansdowne protested that it would be worth

paying money to get rid of the colonies—British Guiana and Trinidad—which would produce sugar that Britain could not consume and would withdraw capital which Britain could not afford." Williams, "Historical Background of British Guiana's Problems," 362.

20. See Benedict Anderson, *Imagined Communities*, rev. ed. (London: Verso, 1991), 6.

21. "Capitulation Articles Should Be of Interest," *Daily Chronicle*, July 4, 1931.

22. See *Daily Argosy*, July 21, 1931.

23. Constance A. E. Theobald, "The Empire of Guiana of the Century," *New Daily Chronicle*, July 21, 1931.

24. Ibid.

25. Colonist, "Early History of British Guiana," *New Daily Chronicle*, July 19, 1931.

26. Ibid.

27. Quoted in Daly, *Short History of the Guyanese People*, 99. Daly argues that the activities of Hugues "contributed to a general unrest among the slaves, and to some daring attacks on plantations by runaway slaves, or Bush Negroes as they were called. The situation seemed sufficiently critical for some planters to consider sending their wives and children to the safety of Barbados. However, the situation was restored by a successful expedition against the Bush Negroes during the summer of 1795, in which the Indians played a major part. An earlier expedition by a small force of Dutch troops without Indian support had resulted in their ambush and slaughter. The expense of these and other defensive measures placed a heavy financial burden on the colony and led to an important change in the method of raising and the spending of taxes." Ibid., 99.

28. Ibid., 100.

29. Ibid., 115. Although the British slave trade was abolished in 1807, it was carried on "under the innocent guise of domestics in attendance upon their owners," until 1823, when the slaves on the East Coast revolted. Most of the slaves came from the other West Indian islands. See also Eric Williams, "The British West Indian Slave Trade after Its Abolition in 1807," *Journal of Negro History* 27, no. 2 (April 1942): 176, 177–78.

30. In keeping with Daly's reading of the 1823 rebellion, I prefer to confer the title of martyr on Quamina rather than on Rev. Smith, as it is customary to do. Daly reasons: "Smith . . . was not so much a martyr as a scapegoat. He was made to suffer for what the planters regarded as the misdeeds and subversive influence of all the missionaries in Demerara-Essequebo. He did not suffer because of his belief, nor by his death did he bear witness to the truth. The person who suffered in this way and who more appropriately could be called the Demerara Martyr, was Quamina. Believing in the doctrines of Christianity, he risked his life and lost it trying to uphold the sixth commandment of the Mosaic Law." Daly, *Short History of the Guyanese People*, 167.

31. See ibid., 167.

32. Williams, "Historical Background of British Guiana's Problems," 371.

33. Quoted in ibid., 374.

34. In 1811 there were 71,180 slaves; in 1817 there were 79,197 slaves; in 1826 there were 68,326 slaves. Eventually, in 1833, compensation was paid on 68,579 slaves.

35. Williams, "Historical Background of British Guiana's Problems," 373.

36. Quoted in Daly, *Short History of the Guyanese People*, 116–17.

37. Quoted in ibid., 117.

38. Ibid., 116.

39. See Anderson, *Imagined Communities*.

40. Roth was the first Silver Medalist of the University College, London; a Demy Scholar of Magdalen College, Oxford University; president of the Anthropological Section of the British Association for the Advancement of Science in Tasmania; and Honorary Corresponding Member of the Berlin Anthropological Society. He worked in Australia before going to Guyana.

41. William I. Gomes, "Dr. Walter Edmond Roth: The Man and His Scientific Work," *Daily Chronicle*, April 2, 1931.

42. Vincent Roth, *A Life in Guyana*, Vol. 1, *A Young Man's Journey, 1889-1923* (Leeds, England: Peepal Tree Press, 2003), 263.

43. *Geographical Journal* 61, no. 6 (June 1923): 458.

44. See P. M. Netscher, *History of the Colonies: Essequebo, Demerara and Berbice*, trans. W. E. Roth (1888; reprint, Georgetown, British Guiana: Daily Chronicle, 1929), translator's preface.

45. W. E. Roth, "Kanaima: Vengeful Spirit of the Guiana Forest," *Daily Chronicle*, June 7, 1931.

46. "Official Thanksgiving Service," *New Daily Chronicle*, July 22, 1931.

47. Ibid.

48. Ibid.

49. Ibid. Although Bishop Parry offered an interesting sermon, it is wise to note his relationship to Afro-Guyanese. According to Norman E. Cameron, "All through the history of the race there have been white writers and speakers who have made disparaging remarks of us. One of these was a Bishop Parry who in 1906 declared that Negroes could be said to be without ancestors and that they were therefore inclined to superstition." Norman E. Cameron, *Thoughts on Life and Literature* (Georgetown, British Guiana: Persick, 1950), 6.

50. "Official Thanksgiving Service."

51. Stoby, introduction to *British Guiana Centenary Year Book*.

52. See Guy de Weever, "The Six Greatest Men of British Guiana," in Stoby, *British Guiana Centenary Year Book*, 110–15. His six greatest men are Laurens Storm van Gravesande, the founder of Demerara; Rev. John Wray, the first London Missionary Society clergyman who went to teach the slaves to read and write; Wolfert Simon van Hoogenheim, "the man who saved Berbice for civilization during the Great Slave Rebellion of 1763"; and Sir Walter Raleigh, "the greatest advertiser, the great visionary, and, probably . . . the greatest optimist British Guiana has ever had." He says of the sixth person: "I can find no sixth man who has had so profound an influence upon his fellows as to sit as peer beside the five whom I have above named."

53. See "Notables of the Century," in Stoby, *British Guiana Centenary Year Book*, 91–106. They include Samuel Lymas Herbert, "the first Negro medical practitioner in British Guiana, born nine years after the emancipation of slavery"; Patrick Dargan, influential politician and legal mind; Dan Sharples, a local educator and father of several accomplished children, among whom was R. G. Sharples, solicitor and painter of the six watercolors that appeared in Webber's *Centenary History*; Kinsell Joseph, a distinguished head teacher; Margaret Burns, a businesswoman who "owned the largest number of properties in the country"; Duncan Macrae Hutson, an outstanding orator and "the acknowledged leader of the bar"; and Isaac Patoir, the founder of the cattle industry in British Guiana.

54. See R. De Kersting, "Orchids: The King of Flowers," in Stoby, *British Guiana Centenary Year Book*, 116.

55. C. A. R., "History and General Knowledge Attractively Served."

56. Ibid.

57. See E. H. Carr, *What Is History?* (New York: Vintage, 1961).

58. "B.G. Centenary History and Handbook," *Daily Argosy*, November 1, 1931.

59. Interview with Edith Dummett, Hillview, Toronto, February 7, 1987.

60. Terrence Roberts, "The Importance of Space in Tropical Painting of the Americas" (unpublished), in author's possession.

61. Ibid.

62. I am indebted to Terrence Roberts for his insight into *Centenary History* and the role that space plays in the imagination of Guyanese writers and artists. Conversation with Roberts at Castilian House, Georgetown, Guyana, January 10, 2006.

63. See Henry G. Dalton, *The History of British Guiana*, 2 vols. (London: Longman, Brown, Green, and Longmans, 1855).

64. Webber, *Centenary History*, 306.

65. See, for example, Netscher, *History of the Colonies*; and James Rodway, *History of British Guiana: From the Year 1668 to the Present*, Vols. 1–3 (Georgetown, Demerara: J. Thompson, 1891-94).

66. Dalton, *History of British Guiana*, 1:2, 59.

67. Ibid., 1:60.

68. Dalton described the African as follows: "Bred up in the lowest state of ignorance and barbarity, under a burning sun, his habits of necessity betrayed an apathy and want of intelligence which were fatal to him. In his country, he had been taught to witness the last degradation of the human character; he inherited from his parents no qualities but those of the abject bondsman; his will, his desires, his actions, were not his own, and he was trained in the belief that he was an inferior being, and a culprit from the day of his birth among the sons of Adam. Examples had made him callous, idle, and obstinate; necessity had made him cunning and artful; want of education had left him helpless, ignorant and brutal. Right and wrong were terms that conveyed no definite meaning to him; he knew only what displeased and what gratified him. Power and authority had made him timid, abject, and debased. He had no object in the world beyond the indulgence of his appetites; he knew his life was one of servitude, but he had no impulse or ambition for freedom. The yoke was fitted upon him, and he to it, taking insensibly the shape of the moral deformity it imposed upon him. It was irksome and galling, but he was too indolent and hopeless to shake it off. Yet under all these blighting disadvantages, he was patient, submissive, affectionate, grateful, and even cheerful." Ibid., 1:53.

69. Webber, *Centenary History*, 59.

70. Ibid., 61–62.

71. Hereafter *Centenary History* will be cited in the text as *CH*.

72. See Webber's description of the "coloured intelligentsia" in *Centenary History*, 307–8.

73. See James, *Case for West-Indian Self-Government*.

74. "Sudden Death of Hon. A. R. F. Webber," *Daily Chronicle*, June 30, 1932.

75. Daly, *Stories of the Heroes, Book 3*, 330; private correspondence with Tommy Payne, January 8, 1987.

76. "Trinidad Scholarships, 1931," *Daily Argosy*, October 25, 1931.

77. Walter Isaacson, *Einstein: His Life and Universe* (New York: Simon and Schuster, 2007), 91–92.

78. Padmore, *Life and Struggles of Negro Toilers*, 28, 56–57.

79. James, *Life of Captain Cipriani*, 1.

CHAPTER 14. GOING DOWN WITH HIS COLORS FLYING

1. In Jamaica, Trinidad and Tobago, and British Guiana, the clamor for payment and/or out-of-pocket expenses for legislators arose in 1931. In Jamaica and Trinidad, motions were made to this effect. In British Guiana, the *Daily Chronicle* editorialized on this issue: "We are not opposed in principle to the system of paying legislators, and in Jamaica where the elected members are to be paid $120 per month; there may be excellent reasons for introducing the system. . . . Being a developed colony there is possibly less need for up-to-date statistics than there is in British Guiana; but we wonder if our northern neighbours would not have been wiser to count their population and postpone paying their legislators for three years." "Elective Salaries and the Census," *Daily Chronicle*, March 2, 1931. See also "Jamaica Electives to Be Paid," *Daily Chronicle*, March 24, 1931. In Trinidad, the unofficial members "unanimously rejected" the government's proposal that an honorarium of $5 be paid to them for their attendance at meetings of the Legislative Council. "It is understood that not only was the objection taken on the ground that it would be inopportune to receive payment for services at this time of economic stress, but they also thought the sum mentioned not in keeping with the dignity of the work they had to perform and they would rather continue to give of their services to the colony free of charge." *Daily Argosy*, November 4, 1931.

2. "Government Between Crown Colony and Representative Government Desired," *Daily Chronicle*, May 30, 1931.

3. Ibid.

4. Ibid.

5. Order 59 read as follows: "The Council shall not pass nor shall the Governor assent to any vote or resolution, the object or effect of which may be to impose any tax or dispose of, or change, any part of the public revenue, or to revoke, alter or vary any such disposition or charge unless such law, vote or resolution shall have been proposed by, or by the direction of, or shall have the express approval of the Governor." Ibid.

6. Ibid.

7. Ibid.

8. Ibid.

9. Ibid.

10. Ibid.

11. Ibid.

12. *New Daily Chronicle*, February 20, 1929.

13. "A United Front," *New Daily Chronicle*, June 23, 1931.

14. Ibid.

15. "Killing By 'Official Majority' the Spirit of a New Manhood," *New Daily Chronicle*, July 14, 1931.

16. Ibid.

17. Ibid.

18. Quoted in the *New Daily Chronicle*, November 20, 1931. Although the sentiments expressed here show Dr. Harland in a positive light, his belief, expressed in another article, that "the negro" was inferior to whites drew a stinging rebuke from C. L. R. James, "The Intelligence of the Negro" in the *Beacon* (1931), a Trinidad magazine. See Reinhard W. Sander, ed., *From Trinidad* (New York: Africana Publishing, 1978), 227–37.

19. *New Daily Chronicle*, November 20, 1931.

20. Ibid.

21. "Crown Colony Maladministration."

22. Ibid.

23. Ibid.

24. Ibid.

25. Ibid.

26. "West Indian Rule," *Daily Chronicle*, June 18, 1931.

27. Ibid.

28. Ibid. The reference here is to those English officials who found themselves in lower level jobs in local administrations.

29. "Literacy of British Guianese," *Daily Chronicle*, April 3, 1932.

30. "West Indian Rule."

31. See Gupta, *Imperialism and the British Labour Movement*, 192.

32. Ibid., 129.

33. James, *Case for West-Indian Self-Government*, 5–6.

34. Gupta, *Imperialism and the British Labour Movement*, 129.

35. "West Indian Rule."

36. Ibid.

37. "Dr. Morgan's Election Expenses," *Daily Argosy*, October 28, 1931.

38. "Webber Explains District Administration," *Daily Chronicle*, July 29, 1931.

39. "District Administration," *Daily Argosy*, July 16, 1931.

40. "The District Administration Scheme," *Daily Chronicle*, August 22, 1931.

41. "Webber Explains District Administration."

42. Ibid.

43. "The Municipal Bye-Election," *Daily Chronicle*, May 5, 1932.

44. "Hon. A. R. F. Webber Defeated by 29 Votes," *Daily Chronicle*, May 10, 1932.

45. Ibid.

46. "Government Expects to Collect $95," *Daily Chronicle*, June 15, 1932.

47. Ibid.

48. "Treatment of Patients at Public Hospitals," *Daily Chronicle*, June 15, 1932.

49. Ibid.

50. Ibid.

51. Ibid. I took the liberty of reporting this language in the first person.

52. *New Daily Chronicle*, May 15, 1932.

53. Ibid.

54. Akbar Shah, "News and Views of Indian Interest," *New Daily Chronicle*, July 3, 1932.

CHAPTER 15. IDEOLOGY, RACE, CELEBRITY

1. Webber, "How I Won My Election," *Daily Chronicle*, November 19, 1921.

2. *Daily Chronicle*, November, 4, 1921.

3. *Report of the West India Royal Commission*, Vol. 2, Appendix C, 135.

4. Ibid., 91.

5. Rodney, *History of the Guyanese Working People*, 203.

6. *Report of the West India Royal Commission*, Vol. 2, Appendix C, 92.

7. Ibid., 90.

8. Although the correct title of this folk song is "Old Black Joe," it has come down to us in the West Indies as "Poor Ole Joe" and is regarded as a "Negro spiritual."

9. *New Daily Chronicle*, February 5, 1926.

10. *New Daily Chronicle*, February 26, 1926.

11. See Ashton Chase, *A History of Trade Unionism in Guyana, 1900–1961* (Demerara: New Guyana, 1964), 76.

12. *New Daily Chronicle*, June 30, 1932.

13. Gupta, *Imperialism and the British Labour Movement*, 6–7.

14. Cole, *Story of Fabian Socialism*, 222.

15. See "PNP Declares Itself a Socialist Organization," in Nettleford, *Norman Washington Manley*, 58–64.

16. "A. R. F. Webber," *Daily Argosy*, June 30, 1932.

17. "The Late Albert Raymond Forbes Webber," *Tribune*, July 3, 1932.

18. "Legislators Pay Tribute to Dead Colleague," *Daily Chronicle*, August 24, 1932.

19. Interview with Clarence Kirton, January 12, 1987, Georgetown, Guyana. See also James, *Beyond a Boundary*, for an examination of how cricket and football clubs reflected the color question during this period.

20. Lutchman, *From Colonialism to Co-operative Republic*, 48; see 47–54 for a discussion of color prejudice in the society at the time.

21. Interview with Bernard Matthews, January 12, 1987, Georgetown, Guyana.

22. See "Louis de Souza," in Daly, *Stories of the Heroes, Book 3*, 267–93.

23. Edward A. Alpers and Pierre-Michel Fontaine, eds. *Walter Rodney, Revolutionary and Scholar: A Tribute* (Los Angeles: Center for Afro-American Studies and African Studies, University of California,

1982), 163. See also "Louis de Souza," in Daly, *Stories of the Heroes, Book 3*. In the Guyana context, the Portuguese were not seen as being white. Even the northern Europeans looked down upon them.

24. Interview with Kirton.

25. Webber, "New York Facts and Fancies."

26. See Nathan Glazer and Patrick Moynihan, *Beyond the Melting Pot: The Negroes, Puerto Ricans, Jews, Italians, and Irish of New York City* (Cambridge: M.I.T. Press, 1963).

27. See *New Daily Chronicle*, July 30, 1932.

28. Gupta, *Imperialism and the British Labour Movement*, 11.

29. Lord Byron, *Don Juan*, ed. T. G. Steffan, E. Steffan, and W. W. Pratt (New Haven, Conn.: Yale University Press, 1973), 101.

30. Webber, *Centenary History*, 331–32.

31. Quoted in Brooke Allen, "Byron: Revolutionary, Libertine and Friend," *Hudson Review* (Summer 2003): 369.

CHAPTER 16. A DEVOTED WEST INDIAN SON

1. Interview with Edith Dummett, Hillview, Toronto, February 7, 1987. All other quotations are taken from this interview.

2. "Thousands Pay Last Tribute to Dead Legislator," *Daily Chronicle*, July 1, 1932.

3. *New Daily Chronicle*, June 30, 1932.

4. "Tribute by a Brother Elective," *Daily Chronicle*, July 2, 1932.

5. "Telegram of Sympathy from Secretary of State for the Colonies," *Daily Chronicle*, July 3, 1932.

6. *New Daily Chronicle*, June 30, 1932.

7. Ibid.

8. "Late Albert Raymond Forbes Webber."

9. "The Late Hon. A. R. F. Webber," *Daily Chronicle*, July 7, 1932.

10. Ibid.

11. Ibid.

12. Ibid.

13. Ibid.

14. "Grenada Tribute to Late Hon. A. R. F. Webber."

15. Interview with Jennifer Welshman, Hillview, Toronto, February 7, 1987.

16. Webber, *Innocent's Pilgrimage*, 75.

17. Forbes Burnham (1923–85) was the prime minister of Guyana from 1964 until his death in 1985.

18. Daly, *Stories of the Heroes, Book 3*, 1

19. Ibid., 2.

20. Alice Walker, *In Search of Our Mothers' Gardens* (San Diego, Calif.: Harcourt Brace Jovanovich, 1983), 92.

BIBLIOGRAPHY

This bibliography is divided into three sections: Webber's significant writings, which are listed chronologically; other texts that were consulted; and reports by various commissions.

SECTION 1

"The Rise and Wane of the Colony's Industries." *Chronicle*, Holiday Number (August 1916).

Those That Be in Bondage: A Tale of Indian Indentures and Sunlit Western Waters. Georgetown, British Guiana: Daily Chronicle Press, 1917.

Glints from an Anvil: Being Lines of Song. Georgetown, British Guiana: Daily Chronicle Press, 1919.

"How I Won My Election." *Daily Chronicle*, 1921.

An Innocent's Pilgrimage: Being Pen Pictures of a Tender-foot Who Visited London for the First Time. Georgetown, British Guiana: New Daily Chronicle Printing, 1927.

"From an Editorial View-Point." *New Daily Chronicle*, 1928.

"New York versus London." *New Daily Chronicle*, 1929.

"Exploring Unbroken British Guiana." *New Daily Chronicle*, 1930.

"Hors D'Oeuvre of the Ocean Passage." *Daily Chronicle*, 1930.

"I Am an Economic Heretic." *Daily Chronicle*, 1930.

Centenary History and Handbook of British Guiana. Georgetown, British Guiana: Argosy, 1931.

SECTION 2

Allen, Brooke. "Byron: Revolutionary, Libertine and Friend." *Hudson Review* (Summer 2003).

Alpers, Edward A., and Pierre-Michel Fontaine, eds. *Walter Rodney, Revolutionary and Scholar: A Tribute*. Los Angeles: Center for Afro-American Studies and African Studies, University of California, 1982.

Anderson, Benedict. *Imagined Communities*. Rev. ed. London: Verso, 1991.

Ayearst, Morley. *The British West Indies: A Search for Self-Government*. Washington Square: New York University Press, 1960.

Backhouse, Roger, and Bradley Bateman. *The Cambridge Companion to Keynes*. Cambridge: Cambridge University Press, 2006.

Benn, Denis. *The Growth and Development of Political Ideas in the Caribbean, 1774–1987*. Mona: Institute of Social and Economic Research, University of the West Indies, 1987.

Bentham, Ernest. "An Open Letter to All Men and Women of the West Indies." *Daily Chronicle*, 1929.

Best, Lloyd. "Economic Theory and Economic Policy in the Twentieth Century West Indies: The Lewis Tradition of Town and Gown." In *Economic Theory and Development Options for the Caribbean: Sir Arthur Lewis Memorial Lectures, 1996–2005*. Kingston, Jamaica: Ian Randle, 2007.

Birbalsingh, Frank. *The People's Progressive Party of Guyana, 1950–1992: An Oral History*. London: Hansib, 2007.

Blake, Kim. "T. E. S. Scholes: The Unknown Pan Africanist." *Race and Class* 49, no. 1 (July–September 2007).

Bolland, O. Nigel. *The Politics of Labour in the British Caribbean: The Social Origins of Authoritarianism and Democracy in the Labour Movement*. Kingston, Jamaica: Ian Randle, 2001.

Brassington, Frank E. *The Politics of Opposition*. Diego Martin, Trinidad: West Indian Publishing, 1976.

Cameron, Norman E. *The Evolution of the Negro*. Vol. 1. Demerara, British Guiana: Argosy, 1929.

———. *The Evolution of the Negro*. Vol. 2. Demerara, British Guiana: Argosy, 1934.

———. "Guianese Literature, Past, Present, and Future." *Daily Chronicle*, 1930.

———. *Guianese Poetry*. Georgetown, British Guiana: Argosy, 1931.

Chase, Ashton. *A History of Trade Unionism in Guyana, 1900–1961*. Georgetown, Guyana: New Guyana, 1964.

Clementi, Cecil. *The Chinese in British Guiana*. Georgetown, British Guiana: Argosy, 1915.

Cole, Margaret. *The Story of Fabian Socialism*. Stanford, Calif.: Stanford University Press, 1961.

Cozier, Tony. "Lara's New World Record." *Trinidad Express*, November 2005.

Crawford, Marlene Kwok. "The Guyana Experience." In *Essays on the Chinese Diaspora in the Caribbean*, ed. Walton Look Lai. St. Augustine, Trinidad: Walton Look Lai, 2006.

Cross, Colin. *Philip Snowden*. London: Barrie and Rockliff, 1966.

Cudjoe, Selwyn R. *Resistance and Caribbean Literature*. Athens: Ohio University Press, 1980.

Dalton, Henry B. *The History of British Guiana*. 2 vols. London: Longman, Brown, Green, and Longmans, 1855.

Daly, P. H. *West Indian Freedom and West Indian Literature: Stories of the Heroes, Book 3*. Georgetown, British Guiana: Daily Chronicle, 1943.

———. *West Indian Freedom and West Indian Literature: Stories of the Heroes, Book 4*. Georgetown, British Guiana: Daily Chronicle, 1951.

Daly, Vere T. *A Short History of the Guyanese People*. Georgetown, Guyana: Vere T. Daly, 1966.

———. *A Short History of the Guyanese People*. Oxford: Macmillan, 1975.

Davies, Paul. *A. J. Cook*. Manchester: Manchester University Press, 1987.

Dev, Ravi. "State and Societal Violence against Indians in Guyana: The Ethnic Security Dilemmas." *Kaieteur News Column*, October 29, 2006.

Edwards, Adolph. *Marcus Garvey: 1887–1940*. London: New Beacon Books, 1967.

Findlay, Ronald. "On W. Arthur Lewis's Contribution to Economics." *Scandinavian Journal of Economics* 82, no. 1 (1980).

Fletcher, C. R. L., and Rudyard Kipling. *A School History of England*. Oxford: Clarendon Press, 1911.

Francis, William, and John Mullin, eds. *The British Guiana Handbook, 1922*. Georgetown, British Guiana: Argosy, 1923.

Fraser, Cary. "The PPP on Trial: British Guiana in 1953." *Small Axe* 15 (March 2004).

Geiss, Immanuel. *The Pan-African Movement: A History of Pan-Africanism in America, Europe and Africa*. Trans. Ann Keep. New York: Africana Publishing, 1974.

Giglioli, George. *Demerara Doctor: The Autobiography of a Self-Taught Physician*. Ed. with a foreword by Chris Curtis. London: Smith-Gordon, 2006.

Glasgow, Roy Arthur. *Guyana: Race and Politics among Africans and East Indians*. The Hague: Martinus Nijhoff, 1970.

Glazer, Nathan, and Daniel Patrick Moynihan. *Beyond the Melting Pot: The Negroes, Puerto Ricans, Jews, Italians, and Irish of New York City*. Cambridge: M.I.T. Press, 1963.

Gupta, Partha Sarathi. *Imperialism and the British Labour Movement, 1914–1964*. 1975. Reprint, New Delphi: Sage, 2002.

Harris, Wilson. "Afterword." In *Those That Be in Bondage: A Tale of Indian Indentures and Sunlit Western Waters*, by A. R. F. Webber. Wellesley, Mass.: Calaloux, 1988.

Harry, Carlyle. *Hubert Nathaniel Critchlow*. Rev. ed. Georgetown, Guyana: Guyana National Service Publishing Center, 1977.

Hill, W. A. "Colonial Policy and Economic Development in the British West Indies, 1895–1903." *Economic History Review* 23, no. 1 (April 1970).

Isaacson, Walter. *Einstein: His Life and Universe*. New York: Simon and Schuster, 2007.

Jagan, Cheddi. *The West on Trial*. New York: International, 1972.

James, C. L. R. *The Case for West Indian Self-Government*. London: Hogarth Press, 1933.

———. *The Life of Captain Cipriani*. Nelson, Lancashire: Coulton, 1932.

———. "The Making of the Caribbean People." *Radical America* 4, no. 4, Special Issue (May 1970).

Jones, Nigel. *Mosley*. London: Haus Publishing, 2004.

Keynes, John Maynard. *The General Theory of Employment, Interest, and Money*. San Diego, Calif.: First Harvest, 1964.

King, Nicole. *C. L. R. James and Creolization: Circles of Influence*. Jackson: University Press of Mississippi, 2001.

Knight, Franklin. "Introduction." In *Richard B. Moore, Caribbean Militant in Harlem: Collected Writings, 1920–1972*, ed. W. Burghardt Turner and Joyce Moore Turner. Bloomington: Indiana University Press, 1988.

Landreth, Harry. *History of Economic Thought*. Boston: Houghton Mifflin, 1976.

Lewis, W. Arthur. "Economic Development with Unlimited Supplies of Labour." *Manchester School of Economic and Social Studies* 22, no. 1 (January 1954).

———. "The Evolution of the Peasantry in the British West Indies." London, 1936.

———. *Labour in the West Indies*. 1938. Reprint, London: New Beacon, 1977.

Lindbeck, Assar, ed. *Nobel Lectures in Economic Sciences, 1969–1980*. Singapore: Word Scientific, 1992.

Loomba, Ania. *Colonialism/Postcolonialism*. London: Routledge, 1998.

Lutchman, Harold. *From Colonialism to Co-operative Republic: Aspects of Political Development in Guyana*. Rio Piedras, Puerto Rico: Institute of Caribbean Studies, 1974.

———. "Middle Class Colonial Politics: A Study of Guyana with Special Reference to the Period 1920–1931." Ph.D. diss., University of Manchester, 1967.

Lynch, John. *Simon Bolivar: A Life*. New Haven, Conn.: Yale University Press, 2006.

Martin, Tony. *Amy Ashwood Garvey*. Dover, Mass.: Majority Press, 2007.

———. *The Pan-African Connection: From Slavery to Garvey and Beyond*. Cambridge, Mass.: Schenkman, 1983.

Meier, Gerald. "Sir Arthur Lewis and Development Economics: Fifty Years On." In *Economic Theory and Development Options*. Kingston, Jamaica: Ian Randle, 2007.

Morel, E. D. *The Black Man's Burden*. London: National Labour Press, 1920.

Netscher, P. M. *History of the Colonies: Essequebo, Demerara and Berbice*. Trans. W. E. Roth. 1888. Reprint, Georgetown, British Guiana: Daily Chronicle, 1929.

Nettleford, Rex, ed. *Norman Washington Manley and the New Jamaica: Selected Speeches and Writings, 1938–68*. Trinidad: Longman Caribbean, 1971.

Padmore, George. *The Life and Struggles of Negro Toilers*. 1931. Reprint, Hollywood, Calif.: Sun Dance Press, 1971.

Peden, George, "Keynes and British Economic Policy." In *The Cambridge Companion to Keynes*, ed. Roger Blackhouse and Bradley Bateman. Cambridge: Cambridge University Press, 2006.

Perkin, Harold. *The Origins of Modern English Society, 1780–1880*. London: Routledge, 2002.

Poynting, Jeremy. "East Indian Women in the Caribbean: Experience, Image, and Voice." *Journal of South Asian Literature* 21, no. 1 (Winter, Spring), 1968.

Prothero, G. W. "British Guiana." In *Handbooks Prepared under the Direction of the Historical Section of the Foreign Office*, No. 135. London: Her Majesty's Stationery Office, 1920.

———. "Introduction to the Guiana Colonies." In *Handbooks Prepared under the Direction of the Historical Section of the Foreign Office*, No. 134. London: Her Majesty's Stationery Office, 1920.

Rabe, Stephen G. *U.S. Intervention in British Guiana: A Cold War Story*. Chapel Hill: University of North Carolina Press, 2005.

Ramdin, Ron. *From Chattel Slave to Wage Earner: A History of Trade Unionism in Trinidad and Tobago*. London: M. Brian and O'Keefe, 1982.

Roberts, Terrence. "The Importance of Space in Tropical Painting in the Americas." Unpublished.

Rodney, Walter. *A History of the Guyanese Working People, 1881–1905*. Baltimore: Johns Hopkins University Press, 1981.

Rodway, James. *History of British Guiana: From the Year 1668 to the Present*. Vols. 1–3. Georgetown, Demerara: J. Thompson, 1891–94.

Rohini, Reno. "The Hon. A. R. F. Webber." *Daily Chronicle*, 1930.

Roth, Vincent. *A Life in Guyana*. Vol. 1, *A Young Man's Journey, 1889–1923*. Leeds, England: Peepal Tree Press, 2003.

Ruhomon, Peter. *Centenary History of the East Indians in British Guiana, 1838–1938*. Georgetown, British Guiana: Daily Chronicle, 1947.

St. Cyr. Eric. "The Theory of Caribbean Economics: Its Origins and Current Status." Occasional Paper 4. Institute of International Affairs, University of the West Indies, St. Augustine, Trinidad, 1983.

Sartre, Jean-Paul. *Colonialism and Neocolonialism*. Trans. Azzedine Haddour, Steve Brewer, and Terry McWilliams. London: Routledge, 2001.

Schevenels, Walther. *Forty-five Years, 1901–1945: A Historical Précis*. Brussels: IFTU Board of Trustees, 1956.

Seecharan, Clem. *Tiger in the Stars: The Anatomy of Indian Achievement in British Guiana, 1919–29*. London: Macmillan Education, 1997.

Seymour, A. J. "The Literary Adventure of the West Indies." *Kyk-Over-Al* 2, no. 10 (April 1950).

Shiels, Drummond. *The Colonies Today and Tomorrow*. London: Longmans Green, 1947.

Skidelsky, Robert. *John Maynard Keynes, 1883–1946*. New York: Penguin, 2003.

Smith, Lloyd Sidney. *Trinidad: Who, What, Why*. Port of Spain: Lloyd Sidney Smith, 1950.

Stoby, E. Sievewright, ed. *British Guiana Centenary Year Book, 1831–1931*. Georgetown, British Guiana: Daily Chronicle, 1931.

Sweezy, Paul. *The Theory of Capitalist Development*. New York: Monthly Review Press, 1970.

Taylor, A. J. P. *The First World War*. New York: Capricorn Books, 1972.

Thorpe, Andrew. "The Industrial Meaning of 'Gradualism': The Labour Party and Industry, 1918–1931." *Journal of British Studies* 35, no. 1 (1996).

Trouillot, Michel-Rolph. *Silencing the Past: Power and the Production of History*. Boston: Beacon Press, 1995.

Walker, Alice. *In Search of Our Mothers' Gardens*. San Diego, Calif.: Harcourt Brace Jovanovich, 1983.

Williams, Denis. *Giglioli in Guyana, 1922–1972*. Georgetown, British Guiana: National History and Arts Council, 1973.

Williams, Eric. "The British West Indian Slave Trade after Its Abolition in 1807." *Journal of Negro History* 27, no. 2 (April 1942).

———. "The Historical Background of British Guiana's Problems." *Journal of Negro History* 30, no. 4 (October 1945).

Wood, Gertie. "A Call to British Guiana Women to Be Militant in Local Politics." *Daily Chronicle*, 1930.
———. "To Guianese Women." *Daily Chronicle*, March 1931.

SECTION 3

Proceedings of the West Indian Conference, London, May–June 1926. London: Colonial Office, 1926.

Report by Hon. E. L. F. Wood, M.P. on His Visit to the West Indies and British Guiana, December 1921–February 1922. London: Her Majesty's Stationery Office, 1920.

Report of the British Guiana Commission. London: Her Majesty's Stationery Office, 1927.

Report of the Sugar Industry of the West Indies and British Guiana, West Indian Sugar Commission, 1929–1930. London: Her Majesty's Stationery Office, March 1930.

Report of the West India Royal Commission. Vol. 2, Appendix C. London: Her Majesty's Stationery Office, 1897.

INDEX